*Manuscript, Print, and the English Renaissance Lyric*

By the same author:

*John Donne, Coterie Poet*

# MANUSCRIPT, PRINT, AND THE ENGLISH RENAISSANCE LYRIC

## Arthur F. Marotti

CORNELL UNIVERSITY PRESS
*Ithaca and London*

First published 1995 by Cornell University Press.

Printed in the United States of America

⊗ The paper in this book meets the minimum requirements of the American National Standard for Information Sciences— Permanence of Paper for Printed Library Materials, ANSI Z39.48–1984.

Library of Congress Cataloging-in-Publication Data

Marotti, Arthur F., 1940–
    Manuscript, print, and the English renaissance lyric / Arthur F. Marotti.
        p.    cm.
    Includes bibliographical references (p.) and index.
    ISBN 0–8014–2291–4 (cloth) — ISBN 0–8014–8238–0 (paper)
    1. English poetry—Early modern, 1500–1700—Criticism,
Textual.   2. English poetry—Early modern, 1500–1700—Manuscripts.
3. Manuscripts, Renaissance—England—History.   4. England—
Intellectual life—16th century.   5. England—Intellectual life—17th
century.   6. Printing—England—History—16th century.
7. Printing—England—History—17th century.   8. Literature
publishing—England—History.   9. Transmission of
texts.   10. Renaissance—England.      I. Title.
PR535.T47M37      1995
821'.040903—dc20                                              94-27160

*For Alice*

# CONTENTS

# CONTENTS

# ILLUSTRATIONS

# PREFACE

THIS BOOK examines the "publication" of English lyric poetry of the sixteenth and seventeenth centuries in manuscript and print. In it I focus on the material forms in which texts are found and on their transmission, reception, and reproduction in order to do the kind of historical-bibliographical work that a number of theorists and scholars have been calling for in recent years. Maria Corti, for example, has argued that what is needed is a new "social history of literature . . . [one that can] take into account the physical means of transmission and transform itself at some point into a social history of writing, with the contributions of several disciplines." Similarly, Roger Chartier writes that "no text exists outside of the support that enables it to be read; any comprehension of a writing, no matter what kind it is, depends on the forms in which it reaches the reader." D. F. McKenzie states that it is impossible "to divorce the substance of the text on the one hand from the physical form of its presentation on the other" and has defined "a *text* as a complex structure of meanings which embraces every detail of its formal and physical presentation in a specific historical context."[1] In short, the various

[1] Maria Corti, *An Introduction to Literary Semiotics*, trans. Margherita Bogat and Allen Mandelbaum (Bloomington: Indiana University Press, 1978), p. 152n; Roger Chartier, "Texts, Printing, Reading," in *The New Cultural History*, ed. Lynn Hunt (Berkeley and Los Angeles: University of California Press, 1989), p. 161; and D. F. McKenzie, "Typography and Meaning: The Case of William Congreve," in *The Book and the Book Trade in Eighteenth-Century Europe*, ed. Giles Barber and Bernhard Fabian (Hamburg: Ernst Hauswedell, 1981), pp. 82, 84, 90. For a discussion directly relevant to the argument I pursue, see also my "Shakespeare's Sonnets as Literary Property," in *Soliciting Interpretation: Literary Theory and Seven-*

manuscript and print forms in which texts were recorded and transmitted can be the basis of a socioliterary history that unlike traditional literary history considers texts in their material specificity (rather than in their edited "ideal" forms), attends to their reception and reproduction in a variety of social and historical circumstances (and not just in the context of the print publication process), and emphasizes an inchoate or developing definition of literature and authorship (rather than a stable definition based on alleged authorial "intentions"). Authorship, textuality, and "literature" itself all look different in this other framework.

In this necessarily selective work, I am primarily interested in the relationship of verse transmission in both manuscript and print to the processes by which literature became institutionalized in the early modern period. The opposition I imply between manuscript transmission of texts and book publication, however, is not a simple one, since the systems affected each other and embraced a wide variety of practices in which texts were treated in different ways. I dislodge poems broadly defined as "lyrics" from the context of a supposedly continuous literary history in order to conduct a historical inquiry not only into how such works functioned as social verse but also into that social history of literature of which Corti speaks. I concentrate particularly on the historical moment in which the interaction of print culture with an overlapping manuscript culture shaped the institution of literature itself and the status of authors, texts, and readers within it.

During the English Renaissance, despite the widespread effects of the Gutenberg revolution, much literature continued to be written for manuscript circulation rather than for print. In fact, it could be said that literature itself did not become institutionalized until more than a century and a half of print culture had passed, during which time two systems of publication coexisted. In the older, manuscript system, the modern boundary between the literary and the nonliterary had not yet solidified, and texts were immersed in social worlds whose conditions enabled them to be produced and consumed.

When lyric poetry is largely occasional and bound to the contexts

---

*teenth-Century English Poetry*, ed. Elizabeth D. Harvey and Katharine Eisaman Maus (Chicago: University of Chicago Press, 1990), pp. 143–73.

of its initial production and reception, manuscript miscellanies and verse anthologies give a better sense of the sociocultural functioning of such literary texts than printed editions do. Printed texts of lyric verse—something of an innovation and a matter also of printers' fortuitous access to the literary communications of restricted social groups and coteries—yield a distorted picture of literary history or of the place of literary texts in the life of the society that produced and consumed them. Manuscripts, on the other hand, better reveal the socioliterary dynamics of particular texts and the social history of literature. It took a relatively long time for anthologies and single-author editions of lyric poetry to become an established feature of print culture in England, and the manuscript system of transmission had a remarkable strength and durability through the first two centuries of English printing. Given this situation and given that few scholars and students of the period are very familiar with the less accessible documents that constitute the uneven record of a post-Gutenberg manuscript culture, I devote more attention in this book to manuscripts than to print. Since roughly the late 1970s, scholars such as Elizabeth Eisenstein, Lucien Febvre and Henri-Jean Martin, Richard Helgerson, Roger Chartier, Richard Newton, Joseph Loewenstein, Martin Elsky, and Wendy Wall have turned their attention to early print culture and to how modern conceptions of textuality, authorship, and readerships were shaped within this context.[2] But apart from those textual scholars who have edited the work of individual authors, few specialists in the field have closely examined this rich manuscript material for what it reveals of the larger social and institutional history of literature. Now that several volumes of Peter Beal's *Index of English Literary Manuscripts* have been published and many manuscripts have been reproduced in the various series brought out by Harvester Microfilms (those, for example, from the British Library, the Bodleian Library, the Cambridge University Library, and the Fol-

---

[2] Partly because Wendy Wall examines gender issues so intelligently and so thoroughly (especially in *The Imprint of Gender: Authorship and Publication in the English Renaissance* [Ithaca: Cornell University Press, 1993], portions of which the author has generously shared with me in manuscript form) and partly because some recent feminist scholars have dealt extensively with women's publishing work in various genres, I have not in this book discussed such authors as Isabella Whitney, Mary Wroth, and Margaret Cavendish (duchess of Newcastle) as fully as I might have. I have, however, paid more attention to the functioning of women in the manuscript system, since this side of the story is less known.

ger Shakespeare Library) scholars have useful guides and easier access to the primary documents needed for research into manuscript literary transmission.

I have divided this book into five chapters and a conclusion. In Chapter 1 I discuss manuscript transmission by turning first to the topic of the occasional character of most English Renaissance lyrics, a feature related to their transmission in shorter or longer manuscript documents to restricted audiences. I deal next with the various sorts of manuscript documents in which poems are found and the various social and institutional contexts in which they were transmitted and collected: the universities, the court, the Inns of Court, and the family. I also touch on middle-class collecting efforts, Catholic manuscript transmission and collection, and women's involvement in the manuscript system. I conclude with a brief discussion of some representative sixteenth- and seventeenth-century manuscript collections.

In Chapter 2 I deal primarily with two kinds of verse that figure more importantly in manuscript than in print collections, the obscene (which was often implicitly political) and the political itself. The first sort of verse is not surprising, given that so many of the manuscript compilations were made at the universities and Inns of Court by young men. I discuss the explicitly political verse found in manuscript collections at much greater length before turning to political and recreational libeling. The largest part of this chapter is devoted to poetry written in response to specific political scandals, the falls of prominent individuals, and the conflicts between Crown and Parliament and between Royalist and Puritan factions. Most of the political and obscene poems I highlight are difficult or impossible to find in the print anthologies of the period. I conclude this chapter with a section devoted more broadly to the poems that seem to have been the most popular ones in the system of manuscript transmission—many of which are virtually unknown to traditional literary history.

In Chapter 3 I focus on the reproductive or cocreative activities of scribes and compilers in the manuscript system. I discuss first the instability and malleability of texts in this medium with various examples, before focusing on some of the transformations of John Donne's verse in the seventeenth century. I follow this with a much longer discussion of "answer poetry"—the sorts of imitative, competitive, parodic verse encouraged by the manuscript system—and of compiler verse generally, the pieces entered into their collections by those who created anthologies of poetry or gathered verse in miscellaneous collections of poetry and prose. Since most of the texts I discuss in this last section are unknown, I quote several in full to produce, in effect, a mini-anthology of compiler poetry for scholars who have not had access to or are unfamiliar with such work.

In Chapter 4, the longest, I initiate the discussion of the incorporation of lyric poetry in print from the mid-sixteenth century to the Restoration. I focus on four important moments in English publication history that affected the literary institutionalization of the lyric and the functioning of authors, publishers, and consumers/readers within print culture: (1) the appearance of the first important poetry anthology in English, *Tottel's Miscellany* (1557); (2) the posthumous editions of *Astrophil and Stella* and of Sir Philip Sidney's other works in the 1590s; (3) Ben Jonson's 1616 folio collection of his poems, plays, and masques; and (4) the posthumous editions of the poems of John Donne and George Herbert in 1633. I consider these as part of a process through which print replaced manuscripts as the normal medium for such literature. In the context of the complex political and cultural conflicts of the mid-seventeenth century, I examine the crucial role played by the printer Humphrey Moseley in the development of printed editions of verse. I also examine the continuing practices of poetry anthologizing and the incorporation of poems in courtesy literature and other self-help publications. I conclude the chapter with a brief examination of some of the features of the physical book which distinguished print from manuscripts, affected how printed poetry was received and used, and represented the significantly different sociocultural positions of the parties to literary production and reception.

In Chapter 5 I concentrate on the changing relationships of writers and publishers with two kinds of "patrons"—old-style socially superior protectors or benefactors and new-style commercial purchases of printed works. I highlight the friction between the two kinds of patronage within the commodifying processes of print culture and the negotiations poets undertook in order to establish for themselves a position of advantage in relation to the printers and publishers, aristocratic patrons, and readers of various social ranks.

In the conclusion I make some observations about the effects of the two systems of literary transmission on each other.[3]

---

[3] After the completion of this book several important and valuable works have appeared

# PREFACE

## A Note on the Transcription of Texts

In citing both manuscript and print texts, I modernize $i/j$ and $u/v$ and convert the long $s$ and old double $v$ to the modern forms. I expand most contractions, converting the $y$ used as a thorn to the modern *th*. I retain original capitalization and punctuation (including the normally light punctuation of manuscript documents). I use angle brackets to mark deleted words or lines and square brackets to indicate omitted words or lines. I mark inserted words, phrases, or lines by enclosing them in insertion carets (e.g., ^doth^).

## Acknowledgments

Some material in this book represents more or less heavily revised versions of the following articles and book chapters. I thank the publishers for permission to reprint:

"Manuscript, Print, and the Social History of the Seventeenth-Century Lyric," in *The Cambridge Companion to English Poetry*, ed. Thomas N. Corns (Cambridge: Cambridge University Press, 1993), pp. 52–79; reprinted with permission of Cambridge University Press.

"The Transmission of Lyric Poetry and the Institutionalizing of Literature in the English Renaissance," in *Contending Kingdoms: Historical, Psychological, and Feminist Approaches to the Literature of Sixteenth-Century England and France*, ed. Marie-Rose Logan and Peter Rudnytsky (Detroit: Wayne State University Press, 1991), pp. 21–41.

"John Donne, Author," *Journal of Medieval and Renaissance Studies* 19 (1989): 69–89.

"Malleable and Fixed Texts: Manuscript and Printed Miscellanies and the Transmission of Lyric Poetry in the English Renaissance," and "Manu-

---

that are directly relevant to its subject matter. I would like to call particular attention to Mary Thomas Crane's *Framing Authority: Sayings, Self, and Society in Sixteenth-Century England* (Princeton: Princeton University Press, 1993), Harold Love's *Scribal Publication in Seventeenth-Century England* (Oxford: Clarendon Press, 1993), and William Ringler's *Bibliography and Index of English Verse in Manuscript, 1501–1558* (London and New York: Mansell, 1992).

# PREFACE

script, Print, and the English Renaissance Lyric," in *New Ways of Looking at Old Texts: Papers of the Renaissance English Text Society, 1985–1991,* ed. W. Speed Hill, MRTS, vol. 107 (Binghamton, N.Y.: Medieval & Renaissance Texts & Studies in conjunction with the Renaissance English Text Society, 1993), pp. 159–73, 209–21. Copyright, Center for Medieval and Early Renaissance Studies, SUNY Binghamton.

"Poetry, Patronage, and Print," *The Yearbook of English Studies* 21 (1991): 1–26.

Over the several years I have spent on this project, I have incurred many debts that I am happy to acknowledge. This book would not have been possible without the pioneering work of such scholars as Peter Beal, Margaret Crum, and Mary Hobbs, as well as that of the many textual scholars whose work I cite. My institutional and personal debts are many. I thank the American Council of Learned Societies for a year-long fellowship in 1988–89 and Wayne State University for its support in the form of research grants, summer research awards, a sabbatical leave, and a fellowship supplement. Over the last few years, I have valued the advice and encouragement of Thomas Berger, Lesley Brill, Jean Brink, Cedric Brown, Ann Coiro, Heather Dubrow, Martin Elsky, Stanley Fish, Margreta de Grazia, Margaret Hannay, Richard Helgerson, W. Speed Hill, Karl Josef Höltgen, Arthur F. Kinney, Jacob Lassner, Joseph Loewenstein, Gerald MacLean, Leah Marcus, Stephen Orgel, G. W. Pigman III, James Shapiro, Nigel Smith, and Wendy Wall. I am also grateful to Andrew Lewis for skillful copyediting. I have presented sections of the work as lectures to receptive audiences at Columbia University, Brooklyn College, Fordham University–Lincoln Center, UCLA, the University of Arizona, and Arizona State University. I owe much to the staffs of the British Library Manuscript Room, the Duke Humphrey Room of the Bodleian Library, the Folger Shakespeare Library, the Huntington Library, and the Wayne State University Library (particularly Donald Breneau). My son Bill, who has both an academic and filial interest in this project, and my son Steve, who, with his brother, taught me how to be a father, have both helped to sustain me emotionally. My greatest debt is to my best friend, to whom I dedicate this book.

ARTHUR F. MAROTTI

*Detroit, Michigan*

# SHORT REFERENCES
## AND
### *ABBREVIATIONS*

Beal           Peter Beal, comp., *Index of English Literary Manuscripts.* London and New York: Mansell, 1980–  . Vol. 1, pts. 1 & 2; vol. 2, pt. 1.

Crum          Margaret Crum, ed., *First-Line Index of Manuscript Poetry in the Bodleian Library Oxford.* 2 vols. Oxford: Oxford University Press; New York: Modern Language Association of America, 1969.

Cummings    Laurence Cummings, "John Finet's Miscellany." Ph.D. diss., Washington University, 1960.

*DNB*           *Dictionary of National Biography*

Grierson     Herbert J. C. Grierson, ed., *The Poems of John Donne.* 2 vols. Oxford: Oxford University Press, 1912.

Harvester    *British Literary Manuscripts from the British Library, London, Series One: The English Renaissance, c. 1500–1700.* Brighton, England: Harvester Press Microform Pubs., 1984.

Hughey      Ruth Hughey, ed., *The Arundel Harington Manuscript of Tudor Poetry.* 2 vols. Columbus: Ohio State University Press, 1960.

# SHORT REFERENCES AND ABBREVIATIONS

| | |
|---|---|
| Add. | Additional |
| Ash. | Ashmole |
| BL | British Library, London |
| Bod. | Bodleian Library, Oxford |
| Camb. | Cambridge University Library |
| Don. | Donation |
| Eng. Poet. | English Poetry |
| Folger | Folger Shakespeare Library, Washington, D.C. |
| Harl. | Harley |
| Harv. | Houghton Library, Harvard University |
| Hunt. | Henry E. Huntington Library, San Marino, California |
| Mal. | Malone |
| Rawl. | Rawlinson |
| Rosenbach | The Rosenbach Museum and Library, Philadelphia |

❦❦❦❦❦❦❦❦❦❦❦❦❦❦❦❦❦❦

*CHAPTER ONE*

# LYRICS
## AND THE
*MANUSCRIPT SYSTEM*

LYRICS were recorded and transmitted in pre-Gutenberg English manuscript culture, but they also had an extended life in manuscript transmission and compilation during at least the first two centuries of print, when the two systems of literary transmission not only competed but also influenced each other and, to a great extent, coexisted by performing different cultural functions. A large body of documents survives, for example, for a broad chronological period from the last years of the reign of Henry VIII through the Interregnum, testifying to the vigorous persistence of post-Gutenberg manuscript culture. As late as the Restoration, when a fair amount of manuscript transcription had been professionalized by scriveners and publishers who ran modern "scriptoria,"[1] manuscript transmission and compilation continued even though print had largely replaced handwriting as the dominant literary medium. Some of the cultural dynamics of the change from medieval to modern are visible in this overlap of manuscript and print in early modern England. Although earlier manuscripts containing lyric verse deserve careful study, they belong to a period before print culture began to have its real impact. I begin instead with those sixteenth-century manuscripts that represent the beginnings of early modern lyric anthologizing.

---

[1] See W. J. Cameron, "A Late Seventeenth-Century Scriptorium," *Renaissance and Modern Studies* 7 (1963): 25–52.

# MANUSCRIPT, PRINT, AND THE RENAISSANCE LYRIC

## The Occasional Character of Renaissance Lyric Verse

In the English Renaissance, the composition of lyric poems was part of social life, associated with a variety of practices in polite and educated circles. Read aloud to live audiences[2] or passed from hand to hand in single sheets, small booklets, quires, or pamphlets, verse typically found its way into manuscript commonplace books rather than into printed volumes—though, of course, printers often eventually gained access to manuscripts preserving the work of single writers or groups of authors and exploited them for their own economic and social purposes. Single poems as well as sets of poems were written as occasional works. Their authors professed a literary amateurism and claimed to care little about the textual stability or historical durability of their socially contingent productions. Though modern scholars treat such works as autonomous pieces of literature separable from the circumstances in which they were created, such poems are best viewed first within the social context that shaped them and the system through which they were originally produced, circulated, altered, collected, and preserved. This focus better suits the particular historical situations of such texts and the culture-specific definition of literature shared by their authors and original audiences.[3]

Lyrics were written in an astonishing number of circumstances in the English Renaissance: these included imprisonment, New Year's gift-giving, and correspondence, along with more conventional situations such as paying compliments and appealing for patronage.

[2] On the custom of oral performance of literature, see William Nelson, "From 'Listen, Lordings' to 'Dear Reader,'" *UTQ* 46 (1976–77): 110–24, and Roger Chartier, "Leisure and Sociability: Reading Aloud in Modern Europe," trans. Carol Mossman, in *Urban Life in the Renaissance*, ed. Susan Zimmerman and Ronald F. E. Weissman (Newark: University of Delaware Press, 1989), pp. 103–20. As Edward Doughtie puts it, "Most of the really vital literary forms of the sixteenth century were written with the possibility of oral performance in mind: sermons, plays, and song lyrics, of course—even romances and long poems were probably read aloud to small groups" in *Lyrics from English Airs, 1596–1622* [Cambridge: Harvard University Press, 1970], p. 36). See also Roger Chartier, *The Cultural Uses of Print in Early Modern France*, trans. Lydia Cochrane (Princeton: Princeton University Press, 1987), pp. 152–55, on the different environments in which texts were read aloud, particularly to illiterate audiences.

[3] See, in particular, the two seminal articles by J. W. Saunders, "The Stigma of Print: A Note on the Social Bases of Tudor Poetry," *Essays in Criticism* 1 (1951): 139–64, and "From Manuscript to Print: A Note on the Circulation of Poetic MSS. in the Sixteenth Century," *Proceedings of the Leeds Philosophical and Literary Society* 6, no. 8 (1951): 507–28. See Alastair Fowler, *Kinds of Literature: An Introduction to the Theory of Genres and Modes* (Cambridge: Harvard University Press, 1982), pp. 219–33, on the historical place of lyric poetry in the hierarchy of literary genres.

Poems were composed in response to themes set by others; they were designed as answers to or parodies of known texts; they were made to fit well-known tunes or to serve as responses to the challenge to extemporaneous composition;[4] they were verse riddles for social diversion, libels or epigrams about known individuals, ghostwritten pieces for use by a patron or employer. Poems appeared not only on paper, but also on rings, on food trenchers,[5] on glass windows (scratched with a pin or diamond),[6] on paintings,[7] on tombstones and monuments, on trees,[8] and even (as graffiti) on London's Pissing Conduit.

George Puttenham's description of the transcription of epigrams and posies identifies such texts as social ephemera. Referring to a poem by Sir John Harington, Puttenham wrote:

This *Epigramme* is but an inscription or writting made as it were upon a table, or in a windowe, or upon the wall or mantell of a chimney in some

---

[4] See, for example, the poem in George Gascoigne's *Discourse of the Adventures passed by Master F.J.*, "In prime of lustie yeares, when Cupid caught me in" (composed to fit a *"Tyntarnell"*) (*George Gascoigne's "A Hundreth Sundrie Flowers,"* ed. C. T. Prouty, University of Missouri Studies, vol. 17, no. 2 [1942; reprint, Columbia: University of Missouri Press, 1970], p. 62), and the poem found in Thomas Pecke's *Parnassi Puerperium* (1659), p. 184, "Verses made Ex tempore, and writ in a Ladies book; occasioned by a Friends recital, of that well-known Fancy of Doctor Corbets: Little Lute, when I am gone, &c. And referring to the Covers of a singing Book, Painted with Slips of Flowers, to several statues, which were there view'd; and bitter Cherrie, tasted of by the Authors, That Lady being absent, &c." ("When my voracious Eyes first lent a Look").

[5] Doughtie notes that "the trenchers for which . . . verses were written were thin wooden discs, usually about six inches in diameter, which were painted and inscribed on one side and plain on the other. After a meal, fruit or cheese would be served on the plain side. They were then turned over and the verses read aloud for the amusement of the company" (*Lyrics from English Airs*, pp. 596–97). He cites the collection of such verse published in *Proceedings of the Society of Antiquaries* (of London), 2d ser., 10 (1885): 207–16, and 12 (1888): 201–23.

[6] Donne's "Valediction: of my Name in the Window" assumes the commonness of the practice; Ruth Hughey notes, for example, that Mary, Queen of Scots, inscribed two lines of a poem found in Tottel on a window of Fotheringay Castle (Hughey, 2:19).

[7] Ruth Hughey notes that Harington composed two poems on a portrait of Seymour that he gave to Queen Elizabeth (*John Harington of Stepney: Tudor Gentleman, His Life and Works* [Columbus: Ohio State University Press, 1971], p. 55). The practice of putting poems in paintings is alluded to in Bod. MS Ash. 38, p. 39, in which there is a transcription of "Certayne verses written by Mr Robert Barker his Majesty's Painter under his Majesty's picture" ("Crownes hath their Compass, length of dayes their date").

[8] In Bod. MS Rawl. Poet. 148, John Lilliat's anthology, the compiler's poem beginning "The sturdie Oke too old to bear" is accompanied by the note "Finding few frute upon the Oke, / This Rithme upon the Ryne he wrote" (*Liber Lilliati: Elizabethan Verse and Song [Bodleian MS Rawlinson Poetry 148]*, ed. Edward Doughtie [Newark: University of Delaware Press; London: Associated University Presses, 1985], p. 62). This is the practice ridiculed by Shakespeare in *As You Like It*.

place of common resort, where it was allowed every man might come, or be sitting to chat and prate, as now in our tavernes and common tabling houses, where many merry heades meet, and scrible with ynke with chalke, or with a cole such matters as they would every man should know, & descant upon. Afterward the same came to be put on paper and in bookes, and used as ordinarie missives, some of frendship, some of defiaunce, or as other messages of mirth. . . .

There be also other like Epigrammes that were sent usually for new yeares giftes or to be Printed or put upon their banketing dishes of suger plate, or of march paines, & such other dainty meates as by the curtesie & custome every gift might carry from a common feast home with him to his owne house, & were made for the nonce, they were called *Nemia* or *apophoreta,* and never contained above one verse or two at the most, but the shorter the better, we call them Posies, and do paint them now a dayes upon the backe sides of our fruite trenchers of wood, or use them as devises in rings and armes and about such courtly purposes.[9]

Although Puttenham alludes to the most casual and ephemeral of poetic productions, his conception of verse as basically occasional was typical for the period.

Consider just one of the common contexts in which lyrics were composed, the prison. It is interesting that so many important poets and public figures wrote prison poetry.[10] While in prison, particularly in the Tower of London, as Ruth Hughey has suggested (1:66), some individuals actually compiled collections of verse such as the main manuscript on which *Tottel's Miscellany* (1557) was based or a large portion of the similar anthology begun by John Harington of Stepney, the Arundel Harington Manuscript. Sir Thomas Wyatt probably composed his translations of the Penitential Psalms and some of his lyric poems while in prison.[11] The earl of Surrey wrote verse when imprisoned on two different occasions.[12] The Protestant martyr Anne Askew

[9] George Puttenham, *The Arte of English Poesie* (1589; facsimile, Menston, U.K.: Scolar Press, 1968), pp. 43–44, 47.

[10] See Julia Boffey, *Manuscripts of English Courtly Love Lyrics in the Later Middle Ages,* Manuscript Studies 1 (Woodbridge, Suffolk: D. S. Brewer, 1985), p. 85, on the "farewell" poem written by condemned prisoners. Derek Pearsall points out that the two best fifteenth-century poets were Lancastrian prisoners, Charles d'Orleans and James I of Scotland (*Old and Middle English Poetry* [London: Routledge, 1977], p. 217).

[11] Most recently, Stephen Greenblatt, in *Renaissance Self-Fashioning from More to Shakespeare* (Chicago: University of Chicago Press, 1980), p. 121, has accepted this suggestion made originally by H. A. Mason in *Humanism and Poetry in the Early Tudor Period* (London: Routledge & Kegan Paul, 1959), pp. 202–9.

[12] According to William A. Sessions, the satire "London, hast thow accused me" "was probably written from Fleet prison in 1543" and Surrey's translations of the psalms and

turned to verse in her dire circumstances, composing a religious ballad before her execution.[13] John Harington of Stepney, a servant of then princess Elizabeth during the reign of Queen Mary, wrote some of the pieces found in the Arundel Harington Manuscript while he was in the Tower.[14] Thomas Seymour (Protector Somerset) composed a prison poem while in the Tower awaiting execution,[15] just as Elizabeth herself translated a poem by Petrarch when she was there.[16] John, earl of Warwick, Lord Robert Dudley, and Sir Walter Ralegh all wrote poems while awaiting execution.[17] John Hoskins, imprisoned along with three other members of the 1614 ("Addled") Parliament for their wittily critical speeches against royal policy, composed both verse and letters in the Tower.[18]

Robert Devereux, second earl of Essex, supposedly wrote "The Passion of a Discontented Mind" the night before he was executed: it is interesting that the printed text lacks the most politically subversive lines of the version preserved in manuscripts, lines 25–30, a stanza addressed to the "faire Queene of mercy and of pittye" (25), "gracious blessed Mary," whose cult Elizabeth secularized for her own purposes.[19] Philip Howard, earl of Arundel, in his prison poem "A

other related poems "were likely written during Surrey's last days in the Tower during the weeks of his trial and before his beheading in January 1547" (*Henry Howard, Earl of Surrey* [Boston: Twayne Publishers, 1986], pp. 83 and 101).

[13] Askew's ballad written in Newgate prison was printed in *The lattre examination of the worthye servaunt of God mastres Anne Askewe* (Wesel, 1547), fol. 63r–v. A modern text is found in *The New Oxford Book of Sixteenth Century Verse*, ed. Emrys Jones (Oxford: Oxford University Press, 1991), pp. 123–24. See Elaine V. Beilen, "Anne Askew's Self-Portrait in the *Examinations*," in *Silent But for the Word: Tudor Women as Patrons, Translators, and Writers of Religious Works*, ed. Margaret Patterson Hannay (Kent: Kent State University Press, 1985), pp. 77–91.

[14] See Hughey, 1:90, 96. In *John Harington of Stepney*, p. 31, Hughey also refers to BL MS Royal 17 A XVII, which has "Certaigne Psalmes of David translated into English meter by Sir Thomas Smith, Knight, then prisoner in the Tower of London, with other prayers and songues, by him made to pas the tyme then, 1549." Smith was a client of Protector Somerset.

[15] See Hughey, 1:341–42.

[16] This is also found in the Arundel Harington Manuscript (Hughey, 1:360–63). See also *The Poems of Queen Elizabeth I*, ed. Leicester Bradner (Providence: Brown University Press, 1964), pp. 13–16.

[17] See Hughey, 1:338–41, for the Warwick and Dudley pieces. Ralegh's prison poems "Give me my scallop shell of quiet," "What is our Life?" and "Even such is time" had considerable popularity in manuscript circulation because of the political notoriety of their author. See the discussion of this phenomenon in Chapter 2.

[18] Louise Brown Osborn, *The Life, Letters, and Writings of John Hoskyns 1566–1638* (1937; reprint, Hamden, Conn.: Archon Books, 1973), pp. 43–44.

[19] See the text of and commentary on this poem in *The Poems of Edward De Vere, Seventeenth Earl of Oxford, and of Robert Devereux, Second Earl of Essex*, ed. Steven W. May, *Studies in Philology*

Fourfold Meditation," also used Mariolatry in a politically subversive way.[20] Some poems by Catholic authors were prized despite the religious affiliation of the poets: John Harington of Stepney transcribed Edmund Campion's prison poem ("Why doe I use my paper ynke and pen") under the heading "Verses made by a Catholique in prayse of Campion that was executed at Tyburne for Treason as ys made knowne by Proclamation" (Hughey, 1:106–11), and John Lilliat put the note "A good verse, upon a badd Matter" before the copy of the poem in his manuscript anthology.[21] The Catholic Chidiock Tichborne's prison poem "My prime of youth is but a frost of cares" proved quite popular in the system of manuscript transmission, in addition to finding its way into print.[22] Whether composed by Protestants or Catholics, such poems carried with them a strong sense of political oppositionalism, for religious or philosophical reflection could serve as an oblique attack on the current regime.[23]

BL MS Sloane 1446 records the following poem along with its circumstances of composition:

---

77, no. 5 (1980): 48–59, 94–106. See also Steven W. May, *The Elizabethan Courtier Poets: The Poems and Their Contexts* (Columbia: University of Missouri Press, 1991), pp. 220–23. This piece, with the ending censored, was published anonymously in London in 1602.

[20] See Howard's prison poem in Bod. MSS Rawl. Poet. 219, fols. 1r ff., and Tanner 118, fols. 44–53, a piece that was passed off as a work by Southwell and printed in 1606 by G. Eld as *A Fourefold Meditation*. In the Rawlinson manuscript, the poem is titled "A poem of the contempte of the world and an exhalation to prepare to dye made by Phillipe [Howard] Earle of Arundell after his attaynder" (fol. 1r). See May, *Elizabethan Courtier Poets*, pp. 214–20, for a discussion of Howard's work. May also points out that Essex knew that Elizabethan culture demanded that, as Sir Henry Lee put it, one substitute "*Vivat Eliza,*" for an *ave mari*" (p. 356).

[21] See Doughtie, *Liber Lilliati*, p. 83, and Hughey, 2:57–66.

[22] For a discussion of Chidiock Tichborne (1558?–1586) and an edition of his poem, see Richard S. M. Hirsch, "The Works of Chidiock Tichborne," *ELR* 16 (1982): 303–18. See also his correction in "The Text of 'Tichborne's Lament' Reconsidered," *ELR* 17 (1987): 277. There is an interesting discussion of Tichborne's elegy in Arnold Stein, *The House of Death: Messages from the English Renaissance* (Baltimore: Johns Hopkins University Press, 1986), pp. 75–83. Tichborne's "Elegie, written with his own hand in the Tower before his execution" was printed in *Verses of Prayse and Joye writen upon her majesties preservation* (London, 1586), but it was also reproduced in many manuscripts as well, such as BL MSS Add. 38823, fol. 30r; Egerton 2642, fol. 256v; and Sloane 1446, fol. 42r–v; and several Bodleian manuscripts (see Crum, p. 591). In the Sloane manuscript it appears two items after a piece by the Jesuit Henry Fitzsimon, "In elder times an auncient custom 'twas" (printed in *The Justification and Exposition of the Divine Sacrament of the Masse* [Douay, 1611]).

[23] In *Secret Rites and Secret Writing: Royalist Literature, 1641–1660* (Cambridge: Cambridge University Press, 1989), pp. 134–37, Lois Potter discusses the "centrality of prison" as both a reality and as an environment for literary composition and anthologizing during the Interregnum, especially for defeated Royalists such as Richard Lovelace.

Mr H: Harrington to the Countess of Bedford hee beinge her kinseman and in prison for debt; his freinds neglecting him for feare of displeasing her in reguard of her distasting and beinge angry at some of his unthriftie courses.

> Reade and pittie as you goe
> these my unhappie rimes
> whoe expect; if you say noe
> no pittie from the times
>
> Sublunary thinges doe move
> as the Caelestiall doe
> and if you'd begin to love
> the world would doe so too
>
> But if you should once begin
> to frowne uppon my state
> the world would then accompt it sinn
> to Cherrish what you hate.
>
> Then lett it not accounted bee
> my faulte: if I doe call
> to save that which is yours in mee
> for then you should save all.
>
> Which though you should refuse to doe
> when sorrowes strikes mee dead
> howe much I serv'd and honour'd you
> shall in my death bee reade.
> (Fols. 46r–v)[24]

The situation of a young spendthrift appealing to a powerful relative for assistance would have interested a whole class of individuals similarly dependent on the system of kinship and patronage.

Thus, lyric poems were occasioned by a range of social practices during the English Renaissance. Such verse was embedded in specific social situations, and writers and audiences responded to it both within the immediate context and in terms of shared sociocultural assumptions. H. A. Mason complained some years ago after examin-

---

[24] See also two Bodleian manuscripts in which this piece appears: Ash. 36, 37, fol. 22v, and Eng. Poet. c.50, fol. 112v.

ing the verse of Sir Thomas Wyatt: "By a little application we could compose a dictionary of conventional phrases which would show that many of these poems of Wyatt's are simply strung together from these phrases into set forms. There is not the slightest trace of poetic activity. The reason, I suggest, is that no poetic activity was attempted. Wyatt, like the other court writers, was merely supplying material for social occasions."[25] Despite his romantic assumptions about creativity, Mason saw the difficulty in separating the poems of someone like Wyatt from the contexts in which they were embedded.

Two passages from the diary of Queen Elizabeth's "saucy Godson," Sir John Harington of Kelston, illustrate the occasional nature of most courtly and satellite courtly poetry in the period. The first recounts an episode of public favor by the monarch: "The Queen stood up and bade me reache forth my arme to reste her theron. Oh, what a swete burden to my next songe.—Petrarcke shall eke out good matter for this businesse." The second identifies the passing on a particular lyric to Elizabeth as a part of a general strategy of securing her patronage and that of her chief ministers:

I muste not forgette to call on the Treasurer [Burghley], he that dothe not love the *man*, will have little favoure with the mistresse, and I am in good likinge withe bothe, praisede be God.—My Lord of Essex is also my friende, and that not in bad sorte. He bides me lay goode holde on her Majesties bountie, and aske freely; I will attende tomorrowe, and leave this little poesie behinde her cushion at my departinge from her presence.

To the Queens Majestie

For ever dear, for ever dreaded Prince,
You read a verse of mine a little since;
And so pronounc'st each word, and every letter,
Your gracious reading grac'st my verse the better:
Sith then your Highnesse doth by gift exceeding,
Make what you read the better for your reading;
Let my poore muse your pains thus farre importune,
Like as you read my verse, so—*read my Fortune.*
From your Highnesse saucy Godson[26]

---

[25] Mason, *Humanism and Poetry*, 171.
[26] *Nugae Antiquae*, ed. Henry Harington (1779; reprint, Hildesheim: Georg Olms, 1968), 1:216–17.

For Harington, as for other courtier poets, poems were an extension of artful, polite behavior and, at the same time, ways of formulating actual or wished-for social transactions. There is a surviving poem by Queen Elizabeth, allegedly stolen from "her Majesties tablet," that is a reply to a courtly solicitation from Sir Walter Ralegh.[27]

More artfully than the sometimes deliberately clownish Harington, men such as Sir Edward Dyer and Sir Walter Ralegh used verse not only to comment on their experience for an appreciative coterie but also, like Harington, to make a direct appeal to the monarch for economic and political favors. Dyer's "Song in the Oke" presented at the Woodstock entertainment of 1575 apparently came when the queen was ready to restore him to her good graces after three years of disfavor.[28] While in disgrace, he had composed a poem that became, in its eloquent expression of politically encoded amorous complaint, a model of the kind of verse that could be written by the frustrated or rejected ambitious courtier, "He that his mirth hath lost," a piece otherwise known as "Dyer's Phancy" in Robert Southwell's parody.[29] Texts written by such nonpublishing coterie authors as Wyatt, Sidney, Dyer, Ralegh, Donne, Carew, and Corbett ought to be examined in terms of the specific historical conditions in which they were produced and received.[30]

Sometimes manuscripts preserve (or invent) specific social occasions for poems that, in print, have a more general meaning. For example, the Carew poem that appeared in the 1640 printed edition of that poet's work under the title "Secresie protested,"[31] was given a very specific context in one manuscript collection, "A gentle man that had a Mistress, and after was constrayned to marry a nother, the first was a frayd that hee would reveale to his new wyfe, their secret Loves wheruppon hee wrights thus to her" (Bod. MS Ash. 38, p. 25).

[27] See L. G. Black, "A Lost Poem by Queen Elizabeth," *Times Literary Supplement*, May 23, 1968, p. 535, and May, *Elizabethan Courtier Poets*, p. 319.

[28] See Ralph Sargent, *At the Court of Elizabeth: The Life and Lyrics of Sir Edward Dyer* (London: Oxford University Press, 1935), p. 36, and E. K. Chambers, *Sir Henry Lee: An Elizabethan Portrait* (Oxford: Clarendon Press, 1936), pp. 90–91.

[29] In the Virtue and Cahill Library MS 8635, Southwell's poem is titled "Dyers phancy turned to a Sinners Complainte" (noted in *The Poems of Robert Southwell, S.J.*, ed. James H. McDonald and Nancy Pollard Brown [Oxford: Clarendon Press, 1967], p. 135). Dyer's poem was especially popular in manuscripts.

[30] For a book-length study of an individual coterie poet, see my *John Donne, Coterie Poet* (Madison: University of Wisconsin Press, 1986).

[31] *The Poems of Thomas Carew with his Masque "Coelum Britannicum,"* ed. Rhodes Dunlap (Oxford: Clarendon Press, 1949), p. 11.

The printed text, which imitates a conceit from Donne's lyric "The Dampe" in its final lines,[32] seems a conventional promise of secrecy in love, whereas the manuscript version is much more dramatic and emotionally complex. When social verse passed in the system of manuscript transmission beyond its original environments of production and reception, it was usually recoded and recontextualized, especially when poems were collected or anthologized in a process that converted them into works of "literature."

## Manuscript Gatherings and Manuscript Books

The transmission of poems in loose sheets and booklets generally preceded their transcription in miscellanies or anthologies.[33] Since such documents are the most perishable of literary records, there are very few surviving examples of this practice: most of those that we have were bound into the larger unit of the manuscript book, although poems in letters and in loose family papers have been preserved. In her study of the circulation of the verse of John Donne and Henry King, Margaret Crum speculates that the former's search in 1614 for his scattered verse resulted in a compilation of loose sheets and booklets of poems that were in circulation and that the papers used by scribes collecting King's verse in their manuscript anthologies were similar documents.[34] The 1640–41 (second) folio of Jonson's works contains an explanation by Sir Kenelm Digby of why poems from the Venetia Digby sequence were missing: "A whole quaternion in the middest of this Poem is lost, containing entirely the three next pieces of it, and all of the fourth (which in order of the whole, is the eighth.) excepting the very end: which at the top of the next quaternion goeth on thus. . . ."[35] Mary Hobbs points to good

---

[32] Ibid., pp. liii–iv.

[33] See Saunders, "From Manuscript to Print," pp. 507–28. G. S. Ivy observes: "In manuscript times, the quire was the basic unit of the book. Most books were probably written by their authors in quires. . . .Miscellaneous manuscripts were compiled by the quire" ("The Bibliography of the Manuscript-Book," in *The English Library before 1700: Studies in Its History*, ed. Francis Wormald and C. E. Wright [London: University of London, The Althone Press, 1958], p. 40).

[34] "Notes on the Physical Characteristics of some Manuscripts of the Poems of Donne and of Henry King," *The Library*, 4th ser., 16 (1961): 121–32.

[35] See *The Complete Poetry of Ben Jonson*, ed. William B. Hunter (1963; reprint, New York: Norton, 1968), p. 256. Hunter explains that a quaternion was "a sheet of paper folded twice to make four leaves." Cf. the discussion of BL MS Harl. 4955 and its relation to Jonson's practice of sending packets of his poems to the earl of Newcastle in *Ben Jonson*,

evidence that Carew's poems circulated first in a manner similar to that of Donne's and King's.[36] In his examination of the Isham manuscripts (Northamptonshire Record Office), Allan Pritchard describes three separate items containing poems by Thomas Pestell, one of Henry King's chaplains, which illustrate some of the forms in which verse was transmitted: the first is "a single sheet of paper folded to make four pages, containing a Latin poem . . . and two English poems"; the second "a little booklet of seven leaves sewn together" with six poems; the third "a similar booklet of twelve leaves" in three sections containing four verse epistles, five "Long-Wingd Epigramms," and forty-two "Short-wingd Epigrams, & Dysticks."[37] In his examination of the continuing practices of manuscript transmission of poems during the Restoration, Harold Love discusses the movement from single-sheet circulation of individual (usually satiric) pieces to larger groupings: "A new poem would be circulated in single copies written on a half sheet folded crossways for pentameters or longways for hudibrastics. The verso of the second leaf was often left blank for addressing as was universal with newsletters. At the next stage groups of poems or single longer poems were issued filling a whole sheet folded as a quarto. The third stage was to assemble large anthologies often covering the productions of several years."[38]

Of course some surviving manuscripts, bound either in their own time or subsequently, constitute gatherings into larger units of loose papers or fascicular collections. Many of these throw light on the transmission processes that precede deliberate collecting efforts. For example, the first thirteen folios of BL MS Add. 28253, Edward Bannister's collection, were originally loose sheets, each folded separately, with descriptions of the individual contents on the back.[39] BL MS Add. 23229, part of the larger collection of papers of Viscount Con-

---

ed. C. H. Herford, Percy Simpson, and Evelyn Simpson, 11 vols. (Oxford: Clarendon Press, 1925–52), 9:4–8.

[36] *The Stoughton Manuscript: A Manuscript Miscellany of Poems by Henry King and his Circle, circa 1636*, facsimile, with an introduction and indexes by Mary Hobbs (Aldershot, U.K.: Scolar Press, 1990), p. xviii.

[37] Allan Pritchard, "Unpublished Poems by Thomas Pestell," *ELR* 10 (1980): 137.

[38] Harold Love, "Scribal Publication in Seventeenth-Century England," *Trans. Camb. Bibl. Soc.* 9, no. 2 (1987): 143. In "Sidney's *Certain Sonnets*: Speculations on the Evolution of the Text," *The Library*, 6th ser., 2 (1980): 430–44, Germain Warkentin discusses the custom of writing poems on folded folio sheets, or bifolia.

[39] See L. G. Black, "Studies in Some Related Manuscript Poetical Miscellanies of the 1580's," 2 vols. (Ph.D. diss., Oxford University, 1970), 1:247.

way (Beal, 1.1.247), has many pages of folded correspondence, some containing poetry. One of the verses sent in correspondence is an obscene poem followed by a note on the other side of the paper from the transcriber: "Pray my Lord tell nobody from whom this Song comes, for I am ashamed to owne it" (fol. 43r–v). BL MS Add. 11743 is a composite volume of verse written by or related to members of the Fairfax family, containing much folded correspondence (Beal, 1.2.526) and incorporating papers of different sizes. Bod. MS Rawl. Poet. 172, which contains transcriptions from the sixteenth through the eighteenth centuries on various paper stocks, has, for example, a folded verse epistle of moral instruction from a father to a daughter written by one "Robert Blakwell." At the beginning of BL MS Add. 15232, the Bright Manuscript, there is a letter to the countess of Pembroke on much higher quality paper than the rest of the manuscript. In his study of Bod. MS Add. B.97, Robert Krueger concludes that Leweston Fitzjames "copied his transcript [of Davies's epigrams] in loose sheets and later had them bound."[40]

Nicholas Burghe's manuscript (Bod. MS Ash. 38) opens with a bifolium containing three poems: the remains of someone's personal wax seal are found on one of the sides of the paper (which is itself smaller than the sheets following). Folger MS V.a.219 contains the following titled sections of loose manuscript pages of poetry bound together: "The Poems of Thom[as] Randolph Gentleman Master of Arts and fellow of Trinitie Coll[ege] in Cambridge" (fols. 18r–25r); "Out of the poems written upon Thom[as] Rand[olph]" (fols. 25v–29r); "Poems of Ed[mund] Waller of Beckonsfeild Esquire" (fols. 29r–32v); and "Ben[jamin] Johnson his poems" (fols. 33r–34v). Bod. MS Rawl. Poet. 26 comprises several different units bound together, some bifolia, some regular folio booklets, some tipped-in quarto pages, and so forth. One of the items seems to reproduce the form in which a poem was sent in correspondence: Corbett's encomiastic poem to Buckingham, beginning "When I can pay my Parents, or my Kinge," is transcribed on fol. 6or with the subscription "Yor Lor[dship's] most humble servant to command. Rich[ard] Corbet . . . Christs-church, this present New-yeares day 1621." Written sideways in the margin is the note "To the Duke of Buckingham. Lord George

[40] Robert Krueger, "Sir John Davies: *Orchestra* Complete, *Epigrams*, Unpublished Poems," *RES*, n.s., 13 (1962): 121.

Villiers"—both the title of the poem and the identification of the addressee of this verse epistle. Rosenbach MS 240/7, containing 127 pages of uneven sheets bound together and written on in three different hands, despite its appearance, presents itself as a single collection, probably a university miscellany, opening with a poem "To the beauteous Reader whomsoever" (Beal, 1.2.12). BL MS Harl. 2253 consists of independent quires bound together. On the basis of his study of the genesis and evolution of the two Dalhousie manuscripts Ernest W. Sullivan II has argued that "Renaissance manuscripts should not be thought of or treated as textual units but as collections of smaller groupings of poems or other materials."[41]

Mary Hobbs discusses the relationship of a number of manuscript collections in terms of the circulation of quires with groups of poems in them: for example, the large manuscript compiled by Peter Calfe (and, possibly, his son of the same name), BL MS Harl. 6917–18, is related to other collections that, like it, are collections of collections.[42] Relating her observations to what David Veith has argued for the circulation of manuscripts in the Restoration period, Hobbs postulates the circulation of short collections of verse "consisting of several sheets quired into a pamphlet, in which poems may occur in roughly the same order."[43] Hobbs also identifies BL MSS Add. 21433 and 25303 and Harl. 3910 as having circulated within the Inns of Court.[44] She makes interesting connections between William Strode's autograph manuscript, Oxford MS CCC 325, and that of his second cousin Daniel Leare, whom he may have tutored at the university, BL

[41] *The First and Second Dalhousie Manuscripts: Poems and Prose by John Donne and Others,* facsimile, ed. Ernest W. Sullivan II (Columbia: University of Missouri Press, 1988), p. 10.

[42] See Mary Hobbs, "Early Seventeenth-Century Verse Miscellanies and Their Value for Textual Editors," *English Manuscript Studies* 1 (1989): 189. There is considerable overlap too with the printed anthology *Musarum Deliciae.* Hobbs writes: "It is . . . remarkable to find in at least six different manuscripts a virtually identical *large* group of poems by Herrick, Thomas Randolph, Carew and James Shirley, together with a body of anonymous lyrics. . . .Two of the manuscripts concerned, Huntington MS HM 172 and Folger MS V.a.96, agree, once more, even in their errors. . . .What seems unprecedented is that the same group of poems, considerably augmented, should turn up again in Bodleian Library MS Eng. poet. c.50, Harvard fMS Eng. 626 and Rosenbach MS 191. They agree in about a hundred poems, almost in the same order, including over thirty by Thomas Randolph. Moreover, the same basic group occurs in Peter Calfe's manuscripts, British Library, Harley MSS 6917–18, possibly in an earlier stage of transmission, as the group is there divided into five smaller ones, interspersed with poems evidently from different sources: Calfe seems to have borrowed and copied collections wholesale, as well as with scrupulous accuracy" (p. 202).

[43] Ibid., p. 195.

[44] Ibid., p. 196.

MS Add. 30982, suggesting that Strode and George Morley, who were both at Christ Church, Oxford, for long periods, allowed students to copy poems from their collections, a situation that could help to account for the large number of surviving manuscripts from that college.[45]

The traces of the processes of literary transmission to be found in manuscript papers, miscellanies, and poetry anthologies are many. They include, for example, information about the source from whom a particular text was obtained. Thus, in Bod. MS Tanner 169, Stephen Powle's commonplace book, Breton's poem "In Sunny beames the skye doth shewe her sweete" is attributed to King James of Scotland, "A passionate Sonnet made by the Kinge of Scots uppon difficulties ariseing to crosse his proceedinge in love & marriage with his most worthie to be esteemed Queene," and it is accompanied by the note "Geaven me by Master Britton who had been (as he sayed) in Scotland with the Kinges Majesty: but I rather thinke they weare made by him in the person of the Kinge" (fol. 43r). Later in the same manuscript, Powle notes after a transcription of another Breton poem, "1617: Oct: 17/ A placed aloane is but an idle worde," "Theis 12 verses weare made and geaven me by Mr Nic. Bretton anno et die supradictis" (fol. 173v).[46] Nicholas Burghe notes at the bottom of one page of his collection, after his transcription of "An Invective of Mr George Chapman against which Ben: Johnson" ("Great Learned wittie-Ben; be pleasd to light"), "more then this never came to my hande, but [the rest was] lost in his sicknes" (Bod. MS Ash. 38, p. 18). A section of the Arundel Harington Manuscript begins with the notation "Certayne verses made by uncertayne autors. wrytten out of Charleton his booke" (Hughey, 1:179).

Sometimes compilers of manuscript collections provide information (or misinformation) about the original context of particular poems. For example, in Bod. MS Add. B.97 Leweston Fitzjames records

---

[45] Ibid., p. 198. Hobbs also relates the Stoughton Manuscript to Folger MSS V.b.43 and V.a.125; BL MSS Add. 25707, Harl. 6917–18, and Sloane 1446; and St. John's Col. Camb. MS 23 (*Stoughton Manuscript*, pp. xv–xvi).

[46] For information about Powle, who served as government official both in London and in his home county, see Virginia F. Stern, *Sir Stephen Powle of Court and Country: Memorabilia of a Government Agent for Queen Elizabeth I, Chancery Official, and English Country Gentleman* (Selingsgrove, Pa.: Susquehanna University Press; London: Associated University Presses, 1992). Stern notes that "Breton was a frequent visitor in Powle's house" (p. 135).

two epigrams along with the contexts to which they originally belonged:

A Poesie, written by a gentleman in the end of a book, which he gave unto his Mistress

> Deere, but remember it is I:
> That for thy love will live, & dye.

> Is it not the tricke of an arrant whore,
> To washe her Arse in the milke & give it to the poore

> written in Essex gallerie by the doore
> of my Ladie of Lecesters chamber
>
> (Fol. 19r)

The scribe who transferred this ephemeral verse to a manuscript collection thus attempted to preserve the information that enabled it to be read in its social contexts. Similarly, in Bod. MS Mal. 19 the poem beginning "Christ rode some 7 yeares since to Court" is introduced with the heading, "Verses found in a box sealed, found at the Court, & delivered to the kinge" (p. 145).[47] There is a note in Bod. MS Rawl. Poet. 26 about the poem "Who doubts of Providence, or God denyes," "Mr Thomas Scott sent these verses by the hand of Dr John White to Sr Walter Raleigh; upon the setting forth of his Booke of the History of the World" (fol. 6v).

The circulation of manuscript collections sometimes left marks within the documents themselves. Humphrey Coningsby, for example, noted after one of the poems in his collection, a unique piece titled "Somn[i]um Affectionale" ("Luld by Conceipte when fancy clozde myne Eyes"), the source from which he obtained the item, "geven H E" (BL MS Harl. 7392, fol. 62r). The unidentified lyric, "Die, die, desire and bid delight adieu," is identified by its source of transmission in BL MS Harl. 3910, "A farewell to desire geven by

---

[47] This poem was attributed to "John Willyams of Essex, Esq. once of Middle temple" and is found also in Bod. MS Rawl. Poet. 26, fol. 188v (Crum, p. 153).

J.T."[48] In BL MS Sloane 396, at the start of a transcription of Matthew Bacon's poems, there is a personal note: "Brother Vessy Matt Bacon desires you to send this up againe to his mothers, when you have sithen usd it, or writt it out. J[eramiel?] T[errent?]" (fol. 2r). In Bod. MS Eng. Poet. c.50, a large folio collection of the mid-seventeenth century in which many hands are represented, there is a note at the end, apparently by one of the transcribers, to someone to whom the volume was being lent: "the manuscript of Judge dodridge will shew you more. vale" (fol. 133v).[49]

At the other extreme from those gatherings of loose sheets and independent quires of writing are those blank or "table" books into which individuals were to transcribe the prose and poetry they wished to have in their personal collections. These ranged from small pocket-size books or notebooks that students and others could use for notes and jottings to quarto and folio volumes that would have made handsome presents and served the needs of more deliberate and serious collectors of texts. One of the items for sale from the pack of Autolycus in Shakespeare's *Winter's Tale*, incidentally, is a "table-book" (4.4.601). Although the custom of transcribing texts in such volumes was much more common in the seventeenth century than in the sixteenth, there are some noteworthy examples of early table books. Laurence Cummings claims, for instance, that Bod. MS Rawl. Poet. 85 was "a bound and foliated book before [John] Finet began making entries" in it (p. 40). Hunt. MS HM 8 evidently began as a blank folio table book. A collection of verse was transcribed in it, and it was then presented as a gift to another person: the title page indicates it is "Frances Aungers booke of the gift of Tomas Buttess . . . the ii day of Jyly Anno Domini 1581."[50]

---

[48] Crum, p. 199. The poem is found in John Finet's anthology, and is part of the related Coningsby collection. According to Cummings, the poem itself may be the composition of an Oxford student (p. 434).

[49] Sir John Doderidge (1555–1628) graduated with a B.A. from Exeter College (Oxford) in 1577, entered Middle Temple, became a member of the Society of Antiquaries, and was chosen M.P. for Barnstaple (in 1588). He became a serjeant-at-law (1604) and was made Prince Henry's serjeant and solicitor general (1604). He was an M.P. from 1603–1611, and opposed King James's claim that the *post-nati* of Scotland were also citizens of England. He was knighted in 1607 and became a justice of the king's bench in 1612. He received an honorary M.A. from Oxford in 1614. He especially accommodated himself to the King's interests in the latter part of his judicial career. He published a number of books and manuals on the law and a history of Wales, Cornwall, and Chester (*DNB*, pp. 1062–63).

[50] Karl Josef Höltgen identifies Thomas Butts as "a wealthy, cultured, charitable, and paternalistic country gentleman of Puritan convictions and with a turn for versifying" and

# LYRICS AND THE MANUSCRIPT SYSTEM

## Types of Manuscript Collections

The manuscripts and manuscript collections in which we find Renaissance lyrics represent the beginnings of the modern poetry anthology. But these documents reveal very different ways of treating verse, ranging from the quite casual to the serious and systematic—from using poems to fill available blank spaces in manuscripts, to incorporating large numbers of them in collections of miscellaneous prose and verse, to actually compiling them in anthologies. These range from casual, personal, or family commonplace-book collections to carefully arranged, sometimes professionally transcribed, volumes.

In her study of fifteenth- and early sixteenth-century manuscripts containing courtly love poems, Julia Boffey notes that in England, unlike France, the practice of assembling carefully planned, sometimes decorated or illuminated, manuscripts of lyric verse did not take hold in the early Renaissance, and so the manuscripts in which one finds courtly poems are not true lyric anthologies but collections of different types in which the transcription of lyrics was, if not an afterthought, at least a casual practice.[51] Boffey notes, "Out of the hundred or so relevant manuscripts, only two complete volumes, BL MSS Add. 17492 and Harl. 682, and one section of a quasi-fascicular manuscript, Bod. Fairfax 16, are made up entirely (or almost entirely) of such poems."[52] Typically, lyrics were inserted in books given over to other sorts of texts. These included manuscripts gathering the work of a single author, such as Chaucer, manuscripts that contain

---

Francis and his brother John Aunger as "the sons of Butts' cousin and executor Richard Aunger, a distinguished lawyer of Gray's Inn. In 1581 Francis Aunger had been presented by Thomas Butts with 'A Boke Off Verses Named Aurum e stercore' collected by Robert Talbott and written in part by Butts (Huntington MS. 8)....He became eventually Master of the Rolls for Ireland and, in 1621, was created Baron Aungier of Longford." The manuscript was evidently part of "a social and cultural milieu dominated by the Puritan landed gentry" ("Sir Robert Dallington [1561–1637]: Author, Traveler, and Pioneer of Taste," *HLQ* 47 [1984]: 151). Höltgen, in private correspondence, has informed me that "in the Will of Thomas Butts, dated 22 May 1592 (Norwich Consistory Court, Liber Appleyard, f. 376v), the testator leaves this manuscript book to Henry Gosnold, son of Mathew Gosnold, late of Hempton....[T]here must have been two copies or versions of this manuscript. Gosnold belongs to a well-known family of Otley Hall, Suffolk. Aunger was the ancestor of the Earls of Longford and of the present Lord Longford....Another version of Robert Talbott's 'Aurum ex stercore' without the additions by Thomas Butts is in MS. Corpus Christi College, Oxford 258, art. 8, and a miscellaneous collection of transcripts in Corpus Christi College, Cambridge 379." I thank Professor Höltgen for his scholarly generosity.

[51] Boffey, *Manuscripts*, pp. 134–35.
[52] Ibid., p. 7.

various verse and prose items of interest to an elite audience, such as those produced by the anthologist John Shirley,[53] and commonplace books in which individuals collected miscellaneous texts in verse and prose, some of them simply practical items such as medical receipts.[54] In academic commonplace books, poems might have been transcribed for recreation, as Boffey suggests, as "light relief,"[55] in texts given over to weightier matters.

The personal miscellany and poetry anthology differed from the professional collection. Historically, these personal collections grew out of medieval florilegia and the practice of keeping commonplace books taught in Renaissance schools.[56] In outlining the sources of the

[53] In the heterogenous collections assembled by the fifteenth-century compiler John Shirley (whose practices were, in a sense, the model for what was done in a print culture by editors like Richard Tottel) lyric poems are interspersed among various other writings of interest to the courtly or marginally courtly audience for whom he presumably produced his work. See ibid., pp. 15–17. In *Poets and Princepleasers: Literature and the English Court in the Late Middle Ages* (Toronto: University of Toronto Press, 1980), p. 132, Richard Firth Green emphasizes Shirley's amateur status: "In his younger days Shirley had been a 'wele cherissed' servant of the earl of Warwick (himself a courtly poet), and it seems quite possible that the scribal activities of his later years were in large measure inspired by a love of courtly literature and an antiquarian's concern to rescue it from obscurity. . . .His two surviving prefaces suggest that he may well have circulated his anthologies more from a desire to popularize his literary enthusiasms than from motives of personal gain." A. I. Doyle suggests that Shirley ran a sort of circulating library, with a clientele however of courtly status and perhaps more as a hobby than a business" ("English Books In and Out of Court from Edward III to Henry VII," in *English Court Culture in the Later Middle Ages,* ed. V. J. Scattergood and J. W. Sherborne [New York: St. Martin's Press, 1983], p. 177). Cheryl Greenberg characterizes Shirley as a professional scrivener and as the proprietor of a bookshop whose operation continued after his death ("John Shirley and the English Book Trade," *The Library,* 6th ser., 4 [1982]: 369–80). Clearly Shirley's anthologies and professionally produced manuscript books that were editions of single authors' works differ from those manuscripts and manuscript collections from the sixteenth and early seventeenth centuries that were part of the system of private manuscript transmission and compilation.

[54] Boffey, *Manuscripts,* pp. 11, 15–19. Boffey distinguishes between the " 'hold-all' anthology" and the commonplace book, the former involving some degree of planning (p. 22). For example, Oxford Balliol MS 354, the commonplace book of the London alderman Richard Hill, contains not only songs and carols, religious poems and prayers, historical poems, ballads, and satirical pieces, but also a selection of tales from Gower's *Confessio Amantis,* the verse legend of Pope Gregory's *Trentale,* two books of courtesy, Lydgate's *Vertues of the Mass* and *The Chorle and the Burde,* treatises on the managing and breaking of horses and on the grafting of trees, various religious and ecclesiastic entries, encyclopedic notes on things curious or useful to know, medical remedies, household precepts, puzzles, riddles, and tricks. See Roman Dyboski, ed., *Songs, Carols and Other Miscellaneous Poems from the Balliol MS. 354, Richard Hill's Commonplace-Book,* EETS, extra ser., 101 (1907) (London: Kegan Paul, 1907), and R. L. Greene, *The Early English Carols* (Oxford: Clarendon Press, 1935), pp. 339–40.

[55] Boffey, *Manuscripts,* p. 25.

[56] On the custom of keeping commonplace books, related to that of compiling anthologies of verse or miscellanies in which poems are included, see R. R. Bolgar, *The Classical Heritage and Its Beneficiaries from the Carolingian Age to the End of the Renaissance* (1954; reprint,

secular lyrics he anthologized, Rossell Hope Robbins pointed to such sources as "The Friar Miscellanies" of the thirteenth century, florilegia used as sources of sermon material, "Minstral Collections" of carols, songbooks, "aureate collections" of poems produced as professional anthologies, and commonplace books kept either by secular or religious persons.[57] The last is the main ancestor of those sixteenth- and seventeenth-century miscellanies and anthologies in which we find lyric poems.

In personal commonplace-book miscellanies one is as likely to find recipes for brandy, household accounts, copies of correspondence, medical information, and business calculations as poetry of various kinds. For example, the miscellany of Simon Sloper (Bod. MS Eng. Poet. f.10), who was educated at Oxford, starts with a transcription of Bacon's essay "Of Great Place" (fol. 2r), "the catalogue of nobilitie" (fols. 3r–5v), sheets on each of the colleges of Cambridge, a list of twenty-six English bishoprics, a table of the reigns of all English kings through Charles I, notes on scriptural commonplaces, and other passages from Bacon's essays. It begins its poetical selections only on fol. 84r, including the transcription of a series of numbered poetry extracts (fol. 87r), before returning toward the end of the manuscript to prose, "Wittie Apothegms or Speeches" (fol. 123r–v) and medical receipts (fols. 125v–30v). Poetry, then, constitutes a minor feature in the miscellany.

Sir Edward Hoby's commonplace book (BL MS Add. 38323) is also

---

New York: Harper & Row, 1964), pp. 265–75, and Peter Beal, "Notions in Garrison: The Seventeenth-Century Commonplace Book," in *New Ways of Looking at Old Texts: Papers of the Renaissance English Text Society, 1985–1991*, ed. W. Speed Hill, MRTS, vol. 107 (Binghamton, N.Y.: Medieval & Renaissance Texts & Studies in conjunction with the Renaissance English Text Society, 1993), pp. 131–47. In her edition of Henry King's poetry, Margaret Crum cites T. W. Baldwin, *Shakespeare's Small Latin and Lesse Greeke* (Urbana: University of Illinois Press, 1944), 1:360, on Westminster School's extending to English the academic exercises in translation, paraphrase, and imitation (*The Poems of Henry King*, ed. Margaret Crum [Oxford: Clarendon Press, 1965], p. 29). Richard Panofsky, "A Descriptive Study of English Mid-Tudor Short Poetry, 1557–1577" (Ph.D. diss., University of California, Santa Barbara, 1975), discusses various forms of verse composition taught in the grammar schools, including the encomium, the epitaph, the theme poem, and "precept poetry" (p. 92).

[57] Rossell Hope Robbins, ed., *Secular Lyrics of the XIV and XVth Centuries*, 2d ed. (Oxford: Clarendon Press, 1955), pp. xvii–xxx. In *Preachers, Poets, and the Early English Lyric* (Princeton: Princeton University Press, 1986), Siegfried Wenzel discusses the preservation of lyrics in sermon collections, preaching notebooks and manuals, and manuscript books of various kinds, as well as in anthologies. He is particularly interested in how short poems were employed in vernacular sermons to support the main themes, to prove points, to deliver messages with strong emotional appeal, and to serve as prayers or as memory aids.

largely a prose miscellany with some poems inserted: it contains lists of peers, officers, M.P.'s, ships of one hundred tons or more, Queen Elizabeth's oration on the last day of the first session of Parliament in 1585 (fol. 25r–v), and many court documents, for example, the Privy Council Petition of Parliament (fol. 82r–v). The whole manuscript demonstrates how a man of the court with little interest in amorous or witty verse could embed moral or politically topical verse in a manuscript largely devoted to copies of official records and documents.[58] It makes sense, in the context of this manuscript, for this man of affairs to record the short poem by the father of his friend Sir John Harington (John Harington of Stepney):

> He that spareth to speake hath hardlie his intent
> He that speaketh and spedeth his speaking is well spent
> He that speaketh and spedeth not, his speaking is but lost
> Yet speaking without speding is but a small cost.
>
> (Fol. 256v)[59]

The long anonymous poem he records, "Since that my eyes are overbolde and make me to offende" (fol. 8r), is in the familiar courtly mode of hermit-like withdrawal from active life.

Folger MS V.a.125, a manuscript headed "A booke of verses collected by mee . . . R Dungarvane," includes recipes for elder ale, cowslip wine, marigold wine, and raspberry wine; at the beginning of the reverse transcription from the back the compiler gives directions for making ink. This is one of the unusual manuscript environments in

---

[58] Sir Edward Hoby (1560–1617) was educated at Eton and Trinity College, Oxford, receiving both a B.A. and an M.A. He entered the Middle Temple sponsored by Lord Burghley, his uncle, and began a long career of court service. He married the daughter of Henry Carey, Lord Hunsdon, was knighted by Elizabeth, and came to the favorable attention of King James of Scotland when he accompanied his father-in-law on a diplomatic mission. He served as M.P. for Queensborough, Kent, in 1586 and in 1588 was M.P. for Berkshire. He was made a J.P. for Middlesex in 1591, was elected M.P. for Kent in 1593, and received the patent for wool merchandising in England. He was M.P. for Rochester in the parliaments of 1597, 1601, 1604, and 1614. He was made a gentleman of the privy chamber by James I. He was a close friend of Sir John Harington and William Camden. He published several theological works as well as translations of French and Spanish works on politics and war (*DNB*, pp. 946–48).

[59] This poem is found also in the "Blage" manuscript and may actually be an answer poem to one of Surrey's (see *Sir Thomas Wyatt and His Circle: Unpublished Poems Edited from the Blage Manuscript*, ed. Kenneth Muir [Liverpool: Liverpool University Press, 1961], p. xiii). It also appears in BL MS Harl. 7392, fol. 59v, and in Trinity Col. Dublin MS D.27, fol. 176v (Hughey, *John Harington of Stepney*, pp. 88, 257).

which we find poems by Donne.[60] The Interregnum manuscript kept by Sir Edward Dering (Hunt. MS HM 41536) contains a diary from October 1656 in the first part and poetry at the back in reverse transcription. BL MS Sloane 739 is basically a medical commonplace book in which extracts from Carew's poems are found (beginning at fol. 103v). BL MS Egerton 4064 contains a large business diary, models of legal and financial documents, and then forty-seven poems by Donne (fols. 231r–99v) in a miscellaneous poetry collection.

Bod. MS Douce 280, the commonplace-book collection of John Ramsey, is a good example of the variety of materials that were gathered in a personal miscellany. This collection contains not only transcriptions from printed literature, such as Spenser's "Mother Hubberd's Tale," "Tears of the Muses," and "The Visions of Petrarch"; songs from published books of songs and madrigals; Francis Sabie's *Fisherman's Tale* (1595) and its continuation, *Flora's Fortune* (1595); individual pieces by the earl of Essex, Robert Southwell, and Ramsey himself; but also "A Rule to find the goulden or prime nomber"; a discussion of the organization of and admissions to Cambridge University; a translation of one book of Caesar's *Commentaries;* medical recipes; lists of the offices of England, of the kings of England since the Conquest, of lords, knights, captains, bishoprics, and counties in England; and comments on theology and on English history and politics. It also has more personal items: a partial autobiography, a family genealogy, a copy of Ramsey's will, a reading program, instructions to his son and heir, and the family coat of arms. Poetry is, of course, a minor feature of this miscellany, but it is certainly embedded in a context of an individual's intellectual, political, and familial, as well as literary interests. When Ramsey lists important authors to read or, as he puts it, "Personages to converse with" (fol. 91v)—including historiographers, musicians, navigators, philosophers, geometricians, arithmeticians, cosmographers, geographers, astronomers, hydrographers, chorographers, and other scholars and travelers—he mentions initially only two poets, Dowland and Daniel, before adding later "Mr Edmund Spencer an admirable Poet" (fol. 103r), many of whose works he copied from their printed versions.

[60] Mary Hobbs identifies the owner of Folger MS V.a.125 as "Richard Boyle, Viscount Dungarvon, [who] used that title only from 1630 until 1642, when he became Lord Burlington" (*Early Seventeenth-Century Verse Miscellany Manuscripts* [Aldershot, U.K.: Scholar Press, 1992], pp. 79–80).

In a later listing of the knights of England he defines Sir Philip Sidney as "Englands Mars & Muse" (fol. 100v).[61]

Leweston Fitzjames, of the Middle Temple a friend of Sir John Davies, transcribed that author's epigrams and *Orchestra* on papers that were then bound into a commonplace book (Bod. MS Add. B.97) that also contains such prose as "Of Behemoth & Leviathan" (fol. 1v), "Examples of Pestilence" (fol. 2r), medical remedies for the cough and for the removal of smallpox spots, a discussion of the law of primogeniture, and various letters in English and Latin.[62] Manuscripts such as Bod. MS Rawl. Poet. 108, BL MSS Add. 30076 and Harl. 677, and Folger MS V.b.93 in whole or in part arrange items under letters of the alphabet to facilitate their use as commonplace collections.

Lyrics were often transcribed in available odd spaces, including the flyleaves of books and manuscripts of various kinds.[63] In Stephen Powle's commonplace book (Bod. MS Tanner 169) poems are largely used as fillers: the book itself is largely given over to prose, such as an argument for marriage, letters (some by Powle himself), medical prescriptions, essays by Sir William Cornwallis, a speech by Queen Elizabeth to Parliament in 1576, a copy of the lengthy prose libel *Leicester's Commonwealth,* and a long (self-justifying) autobiographical statement (fols. 149r–73v) that Powle addressed to his father.[64]

Although the norm in the manuscript system of transmission was to mix the works of individual authors, there were, from a very early date, a number of manuscripts wholly or largely given over to the work of single poets. BL MS Egerton 2711, for example, is, for the most part, a collection of Wyatt's verse, incorporating that poet's autograph corrections.[65] Similarly, the (rediscovered) BL MS Add. 58435 is an autograph notebook by Robert Sidney, the brother of Sir

---

[61] On the contents of this manuscript, see Edward Doughtie, "John Ramsey's Manuscript as a Personal and Family Document," in Hill, *New Ways of Looking at Old Texts,* pp. 281–88.

[62] See Krueger, "Sir John Davies," pp. 17–29, 113–24.

[63] See Boffey, *Manuscripts,* pp. 27–29. Peter Dronke discusses the insertion of vernacular poems in odd spaces in medieval Latin manuscripts in his *Medieval Latin and the Rise of the European Love-Lyric,* 2d ed., 2 vols. (Oxford: Clarendon Press, 1968).

[64] This is subscribed at the end "Begunne, & ended in 16 Mornings, 1581, May 22. Dated to my Father the 20. of June, 1581: penned in a water-bath at Argentine called Strasborge in Alsatia, being an extreame hott Summer: but perused and inlarged at sondry tymes sithence" (fol. 173v). Cf. Stern, *Sir Stephen Powle,* pp. 38–42.

[65] See Richard Harrier, *The Canon of Sir Thomas Wyatt's Poetry* (Cambridge: Harvard University Press, 1975), pp. 1–15.

Philip, who transcribed his own verse and continued to revise it.[66] BL MS Egerton 3165 contains, on the first 113 of its 115 leaves, one hundred poems by Sir Arthur Gorges, with revisions entered by the author, ninety-eight of which were entered by two scribes and the last two by Gorges himself.[67] Fulke Greville's revision of a scribal copy of his poems is found among the Warwick manuscripts (BL MSS Add. 54566–71).[68] BL MS Add. 12049 is a copy of Sir John Harington's epigrams made for Prince Henry.[69] Oxford MS CCC 325, in the hand of William Strode, contains mainly his own poetry, as well as the work of others.[70] BL MS Lansdowne 777 contains the collected verse of William Browne of Tavistock.[71] Bod. MS North Add. e.1 & 2 are Dudley North's miscellanies representing the writing he gathered for publication in *A Forest of Varieties* (1645) and *A Forest Promiscuous of Several Seasons Productions* (1659).[72] Bod. MS Eng. Poet. e.30, an anthology copied by Henry King's amanuensis, Thomas Manne, contains fifty-four of King's poems along with corrections by King himself.[73] Peter Beal describes BL MS Add. 37157 as "[Sir Edward] Herbert's own 'official' collection of his poems . . . bound up in a composite volume of Herbert family papers . . . a fair copy made by amanuensis, who often left spaces for letters or words he evidently could not decipher in his copy-texts; Herbert then went through the MS filling in the spaces and making a number of minor autograph corrections and revisions" (Beal, 1.2.167). The Westmoreland Manuscript (N.Y. Pub-

---

[66] See *The Poems of Robert Sidney,* ed. P. J. Croft (Oxford: Clarendon Press, 1984), pp. 3–16, 115–23.

[67] See *The Poems of Sir Arthur Gorges,* ed. Helen Estabrook Sandison (Oxford: Clarendon Press, 1953), p. xxvii.

[68] See *The Poems and Dramas of Fulke Greville,* ed. Geoffrey Bullough, 2 vols. (New York: Oxford University Press, 1945), 1:29.

[69] Edwin Wolf II writes that this is "Harington's text as he wished it to be known in 1605" ("The Textual Importance of Manuscript Commonplace Books of 1620–1660," *Bibliographical Soc. of the Univ. of Virginia* [1949]: 4). Wolf notes three separate autograph manuscripts of Harington's epigrams, as well as single-author collections for Wotton, Donne, Browne, King, Carew, and Randolph (pp. 3 and 8). For transcripts of poems from the British Library manuscript and from Folger MS V.a.249 excluded from printed editions of Harington, including the modern one, see R. H. Miller, "Unpublished Poems by Sir John Harington," *ELR* 14 (1984): 148–58.

[70] See *The Poems of Richard Corbett,* ed. J.A.W. Bennett and H. R. Trevor-Roper (Oxford: Clarendon Press, 1955), p. lxii, and M. A. Forey, "A Critical Edition of the Poetical Works of William Strode, Excluding *The Floating Island*" (B.Litt. thesis, Oxford University, 1966).

[71] Wolf, "Textual Importance," p. 10.

[72] See Margaret Crum, "Poetical Manuscripts of Dudley, Third Baron North," *Bodleian Library Record* 10 (1979): 98–108.

[73] *Poems of Henry King,* ed. Crum, pp. 48–49, and Crum, "Notes," pp. 121–32.

lic Library) consists of the transcriptions of groups of Donne's elegies, satires, divine poems, paradoxes, and problems by his friend Rowland Woodward.[74] George Herbert's work survives in two important manuscript collections, the Williams Manuscript (Dr. Williams Libr. MS Jones B 62) and Bod. MS Tanner 307.[75] Herbert left the publication of his work to the discretion of a literary executor, not foreclosing the possibility of its appearance in print. The minor religious poet Henry Colman, however, had his poems done up in a manuscript book that was designed to imitate and rival the products of print technology, "Divine Meditations by H: C: Philomusus" (Bod. MS Rawl. Poet. 204).[76]

There are large collections of individual authors' poems in particular manuscript anthologies, especially the verse of John Donne, which is found in more surviving manuscript documents than the work of any other English Renaissance poet.[77] The Leconfield Manuscript transcribed for Donne's patron Henry Percy, earl of Northumberland (Cambr. MS Add. 8467),[78] and the Bridgewater Manuscript (Hunt. MS EL 6893), transcribed for Donne's friend John Egerton, later earl of Bridgewater, have sizeable groups of Donne's poems embedded within larger collections. A number of manuscript collections, like these, were transcribed for aristocrats. For example, the first part of the Haslewood-Kingsborough Manuscript, C. M. Armitage argues, was transcribed before Donne's death in 1630 for Edward Denny, earl of Norwich, by Charles Cokes.[79] So too BL MS Harl. 4955 contains a very large section with Donne's poems (fols.

[74] See the discussion of this manuscript in John Donne, *The Divine Poems*, ed. Helen Gardner, 2d ed. (Oxford: Clarendon Press, 1978), pp. lxxviii–lxxxi.

[75] See *The Williams Manuscript of George Herbert's Poems*, facsimile, with an introduction by Amy N. Charles (Delmar, N.Y.: Scholars' Facsimiles & Reprints, 1972), and *The Bodleian Manuscript of George Herbert's Poems: A Facsimile of Tanner 307*, facsimile, with an introduction by Amy M. Charles and Mario A. Di Cesare (Delmar, N.Y.: Scholars' Facsimiles & Reprints, 1984).

[76] See the recent edition of this manuscript: Henry Colman, *Divine Meditations (1640)*, ed. Karen E. Steanson (New Haven: Yale University Press, 1979).

[77] At least 246 manuscripts containing Donne's poems have been identified and more continue to be discovered. See Ted-Larry Pebworth, "Manuscript Poems and Print Assumptions: Donne and His Modern Editors," *John Donne Journal* 3 (1984): 20. Peter Beal has remarked that "probably more transcripts of Donne's poems were made than of the verse of any other British poet of the 16th and 17th centuries" (Beal, 1.1.245).

[78] See Dennis Flynn, "Donne and the Ancient Catholic Nobility," *ELR* 19 (1989): 305–23, for a discussion of Donne's early connections with a group of Catholic noblemen, including Percy.

[79] C. M. Armitage, "Donne's Poems in Huntington Manuscript 198: New Light on 'The Funerall,' " *SP* 63 (1966): 697–707.

88r–144v), followed by a run of poems by Francis Andrews (fols. 145r–72r). Similar gatherings of other poets' works exist, for example, for Henry Constable (Vict. and Albert Museum MS Dyce 44, fols. 12–43), Nicholas Breton (BL MS Add. 34064, fols. 1–26, 41–54),[80] and Thomas Carew (in Bod. MS Don. b.9 and Rosenbach MS 1083/17).[81]

## Some Physical Features of Manuscript Collections

Each handwritten copy of a poem is unique, whereas printed texts are meant to be identical. Handwriting itself was further individualized by the personalized versions of secretary, italic, or hybrid scripts. John Ramsey gives an account of his life at the beginning of his manuscript miscellany (Bod. MS Douce 280) in which he explains that he was wounded in his right hand in a duel. His handwriting changes dramatically from secretary script, presumably written with the right hand before his injury, to italic script done with the left hand, and finally to a much less legible hand as palsy degrades the writing still further.[82] Some manuscripts contain practice writing by children, who were set to copy texts by parents and tutors, often many times over.[83]

Women were usually taught to use italic, rather than secretary, script. Citing Martin Billingsley, who notes in *The Pens Excellencie* that the italic was taught to women because it was the easiest script, Giles E. Dawson and Laetitia Kennedy-Skipton point out that the mass of contemporary manuscript evidence indicates that women almost inevitably used this hand.[84] There are gender markers in some manuscript collections or portions of them. For example, in BL MS Egerton 2711 there is an answer poem to Wyatt's "Madame withouten many Wordes" in an italic hand, probably written, Richard Harrier suggests,

---

[80] See William Ringler, "Bishop Percy's Quarto Manuscript (British Museum MS Additional 34064) and Nicholas Breton," *PQ* 54 (1975): 26–39.

[81] See *Poems of Carew*, ed. Dunlap, pp. lxviii–lxix. Dunlap calls the first half of Don. b.9 the "only . . . collection devoted almost exclusively to his work" (p. lxix); it contains forty-two poems by Carew, including seven of the nine Psalm translations. See also Beal, 2.1.45.

[82] For an interesting recent discussion of handwriting and individual character, see Jonathan Goldberg, "Hamlet's Hand," *Shakespeare Quarterly*, 39 (1988): 307–27. See also his *Writing Matter: From the Hands of the English Renaissance* (Stanford: Stanford University Press, 1990).

[83] See Janet Backhouse, "An Elizabethan Schoolboy's Exercise Book," *Bodleian Library Record* 9 (1978): 323–32.

[84] Giles E. Dawson and Lactitia Kennedy-Skipton, *Elizabethan Handwriting, 1500–1650, A Manual* (New York: Norton, 1960), p. 10. Cf. Goldberg, *Writing Matter*, p. 138.

by a woman in the late sixteenth or early seventeenth century.[85] Sir John Harington's daughters Frances and Ellina transcribed poems in italic in BL MS Add. 36529.[86] Mary Lamb argues that the anonymous composer of the three holograph poems in the Bright manuscript was a female member of the Sidney family because they are in an italic script.[87] The authorial holograph of Lady Mary Wroth's poems (Folger MS V.a.104) is written in a formal italic hand.[88] The daughter of Sir Thomas Browne, Mrs. Elizabeth Lyttleton, transcribed poems in her commonplace book in italic hand (Cambr. MS Add. 8460), with a heavy concentration on religious verse. Nicholas Ferrar's nieces, Anna and Mary Collett, were probably the main copyists responsible for the beautiful Bod. MS Tanner 307 manuscript of Herbert's poems, the fair copy of *The Temple* sent to the printer in 1633, written in a calligraphic hand characteristic of manuscripts produced at Little Gidding.[89]

Men, however, especially aristocrats, also came to use italic script, and, by the early seventeenth century, many chose italic or hybrid secretary-italic forms.[90] In discussing Wyatt's autograph manuscript (BL MS Egerton 2711), Richard Harrier points out that the poet "wrote two hands, secretary and italic, the latter usually called forth by Latin or by technical language."[91] Ruth Hughey notes (2:120) that Sir John Harington sometimes used this hand.

Handwritten texts could be treasured for their personal associa-

---

[85] Harrier, *Canon of Wyatt's Poetry*, p. 12.

[86] On fol. 29v the names "Francis Haryngton" and "Ellina Harrington" appear. On fol. 82r "Ellina Harrington" is written in italic after a poem transcribed in secretary script. See Hughey, 1:41.

[87] Mary Lamb, "Three Unpublished Holograph Poems in the Bright Manuscript: A New Poet in the Sidney Circle?" *RES*, n.s., 35 (1984): 301. This is reprinted in her *Gender and Authorship in the Sidney Circle* (Madison: University of Wisconsin Press, 1990), pp. 194–228.

[88] See *The Poems of Lady Mary Wroth*, ed. Josephine A. Roberts (Baton Rouge: Louisiana State University Press, 1983), p. 61. Roberts claims that Lady Mary Wroth "clearly reserved her meticulous italic script for preparation of fair copies of her poems and for correspondence with persons of high rank" (p. 61) and distinguishes between her formal italic script and the cursive italic she used in other documents.

[89] See Amy M. Charles, *A Life of George Herbert* (Ithaca: Cornell University Press, 1977), p. 183.

[90] Goldberg discusses how the italic humanist hand came into favor in the sixteenth century among the aristocracy and in academic circles: "By the close of the century, those with claims to high literacy could manage at least to produce their signatures in this culturally prestigious hand" (*Writing Matter*, p. 51).

[91] Harrier, *Canon of Wyatt's Poetry*, p. 10. In *Verse Miscellany Manuscripts*, pp. 64 and 75, Hobbs discusses a single scribe's alternation of two distinct hands in the fourth section of BL MS Add. 25707 and in BL MS Add. 30982.

tions. Sir Stephen Powle wrote, for example, in his commonplace book after the text of Tichborne's poem, "My prime of youth is but a frost of cares," "Written by him sealfe. 3. dayes before his exequution: I have the originall written with his owne hande" (Bod. MS Tanner 169, fol. 79r). Peter Beal cites (in Edmund Blunden's translation) Donne's Latin poem to Dr. Andrews revealing that poet's preference for manuscripts over printed books:

> What Printing-presses yield we think good store,
> But what is writ by hand we reverence more:
> A Book that with this printing-blood is dyed
> On shelves for dust and moth is set aside,
> But if't be penned it wins a sacred grace
> And with the ancient Fathers takes its place.
>
> (1.1.245)

Manuscripts were especially valued when transcribed calligraphically. In her study of the manuscripts associated with Henry King's amanuenses, Mary Hobbs notes that they "produced calligraphic works of art fit to be placed on library shelves next to printed books. The Poems are well-spaced, with carefully centered titles; each page has a catch-word at the foot; ligatures join the letters 's' and 'c' to the long consonants such as 'l,' 't' and 'h,' and important words and phrases are emphasized by a bolder stroke of the pen."[92]

In his discussion of handwritten documents, Harold Love emphasizes the elements of residual orality, the "power of chirography to convey presence" in the face of the growing authority of the print medium.[93] Peter Lucas points out that "the hierarchical position of the script in which the manuscript is written corresponds to the hierarchical position in society of the patron to whom it is sent" so "one of the things that a patron could get out of his patronage was a manuscript which even in its style of handwriting reflected something of the patron's social position."[94]

The layout of a manuscript differs from that of a printed text. Especially when the manuscript transcriber was an amateur, the lines

---

[92] Hobbs, *Stoughton Manuscript*, p. x.

[93] Harold Love, "Manuscript versus Print in the Transmission of English Literature, 1600–1700," *Bibliographical Soc. of Australia and New Zealand* 9 (1985): 98.

[94] Peter Lucas, "The Growth and Development of English Literary Patronage in the Later Middle Ages and Early Renaissance," *The Library*, 6th ser., 4 (1982): 229–30.

were apt to be irregular rather than rectilinear, though some manuscripts have lined or folded pages and many have ruled margins. In his commendatory epistle to Thomas Watson's *Hekatompathia* (1582), John Lyly calls attention to the difference between "crooked" handwritten love poems and the perfectly aligned printed texts, explaining that he was reluctant to publish his own love lyrics because in print they would have lost some of the expressiveness of transcribed verse: "Seeing you have used mee so friendly, as to make me acquainted with your passions, I will shortly make you pryvie to mine, which I would be loth the printer should see, for that my fancies being never so crooked he would put them in streight lines, unfit for my humor, necessarie for his art, who setteth downe, blinde, in as many letters as seeing" (sig. A5v). In Gascoigne's "Dan Bartholomew of Bathe" the lover complains when his mistress prefers printed poems of a rival to his handwritten ones: "The rymes which pleased thee were all in print / And mine were ragged, hard for to be red."[95]

In manuscripts, scribes could alter the size of their handwriting to fit poems into available spaces. For example, in Nicholas Burghe's anthology (Bod. MS Ash. 38), after the first fourteen lines of a poem beginning "How comes the worlde soe sad for whom doth death" (p. 97), an elegy on Ben Jonson by George Stutvile, the writing is reduced to fit the rest of the piece on the page. There was less flexibility in published books. The exigencies of page and type size, for example, forced the printer of Barnabe Googe's *Eglogs, Epytaphes, and Sonettes* (1563) to break each heptameter, hexameter, and pentameter line after the fourth foot and to set it as two lines.[96] This constraint operated as late as John Donne Jr.'s misleadingly presented 1660 "edition" of the poems of Pembroke and Rudyerd (a belatedly published poetry miscellany); in it each line of the poulter's measure in Dyer's famous manuscript-circulated poem "He that his mirth hath lost" is printed as two.[97]

Some professionally transcribed manuscripts of verse include ru-

[95] *George Gascoigne's "A Hundreth Sundrie Flowres,"* ed. Prouty, p. 212.

[96] Barnabe Googe, *Eglogs, Epytaphes, and Sonettes* (1563), facsimile, with an introduction by Frank B. Fieler (Gainesville, Fla.: Scholars' Facsimiles & Reprints, 1968), p. xii.

[97] *Poems, Written by the Right Honorable William Earl of Pembroke . . . Whereof Many of which are answered by way of Repartee, by Sir Benjamin Ruddier, Knight. With several Distinct Poems, Written by them Occasionally, and Apart* (London, 1660). This is the first printing of Dyer's well-known poem. Bod. MS Rawl. Poet. 85 also has a version of this work lineated in the same way (fols. 109r–12v).

dimentary forms of ornamentation and deploy poems on the page with some sense of aesthetic design. In Bod. MS Rawl. Poet. 31, a vellum-bound, carefully ordered text in the hand of a professional scribe, there are ornamental divisions between its poems. This is also true of BL MS Add. 22118. In BL MS Add. 33998, a professionally transcribed anthology, the title of each poem and the names of the authors of those pieces for which there are ascriptions are enclosed in hand-drawn boxes. Some manuscripts retain features of older calligraphically produced artifacts: BL MS Egerton 2642, for example, a miscellany containing a book of heraldry as well as funeral verse, epitaphs, and moral, satiric, and epigrammatic poetry from the 1570s and 1580s is a rubricated manuscript.[98] Generally, however, there is a marked difference between the iconicity of ornamented or unornamented texts in printed editions and the appearance of the same texts in manuscript collections where their physical appearance does not call attention to them as aesthetic objects. In an authorial manuscript to be used to produce an edition of his poem on Baron Chichester, Christopher Brooke includes a note to the printer giving instructions for the presentation of his verse in the printed edition: "Let this Poem be printed with a Margent of black above, and beneath; and but 12 or 14 lynes on a side at the most; the distinctions *duely* observed; and some Judicious man to correct the Proofes by the Copie C: B:" (BL MS Egerton 2405, fol. 1r). This manuscript also contains a much longer note "To the Gentlemen that shall licence this Poem for the Presse," defending the satirical elements in his poem and the rightness of his motives, ending with instructions to "take out or dash [this letter] with your pen, Lest the Printer should be so grosse to print it with the rest" (fol. 25r). Often the final gatherings in printed editions left room for augmenting the verse of a single poet with the work of others, just as the process of collecting verse in blank books, for example, often produced empty spaces throughout a manuscript, into which texts could be copied later.

Whereas each printed book had pages of uniform size (most poetry texts appearing in quarto or octavo), bound manuscripts sometimes included different-size papers or quires. In physical format manuscript collections differed from printed ones in other ways: for ex-

---

[98] Black states that "Egerton 2642 [was] . . . collected by Robert Commaundre, Rector of Tarporley (Cheshire) and Chaplain to the Lord President and Council of the Marches of Wales in Sir Henry Sidney's time" ("Studies," 1:104).

ample, some were transcribed from the end as well as from the beginning. For example, in Bod. MS Eng. Poet. e.14 the material runs from the start on fols. 1–76 and, inversely and in reverse, from the end from fols. 101v through 76v. In Bod. MS Rawl. Poet. 212 for the most part the poetry is relegated to the section of the miscellany done in reverse transcription. In Folger MS V.a.103 there are two verse anthologies, the first through fol. 82, in which, according to Michael Rudick, 160 poems are "arranged by kinds and subject matters,"[99] the second a later mixed verse and prose collection transcribed in reverse from the last folio of the manuscript. Some (or most) manuscripts have different hands and sizes of writing, and some utilize double columns or sideways transcription.[100] Whereas printed texts were produced in a relatively short time, manuscript collections typically took shape over an extended period, in some cases over a century.[101]

## The Social Contexts of Manuscript Compilation

Manuscript miscellanies and poetical anthologies were kept mainly by individuals or groups of people associated with the following environments: the universities, the Inns of Court, the court, and the household or the family (by both aristocratic and middle-class individuals and their extended social circles). Harold Love calls such groups "scribal communities" and sees the circulation of manuscripts as "a mode of social bonding" in which the "very choice of scribal publication in preference to print might well be dictated by a sense of identification with a particular community and a desire to nourish its corporate ideology."[102] The few surviving medieval ancestors of the Renaissance manuscript collections were associated with religious establishments and with the households of provincial gentry. For example, Rossell Robbins claims that BL MS Harl. 2253 was "compiled

[99] Michael Rudick, "The Poems of Sir Walter Ralegh, An Edition" (Ph.D. diss., University of Chicago, 1970), p. 246.
[100] Double columns are used in Bod. MS Ash. 38, pp. 113–27, and also in Hunt. MS HM 198, pt. 1.
[101] For example, BL MS Add. 30982 runs from the early Jacobean era through the late seventeenth century. Bod. MSS Rawl. Poet. 26 and 172 also contain transcriptions made over an extended period.
[102] Love, "Scribal Publication," p. 146.

by monks at Leominster.''[103] Camb. MS Ff.1.6 is a fascicular manuscript that was kept by the Findern family of Derbyshire in the late fifteenth and early sixteenth centuries.[104] Some of these documents were associated with royalty and the nobility, some with members of the courtly establishment, and some with provincial landed gentry whereas others were connected with middle-class Londoners, with the clergy, and with university students and faculty.[105] The surviving sixteenth-century manuscript collections, however, were connected mainly with the universities, the Inns of Court, the court, and aristocratic households. Some documents show signs of involvement with more than one of these milieus and, of course, especially family collections passed into the hands of the next generation following that of the original compiler(s).

## The Universities

The majority of manuscript miscellanies and poetry anthologies from the sixteenth and seventeenth centuries originated in university settings, with Oxford collections, particularly in the seventeenth century, far outnumbering those from Cambridge. Two major Elizabethan anthologies of this type survive. It is interesting that both bear traces of the connections between the academic and courtly or cosmopolitan environments: Humphrey Coningsby's manuscript (BL MS Harl. 7392), a collection of poems begun by him at Oxford in the early 1580s and continued in London, where he had contact with the Inns of Court,[106] and John Finet's manuscript (Bod. MS Rawl. Poet. 85), begun at court and continued at Cambridge in the late 1580s.[107]

---

[103] Robbins, *Secular Lyrics*, pp. xvii–xviii; cf. the texts in *English Lyrics of the Thirteenth Century*, ed. Carleton Brown (1932; reprint, Oxford: Clarendon Press, 1962). Pearsall, however, in *Old and Middle English Poetry*, p. 121, dates this 1330–40 and associates it with the aristocratic Mortimer family from Hertforshire and with Adam de Orleton, bishop of Hereford, connecting this collection with the troubadour and goliardic tradition, with "a class of clerical jongleurs, imitators of the courtly tradition" (p. 129).

[104] See *The Findern Manuscript: Cambridge University Library MS. Ff.1.6*, introduction by Richard Beadle and A.E.B. Owen (London: Scolar Press, 1978), and Rossell Hope Robbins, "The Findern Anthology," *PMLA* 69 (1954): 610–42. Ralph Hanna III argues that the old notion of this manuscript as a compilation of booklets is correct ("The Production of Cambridge University Library MS. Ff.i.6," *Studies in Bibliography* 40 [1987]: 62–70).

[105] See Boffey, *Manuscripts*, pp. 113–41.

[106] See Black, "Studies," 1:41–54, and Cummings, pp. 60–61.

[107] These two anthologies share a central group of forty-seven poems: see Cummings, pp. 60–61, and Black, "Studies," 2:335–47.

The great period for university anthologies, however, was the seventeenth century, particularly from about 1620 to the mid-1640s. Of these surviving manuscripts, an extraordinary number originated at Christ Church, Oxford. Mary Hobbs, who has studied the relationships among these documents, highlights the importance of practices of verse composition encouraged at Westminster School, where many Christ Church poets were educated, and traces the influence of such individual poets as George Morley, Brian Duppa, Richard Corbett, William Strode, and William Cartwright on the development of circulating groups of poems that entered into the expanding collections of this period.[108] Raymond Anselment points out the Westminster–Christ Church connection, noting that Westminster annually sent three students to Christ Church and that Westminster "had a reputation for producing men of letters as well as religious and academic leaders," including such writers as Cartwright, Randolph, King, Strode, Jonson, George Herbert, and Cowley. He credits Lambert Osbaldeston, who succeeded Lancelot Andrews as head at Westminster from 1622 to 1638, with guiding "the generation of writers who appear so prominently in the Oxford collections" of printed panegyric verse, most of whom also appeared in the manuscript anthologies. He also calls attention to Brian Duppa, vice-chancellor of Oxford University, who encouraged Oxford authors.[109] One can number among these Christ Church anthologies BL MSS Add. 30982 and 58215, Egerton 2421, and Sloane 1792; Bod. MSS Eng. Poet. e.14 and e.30; Folger MSS V.a.97, V.a.170, V.a.262, V.a.345, and V.b.43; Rosenbach MSS 239/22 and 239/27; and Westminster Abbey MS 41.[110] Folger MS V.a.262, for example, has on the page preceding its verse anthology, "Divers Sonnets & poems compiled by certaine gentil Clerks and Ryme-Wrights," testifying to the shared practices of poetry anthologizing at the university. Folger MS V.a.345, another Christ Church collection, is written in many different hands. Compilers of poetry anthologies were associated with other Oxford col-

---

[108] See Hobbs, *Verse Miscellany Manuscripts*, pp. 82–85 and 116–23, as well as her Scolar Press edition of the Stoughton manuscript and her article, "Early Seventeenth-Century Verse Miscellanies."

[109] Raymond A. Anselment, "The Oxford University Poets and Caroline Panegyric," *John Donne Journal* 3 (1984): 184–86. Crum lists the following Westminster-trained poets: Dryden, Jonson, Cowley, G. Herbert, Randolph, Alabaster, Strode, Corbett, Cartwright, G. Fletcher, Martin Llyellyn, and J. Mayne (*Poems of Henry King*, p. 5).

[110] Hobbs discusses the Westminster Abbey Manuscript of George Morley's verse as a seminal collection (*Verse Miscellany Manuscripts*, pp. 116–18).

leges, especially New College[111] and St. John's, but Christ Church was the social hub of this activity. Richard Corbett and William Strode, whose poems are represented in many seventeenth-century manuscript collections, were both associated with Christ Church. Corbett, who spent thirty years at the university, was made dean of Christ Church in 1620, bishop of Oxford in 1628 (with the patronage of the then-declining duke of Buckingham), then bishop of Norwich in 1632. Strode was a public orator at the university and Corbett's chaplain, accompanying him finally to Norwich.[112] Many Oxford anthologies, not unexpectedly, contain verse of local or topical interest, especially short satiric poems on deceased or disgraced college figures. BL MS Egerton 2421, for example, has the following topical pieces: "On Feild & Day standing to bee Proctours" (fol. 4r); "On Owen butler of Christ Church in Oxford" (fol. 16r); "On John Dawson Butler of Christ Church 1622" (fol. 16r–v); "On the death of Ben: Stone of New: Coll: in Oxon" (fol. 17r–v); "On Tom: Christchurch great bell newfounded: to young Tom" (fol. 19r); "On Master Sanburne Sheriffe of Oxforde" (fol. 20r); "On the piece of noble worthy lady Paulet" (fols. 29r–32r).[113] After John Clavell, a purser at the university, ran afoul of the law for financial misdealings, was condemned on 30 January 1625/6, then received a royal pardon from Charles I, poems by and about him were copied in a relatively large number of manuscripts.[114]

The manuscript compilations of verse in this period which originated in Cambridge also contain poems satirizing university figures. BL MS Add. 44963, for example, compiled by Anthony Scattergood of Trinity College, Cambridge, has many poems of parochial interest, as does BL MS Add. 22603, a mid-seventeenth-century manuscript;[115] Bod. MS Eng. Poet. f.25 is a Cambridge miscellany of university ex-

---

[111] This school, with close ties to Winchester School, which encouraged the writing of vernacular verse, also fostered poetic composition and compilation (ibid., 89). Hobbs refers to Bod MSS Mal. 19 and Rawl. Poet. 84 as well as to Harv. fMS Eng. 686 as manuscripts connected to New College.

[112] See the life of Corbett in *Poems of Corbett*, ed. Bennett and Trevor-Roper, pp. xi–xli and xxxiii.

[113] A gift of needlework that Lady Paulet gave to the university (Crum, p. 695).

[114] For example, the poem Clavell wrote petitioning the king for pardon is found, with or without an answer poem in Bod. MSS Add. A.301, fol. xii; Douce f.5, fol. 16; Eng. Poet. c.50, fol. 24v; Eng. Poet. e.14, fol. 81v; Eng. Poet. f.10, fol. 92v; and Rawl. Poet. 84, fol. 73v rev. and in BL MSS Add. 25707, fol. 73v, and 44963, fol. 39v.

[115] See *The Poems of John Cleveland*, ed. Brian Morris and Eleanor Withington (Oxford: Clarendon Press, 1967), p. lii.

ercises and poems.[116] Archbishop Sancroft's manuscripts, Bod. MS Tanner 465 and 466, have Cambridge associations.[117] John Milton's early poem on Hobson the carrier of Cambridge shows up in Bod. MS Rawl. Poet. 26 (fol. 64v).[118] But, of course, certain topical pieces circulated among students at both universities: for example, satiric epitaphs on Edmund Pricke of Christ's College, Cambridge, and his namesake at Christ Church, Oxford, and poems about disastrous academic performance before King James of Barten Holiday's comedy *Technogamia*.[119]

Since students at the universities, however, came from different levels of the social hierarchy, it is fair to say that in this environment the practices of manuscript transmission cut across social classes most dramatically. In fact, one of the obvious reasons for the persistence of the manuscript system of literary transmission through the seventeenth century was that it stood opposed to the more democratizing force of print culture and allowed those who participated in it to feel that they were part of a social as well as an intellectual elite. For example, a short poem found on the first page of a large, collaborative Christ Church (Oxford) anthology was obviously composed by a student who was not a member of the upper classes, someone who identified himself primarily as a scholar:

> My wits my wealth, my learning is my lands
> My gownes my goods, my bookes for buildings stand,
> Arts are my acres, tongues my tenements,
> Pens are my ploughes, my writings are my rents.
> (Folger MS V.a.345, fol. [*]r)

---

[116] Ibid., p. liii.

[117] For a discussion of an interesting Cambridge manuscript, see Ted-Larry Pebworth and Claude J. Summers, "Recovering an Important Seventeenth-Century Poetical Miscellany: Cambridge ADD. MS 4138," *Trans. Camb. Bibl. Soc.* 7, no. 2 (1978): 156–69.

[118] In "Milton and Class Identity: The Publication of *Areopagitica* and the 1645 *Poems*," *Journal of Medieval and Renaissance Studies* 22 (1992): 287, Ann Baynes Coiro notes the following articles on this poem: "William R. Parker, "Milton's Hobson Poems," *MLR* 31 (1936): 395–402; G. Blakemore Evans, "Milton and the Hobson Poems," *MLQ* 4 (1943): 281; Willa McClung Evans, "Hobson Appears in Comic Song," *PQ* 26 (1947): 321–27; and G. B. Evans, "Some More Hobson Verses," *MLQ* 9 (1948): 10, and "A Correction to Some More Hobson Verses," *MLQ* 9 (1948): 184.

[119] For the Pricke poems, see the items Crum lists as A1362, O1094, S984, T607, T1445, and T1481; for poems about Barten Holiday's play, B384, B520, C229, N237b, T266, T392, W615–16, W957, and W2255.

This piece says much about the social status of at least some of the students who participated in the system of manuscript transmission: their social and political conservatism might have been more a sign of their sociopolitical ambitions than the defensive gestures of a privileged class. Whether or not they were from the ranks of the gentry, Oxford and Cambridge students who compiled miscellanies and anthologies thought of themselves as engaging in the leisure activities of the educated gentleman.

## The Inns of Court

Many manuscripts were associated with the Inns of Court, a social and cultural milieu in which both political consciousness and literary activity were quite high, especially at the end of the sixteenth century and the beginning of the seventeenth.[120] Many university students who started manuscript miscellanies or poetry anthologies continued to add to their collections when they entered new environments. One of the most typical movements was from the university to the Inns of Court. Rosenbach MS 1083/15 from the last decade of the sixteenth century through the first quarter of the seventeenth is a large poetry collection connected with both Oxford and the Inns.[121] Robert Bishop's commonplace book (Rosenbach MS 1083/16) reflects the compiler's Oxford and Inns of Court background: titled "Miscellanies, or a Collection of Divers witty and pleasant Epigrams, Adages, poems, Epitaphes &c: for the recreation of the overtraveled Sences 1630," this anthology of 396 poems is a fine representative of the university and Inns of Court compilations of the period.[122] Bod. MS Eng. Poet. e.14 has many Oxford associations, beginning with a transcription of Richard Corbett's "Iter Boreale," a long poem that recurs in a surprising number of manuscript collections, but it also has signs of having being used in an Inns milieu: it contains, for instance, two

---

[120] See Philip Finkelpearl, *John Marston of the Middle Temple: An Elizabethan Dramatist in His Social Setting* (Cambridge: Harvard University Press, 1969), pp. 3–80, and Wilfred R. Prest, *The Inns of Court under Elizabeth I and the Early Stuarts* (London: Longman, 1972).

[121] See James Sanderson, "An Edition of an Early Seventeenth-Century Manuscript Collection of Poems (Rosenbach MS. 186 [1083/15])" (Ph.D. diss., University of Pennsylvania, 1960) and "Epigrammes P[er] B[enjamin] R[udyerd] and Some More 'Stolen Feathers' of Henry Parrot," *RES*, n.s., 17 (1966): 241–55. In *Verse Miscellany Manuscripts*, pp. 90–93, Hobbs discusses manuscripts associated with legal circles, such documents as BL MSS Add. 21433 and 25303, Harl. 3910 and 6057, Sloane 1446, and Folger MS V.a.262.

[122] See David Coleman Redding, "Robert Bishop's Commonplace Book: An Edition of a Seventeenth-Century Miscellany" (Ph.D. diss., University of Pennsylvania, 1960).

poems "On Charls the Porter of Lincolns Inn" (fols. 11r and 13v–14r). BL MS Sloane 1446, which Beal says was "probably compiled by Francis Baskerville of Malmesbury, Wiltshire" (1.2.273),[123] has Christ Church (Oxford) pieces and Inns of Court material. Mary Hobbs divides the manuscript into two sections, the first (fols. 1r–64v) written in a "mixed hand, chiefly secretary" having to do with Oxford, the second (fols. 64v–94r) in a "very rounded italic hand" transcribing an Inns of Court collection related to the contents of BL MSS Add. 21433 and 25303.[124] This document also begins with Corbett's "Iter Boreale" and contains a rare copy of Milton's "On the Marchionesse of Winchester whoe died in Childbedd. Ap: 15.1633" (fols. 37v–38v). This collection is a good example of the social diffusion and conflation of verse from different sources, starting with poems derived from the local circulation of manuscript material at Oxford and moving to the more politically charged environment of London: some of the groupings of poems in the second part of this anthology are topical. A fair number of pieces, not listed as appearing in the Bodleian manuscripts indexed by Margaret Crum, are signed "F.B.," and were probably written by the compiler. Bod. MS Add. B.97, as noted above, is a commonplace book kept by Leweston Fitzjames first at Oxford, then at the Middle Temple. Both as a student and as a more mature man, Fitzjames made his commonplace book a mirror of his intellectual, literary, professional, and practical interests.

Other manuscripts were probably begun at the Inns of Court. The Farmer-Chetham Manuscript (Chetham's Lib., Manchester MS Mun. A.4.150), for example, mixes poems with political prose, opening with material having to do with such sensational public events as the arraignment for treason of the earls of Essex and Southampton and the trial and imprisonment of Sir Walter Ralegh. Its poems include Sir John Davies's "Gulling Sonnets" and selected epigrams (written at the Middle Temple), pieces by Donne and Ralegh, and older verse by Oxford and Sidney.[125] Bod. MS Don. c.54 is a miscellany of verse and prose owned by Richard Roberts, identified by Robert Krueger

---

[123] According to Hobbs, BL MS Sloane 1446 is an Inns of Court manuscript and Baskerville was a member of the Long Parliament (*Stoughton Manuscript*, p. xv). See also her *Verse Miscellany Manuscripts*, pp. 74–78.

[124] Hobbs, *Verse Miscellany Manuscripts*, pp. 74–75.

[125] See *The Dr. Farmer Chetham MS*, ed. Alexander B. Grosart (Manchester: Chetham Soc. Pub., vol. 89, 1873).

as a Welshman who became a judge and was part of "a circle of legal acquaintances that exchanged verses with one another" in Jacobean London.[126] His manuscript compilation is unusual in that it includes a long final section of poems in Welsh from friends in his native Wales. It contains politically sensitive libels against such figures as Edward Coke (fol. 6v), Robert Cecil (fol. 20r), and Robert Carr, the earl of Somerset (fol. 22v), and poems by such authors as Ralegh, Jonson, Joshua Sylvester, Davies, and Donne. Revealing an interest in the social networks in which he was involved, Roberts makes sure to list in the margin the names of the people who took part in the witty recreations referred to in Hoskins's Latin poem *Convivium Philosophicum* (fols. 21r–22r): "Christopher Brooke," "John Dun.," "Lionel Cranfield," "Arth[ur] Ingram," "Robert Phillips," "Henrie Nevill," "Connocta" [Connaught], "Hoskins," "Ric[hard] Marten," "Henry Goodier," "John Weste," "Hugh Holland," "Inigo Jones," "Tho[mas] Coriat," and "Edw[ard] Ratcliff," all members of a London social circle sometimes mistakenly called the Mermaid Club.[127]

Particular collections are associated with lawyers and government officials. For example, as noted earlier, Hunt. MS HM 8 was owned by the lawyer who became Master of the Rolls for Ireland, Francis Aunger.[128] Oxford All Souls Libr. MS 155, is a 413-leaf folio copied from the papers of Sir Christopher Yelverton, who was Speaker of the House in the 1597 Parliament; though largely comprised of prose, it also has some verse, including pieces by Sir John Davies, who functioned in an Inns environment.[129] Another successful lawyer, Chaloner Chute, owned a large folio manuscript poetry collection (BL MS Add. 33998) compiled especially for him sometime in the 1630s (Beal, 2.1.259).

*The Court*

Although much poetic composition is associated with the court, many fewer poetry anthologies survive from this environment than

---

[126] *The Poems of Sir John Davies*, ed. Robert Krueger, with introduction and commentary by the editor and Ruby Nemser (Oxford: Clarendon Press, 1975), p. 438.

[127] See I. A. Shapiro, "The Mermaid Club," *MLR* 45 (1950): 6–17, 58–63; R. C. Bald, *John Donne, A Life* (New York: Oxford University Press, 1970), pp. 193–95; and Annabel Patterson, "All Donne," in *Soliciting Interpretation: Literary Theory and Seventeenth-Century English Poetry*, ed. Elizabeth D. Harvey and Katharine Eisaman Maus (Chicago: University of Chicago Press, 1990), pp. 37–67.

[128] See note 50.

[129] See *Poems of Davies*, ed. Krueger, p. 445.

from the universities and the Inns of Court. The first forty-nine poems of John Finet's anthology were probably transcribed while he was at the court of Elizabeth (Bod. MS Rawl. Poet. 85) in the 1580s.[130] The Haringtons, father and son, were both courtiers and gathered their verse in courtly milieus in the Arundel Harington Manuscript. Anne Cornwallis, who was active in the social life of the court, compiled a short verse anthology (Folger MS V.a.89).[131] Richard Edwards, Master of the Children of the Chapel Royal, compiled the (lost) poetry anthology on which *The Paradise of Dainty Devices* (1576) was based.[132] Even Henry Stanford's anthology, compiled while he was in the service of various aristocratic employer-patrons (Cambr. MS Dd.5.75) is at least in part a courtly document: L. G. Black points out that its section of courtly poetry begins with the same item found at the start of Humphrey Coningsby's collection, Dyer's "He that his mirth hath lost."[133] Some family collections or collections associated with both family members and friends involved individuals active in courtly settings.

Certainly the most interesting surviving sixteenth-century courtly manuscript is the famous Devonshire Manuscript (BL MS Add. 17492), a document that has been discussed primarily in relation to the canon of Sir Thomas Wyatt's poetry.[134] Although of the early Wyatt manuscripts it is, perhaps, textually the least reliable source of Wyatt poems and of Wyatt ascriptions, it is the manuscript that best demonstrates the immersion of this poet's verse in a collection of miscellaneous poetry developing within a distinct social group. Julia Boffey describes how the collection developed and circulated:

> Its one hundred and sixty-seven courtly lyrics . . . were copied by at least twenty-three hands. Some of the signatures and names in the manuscript

[130] See Cummings, p. 40.

[131] I discuss this manuscript further in "Women and the Manuscript System," this chapter.

[132] Hyder Rollins, ed., *The Paradise of Dainty Devices, 1576–1606* (Cambridge: Harvard University Press, 1927), p. xiii.

[133] Black, "Studies," 1:55–59. See also Cummings, pp. 62–63, and Steven W. May, *Henry Stanford's Anthology: An Edition of Cambridge University Library Manuscript Dd.5.75* (New York: Garland Press, 1988).

[134] See Harrier, *Canon of Wyatt's Poetry*, pp. 23–54; *Collected Poems of Sir Thomas Wyatt*, ed. Kenneth Muir and Patricia Thomson (Liverpool: Liverpool University Press, 1969), pp. xiii–xv; Kenneth Muir, "Unpublished Poems in the Devonshire MS," *Proc. of the Leeds Philos. and Lit. Soc.* 6, no. 1, pt. 4 (1947): 253–82; and Raymond Southall, *The Courtly Maker: An Essay on the Poetry of Wyatt and His Contemporaries* (Oxford: Basil Blackwell, 1964), pp. 171–73 and passim.

(particularly those of Mary Shelton, Margaret Howard, and Mary Fitz-roy . . .), together with the details of its later history, associate it clearly with the court of Henry VIII, and in particular with a group of friends who were in close contact during the early 1530s in the service of Anne Boleyn. The stints of copying, and the fact that the manuscript seems to have returned at intervals to Mary Shelton, who acted as a kind of overseer, suggest very forcibly that it circulated in the manner of an autograph album, and that the times copied into it were designed to have some piquant personal relevance which would be appreciated by its closely-knit group of readers and contributors.

As the collection was passed around in this way among men and women whose amorous relationships in "real life" are partially documented, it is hardly surprising that they chose for the most part to copy into it lyrics on the subject of love—love among courtiers, expressed in a refined and formal way. Some of the contents actually take the form of communications between them. Once this kind of tone had been established in such a collective compilation, too, it was surely likely to be maintained, even by those who had no pressing reason to send love epistles in such tantalizingly semi-secret circumstances: love lyrics like these have been a perennially popular means of leaving one's mark in an autograph album. The Devonshire manuscript, then, comes to seem less like a collection of courtly love lyrics put together for the purposes of compiling a 'book,' and more like a sequence of letters, with a particularly although not exclusively, personal application.[135]

Associated by scholars with women connected with the Howard family—particularly Mary Shelton, Mary Fitzroy (née Howard), and Margaret Douglas—this manuscript reveals how such a document could serve as the medium of socioliterary intercourse within a restricted social group and the repository of texts generated within such an environment. Although Wyatt's name appears most frequently in the collection, some other names and initials figure significantly, including Mary Shelton, a woman who transcribed as well as composed some of the verse; "madame de Richemont," Mary Howard, sister of the earl of Surrey, who married Henry Fitzroy, duke of Richmond;[136] Richard Hatfield; Anthony Lee; "A.J."; "J[ohn] H[arington]"; "Harry Stuart," Lord Darnley, son of Margaret Douglas and her later

---

[135] Boffey, *Manuscripts*, pp. 8–9.
[136] See Harrier, *Canon of Wyatt's Poetry*, p. 26. John King names her (as duchess of Richmond) as one of the two great patronesses of Protestant writing in the reign of Edward VI (*English Reformation Literature: The Tudor Origins of the Protestant Tradition* [Princeton: Princeton University Press, 1982], p. 106).

husband Matthew Stewart, earl of Lennox; and "T[homas] H[oward]." In addition to these poets, Thomas Clere and Henry Fitzroy, with whom Mary Shelton and Mary Fitzroy were linked, were probably represented in the anthology.[137] In terms of the provenance of the manuscript, Richard Harrier claims that the book itself "was probably purchased in London by Henry Fitzroy about 1533 and was first used by him and his connections, among whom were Mary Howard and her friend Mary Shelton . . . [remaining] primarily a Howard family album." Mary Shelton had it in her possession and, after it circulated among others in the social circle, she later "mark[ed] certain poems for copy, memorization, or musical performance." Later "Lady Margaret Douglas must have taken the volume with her when she married Matthew Stewart, earl of Lennox, in 1544. At her death it was probably left to Charles Stuart, younger brother of Lord Darnley."[138]

An author-centered focus on the Devonshire Manuscript (e.g., the Muir-Thomson edition of Wyatt's poetry) distorts its character in two ways: first, it unjustifiably draws the work of other writers into the Wyatt canon, and, second, it prevents an appreciation of the collection as a document illustrating some of the uses of lyric verse within an actual social environment. It also has discouraged our seeing Wyatt's poems themselves as typical lyric utterances that could be used by individuals other than their author for their own purposes. In the Devonshire Manuscript, literary appropriation, in fact, is illustrated in other ways by Lady Margaret Douglas's and Lord Thomas Howard's use of verse from the 1532 Thynne edition of Chaucer as a private code.[139] This feature of the collection is a sign that the Devonshire Manuscript, in effect, is a bridge between late medieval courtly coterie communication and later practices of manuscript compilation.

### The Family

Outside the two universities, the Inns of Court, and the court, the main environment with which manuscript compilation of poetry was

---

[137] See Harrier, *Canon of Wyatt's Poetry,* p. 23.

[138] Ibid., pp. 27–28.

[139] See Ethel Seaton, "The Devonshire Manuscript and Its Medieval Fragments," *RES,* n.s., 7 (1956): 55–56, and Richard Harrier, "A Printed Source for 'The Devonshire Manuscript,' " *RES,* n.s., 11 (1960): 54.

associated was the family, especially the households of the nobility and gentry. Many family miscellanies and poetry anthologies survive, especially from the seventeenth century. Some of them passed from one generation to the next. BL MS Add. 61822 was assembled by William Briton (of Kelston) and his father.[140] BL MS Add. 27407 was used by Peter Le Neve (1661–1729) and his brother Oliver (Beal, 1.2.402). Bod. MS Rawl. Poet. 84 was connected with the Paulet family (Beal, 1.2.242) and Bod. MS Don. e.6 was probably compiled by members of the Cartwright family of Aynho, Northamptonshire (Beal, 2.1.247). Bod. MS Eng. Poet. f.9, a very large collection of Donne poems mixed with the verse of such other authors as Jonson, Wotton, Ralegh, Ayton, Pembroke, and Rudyerd, has its owner's name and social rank on the first page ("1623. me posidett Hen: Champernoune De Dartington in Devonina: generosus"). It also contains a comical epitaph by one of Champernowne's relatives, "Edward Champernowne."[141] BL MS Add. 25707 is a miscellany associated with the Skipwith family of Cotes, Leicestershire: it incorporates the verse of at least three family members (William, Henry, and Thomas Skipwith).[142] Gatherings of family papers, such as those associated with Viscount Conway (BL MS Add. 23229), represent manuscript compilation of a looser sort. So too, a manuscript such as Bod. MS Eng. Poet. c.53, connected with the Lingard-Guthrie family, represents the gathering together of pages of folded correspondence into one collection (Beal, 2.1.554). Some of these manuscripts contain fragments of family history. Bod. MS Rawl. Poet. 209, a verse miscellany partly compiled after 1646 by John Peverell, is one example: fols. 28–29 have information about the compiler's family background; on fol. 29v

---

[140] William Ringler's typescript account of this manuscript is found among his papers at the Huntington Library; boxes 40–46 contain Ringler's notes on various manuscripts. I have profited from consulting Ringler's notes for some of the manuscripts discussed in this study.

[141] See Beal, 1.2.252, 466. One of the interesting pieces in this collection is the letter between the fictionalized Sir Philip Sidney and Penelope Rich (pp. 222–41). This has been reproduced in Josephine A. Roberts, "The Imaginary Epistles of Sir Philip Sidney and Lady Penelope Rich," *ELR* 15 (1985): 59–77.

[142] For a discussion of this manuscript or of the Skipwiths, see Hobbs, *Verse Miscellany Manuscripts*, pp. 62–67; Beal, 1.1.252 and 2.1.42; and Philip Finkelpearl, *Court and Country Politics in the Plays of Beaumont and Fletcher* (Princeton: Princeton University Press, 1990), p. 26. In "A W. S. Manuscript," a letter published in *TLS*, June 10–16, 1988, Mary Hobbs asserts that this manuscript "appears to contain *five* separate Skipwith collections, bound together" (p. 647). See also James Knowles, "WS MS," *TLS*, April 29–May 5, 1988, pp. 472, 485.

is written "John Peverell Booke 1674" (Beal, 2.1.41). Of course, a blank book or table book in a family's possession might start out being used for miscellaneous contents and then incorporate selections of poetry or, conversely, begin as a poetry collection and be used subsequently for other purposes. Hunt. MS 46323, a manuscript associated with the Calverley family in the Caroline period is an example of the latter: it began as an anthology of verse and then, later, a new hand added a legal treatise and other prose (Beal, 1.2.15 and 2.1.557).

Given the demographic facts of literacy and high cost of paper and of blank "table books," it was unlikely that the practices of manuscript transmission and collection of verse extended very far below the ranks of the gentry, but there are some surviving manuscripts kept by individuals of the "middle class" (outside the university setting) which demonstrate the downward reach of this cultural practice. In her study of late medieval and early sixteenth-century manuscripts in which courtly lyrics are found, Julia Boffey notes that several of these documents belonged to middle-class Londoners, mainly merchants, whom she calls "a much more literate and educated section of society than has often been supposed."[143] These manuscripts are mainly collected works of particular authors or miscellanies of verse and prose rather than poetry anthologies as such. Boffey cites the examples of Camb. MS Pepys 2006, a collection of Chaucerian works owned by the mercer William Fetplace; Bod. MS Rawl. C.86, a large anthology owned by William Warner, merchant taylor; BL MS Harl. 541, associated with the family of the mercer Sir Thomas Frowyk; Camb. MSS TCC R.3.19 and R.3.21, the latter belonging to Roger Thorney, another London mercer; BL MS Harl. 2252, the commonplace book of John Colyns; and Bod. MS Rawl. C.813, connected with John Morris, who was Henry VIII's Chamberlain of the Exchequer.[144] Carol M. Meale has studied the Colyns manuscript closely as an example of a collection that was built "by assembling a large stock of paper, probably all blank, around a core of two commercially-produced booklets, some time after 1517" containing two romances to create "the book as a single entity."[145] Among the items collected

---

[143] Boffey, *Manuscripts*, p. 125.
[144] Ibid., pp. 125–27.
[145] Carol M. Meale, "The Compiler at Work: John Colyns and BL MS Harley 2252," in *Manuscripts and Readers in Fifteenth-Century England: The Literary Implications of Manuscript Study*,

in Colyns's commonplace book are two Skelton poems, *Speke, Parrot* and *Colyn Cloute*, the former not appearing in print until 1545.[146] BL MS Add. 30076 was compiled by Robert Dobbes, vicar of Runcorn, Cheshire, at the start of the seventeenth century (Beal, 1.2.100); BL MS Sloane 542, which has contents related to Oxford and to typical student preoccupations, was owned by a physician Nathaniel Highmore (1613–85) (Beal 1.2.139);[147] and BL MS Egerton 2230 is a verse anthology kept by Richard Glover, a London pharmacist (the first page announces "E. Libris Richardo Glovero pharmacopol. Londonieni . . . 1638") (Beal, 2.1.246). Antiquarians such as John Hopkinson (Bod. MS Don. d.58) and Marmaduke Rawden (BL MS Add. 18044) also kept collections.[148]

The initial compiler of BL MSS Harl. 6917/18, Peter Calfe, might have been a London apothecary. Mary Hobbs identifies him as the "son of a naturalized Dutch merchant in London" and a "near neighbour" of Thomas Manne, one of Henry King's amanuenses.[149] Hunt. MS HM 93 is a commonplace book of poetry and prose, "Dayly Observations both Divine & Morall / The First part. by Thomas, Grocer, Florilegius"—a decidedly middle-class florilegium full of proverbial wisdom and pithy sayings, the bourgeois counterpart of the poetical anthologies of the upper classes, with some contents, such as Herrick's poems (pp. 4–27), lifted from the elite tradition. The collection contains several sermons, along with such other works as Winstanley's *Muses Cabinet* (pp. 109–15), May's epigrams (pp. 116–19), selections from Dubartas (pp. 129–49), Fletcher's piscatory eclogues (pp. 150–67), Richard Fleckno's poems (pp. 158–60), selections from Fletcher's *Purple Island* (pp. 160–65) and from Wotton's *Remains* (pp. 183–86) and "Dr Aglets poems" (pp. 209–10). The compiler's tastes reflect the religious, moral, and utilitarian biases of

---

ed. Derek Pearsall (Woodbridge, Suffolk: D. S. Brewer; Totowa, N.J.: Biblio Distribution Services, 1983), p. 93.

[146] Ibid., p. 95.

[147] Nathaniel Highmore (1613–1685) was born in Dorsetshire, educated at Trinity College, Oxford (1632–39), graduated M.A. in 1641 and M.D. in 1642, staying on in Oxford for some time afterward and becoming friends with Harvey. He later practiced in Sherburne, Dorset, publishing a number of medical treatises, including "A History of Generation" in 1651 (*DNB*, pp. 829–30).

[148] For a discussion of Rawden, see H. F. Killick, "Memoirs of Sir Marmaduke Rawden, Kt. 1582–1646," *Yorkshire Archaeological Journal* 25 (1919): 315–30.

[149] Hobbs, *Stoughton Manuscript*, pp. xv and 309. See also her discussions in "Early Seventeenth-Century Verse Miscellanies," pp. 182–210, and *Verse Miscellany Manuscripts*, pp. 67–71.

his class, but the practice of this grocer-florilegist is one borrowed from his social superiors.

### Catholic Family and Social Circles

A fair number of surviving miscellanies and poetry anthologies can be associated with Catholic families and individuals. Since the censored public sphere of print was not especially receptive to Catholic poetry and prose, in a period in which Catholics, especially recusant Catholics, were a persecuted minority, they found the older manuscript system of transmission especially congenial.[150] The sixteenth-century family manuscript, BL MS Cotton Vespasian A.25, for example, is a recusant manuscript that includes some poems with the kind of strongly Catholic point of view it would have been dangerous to articulate publicly.[151] It has a collection of songs and ballads, many of which are concerned with the religious commitment of the compiler—for example, a poem attacking Protestant iconoclasm, "The lamentation of the crosse"; two religious songs by the recusant clergyman Peter Hartforth; and a ballad on the Northern Rebellion of 1569, "A Ballet of the deathe of Ratlyffe which rosse with the earle of northumberland lord pearse which he maide a lytle spaice before he was handged."[152]

Bod. MS Ash. 48 contains prose and verse from the mid-to-late sixteenth century, including some poems by Henry Lord Morley;[153] Hyder Rollins identifies BL MS Add. 38599 as a Catholic miscellany

---

[150] For a discussion of how Catholics relied on manuscript transmission, see Nancy Pollard Brown, "Paperchase: The Dissemination of Catholic Texts in Elizabethan England," *English Manuscript Studies 1100–1700* 1 (1989): 120–43. The poetry of the Catholic convert William Alabaster, which circulated in manuscript, but was not printed, is a good example of the restricted transmission of Catholic verse: see *The Sonnets of William Alabaster*, ed. G. M. Story and Helen Gardner (Oxford: Oxford University Press, 1959), pp. xxxvii, xliv–xlvii.

[151] This has been edited by Peter J. Seng as *Tudor Songs and Ballads from MS Cotton Vespasian A-25* (Cambridge, Massachusetts, and London: Harvard University Press, 1978).

[152] These poems are found in ibid., pp. 96–98, 76–77, 123–24, and 93–96. Seng points out that the first is found in a longer version in another recusant manuscript, Harv. MS Eng. 749.

[153] This manuscript also has a number of anti-Catholic pieces as well and is written in many hands. See Hyder Rollins, "Concerning Bodleian MS. Ashmole 48," *MLN* 34 (1919): 340–51. Natascha Wurzbach notes of this manuscript: "This is a collection of verses presumed to have been put together by the itinerant singer Richard Sheale in the mid-sixteenth century" (*The Rise of the English Street Ballad, 1550–1650*, trans. Gayna Walls [Cambridge: Cambridge University Press, 1990], p. 2). According to John King, this manuscript demonstrates the "survival of old oral traditions that the Protestants could not suppress" (*English Reformation Literature*, p. 217).

of the Shanne family of Yorkshire.[154] Bod. MS Eng. Poet. e.122 is a recusant collection supposedly in the handwriting of Laurence Anderton, S.J.; BL MS Add. 15225, many of whose ballads were printed by Hyder Rollins,[155] and Folger MS V.a.137, which contains a (twenty-four stanza) "sonnet in praise of our blessed ladie" (pp. 83–90) and a series of religious ejaculations (pp. 164–65), are both Catholic collections. Thomas Wenman's manuscript, BL MS Egerton 2403 (Beal, 1.1.108), begins with "The sad Complaint of mary Queen of Scotts who was beheaded in England in the reign of Queen Elizabeth": a poem of 186 stanzas (fols. 2r–32v). It is followed by a number of religious lyrics, including some composed by the Catholic compiler himself.[156] At one end of the manuscript, at the start of a reverse transcription is a title page advertising the owner's religious allegiance: "THOMAS WENMAN, BONUS— / HOMO TIMENS DEUM / J H S MARIA / 1601 / Londini datum / die 10 Jullii" (fol. 51v rev.). Above the "H" in "J H S" is the figure of the cross.

The mid-seventeenth-century manuscripts associated with the Astons of Tixall contain a rich record of private manuscript circulation of verse and prose correspondence within an extended Catholic family.[157] The particular manuscript compiled by Constance Aston Fowler between 1635 and 1640 (Hunt. MS HM 904), for example, preserves the courtship verse of the compiler's brother Herbert Aston and his wife-to-be Katherine Thimelby as well as an anthology of other poetry by friends and family members along with selected work of better-

---

[154] Hyder Rollins, "Ballads from Additional MS. 38,599," *PMLA* 38 (1923): 133–52.

[155] See Hyder E. Rollins, ed., *Old English Ballads: 1553–1625. Chiefly from Manuscripts* (Cambridge: Cambridge University Press, 1920), pp. xxvii–xxx, for a description of the manuscript.

[156] See the discussion of these in Chapter 3.

[157] See the edition of poetry from the Aston family manuscripts: *Tixall Poetry: With Notes and Illustrations,* ed. Arthur Clifford (Edinburgh: James Ballantyne, 1813). Clifford describes the poetry collections he found among the family manuscripts as follows: "1. A small thin quarto, stitched, but without a cover, on the outermost leaf of which is written, 'Her. Aston, 1658'; 2. A still smaller quarto, which has no cover, but opens with a little poem with this title, 'Mrs. Thimelby on the Death of her only Child'; 3. A small, but thick folio, covered with yellowish parchment, much discoloured; on the outside of which is written, 'William Turner his book, 1662': and on the inside of the under part of the cover, over which the last leaf has been pasted, 'Catherin Gage's book'; 4. A large quantity of loose scraps of paper, sheets, half-sheets, backs of letters, and the like scribbled over with verses" (p. x). These items, in an old family trunk, represent the full range of physical artifacts connected with manuscript transmission, from single sheets, to quarto booklets, to large, bound folio collections. Yale Osborn Col. b 4, a verse miscellany compiled by Herbert Aston, may be the first of these manuscripts described by Clifford. BL MS Add. 36452 is another. I cite most of the Tixall poems from Clifford.

known writers such as Robert Southwell, S.J., Henry King, Ben Jonson, and Richard Fanshawe.[158] One of the family poets included in the Aston family manuscripts, Edward Thimelby, refers to "our soft-pend Crashaw," contrasting this Catholic author with those Cavalier "toyling witts" (Clifford, *Tixall Poetry*, p. 40) who were within the mainstream secular tradition. Alluding to the secularization of religious imagery in seventeenth-century erotic verse, in another poem, Thimelby complains:

> A rapture, alter, sacrifice, a vowe,
>   A relique, extacye, words baudy now,
>   Our fathers could for harmeles termes allow.
> But now the very spring of poesy
>   Is poysond quite, and who would draigne it dry,
>   Must be a better Hollander then I.
>
> (Ibid., p. 42)

Alienated from the libertine Cavalier verse, and obviously referring to such works as Carew's erotic poem "The Rapture," Thimelby reiterates the position Robert Southwell articulated in the 1590s in his rejection of secular for religious verse.[159] Thimelby does, however, allow himself to write occasional, complimentary secular poetry. Like the other members of this Catholic circle of family and friends, he kept his works within the protective social confines of private manuscript circulation.

The second part of the Haslewood-Kingsborough Manuscript (Hunt. MS HM 198, pt. 2) contains a section of Catholic poems, including pieces "To our blessed Ladie in Honor of her Assumption"

---

[158] See Jenijoy La Belle, "The Huntington Aston Manuscript," *The Book Collector* 29 (1980): 542–67, for an interesting analysis of this manuscript and the related treatment of the Constance Fowler–Herbert Aston relationship in her article "A True Love's Knot: The Letters of Constance Fowler and the Poems of Herbert Aston," *JEGP* 79 (1980): 13–31, which prints a transcription of some of Herbert Aston's poems. This particular manuscript was not included in Clifford's *Tixall Poetry*. See also Dennis Kay, "Poems by Sir Walter Aston, and a Date for the Donne/Goodyer Verse Epistle 'Alternis Vicibus,' " *RES*, n.s., 37 (1986): 198–210. The manuscript of Henry Rainsford, whose family was connected with the Astons, indicates that a larger social circle participated in the circulation of literary texts: see Peter Davidson, "The Notebook of Henry Rainsford," *N&Q* 229 (1984): 247–50.

[159] See Southwell's manifesto in "The Author to his loving Cosen," in which he condemns secular love poetry: "Poets by abusing their talent, and making the follies and fayninges of love, the customary subject of their base endevours, have so discredited this facultie, that a Poet, a Lover, and a Liar, are by many reckoned but three wordes of one signification" (*Poems of Southwell*, ed. McDonald and Pollard Brown, p. 1).

(fol. 88v), "To St Michaell Th'archangell" (fol. 88v), "To my Angelus Custos" (fol. 89r), and "To St. George" (fol. 90r), the last possibly a poem to the patron saint of the Catholic author. The poem "Upon the Sight of Dover Cliffs from Callis," suggests that the poet was a Catholic exile:

> Better it were for me to have binn blinde:
> then with sadd eyes to gaze upon the shore
> of my deare countrey, but now mine no more
> which thrusts me thus, both of sight, and minde.
>
> Better for me to have in cradle pined
> then live thus longe to choake upon the coare
> of his sadd absence, whom I still adore
> with present hart, for harts are not confind
>
> Poore hart, that dost in so high tempest saile
> against both winde and Tide, of thie friends will
> what remedie remaines, that cann availe
> but that thou doe with sighes, the sailes fullfill
>
> Untill they splitt, and if the body die
> Tis well ymployd, the soule shall live thereby.
>
> (Fol. 95r)

The piece does not merely treat the conventional theme of love in absence; it seems to protest a forced separation from the author's native country. In the Elizabethan period, of course, the Catholic poet Henry Constable was a good example of a Catholic writer forced into continental exile: it is interesting that his poems, like Southwell's, continued to circulate in the manuscript system after their publication.[160]

---

[160] *The Poems of Henry Constable*, ed. Joan Grundy (Liverpool: Liverpool University Press, 1960), pp. 34–45, 84–92. It is important to note that despite their publication in the 1590s, the poems of Robert Southwell, S.J., continued to circulate in Catholic circles and were gathered in manuscript collections. In their edition of Southwell, McDonald and Pollard Brown show little interest in the commonplace-book anthologies in which this author's poems appear because, as they say, these manuscripts "are of interest only as they shed light upon the manner of the transmission of texts" and have no "textual authority" (*Poems of Southwell*, pp. li–lii). In discussing Bod. MS Eng. Poet. b.5, F. M. McKay says of the Southwell poems in that manuscript: "Could more instances such as that provided by Eng. poet. b. 5 be found, one might be able to establish that although by 1650 there had been twenty editions of Southwell's poetry it was still circulating in manuscript" ("A Seventeenth-Century Collection of Religious Poetry," *Bodleian Library Record* 8 [1970]: 187).

Bod. MS Eng. Poet. b.5. is a fascinating example not only of Catholic anthologizing but also of middle-class participation in a literary system closely associated with the social elite. Complied by Thomas Fairfax, a yeoman from Warwickshire, who transcribed religious verse in the 1650s, this manuscript is the work of a recusant who refused to take the "Oath of Abjuration" mandated by the Long Parliament. As F. M. McKay describes this document:

> Apart from a few prose extracts, the collection is made up of poems, most of which are of a religious nature. None is ascribed to its author. Nearly all the poems are of Recusant origin and those of greatest interest are the numerous carols and ballads and the thirty-two poems of Robert Southwell. . . . Since many of these poems are songs, whether hymns, ballads, or carols, and frequently the appropriate tune is named in the manuscript, they were probably sung on the occasions Fairfax and his friends came together. The religious character of the manuscript reflects the moral earnestness of its compiler, an earnestness deepened by the sadness of his life. Eng. poet. b. 5 reflects the taste of a middle-class Recusant, and perhaps of his friends, in a small Warwickshire village during the period of the Commonwealth.[161]

Although the usefulness of the system of manuscript transmission and collection of verse to recusant Catholics is obvious, the question of class is an interesting one in this document.

## Women and the Manuscript System

Although the keeping of commonplace books was taught to males in grammar schools and the practice of compiling miscellanies and poetry anthologies flourished in the all-male social worlds of the universities and the Inns of Court, some women contributed to or owned (or both) poetry collections in courtly, familial, and other restricted environments. Women engaged in correspondence and, very early on, took up the practice of keeping personal diaries.[162] They were the recipients of individual poems, groups of poems, and whole manuscript collections. In great houses and in courtly circles, they had

---

[161] McKay, "Seventeenth-Century Collection," pp. 187, 191.

[162] See Sarah Findley and Elaine Hobby, "Seventeenth-Century Women's Autobiography," in *Literature and Power in the Seventeenth Century,* ed. Francis Barker et al. (Colchester: University of Essex Press, 1981), pp. 11–36.

access to and sometimes added poems to manuscript compilations. Thomas Nashe complained about the restriction of Sidney's poems to manuscript transmission by citing the example of manuscript verse "imprisoned in Ladyes casks."[163] Henry King wrote a poem "To a Lady" on the uses to which this woman might put a blank table book she received as a gift:

> When your fair hand receives this Little Book
> You must not there for Prose or Verses look.
> Those empty regions which within you see,
> May by your self planted and peopled bee.
> And though wee scarse allow your Sex to prove
> Writers (unlesse the argument be Love)
> Yet without crime or envy You have roome
> Here both the Scribe and Author to become.[164]

Women could both collect and add to the body of poetry they transcribed in their personal anthologies. In some cases, women started or were presented whole collections of poems. Margaret Ezell has argued, in fact, that, because it has focused primarily on print culture and largely ignored women's participation in the coterie circulation of work in manuscript, feminist scholarship has drastically underestimated the literary activities of Renaissance women.[165] As producers of writing, women were much more active in the system of manuscript transmission than in print.

Women identified as owners of manuscript collections include Anne Cornwallis, daughter of Sir William Cornwallis and later wife to the seventh earl of Argyll (Folger MS V.a.89);[166] Eleanor Gunter, sister

[163] G. Gregory Smith, ed., *Elizabethan Critical Essays* (London: Oxford University Press, 1904), 2:224. See also the discussion of women's private keeping of poems and miniatures in Patricia Fumerton, " 'Secret Arts': Elizabethan Miniatures and Sonnets," *Representations* 15 (Summer 1986): 57–97.

[164] *Poems of Carew,* ed. Dunlap, p. 154. This passage is cited by Margaret Crum, "Notes," p. 121.

[165] Margaret Ezell, " 'To Be Your Daughter in Your Pen': The Social Functions of Literature in the Writings of Lady Elizabeth Brackley and Lady Jane Cavendish," *HLQ* 51 (1988): 281–96. See also her article "The Myth of Judith Shakespeare: Creating the Canon of Women's Literature," *NLH* 21 (1990): 579–92.

[166] See William H. Bond, "The Cornwallis-Lysons Manuscript and the Poems of John Bentley," in *Joseph Quincy Adams Memorial Studies,* ed. James G. McManaway, Giles E. Dawson, and Edwin E. Willoughby (Washington, D.C.: Folger Shakespeare Library, 1948), pp. 683–93.

of Edward Gunter of Lincoln's Inn (Bod. MS Rawl. Poet. 108);[167] Lady
Ann (Harris) Southwell (1573–1636), whom Peter Beal identifies as
the daughter of Sir Thomas Harris of Cornworthy, Devon (1.2.391)
(Folger MS V.b.198);[168] Mrs. Elizabeth Lyttleton, daughter of Sir Thomas Browne (Cambr. MS Add. 8460); Margaret Bellasys (BL MS Add.
10309), the daughter of Thomas, Lord Fauconberg (1577–1653), a
Royalist turned Cromwell supporter (Beal, 1.2.452);[169] and, as noted
above, Constance Fowler, daughter of Sir Walter Aston of Tixall, Staf-
fordshire (Hunt. MS HM 904). BL MS Add. 36529, an early manuscript containing poems by such authors as Wyatt, Surrey, John
Harington of Stepney, Sir John Cheke, all written before 1565, is a
manuscript probably kept by women of the Harington family.[170] BL
MS Harl. 3357 is marked "Henrietta Holles her book Given by her
father."[171] BL MS Add. 4454 is a personal miscellany kept by Katherine Austen in a four-year period in the mid 1660s.[172] References to
family members abound in this document. Aberdeen Univ. Lib. MS
29, marked "Elizabeth Len hir booke," is a mid-seventeenth-century
verse miscellany owned by Elizabeth Lane and John Finch (Beal,
1.2.148). BL MS Add. 44963 is a commonplace book of Anthony
Scattergood that passed into the ownership of someone who was
probably his daughter: the last page has the note "Elizabeth Scattergood her booke/ 1667/8" (fol. 137v).[173]

[167] See Falconer Madan, *Summary Catalogue of Western Manuscripts in the Bodleian Library at Oxford* (1895; reprint, Munich: Kraus-Thomson, 1980), no. 14601.
[168] This folio commonplace book of verse and prose, titled "The workes of the Lady Ann Sothwell: December 2 1626" (fol. 1r), includes the compiler's own poetry. Her 101-stanza poem on the Decalogue is recorded in BL MS Lansdowne 740, a manuscript largely composed of poems by Donne and by members of his coterie. Lady Southwell's manuscript book is being edited for the Renaissance English Text Society by Jean Klene. See Klene's paper, "Recreating the Voice of Lady Anne Southwell," in Hill, *New Ways of Looking at Old Texts*, pp. 239–52.
[169] The first thirty-nine folios contain characters, followed by poems. Some of the latter are quite bawdy, including "Gnash his Valentine" (fols. 137v–39v) and a piece on a wom-an's attraction to a man with a big nose, but small penis. The collection also contains a large number of love lyrics and epigrams.
[170] See Ruth Hughey, "The Harington Manuscript at Arundel Castle and Related Doc-uments," *The Library*, 4th ser., 15 (1935): 408–14, for a discussion of this manuscript.
[171] The British Library Catalogue notes that "John Holles is the last Duke of that name. She married the late Edward Harley Lord Oxford, Son of Robert Harley, first Lord of that Family" (see Harvester, p. 196).
[172] She is identified as the daughter of Robert Wilson and the widow of the Oxford-educated Thomas Austen, who died in 1658 (Harvester, p. 107).
[173] Anthony Scattergood was educated at Trinity College, Cambridge, and the manu-script, which contains poems in Latin, Greek, and English as well as academic exercises, was compiled in the 1630s (Beal, 1.2.271).

Some of the manuscripts connected with the Catholic Aston family, were compiled by women—most notably Constance Aston Fowler, Katherine Thimelby, and Gertrude Aston Thimelby. Constance Fowler's manuscript (Hunt. MS HM 904) is a Catholic family commonplace book with a mixed religious and secular collection. Pieces by such authors as Henry King, Jonson, Thomas Cary, and Richard Fanshawe appear to be interpolations in an anthology of religious verse and private poems written by or about family members.[174]

In one of her letters to her brother Herbert, who was on the Continent, Constance Aston Fowler begged him for some of his poetry: "Send me some verses, for I want some good ones to put in my booke" (Clifford, *Tixall Poetry*, p. xxii). Herbert himself later wrote in a letter to his sister that his wife, Katherine Thimelby, was making an anthology of his poems, requesting that Constance send copies of any of the items not recorded in a list he provided:

> My Mistress havings nothinge els to doe this winter, hath made a slight collection of all my workes. Wherefore you must make an inquiry into all your papers, and if you find any of mine that beginn not as this note, you must send them her by the first opertunity, that is, by Cannal [Canwell, near Lichfield] to us. . . .These I remember you have: To my Lady St Allbon's Death. If Love be a Pilgrimage, &c. On the Barr betwene. Laeta, the above, and the Reliquary. (Ibid., pp. xxii–xxiii)

This is a good example of how a young woman assembled an anthology of poems in the context of family relations, personal devotional and literary interests, and Catholic royalist politics.[175] Courtship poems, for example, exhanged between her brother Herbert Aston and Katherine Thimelby are preserved alongside the well-known work of poets who appear throughout the system of manuscript transmission.

In her manuscript among the Aston family papers, Catherine Gage collected verse from the larger environment of print and manuscript

---

[174] According to La Belle, the second hand in the manuscript, which only transcribed religious poems, mostly Catholic ballads, is not Constance's and is probably that of her elder sister Gertrude, who later became a nun ("Huntington Aston Manuscript," p. 544).

[175] Margaret Ezell states that "Constance Aston Fowler was the hub of a literary group which included Lady Dorothy Shirley, Katherine Thimelby, and Gertrude Aston, in addition to Fowler's brother Herbert Aston and the Cavalier poet Sir Richard Fanshawe" ("Myth of Judith Shakespeare," p. 589).

circulation.[176] She favored love poetry, but by arranging the verse as a series of numbered selections titled to conform to conventional situations, she presented poems by such authors as Ralegh, Pembroke, Shirley, Fletcher, Davenant, Dryden, Katherine Philips, and Rochester anonymously, along with a large amount of unidentifiable verse, as components of a collection she herself designed.[177] Thus (Ralegh's?) "Like to a Hermite poore in place obscure" becomes "Despair" (pp. 115–16) and a song of Dryden's from *The Maiden-Queen* (1668), "I feed a flame within," becomes "Concealed Love" (pp. 146–48). In a largely Restoration context, this Catholic aristocrat put together her own connoisseur collection.

Most of the manuscripts associated with women contain devotional pieces. Ringler notes that BL MS Add. 10037 is a short twelve-folio pamphlet of eleven devotional poems by Jane Seager in her own hand.[178] Elizabeth Lyttleton's book opens with religious poems (pp. 3–5) and contains many other religious pieces, including an interesting parody of the popular lyric, "Like to a Hermite poore in place obscure":

> Like Christian well resolv'd in place obscure,
> I mean to spend the Remnant of my Days
> in unfrequented Paths of Folk impure
> to meditate on my Redeemers praise:
>     and at thy Gates, o Death, Ile linger still
>     to Let out life, when God and nature will.
>
> A Mourning Weed my Body shall attire,
> my staff the Cross of Christ where on Ile stay,
> of true Repentance Linkt with Christ desire
> the Couch is made, where on my limbs Ile lay:
>     and at [etc.]
>
> My Food shall be of Christian Manna made
> my drink the streams flowed from my Saviours side
> and for my light, through Earths erroneous shade

---

[176] Clifford, *Tixall Poetry*, p. 365, identifies her as Lady Aston, daughter of Sir Thomas Gage, baronet of Firle in the county of Suffolk, and second wife of Walter, third Lord Aston.

[177] See ibid., pp. 109–205.

[178] I cite Ringler's notes from the Huntington Library collection of his papers.

the beames of Grace shall be my safest Guide
and at [etc.]
(Camb. MS Add. 8460, pp. 61–62)[179]

A courtier's disingenuous announcement of his retirement from the field of political competition here is transformed into a private religious exercise. Henrietta Holles's book (BL MS Harl. 3357) also contains much religious verse.

Bod. MS Firth e.4, a manuscript probably produced for Lady Harflete,[180] contains a large number of songs and answer poems. It opens with a dedication to Lady Harflete herself:

1: To the Incomparably vertuous Lady
the Lady Harflett

Loe here a sett of paper-pilgrimes sent
From Helicon, to pay an Homage-rent
To you theyre sainte: each brings by arts command
A gemme, to make a bracelet for your hand.
          you'le crowne theyre journey, if free entrance lies
          At those same Christall portals of your eyes.
Or here's a garden, planted by the care
Of fancee: every elegie drawes some teare
To water it, verses which diviner bee,
Are wholesome hearbes: others more light, and free,
Are painted flowers without smell: Here's fixt
A band of Roses; violets there are mixt,
          In the the cheife perfection of all standes.
          If you'le but add the Lillies of your hands.
Or here's a feast, where poets are the Cookes.
Fancies are severall dishes; Its that lookes
For brisker wine, findes onely lovers teares.
Drawne out by spungie greife, or palsie feares:
Pallas serves in her olives; Thetis bringes

---

[179] This poem is found in neither Bodleian nor British Library manuscripts. The Cambridge manuscript also has poems by Donne, Corbett, Wotton, Cartwright, Ralegh, and others, including a piece by Katherine Phillips. In *Verse Manuscript Miscellanies*, p. 2, Hobbs notes a religious poem about Good Friday written by the poet Henry King's sister Anne, which can be found in Bod. MS Rawl. D. 398, fol. 235.

[180] Morris and Withington identify her as "the wife of Sir Christopher Harflete of Canterbury" (*Poems of Cleveland*, p. liii). In his edition of Crashaw's poetry, L. C. Martin describes another manuscript (BL MS Add. 33219) "bound in silvered silk" that was probably "designed as a gift to a lady," possibly by Crashaw himself (*The Poems English, Latin and Greek of Richard Crashaw*, ed. L. C. Martin [Oxford: Clarendon Press, 1957], pp. lxxiii–iv).

In stead of fish, her Venus from her springes.
Those thankfull paire of wonted Graces, bee
In this same banquet, multipli'd to three.
    you are that guest, whom all doe humbly pray
    you'de not let harsh detraction take away.
But this same word detracts, 'tis more then bold
that thinks this sun, will not turne earth to gold
Which changing powre theese poets come to try
Knowinge your favour's skil'd in chimicie
theyre soule lies in your breath, if this allow;
They made the verses, but the poets you
Or if they shall with a more harsh gale meete,
theyre paper serves, but for theyre windinge-sheete:
In you theyse fortunes lie, you you alone;
The Muses stand for ciphers, add but one
(your noble selfe) to those, theyre noughts; and then
the number of the Muses wilt bee ten.
    Or if you will not daigne a Muses name
    yet let the Muses commit yours to fame.

This poem, which presents a collection of both secular and religious verse, assumes that its addressee has sophisticated literary taste and a connoisseur's appreciation of the anthology's contents. As a patroness, she is a sponsor of poets, figuratively a tenth muse, and the owner of the texts presented to her as a gift. It is interesting that the first poem that follows is Ralegh's "Lie," which is also the first poem in Lady Anne Southwell's commonplace book (Folger MS V.b.198).

Although Isabella Whitney, Emilia Lanyer, and (possibly) Lady Mary Wroth are remarkable early examples of women who decided to transfer their own poetry to the medium of print, they are exceptional cases: it is rare to find published poems by women authors before the mid-seventeenth century, when Lady Margaret Cavendish, duchess of Newcastle, brought out her poems (*Poems and Fancies, written by the Right Honourable, The Lady Newcastle* [London, 1653]). Poems by women circulated more freely, however, in the manuscript system and survive in a number of collections. It is quite possible, moreover, that many anonymous pieces found in manuscript collections were also composed by women.[181] For example, Richard Harrier suggests

---

[181] For a discussion of one manuscript preserving women's writing, Bod. MS Rawl. Poet. 16, "Poems, songs, a Pastoral & a Play" by Lady Elizabeth Brackley and Lady Jane Cavendish, see Ezell, " 'To Be Your Daughter in Your Pen,' " pp. 281–96.

that the poem in the Devonshire Manuscript beginning "Farewell all my wellfare" (fols. 9v–10r) is "written from a woman's point of view" and that it "reads like a fifteenth century song or imitation of it by a woman."[182] BL MS Royal 12 A.I–IV is a mid-sixteenth century manuscript including juvenilia of Lady Mary Fitzallen.[183] Bod. MS Rawl. Poet. 26 notes with reference to the political answer poem that begins "Contemne not gratious king, our playnts and teares," "These are sayd to be done by a Lady" (fol. 20r).[184] We know that, especially in courtly settings, women had the opportunity to take part in the composition of and exchanges of verse.[185]

The Devonshire Manuscript (BL MS Add. 17492) includes the love poems exchanged by a married couple, Lady Margaret Howard and Lord Thomas Howard. Lady Margaret, who was the niece of King Henry VIII, contracted an unauthorized marriage with Lord Thomas Howard—an act for which the couple was punished severely. In a run of poems dealing with the situation of the lovers' imprisonment after the discovery of their marriage, Margaret Douglas answers her husband's pained epistles with her own expressions of sympathy and fidelity, which profess unwavering love and resistance to the coercion of the authorities. The piece beginning "I may well say with joyful harte,"[186] done in the serviceable plain style of early Tudor verse, has

---

[182] Harrier, *Canon of Wyatt's Poetry*, p. 41.

[183] These are identified as "Exercises in *Latin* translation, written as new-year's gifts to her father by Lady Mary Fitzalan, younger daughter of Henry Fitzalan, Earl of Arundel. The first two were written after, the last two before, her marriage (*circ.* 1554) with Thomas Howard, Duke of Norfolk; she died (aged 17) in 1557" (Harvester, p. 116).

[184] Crum says this poem answers O 803 and is also found in Bod. MSS Ash. 36, 37, fol. 59; Eng. Poet. c.50, fol. 25v; and Rawl. Poet. 152, fol. 4r (p. 175).

[185] See, for example, the discussion of Lucy, countess of Bedford, in my *John Donne*, pp. 202–32, and Barbara Kiefer Lewalski, "Lucy, Countess of Bedford: Images of a Jacobean Courtier and Patroness," in *Politics of Discourse: The Literature and History of Seventeenth-Century England*, ed. Kevin Sharpe and Steven N. Zwicker (Berkeley and Los Angeles: University of California Press, 1987), pp. 52–77. Much attention has been given recently to the manuscript and print remains of Lady Mary Wroth's poetry and prose. Jeff Masten has argued that the holograph of her poems (Folger MS V.a.104) was for her own use and that "the poems themselves—like the anomalous manuscript in which they are inscribed—encode a withdrawal from circulation. . . . [The poems] articulate a woman's resolute constancy, self-sovereignty, and unwillingness to circulate among men; they gesture toward a subject under self-control. In their insistent privacy and refusal to circulate, the poems reproduce the actual situation of their writing" (" 'Shall I turne blabb?': Circulation, Gender, and Subjectivity in Mary Wroth's Sonnets," in *Reading Mary Wroth: Representing Alternatives in Early Modern England*, ed. Naomi J. Miller and Gary Waller [Knoxville: University of Tennessee Press, 1991], p. 69).

[186] Muir, "Unpublished Poems," p. 264. I cite this edition for the Douglas and Howard poems. See Muir's discussion of these on pages 254–57. BL MS Egerton 2642 contains poems by another woman caught in the middle of political machinations: "Certain verses

a certain romantic and personal value in the protective confines of a poetical collection restricted to a sympathetic audience. Late in the Devonshire Manuscript, there is a testament poem addressed to her father in which she defends her elopement as an act that "prosedeth off lovers Fervence / And off my harts constancy" (Muir, "Unpublished Poems," p. 277). She may also have written the poem beginning "My hart ys set nat to remove" (p. 276), which has a female speaker. After Lord Thomas Howard's death in prison and after Margaret's marriage to the duke of Lennox, such poems would have been kept particularly close in a manuscript that her own son, Lord Darnley (husband of Mary, Queen of Scots, and father of James I), could later use for one of his own love poems.[187]

Many poems in the Devonshire Manuscript either attack or defend women, a trend found in many other manuscripts. Trinity Col. Camb. MS R.3.19 similarly combines attacks on and defenses of women.[188] Roman Dyboski notes the presence of misogynistic poetry in Richard Hill's commonplace-book collection.[189] BL MS Cotton Vespasian A.25 has a song in praise of women answered by one criticizing them.[190] Apart from those Wyatt lyrics that either compliment or satirize women's behavior, the Devonshire Manuscript contains both particular and general attacks on women for "newfangilnes" (Muir, "Unpublished Poems," p. 273) and for being fair without and foul

---

written by . . . Lady Jane [Grey] before her deathe unto the Lord Guylford Dudley her husband who was executed upon the scaffold at Tower Hill . . . a litle before the death of the same Lady Jane" (fol. 213v). These include the following moral pieces:

> Bee constant, bee constant, feere not for payne,
> Christe hath redeamed thee, and heaven is thy gayne
>
> Do never thinke it straunge,
> Though nowe I have mysfortune
> For if that fortune chaunge:
> The same to the may happen.
>
> Yf God do Helpe thee: Hate shall not hurte thee!
> Yf god do fayle thee, then shall not Labor prevayle thee.

These conventional poetic sentiments from the woman who was put forward by the Northumberland faction as queen of England after the death of Edward VI resemble other prison poems in their retreat into Christian fortitude.

[187] See "My hope is yow for to obtaine" in Muir, "Unpublished Poems," p. 272, possibly written to Mary, Queen of Scots.

[188] Boffey, *Manuscripts*, p. 19.

[189] Dyboski, *Richard Hill's Commonplace-Book*, pp. xxvi–xxvii.

[190] Seng, *Tudor Songs and Ballads*, pp. 35–39.

within (pp. 273–74). There is a punctuation-game poem by Richard Hatfield that converts a seeming praise of women into an attack on them (pp. 260–61). But there are also such defenses of women as the following lines, provided, of course, they are not given an ironic reading:

> Womans herte unto no creweltye
>     Enclynyd ys, but they be charytable,
> Pytuous, devoute, ful off humylyte,
>     Shamefast, debonayre and amyable,
>     Dredeful and off wordes measurable:
> What women these have not paraventure
> Folowyth not the way off her nature.
>
> (Ibid., 278)

The faithfulness of women is hyperbolically (and positively) defined in another piece that reflects metapoetically on the medium through which it is expressed:

> Yff all the erthe were parchment scrybable
> Spedy for the hande, and all maner wode
> Were hewed and proportyoned to pennes able,
>     Al water ynke, in damme or in flode,
>     Every man beyng a parfyte scribe or goode,
> The faythfulnes yet and prayse of women
> Cowde not be shewyd by the meane off penne.
>
> (Ibid.)

Just as misogynistic pieces are counterbalanced by poems in praise of women, so too the love poems, following the Wyatt model, set amorous compliments and complaints against palinodes and renunciations of love.[191]

Folger MS V.a.89, which includes Anne Cornwallis's short collection of verse from the late Elizabethan period, contains an interesting poem attributed to Ann Vavasour, with whom the earl of Oxford had

---

[191] On at least one occasion an educated woman replied to a misogynistic poem written by a man. In *Elizabethan Courtier Poets*, p. 246, May reprints Lady Mary Cheke's poem answering Sir John Harington's epigram "Of a certayne man" ("That no man yet could in the bible finde"). May uses as copytext Victoria and Albert Museum Dyce MS 44, fol. 72v. Lady Cheke, May notes, was the daughter of Richard Hill, "sargeant of the wine cellar to Henry VIII" (p. 245).

a scandalous affair in the early 1580s, a lyric in which the female speaker discourses on the danger of revealing one's love in the repressive environment of the Elizabethan court:

> Thoughe I seeme straunge sweete freende be thou not so
>  Do not anoye thy selfe with sullen will
> My harte hathe voude allthoughe my tongue sayes noe
>  To rest thyne owne in freendly liking styll.
> Thou seest me live amongste the Lynxes eyes
>  That pries and spies eche privy thoughte of mynde
> Thou knowest ryghte well what sorrowes maye aryse
>  Ife once they chaunce my setled lookes to fynde
> Contente thy selfe that once I made an othe
>  To sheylde my selfe in shrowde of honest shame
> And when thou lyste make tryall of my trouthe
>  So that thou save the honoure of my name
> And let me seme althoughe I be not coye
>  To cloak my sadd conceyte with smylinge cheere
> Let not my jestures showe wherin I joye
>  Nor by my lookes lett not my love apeere.
> We seely dames that false suspecte, do feare
>  And live within the mouthe of envyes lake
> Must in oure heartes a secrete meaning beare
>  Far from the shewe that outwardlye we make
> Goe wher I lyke, I lyste not vaunte my love
>  Where I desyre there moste I fayne debate
> One hathe my hande an other hathe my glove
>  But he my harte whome most seem most to hate
> Thus farwell freende I will continewe straunge
>  Thou shalte not heere by worde or writinge oughte
> Let it suffice my vowe shall never chaunge
>  As for the rest I leave It to hy thoughte.

vavaser[192]

Although this piece is subscribed "La[dy] B to N" in BL MS Harl. 6910 (fol. 145r) and, as Cummings points out (p. 225), there are elements in the poems that conflict with the circumstances of Ann Vavasour's life, the important thing is not the identification of the author, but the representativeness of the utterance: the poem occurs

---

[192] I have altered Cummings's transcription (pp. 220–21) of the version in the Finet anthology to conform to the variants found in the Cornwallis manuscript. For a discussion of the Cornwallis manuscript, see Bond, "Cornwallis-Lysons Manuscript," pp. 683–93.

in at least five manuscripts.[193] John Finet's anthology has a poem ascribed to one "Mistress M. R." lamenting the vulnerable position of women whose honor is continually under attack by erotically aggressive men, "Howe can the feeble forte butt yeelde att last" (Bod. MS Rawl. Poet. 85, fol. 114r–v; cited in Cummings, pp. 772–73). The social rhetoric and situational appropriateness made these two courtly poems collectable.

Mary Lamb argues for female authorship of three anonymous love poems in the Bright Manuscript connected with the Sidney family (BL MS Add. 15232).[194] Lady Mary Wroth, Sir Robert Sidney's daughter and Sir Philip Sidney's niece, circulated her verse in manuscript within her family and a circle of friends that included Ben Jonson, who copied some of her poems and admired her poetic abilities.[195] Among the poems Clifford gathers in that part of *Tixall Poetry* labeled "Poems by the Honourable Mistress Henry Thimelby" are pieces "on the Death of her Only Child," "To her Husband, on New-Years-Day, 1651," "Upon a Command to Write on my Father," "To my Brother and Sister Aston, on their Wedding-day, Being Absent," and the following Jonsonian epitaph:

> To Sir William and my Lady Persall,
> uppon the death
> of their Little franke
>
> Happy parents, mourne no more,
> You this jewell but restore:
> Nor yet question Heavens will,
> Why he was not lent you still.
> As you merited that grace,
> So his innocence the place
> We all ambition; nor could you
> Covet yours to bar his due.
> Say in him we know did meete
> All was good, and all was sweet,
> Does this aggravate your cross?
> Your gaine is greater then your loss.
> For, alas! what did he here?

---

[193] In addition to Bod. MS Rawl. Poet. 85, Cummings also cites Bod. MS Rawl. Poet. 172, BL MSS Harl. 6910 and 7392, and Folger V.a.89 (p. 222).

[194] Lamb, "Three Unpublished Holograph Poems," pp. 301–15.

[195] See *Poems of Lady Mary Wroth*, ed. Roberts, pp. 17, 19, 42.

> Please your eye, delight your eare:
> He your senses' welcome guest,
> Treates your soules now with a feast.
> Tis his powerfull praiers give you
> All good here, and heaven too.
> Yet hence your comfort most will rise,
> God loves the child that quickly dies.
> (Clifford, *Tixall Poetry*, pp. 99–100)

Such female-authored verse stayed close to immediate relations with family and friends, brought forth by such common occasions as births, deaths, marriages, and New Years' greetings.

Gertrude Aston, who became a nun in her widowhood, wrote appropriately devotional verse, such as the following:

### On Saint Catherines Day

> You glorious saint, tho borne of royall blood,
> All greatness scorn'd but that of being good.
> Tho learn'd in many knowledges, were still,
> Best knowing, and most practising God's will.
> And tho more fayre than is the rosy morne,
> The charmes of vertue did you most adorne.
> Pray, I not great, not wise, not fayre may seeme,
> In the world's false, but in heaven's just esteeme.
>                                    GERT. ASTON
>                                    (Ibid., 226)

Clearly in this seventeenth-century Catholic family, there were many women who collected, transmitted, and composed verse—all of whom confined themselves to the manuscript system.

One of the difficulties in searching for poems written by female authors is, of course, caused by the practice of male authors' composing pieces spoken by female personas. The earl of Oxford, for example, scripted an echo poem for his mistress Ann Vavasour to follow his lyric, "Sittinge alone my thought in melancholye moode" ("'O heavens,' quoth she, 'who was the first that bed in me this fevere'").[196] Poems by Queen Elizabeth survive, including a wittily

---

[196] May, *Elizabethan Courtier Poets*, pp. 282–83, transcribed from Anne Cornwallis's collection (Folger MS V.a.89, fol. 9).

condescending reply to a courtly solicitation by Sir Walter Ralegh,[197] but even in her case there is an example of a poem written by someone else in her person, "When I was fair and young," a lyric whose message is that the queen will regret not yielding to importunate suitors. This is the first poem in John Finet's anthology, "Verses made by the queine when she was supposed to be in love with mountsyre" (fol. 1r), an identification that associates the lyric with Elizabeth's byzantine marriage negotiations with the duke of Anjou.[198]

Throughout the period with which this book is concerned, women figure in important ways as the owners, compilers, and contributors to the manuscript miscellanies and poetry anthologies. Both the relative privacy of manuscript transmission and the relative hostility of print culture to women's writing affected women's choice of the manuscript medium of communication. Were literary histories more attentive to manuscript evidence and less dependent on the products of print culture, women's activities as authors, compilers, and owners of literary texts would be more visible.

## Sixteenth-Century Manuscript Collections

Very few manuscript poetry anthologies from the sixteenth century survive. Of these collections, four in particular stand out: the Arundel Harington Manuscript, John Finet's anthology (Bod. MS Rawl. Poet. 85), Humphrey Coningsby's anthology (BL MS Harl. 7392), and Henry Stanford's manuscript (Camb. MS Dd.5.75). In many ways, these anthologies of sixteenth-century verse are more interesting than anything comparable in print at the time.

The first of these, the Arundel Harington Manuscript, presented in an exhaustively annotated modern edition by Ruth Hughey, is a courtly anthology assembled over some sixty years John Harington of Stepney, a pre-Elizabethan client of Protector Somerset who entered the service of Queen Elizabeth, and his son, Sir John Harington of Kelston, who composed epigrams and the Menippean satire *The Met-*

---

[197] See Black, "Lost Poem." p. 535, and May, *Elizabethan Courtier Poets*, p. 319.

[198] See *Poems of Queen Elizabeth I*, ed. Bradner, pp. 5, 73. May, however, claims this poem should be assigned to Elizabeth (*Elizabethan Courtier Poets*, p. 317). For a general discussion of poems with female speakers, see Gail Reitenbach, " 'Maydes are simple, some men say': Thomas Campion's Female Persona Poems," in *The Renaissance Englishwoman in Print*, ed. Anne M. Haskelhorn and Betty S. Travitsky (Amherst: University of Massachusetts Press, 1990), pp. 80–95.

*amorphosis of Ajax* and translated Ariosto's *Orlando Furioso*. Although its early contents put it in a family of collections that includes the Wyatt autograph manuscript (BL MS Egerton 2711) and *Tottel's Miscellany* (1557),[199] its later texts range through the poetry of the second half of the Elizabethan period. It is thus a broadly based chronological collection of sixteenth-century verse of various kinds and styles: it includes older moral, religious, and complaint verse as well as more stylish or avant-garde courtly lyrics of the last part of the century, pieces by such poets as Wyatt, Surrey, and John Harington of Stepney on the one hand, and Ralegh, Sidney, Dyer, Daniel, Greville, Constable, and Sir John Harington of Kelston, on the other.[200]

Ruth Hughey suggests that this manuscript anthology offers scholars the opportunity to study "changing taste and poetic development from about 1540 to 1600" (1:68). It reflects the social and political dynamics of the court and the semiotic encoding of poetic texts in that environment. Originally begun probably while the elder Harington was a prisoner in the Tower, the collection developed under the supervision of a father and son who were deeply involved in the Tudor court and government. Hence, it is not surprising to find in the anthology such poems as the elder Harington's piece in praise of the Princess Elizabeth's maids of honor, "The great Dyana, chaste" (Hughey, 1:299–301); "A sonet writen upon my Lord Admiral Seymour" (1:79); George Blage's satiric epitaph about his political enemy, the earl of Southampton, "From vyle estate, of base and low degree" (1:344 and 2:441–43); Sir Henry Goodyer's poem about Mary Stuart's troubles in 1572, "If fortune good could answer present ill" (1:179–80 and 2:193–99), followed by an answer poem by Thomas Norton (1:180–82, 2:199–201); Queen Elizabeth's own poem about the Northern Rebellion, "The dread of future foes" (1:276–77); and a number of (less politically overt) courtly poems such as Dyer's "He that his myrthe hath lost" (1:182–84).[201]

[199] See the discussion of this manuscript in Hughey, 1:3–75, and in Harrier, *Canon of Wyatt's Poetry*, pp. 16–22. Harrier, in relating the Arundel Harington Manuscript to both BL MS Egerton 2711 and *Tottel's Miscellany*, suggests that John Harington of Stepney probably edited the collection printed by Tottel. He agrees with Hughey that the Arundel Harington Manuscript "was in a medial position" between the Egerton manuscript and Tottel and was likely "the basis for the edited copy from which [Tottel] was printed" (pp. 19–20).

[200] The present manuscript contains 145 leaves of the original, from which some 83 leaves were removed, most of these excisions made in the compiling of the eighteenth-century collection of Harington family papers, *Nugae Antiquae* (Hughey, 1:11, 18).

[201] For a discussion of another Harington poetry manuscript (BL MS Add. 36529) con-

The younger Harington, through social connections, had access to Sir Philip Sidney's *Astrophil and Stella* before its publication and began, but did not continue, a transcription of the poems under the heading "Sonettes of Sir Phillip Sydneys *uppon* to the Lady Ritch" (Hughey, 1:254). He also transcribed before their publication twenty poems under the heading "Master Henry Conestables sonets to the Lady Ritche. 1589" (Hughey, 1:244). Other Sidney poems, from *Certain Sonnets* and the *Arcadia*, Ralegh's epitaph on Sidney, poems by Daniel and Spenser, and poems to the countess of Pembroke indicate Harington's strong interest in the Sidney circle and the Sidney influence. Like his father, the younger Harington also used the manuscript as a repository of some of his own poems and translations, associating himself with the new fashions of poetry of the second half of the Elizabethan era. For both father and son, anthologizing verse was a personal act that proclaimed membership in courtly society and participation in the recreations of an educated elite. Poems were obviously chosen for their social and political allusiveness as much as for their style and moral or philosophical content: the Arundel Harington Manuscript, thus, was as much a personal and family document embedded in the life experiences and social milieus of the compilers as a collection meant to preserve ephemeral poems within an emerging institution of literature where they could have a recognized enduring worth.

Bod. Rawl. Poet. 85 is an unusually rich Elizabethan manuscript anthology compiled by John Finet, who collected verse both at St. Johns College, Cambridge, and at the Elizabethan court in the late 1580s and early 1590s. The compiler later found a place in the early Stuart court as chief secretary to Robert Cecil and as master of ceremonies for both James I and Charles I. Laurence Cummings, not unjustifiably, calls the anthology of verse in this manuscript "the best such miscellaneous collection in England between Tottel's in 1557 and *England's Helicon* in 1600 or the *Poetical Rhapsody* in 1603 (p. 6).[202] Because it was compiled by Finet at the university as well as at the court, perfunctory, trivial, and occasional writing by fellow students

sisting of verse written before 1565, including many by the earl of Surrey, see Hughey, 1: 40–44.

[202] See Cummings, pp. 61–62, and Black, "Studies," 1:64–68. Of the other Elizabethan manuscripts, Marsh Library Dublin MS Z3.5.21, comprising both verse and prose compiled in the 1580s, is also a Cambridge collection.

is mixed in with the work of such courtly writers as Oxford, Ralegh, Breton, Sidney, Dyer, Gorges, Spenser, and Queen Elizabeth herself. In one of the sections of the anthology compiled at Cambridge the occasional nature of the university verse is evident in, for example, Robert Mills's poem, "Ware the water" (fols. 78v–80v): "Written upon this occasion a certayne companye of youthese (schollers in Cambridge) rowinge downe the ryver on daye in a boate for their pleasure the boote chaunced by mischaunce to be torned over wherby some were in dawnger of drownynge and amongste the rest the forsayde author Robert Mylls one of that company (not one of them that had escaped dryest) havynge watter enoughe herebye offred upon the request of his freend J[ohn] F[inet] aforsayde, inveyghed agaynste the watres as foloweth" (fol. 78v; Cummings, p. 577). From a social-historical point of view, such anthologizing is fascinating, partly because we can detect the young compiler's movement from the court to the university and back to the court again. The obscene and misogynistic humor found in some of the poems collected in a student environment contrasts, for example, with the amorous courtesy of the courtly lyrics.

Almost all of the writers collected by Finet are amateurs, but there is a real difference between the polished work of poets such as Dyer, Spenser, and Sidney and the student exercises of his friends James Reshoulde and Robert Mills. The academic poets do, however, make a point of imitating some of the courtly writers, and thus testify to the general interest in courtly writing in the manuscript system as well as in the growing market for printed literature. For example, the crossed-out piece "Forsaken fyrst and now forgotten quyte" (fol. 83v), as Cummings notes, "echo[es] a passage in Dyer's *Fancy*" (p. 399). James Reshoulde wrote his "Eccho made in imitation of Sir P. Sidneys echo going before, pagi. 5" (fol. 85r).[203] There are several Spenserian imitations (fols. 85v–89v; Cummings, pp. 620–35) as well as a quatrain that may be imitating a poem written by King James in 1582, "Since thought hath leve to thynke att least" (fol. 114v; Cummings, pp. 776).[204] Finet himself valued the poems of Sidney, twenty-

---

[203] The original fifth page is missing from the manuscript; the poem Reshoulde imitated may be the *Arcadia* poem beginning "Fayre Rockes, goodly Rivers, Sweet Woodes, when shall I see peace?" (Cummings, p. 619).

[204] Ibid., p. 778, refers to the poem "Since thought is free, think what thou will" in BL MS Add. 24195.

three of whose pieces from the *Arcadia, Certain Sonnets,* and *Astrophil and Stella* are found in his anthology, obviously chosen for their extraordinary literary quality rather than because he had ongoing social relations with their author.[205] The quality of Finet's selections is high, and the poems were compiled at a time when virtually none of them was in print. Cummings assigns 49 of the 149 poems found in this manuscript to Sidney, Dyer, and Spenser and attributes a number of other poems to their influence. Finet was literarily au courant, and he showed little interest in the old-fashioned verse of the previous decades (Cummings, pp. 21–22, 25).

Humphrey Coningsby's manuscript (BL MS Harl. 7392) is a miscellany that contains a sixteenth-century anthology of 127 numbered poems (fols. 12r–78v) plus some other verse items (for a total of 148), sharing 46 poems with Finet's collection. The manuscript opens with a booklet in which is transcribed a collection of epigrams titled "Morris Waspes"[206] (fols. 1r–9v) on paper stock differing from the rest of the manuscript; after the poetry anthology, the paper used for fols. 79r–151 changes again and the transcription of two Italian burlesques is in a different hand; the central anthology looks like an intact item joined to two other units. L. G. Black notes that there are more Dyer poems in this manuscript than in any other source (ten ascribed and one doubtful). It also has five ascribed Oxford poems (and five unascribed); three ascribed Ralegh poems (and one unascribed); four probable Gorges lyrics (one ascribed to him, two to Ralegh, and one to Sidney); three poems ascribed to Queen Elizabeth; three probable, but unascribed, Breton poems; five ascribed Sidney lyrics (and five unascribed ones); and other poems assigned to individuals identified as "Russell," "L. Con. de E & L," "Ro: Poo:" or "R.P.," "Joh[n] Ed[monds]" or "J.Ed.," "Ty. So.," "N.S.," "E.E.," "H.E.," "H.W.," "K.W.," "E.N.," "R.N.," "J. [or I] F.," "Mrs. C. N.," and "H[umphrey] Con[ingsby]." L. G. Black identifies the compiler of the manuscript, Humphrey Coningsby, as a person who matriculated at Christ Church, Oxford, in 1581 and was a member of Parliament for St. Albans in 1584. His cousin, Sir Thomas Coningsby, accompanied Sir Philip Sidney on his grand tour of the Continent.[207]

---

[205] Ibid., pp. 9–14, points out that, among the poems from the *Arcadia,* some are in versions midway between those of the unrevised *Old Arcadia* and those of the *New Arcadia.*

[206] This is William Goddard's *Neaste of Waspes,* printed in 1615.

[207] I summarize information provided by Black, "Studies," 1:42–54, 2:348–54. See also

One of the noteworthy things about Coningsby's poetry collection (which was completed by the mid-1580s) is that it contains both traditional and avant-garde verse—for example, old-fashioned poems by Oxford and Dyer and pieces found also in the popular printed anthology *The Paradise of Dainty Devices*,[208] as well as new-style work by such poets as Sidney, Gorges, and Ralegh. Some of its contents appeared in printed anthologies of the 1590s, such as *Brittons Bowre of Delights* (1591), *The Phoenix Nest* (1593), and *The Arbor of Amorous Devices* (1594).[209] The first numbered poem in the anthology is Dyer's representative love complaint, "He that his mirth hath lost" (fols. 12r–15r). Items in the same idiom include the other Dyer poems; Oxford's "When werte thou borne desyre" (fol. 18r); a piece attributed to Queen Elizabeth, "When I was fayre & yong then favour graced me" (fol. 21v); and Ralegh's "Calling to minde, mine ey went longe abowte" (fols. 36v–37r) and "Farewell false Love, thou Oracle of Lyes" (fol. 37r–v). The collection also has the topical "Cambridge Libell" usually attributed to Stephen Vallenger (fols. 54v–58v), accompanied by marginal identifications of satirically targeted individuals.

Black calls the Coningsby's anthology "an Oxford counterpart to the Cambridge RP 85,"[210] and the presence of this particular libel probably reflects university rivalries. University friendships account for the presence of poems by such men as St. Loe Kniveton and John Edmonds,[211] but like so many contemporary and later poetry collections, Coningsby's bears the marks of the compiler's movement be-

---

*The Poems of Sir Philip Sidney*, ed. William Ringler (Oxford: Clarendon Press, 1962), p. 557, and Cummings, pp. 60–61. Lawrence Stone and Jeanne C. Fawtier Stone provide some additional information about Coningsby, who was the grandson of a namesake who was Chief Justice of the King's Bench under Henry VIII, who left him, though he was "the younger son of a younger son," the property of Penn's Place. "This enabled Humphrey to set himself up as a country gentleman in considerably greater style than his father" (*An Open Elite? England 1540–1880* [Oxford: Clarendon Press, 1984], p. 114).

[208] These include (Robert Pooley's?) "YF Fortune may enforce, that carefull hurt to cry" (fols. 18v–20v), (William Hunnis's?) "Behould the blaste that blowes" (fol. 30v), and (John Thorn's?) "The study Rocke for all his strength" (fol. 72r).

[209] In fact, Robert Allot, identified as the source of a number of the poems in Coningsby's anthology, was connected with the fin-de-siècle publication, *Wits Theater* (1599). See Hyder E. Rollins, ed., *England's Helicon, 1600, 1614*, 2 vols. (Cambridge: Harvard University Press, 1935), 2:48–49. Rollins identifies Allot as possibly "Robert Allot of Derby, Lincolnshire, who was admitted to the Inner Temple in November, 1584."

[210] Black, "Studies," 1:50.

[211] Ibid., pp. 50, 54.

yond the university to London—in this case, to an Inns of Court environment, where he obtained a number of poems from Robert Allot. Black notes that the second half of the collection has the marks of the Inns environment,[212] including, one supposes, the sexist bawdy poem spoken by a young virgin delighted by the discovery of heterosexual pleasure, "When yonger yeres could not my mind acquaint" (fol. 74v), a piece arguing against virginity. The topical poem about the switch of allegiances of John and Laurence Dutton and the players they managed from the earl of Warwick's to the earl of Oxford's acting company (fol. 59r), a piece apparently unique in this manuscript, is the product of London gossip.[213] Most of the collection reveals a court-centered focus typical of ambitious, well-educated Elizabethans. And the prominence in it of such courtly writers as Oxford, Dyer, Ralegh, Gorges, and Sidney is not surprising. But perhaps one of the most interesting features of Coningsby's manuscript for modern readers is the presence in it of a large number of apparently unique, and mostly unpublished, verse, work written not only by the compiler himself but also by colleagues, friends, and other contemporaries.[214] In such an environment, self-conscious "high-literary" texts are mixed with more or less polished amateur and private productions, the unifying principle of the collection being the social relations, political interests, and literary tastes of the compiler. In a more developed literary system, texts came to be deprivatized and arranged in various conventional ways: this is, of course, what starts to happen in print in the late Elizabethan period in both the poetry anthologies and single-author editions that flooded the market.

Camb. MS Dd.5.75, Henry Stanford's anthology, has an interesting combination of contents: politically topical verse, including poems on Mary, Queen of Scots, and the earl of Leicester; poems of compliment by Stanford and the young pupils he tutored; courtly verse by Sidney, Dyer, Breton, Gorges, and others; riddles, satires, libels, and obscene epigrams; and a speech of Queen Elizabeth's. It has items copied

---

[212] Ibid., p. 54.

[213] See the discussion of this in E. K. Chambers, *The Elizabethan Stage*, 4 vols. (Oxford: Clarendon Press, 1923), 2:98–99.

[214] A check against Crum's *First-line Index* and Black's incomplete, but useful, index of verse in sixteenth-century manuscripts ("Studies," 2:395–451) reveals some seventy poems of this sort, most of them unascribed or with authors identified only by initials.

from printed texts as well as those taken directly from the system of manuscript transmission.[215] Its general Elizabethan collection resembles those of Finet and Coningsby, but as May has noted, it also has an unusually large number of poems by the compiler himself and by the children who were his young charges in the aristocratic households in which he served as a tutor.[216] Stanford's manuscript is an interestingly varied anthology, marked by the social-historical circumstances of its compiler.[217]

## Seventeenth-Century Manuscript Collections

Most of the manuscript miscellanies and poetry anthologies discussed in this study are from the seventeenth century, for despite the growing influence of print culture, this period generated an extraordinarily large number of such collections. Peter Beal has identified the 1620s and 1630s, in particular, as "the golden age of MS verse compilation," attributing this dramatic increase in the practice both to the influence of the published collections of such authors as Jonson, Spenser, Shakespeare, and Daniel, as well as to "the spirit of nostalgia for the culture of the previous (Elizabethan) generation" (1.1.246). Many large collections, in fact, were assembled through the 1640s, 1650s, and into the Restoration period, at which time the reestablishment of the monarchy significantly changed the sociopolitical context of manuscript transmission and compilation and the

---

[215] See May's discussion of this manuscript (*Henry Stanford's Anthology*, pp. vii–lxiv), and the treatment of it in Cummings, pp. 62–63, and Black, "Studies," 1:55–59. May notes that pieces were copied from *The Paradise of Dainty Devices* (1576), Baldwin's *Moral Philosophy* (1547), and Young's *Diana* (1598).

[216] See May, *Henry Stanford's Anthology*, pp. viii–xv, and L. G. Black, "Some Renaissance Children's Verse," *RES*, n.s., 24 (1973): 1–16.

[217] Marsh Lib. Dublin MS Z3.5.21 is another important sixteenth-century collection (discussed by Black in "Studies," 1:64–68, and Cummings, pp. 61–62): fols. 1–34 contain forty-eight items in different hands, constituting an Elizabethan anthology of poems from the 1570s or earlier. Inner Temple MS 538 (The Petyt Manuscript) ought also to be noted. It contains eighteen (mostly prose) miscellaneous items, some originally constituting separate booklets, one an old smudged pamphlet of verse (fols. 284–301). It has such items as three psalm translations by Mary Sidney, countess of Pembroke; epigrams by Sir John Harington; Nashe's "Choice of Valentines"; and an Oxford libel by Thomas Bastard, "Fy, bretheren schollers, fy for shame." I am reluctant to include BL MS Add. 34064 in this list of sixteenth-century anthologies. A sizeable portion of this document looks like it was transcribed in a modern imitation of an Elizabethan hybrid secretary-italic hand (fols. 27–40v). This point is made by Cummings, p. 68, and I agree.

number of such collections dropped markedly. The larger manuscript collections of poetry compiled between 1620 and 1660 are particularly interesting documents, especially given the relative paucity and low quality of the printed anthologies of the period.

The two quarto anthologies assembled by Peter Calfe and his son (BL MSS Harl. 6917–18), for example, constitute a remarkably rich collection of verse.[218] The first was transcribed during the 1640s in a period that ends with Charles I's execution (January 30, 1649); the second contains poems from that point through the death of Mrs. Sarah Gilly of Tottenham (August 14, 1659), who is mourned in the last piece of the collection.[219] The first quarto manuscript has over 213 poems on some 106 folios, the second a similar number on two-hundred pages. The first manuscript, in a single hand, is a general anthology of the sort that might have been printed in the late Elizabethan period; it represents a conscious act of anthologizing, the poems being numbered and, where possible, identified by author. (It begins with eleven numbered poems, then restarts the numbering system on fol. 7r.) Each poem has a title and is separated from the next by a horizontal rule. Calfe prefixes his first anthology with a first-line index of 198 poems. The two authors who are represented by a large number of items are Carew (thirty-four poems)[220] and Henry King (seventeen), the latter's work joined also by the verse of other members of his family (Philip King, three poems; John King, six; William King, one). The presence of the King poems, at least, is explained by the connection between Peter Calfe and Thomas Manne, who was King's amanuensis, through whom Calfe probably gained access to King family manuscripts.[221]

---

[218] Hobbs notes that Peter Calfe, the copier whose signature is on the flyleaf of both Harley MS 6917 and its continuation, Harley MS 6918 . . . was the son of a Dutch merchant in London and in the late 1630s lived in Wood Street, just around the corner from the scribe of *TM* [BL MS Add. 58215], Thomas Manne. . . . Given the close-knit character of London literary and musical circles, in which both men evidently moved, it is indeed possible that Calfe had direct access to Manne's manuscript" ("Early Seventeenth-Century Verse Miscellanies," p. 189). Cf. Hobbs, *Verse Miscellany Manuscripts,* pp. 67–71.

[219] Hobbs, "Early Seventeenth-Century Verse Miscellanies," p. 124.

[220] Dunlap notes that "Harl. 6917 . . . contains thirty-five of Carew's poems in two groups, the order in each being nearly the same as that of the 1640 edition. Its variant readings are for the most part plausible, and probably authentic; the total impression is that of versions preliminary to those printed in 1640" (*Poems of Carew,* p. lxxiv).

[221] Hobbs also points out that Calfe's manuscript has a group of about one hundred poems in common with Bod. MS Eng. Poet. c.50 (another large collection), Harvard fMS

The forty authors whose work can be identified in this anthology include both well-known poets (such as Herrick, Cleveland, Davenant, Ralegh, Jonson, Godolphin, and Suckling) and lesser-known figures (such as R. Clarke, T. Maisters, J. Rutter, T. Hickes, T. Freeman, and Harvey Martin). Some seventy poems are not easily identifiable. It is one of a very few manuscripts containing English poems by Crashaw: seven lyrics on fols. 52r–56v and 58r–6or, including an epithalamion not found in the printed editions or in other manuscripts ("Come virgin Tapers of pure waxe").[222]

The second Calfe anthology is a classic Royalist collection, with both anti-Puritan and anti-Parliament pieces and patriotic Royalist exhortations. The largest number of poems by a single author belongs to Cleveland (fifteen). The other verse includes items by Donne, Cowley, Randolph, Herrick, Henry King, Felltham, Strode, Fanshawe, Carew, and Lovelace (among others) as well as poems written by the compiler himself (at the end of the manuscript (fols. 96r–102r).[223] Given when the second collection was probably compiled, it is not surprising that it should contain more political poems than the earlier collection. For example, one of the last pieces in the collection before Calfe's own poems is Lovelace's prison poem (fol. 94v) in a version differing from that printed in *Lucasta. Posthume Poems* (1649).

The first part of the Haslewood-Kingsborough Manuscript (Hunt. MS HM 198, pt. 1) is a folio collection with some 205 numbered pages containing approximately that many poems. C. M. Armitage claims it was transcribed for Edward Denny, earl of Norwich, some time before his death on September 27, 1630.[224] Denny's poem "To the Lady Mary Wroth for writeing the Countes of Montgomeryes Urania," in fact, a piece arguing against permitting women to publish, is included in the collection (p. 164).[225] Although scholars have exam-

---

Eng. 626, and Rosenbach MS 191, but they are "divided into five smaller ones, interspersed with poems evidently from different sources." She postulates that "Calfe ... borrowed and copied collections wholesale, as well as with scrupulous accuracy" ("Early Seventeenth-Century Verse Miscellanies," p. 202).

[222] *Poems of Crashaw*, ed. Martin, p. lxxvii. Martin's transcription is on pp. 406–9 of his edition.

[223] *Poems of Cleveland*, ed. Morris and Withington, p. liv. Morris and Withington date this manuscript later than BL MS Harl. 6917 (after 1641).

[224] Armitage, "Donne's Poems," pp. 697–707. See also the discussion of this manuscript in Herbert Berry, *Sir John Suckling's Poems and Letters from Manuscript* (London: University of Western Ontario, 1960), pp. 33–38.

[225] Lord Denny attacked Lady Mary Wroth's *Urania* because he recognized that he, his daughter, and her husband (Lord Hay) were depicted negatively in this *roman à clef*. His

ined this manuscript mainly because it contains some sixty-five poems by Donne, there are other features that make it both representative and revealing as a collection of the 1620s. Donne's work is mixed with that of other members of his social network. The anthology contains a number of misattributed pieces—many, for example, by Donne's friends.[226] It also has pieces associated with particular Donne poems, such as Sir Edward Herbert's "Whoe so termes Love A fire" (p. 174) and (Beaupre Bell's?)[227] "When I doe love I would not nigh [?] to speed" (p. 173).

The collection has a large number of political poems, starting with the famous "Parliament Fart" (pp. 3–4).[228] These also include William Drummond of Hawthornden's poem "The Five Sences" (pp. 30–32); William Lewis's poem on Bacon's fall, "When you Awake dull Brittons and behould" (pp. 37–40); two pieces on the the notorious countess of Somerset, "From Catherines docke theer launcht A pritty Pinke" (pp. 19–21) and "She that with Troupes of Bustuary Slaves" (pp. 33–34); a number of poems to and about the duke of Buckingham (pp. 6–8, 44–46, 96, 156–59, 174); a poem about Lionel Cranfield's fall (pp. 56–58); the famous "Commons Petition" (pp. 62–63); Corbett's "Iter Boreale" (pp. 109–13); an old satiric piece written against the Catholic Henry Howard, earl of Northampton, "Great Archpapist learned Curio" (p. 164); and other political-religious pieces (pp. 184–89).

The anthology has many of the often-transcribed poems by such

---

poem ("Hermaphrodite in show, in deed a monster") excoriates Lady Mary Wroth for her "hermaphroditic" act of becoming a published woman author. Lady Mary retaliated in an answer poem that matches Denny's piece line for line. See the texts printed in *Poems of Lady Mary Wroth*, ed. Roberts, pp. 32–35. Roberts notes that Denny's poem appears in the Clifton Hall Manuscripts (Univ. of Nottingham Libr., item C1 LM 85/1–5), where it is titled "To Pamphilia from the father-in-law of Seralius," and in BL MS Add. 22603, fols. 64v–65r.

[226] These include John Roe's "Men write that love and reason disagree" (pp. 74–76); "Sleepe next society" (pp. 76–77); "If great men wronge me I will spare my selfe" (pp. 76–77); "An Ellegy to Sir Thomas Roe: 1603" ("Dear Tom: / Tell her if she to hired servants showe," pp. 168–69; Grierson, 1:416); "An Ellegy to Mistress Boulstred: 1602" ("Shall I goe force and Elegye? abuse," p. 169; Grierson, 1:410); "Send me some token that my hope may live" (p. 170); "Come Fates I feare you not, all whome I owe" (p. 172); and "R[owland] W[oodward] frenship & frends" ("Frendship we may on Earth as easy find," p. 174). The last poem was printed in *Poems of Pembroke and Ruddier*, p. 48 (see note 97).

[227] "BB" appears in the margin, along with "LC," the latter probably, the person from whom this and other texts were obtained, possibly Lionel Cranfield.

[228] See the discussion of this poem in Chapter 2.

authors as Jonson, Beaumont, Carew, Herrick, Corbett, Strode, and Randolph: for example, two of Jonson's Venetia Digby poems, "The boddye" and "The Minde" (pp. 54–56); Beaumont's poem on the Lady Markham, "As unthrifts mourne in strawe for their Paund beds" (pp. 10–11); the witty piece "If the one eyde boy, borne of A one ey'd mother" (p. 11); and Carew's poem "A Rapture" (pp. 117–20). Most of these were copied before they appeared in printed editions and, in the case of Herrick's poem "The Description of A Woman" ("Whose head befringed with bescattered tresses," pp. 8–10), we have a poem omitted from the main seventeenth-century printed edition of an author's work.[229]

The collection has a fair number of answer poems, including a run of eight such pieces by William Herbert, earl of Pembroke, and Sir Benjamin Rudyerd (pp. 138–47), one of the largest blocks of their verse outside the 1660 "edition" of their poems. Other answer poems are "Randolph's answer to Benn Johnsons Ode [to Himself]" (pp. 115–16), "Doctor Price his answer to Corbetts reply on his Anniverse upon Prince Henry" (pp. 136–37) and "Doctor Corbetts reply" (p. 137), and Suckling's answer to John Mennis's "Upon Sir John Sucklings Hundred Horse," "I tell the foole who ere thow bee" (p. 160). Hunt. MS HM 198, pt. 1, is, in sum, a remarkably full and rich early Stuart anthology of verse, an album of the sort treasured by the social and intellectual elites.

Bod. MS Ash. 38, identified by Peter Beal (1.2.10 and 2.1.40) as the manuscript of Nicholas Burghe, who was a Royalist captain in the Civil War, is a large folio poetry anthology of some 243 leaves. Brian Morris and Eleanor Withington claim the first 165 pages were probably transcribed before 1638 and the rest of the manuscript written between 1640 and 1660.[230] Whatever the actual dates, this manuscript is one of the richest collections of the mid-seventeenth century, comprising hundreds of poems by a wide range of well-known poets such as Donne, King, Carew, Herrick, Jonson, Strode, Corbett, Randloph, Ralegh, Beaumont, Wotton, and [John] Shirley, as well as lesser-known figures such as Thomas Jay, John Heape, Alexander Gill, Henry Shirley, Thomas Jordan, Simeon Steward, J. Shanke, Robert Markham, and Simon Butteris [or Butterix]. Burghe did not copy

---

[229] This piece was not printed in *Hesperides* (1648), but it did appear in the 1645 version of *Wits Recreations* and, as noted by Beal (2.1.558), in four other manuscripts.

[230] *Poems of Cleveland*, ed. Morris and Withington, pp. lii–liii.

very many poems of any one author—Jonson, Carew, and Herrick having the largest number, but no more than about ten each. He also included several of his own compositions.[231] The manuscript includes political verse on the Somerset marriage and the trial for the murder of Sir Thomas Overbury, on the duke of Buckingham, on Puritans and social upstarts; misogynistic verse; many songs; and over two hundred epitaphs and funeral elegies (many of the former evidently copied from the 1637 edition of Camden's *Remains Concerning Britain*). The large body of commemorative verse, an unusual number of elegies and epitaphs, is a sign of this document's place in a system of communication within a social elite that favored rituals celebrating its members.

Although reflecting the personal tastes and Royalist political bias of its compiler, Burghe's ample anthology nonetheless surpasses most mid-century printed collections in variety and quality: in effect, the kind of collection represented by Davison's anthology *A Poetical Rhapsody* (1602) only took shape during the period of the Civil War and Interregnum within the manuscript system. Printed anthologies, such as *The Harmony of the Muses* (1654) and *Parnassus Biceps* (1656) look skimpy by comparison with collections such as those assembled by Burghe, Calfe, and the compiler of the first part of the Haselwood-Kingsborough Manuscript. The literary history of the period, then, should take into account such manuscript compilations instead of basing its narrative almost exclusively on the products of the printing press, for printed literature only presents part of the story, and it creates a false sense of the separateness of literary texts from the social worlds in which they were so obviously immersed in the system of manuscript transmission.

---

[231] See the discussion of compiler verse in Chapter 3.

*CHAPTER TWO*

# SEX, POLITICS,
## AND THE
### *MANUSCRIPT SYSTEM*

THE MANUSCRIPT collections of the sixteenth and seventeenth centuries contain a wide range of texts written by well-known
professional or amateur poets as well as by less well known or
anonymous ones. The thematic variety of the verse is great, reflecting
not only the many occasions for which poetry was composed, but also
the interests and preoccupations of the members of the academic
and social elite. Given the relative youthfulness of the majority of the
collectors of verse, many of whom were at one of the two universities
or the Inns of Court, it is not surprising that amorous verse constitutes
a large portion of the total: love poems are found in great numbers
in most manuscript collections. Before surveying, at the end of the
chapter, some of the texts that seem to have been most popular in
the manuscript system, pieces that are important because they reveal
much about the tastes and preoccupations of manuscript scribes and
compilers, I would like, first, to concentrate in this chapter on two
types of verse that were more visible in the manuscript system than
in print, the obscene and the political, for their prominence distinguishes manuscript collections from printed anthologies and single-
author editions.

In the relatively private or closed system of manuscript transmission
and compilation, poems dealing with sex and politics constituted a
large percentage of the circulating verse. Pieces that would have been
censored in the more public medium of print were better suited to
the socioliterary environment of the manuscript system. University
and Inns of Court students could transmit and transcribe obscene

(usually either socially iconoclastic or snobbish) pieces in manuscript, free of the censorship that, for example, kept three of Donne's bawdy love elegies from the posthumous 1633 collected edition of that poet's work.[1] Similarly, given the danger of libeling or of public political criticism and comment,[2] the manuscript system was a safer place than print for satiric and serious political poetry. Both types of verse suited the circumstances of restricted communication characteristic of the system of manuscript transmission.

## Obscenity and the Manuscript System

Since the manuscript transmission of verse was most frequently associated with all-male environments such as the universities and the Inns of Court, it is not surprising to find a large amount of bawdy and obscene verse in manuscript collections. Such poetry may have signaled social iconoclasm, neurotic misogyny, adolescent sexual awakening, class antagonism, anti-Puritan attitudes, or, more basically, the social bonding of those who engaged in coterie exchange of verse.[3] Since much witty obscene verse was satiric or libelous or both, it was better suited to the environment of manuscript transmission than to print. In the moral climate of the sixteenth century, when poets were forced to justify *any* secular verse, obscene texts had a patently transgressive character. Like the published erotic epyllia of the 1590s and the censored edition of Marlowe's translation of the Ovid's *Amores* (1599), bawdy or obscene epitaphs, epigrams, songs, love elegies, and lyrics lay beyond the boundaries of the officially approved territory of literature, but since they were basically confined to the processes of social intercourse of which manuscript communication was a part, they stood apart from those canonizing processes that were beginning to operate in print culture. Such work became

---

[1] The ecclesiastical censors removed "Going to Bed," "Loves Warre," and "Loves Progress" from the collection of poems published by Marriot in 1633. These pieces, however, had a long life in the system of manuscript transmission.

[2] George Wither, for example, was imprisoned in Marshalsea after the publication of *Abuses Stript and Whipt* (1613), proving how dangerous it was to publish satire in the Stuart period. See William B. Hunter Jr., ed., *The English Spenserians: The Poetry of Giles Fletcher, George Wither, Michael Drayton, Phineas Fletcher, and Henry More* (Salt Lake City: University of Utah Press, 1977), p. 111. Hunter suggests the earl of Northumberland had Wither incarcerated and King James had him freed.

[3] See my discussion of the sociocultural significance of erotic verse in an Inns of Court environment in *John Donne*, pp. 44–82 (see Chap. 1, n. 30).

an issue only much later, when, for example, the publisher of the Interregnum anthology *Sportive Wit* (1656) threw obscene texts in the face of the Puritan authorities as a gesture of political defiance.[4]

Undergraduate miscellanies and poetical anthologies contain much bawdy and obscene verse. For example, John Finet's collection has a version of a bawdy poem spoken by a woman half-reluctantly having sex:

Lasciva est nobis pagina vita proba est

Naye, phewe nay pishe? nay faythe and will ye, fye.
A gentleman deale thus? in truth ille crye.
Gods bodye, what means this? naye fye for shame
Nay, Nay, come, come, nay faythe yow are to blame.
Harcke sombodye comes, leave of I praye
Ile pinche, ille spurne, Ile scratche, nay good awaye
In faythe you stryve in vayne, you shall not speede.
You mare my ruffs, you hurte my back, my nose will bleed
Looke, looke the doore is open some bodye sees,
What will they say? nay fye you hurt my knees
Your buttons scratche, o god what coyle is heere?
You make me sweate, in faythe here is goodly geare
Nay faythe let me intreat leve if you lyste
You marr the bedd, you teare my smock, but had I wist,
So muche before I woulde have kepte you oute.
It is a very proper thinge indeed you goo aboute.
I did not thinke you woulde have used me this.
But nowe I see to late I tooke my marke amysse
A lytle thinge would mak us two not to be freends.
You use me well, I hope yow will make me amends.
Houlde still Ile wype your face: you sweat amayne
You have got a goodlye thinge with all this payne.
O god how hott I am come will you drincke
Ife we goe sweatinge downe what will they thinke
Remember I praye howe you have usde me nowe
doubte not ere longe I will be quite with you.
Ife any one but you shoulde use me so
Would I put by this wronge? in faythe sir no
Nay goe not yet: staye supper here with me
Come goe to cardes I hope we shall agree.

(Fol. 4r; Cummings, pp. 107–8)

[4] See the discussion of this in Chapter 4.

This poem sets a sexual encounter between a half-willing upper-class woman and a single-minded man in social circumstances in which the couple should fear discovery: it comically juxtaposes sweaty sex with the language of social decorum belonging to a polite environment in which a card-playing gentleman and a woman of fashion (who can order supper to be served in her own bedroom) play out a sexual/social game. The female narrator, like Henry Fielding's Shamela, also makes it possible for the writer to highlight the comic desperation of male erotic aggression. This much-copied piece occurs in manuscript collections through the mid-seventeenth century, but reached print only in two late Interregnum anthologies, *The Harmony of the Muses* (1654) and *Sportive Wit* (1656).[5] In BL MS Add. 22603, a Cambridge man's collection (Beal, 1.2.132, 2.535), this poem (fol. 61r–v) is framed by a short prologue and epilogue characterizing the episode as a woman's dream, then is followed by Edward Denny's misogynistic poem written against Lady Mary Wroth's composition of *Urania* and by a bawdy poem titled "Venus sports" (fol. 65r–v). Other, imitative poems, such as the bawdy song found in Bod. MS Don. c.54, fol. 25v ("Fie awaie what mean you by this") and the short dramatic poem "O quicklye, o quickly, o quickly sweete boye a done" (Folger MS V.a.399, fol. 13r) were spawned by this piece.

Undergraduate collections are full of recreationally obscene epigrams, some concerning notable academic personages and others about lower-class characters well known in their environment. For example, Anthony Scattergood's Cambridge anthology puns on the names of a recently married couple:

On the marriage of Master Turbott with Mistress Hill

What are Deucalion's dayes return'd, that wee
A Turbott swimming on a Hill do see?
And yet this Hill, though never tir'd with standing
Lay gently downe to give the Turbott landing.

---

[5] See Cummings, p. 109, who cites Bod MSS Mal. 19 and Rawl. Poet. 199 and BL MSS Add. 22582, 22602, and 30982, Egerton 923 and 2421, Harl. 6057, and Sloane 542 and 1792, as well as eight Rosenbach and Folger manuscripts. The poem is also found in Bod. MS Ash. 38, p. 150.

What can wee in these dayes so strange report,
When fishes leave the sea on Hills to sport?
(BL MS Add. 44963, fol. 37r)[6]

Folger MS V.a.399 contains a large number of bawdy poems, including one about a farting match between a lady and her maid (fol.
10v), a bawdy poem using legal terminology, "A perfect president of
a deede of Intayle" (fol. 14r–v), and a copy of "Nashe's Dilldo" (fols.
53v–57r), as that poet's "Choice of Valentines" was known. Such
work was especially popular in Inns of Court circles. Rosenbach MS
1083/17, an Inns of Court collection, contains a great deal of obscene verse, including some apparently unique pieces: for example,
"Riddle me Rachell what [is] this / that a man handles when he does
pisse" (a set of metaphoric variations about the male sex organ) and
"Now riddle me Robin & tell me this much / Quid significat a Cut
in Dutch" (the counterpart poem on the vagina).[7] The Farmer-
Chetham manuscript has a partly censored version of a misogynistic
epigram satirizing the use of cosmetics,[8] which appears in several
other manuscripts, including the Oxford commonplace book, Rosenbach MS 1083/16, which has the complete version with the last two
words scored out:

> We Maddams that doe Fucus use
> greatly Muse
> Being ripe fruite you doe not plucke us,
> Since characters in redde and white
> plainely write
> On our painted faces <fuck us>.
>
> (P. 33)[9]

In his edition of Robert Bishop's commonplace book (transcribed
about 1630), a manuscript with connections to both Oxford and the
Inns, David Redding calls attention to the compiler's fascination with

---

[6] This poem is also found in Bod. MS Eng. Poet. f.25, fol. 10, and Rawl. D. 1092, fol. 272.

[7] Sanderson, "An Edition," pp. 372–76 (see Chap. 1, n. 121).

[8] See Grosart, *Dr. Farmer Chetham MS*, p. 82 (see Chap. 1, n. 125).

[9] See also Bod. MSS Eng. Poet. e.14, fol. 10, and Tanner 169, fol. 68v. Crum, p. 1017, notes that the latter attributes the poem to "Mr. F. Davison" and dates it "30 Ap. 1615," which suggests, perhaps, a connection with Frances Howard (countess of Somerset) and the Overbury murder scandal.

bawdy verse; the first section of the anthology contains mostly obscene and misogynistic pieces.[10] As the love lyric, partly in response to the influence of Donne and Jonson, grew bawdier in the seventeenth century and as the licentiousness that came to mark the style of Cavalier writers became a kind of political badge, witty obscene verse came to be associated with the lifestyle of (usually Royalist) gentlemen, one feature of a kind of sexist and classist condescension whose cultural visibility was high throughout the Restoration period. And so, for example, among the Conway papers we find an obscene poem one aristocratic correspondent cautiously shared with another:

> The London Lasses are so stoute
> they care not what they doe
> they will not Lett you have aboute
> Under a crowne or two
>
> They dawbe their Chops & Curle their Lockes
> their breathes perfume they doe
> their tayles are pepperd with a pox
> & that you'are welcome too.
>
> Then give me the Country bucksome Lasse
> hott piping from the Cowe
> shell take a touch uppon the grasse
> I merry & thank you too
>
> her Colours as fresh as roose in June
> her skin as soft as silke
> Sheele doe her business to some time
> and freely spend her milke.
>
> (BL MS Add. 23229, fol. 43r)[11]

In an aristocratic miscellany owned by Horatio Carey in 1642, Rosenbach MS 1083/17, a collection that opens (appropriately) with

---

[10] Redding, "Robert Bishop's Commonplace Book," pp. lxix–xx (see Chap. 1, n. 122). Redding notes the similarity of contents between Bishop's collection and the following manuscripts: Rosenbach MS 189, Folger MSS V.a.162, V.a.262, and V.a.345, and Bod. MSS Don.d.58 and Eng. Poet. e.14. He also remarks that many of the bawdy poems found in these and in Bishop's collection turned up in printed miscellanies such as *Wits Recreations, Wit Restor'd,* and *Musarum Deliciae.*

[11] This poem does not occur in any Bodleian manuscript. See "Manuscript Gatherings and Manuscript Books" in Chapter 1 for the compiler's statement expressing embarrassment in forwarding this bawdy piece.

fifteen pages of epitaphs on famous persons, there is an interesting rare and anonymous poem that reveals the contemporary taste for refined bawdry:

### A Privat discourse with a Mistress

Come Ladie come your leggs display
And lett me clime your milkie way
That leadeth unto Cupids grove
Where I may swell in joyes of love
here's no envious Eye nor Nett
Such as the Smith for Venus sett
The gods themselfs shall thee not see
my self will be a vayle for thee
Why shouldst thou feare to loos the toy
Wherin cold virgins so much joy
A Maydenhead, for know when death
By fates command shall take thy breath
which much perfume Joves starry Court
The wormes shall in the Caskett sport
Wherein that hidden pearle doth ly
And feed out with rude gluttony.
Thou lett me tast the sweets that lie
Within Loves jucy treasury.

(Fol. 91r–v)

Followed by the transcription of another seduction poem, one of Jonson's Celia lyrics (in this version, beginning "Come sweet Mistress lett us prove"), this lyric, which bears an interesting stylistic resemblance to Marvell's "To His Coy Mistress," is very much at home in the collection in which it is placed.[12]

As students, as residents of the Inns of Court, as courtiers, or as London or provincial gentlemen, seventeenth-century manuscript scribes and compilers seem to have been especially fond of obscene and bawdy verse. Carew's prurient lyric, "The Rapture," for example, became one of the most popular pieces for transcription in manuscript collections. It is no surprise then, that the printed anthologies, from *Wits Recreations* (1640), to *Musarum Delicae* (1655), *Sportive Wit*

---

[12] For discussions of this manuscript, see Beal, 2.1.45 and 2.1.543, and Gary Taylor, "Some Manuscripts of Shakespeare's Sonnets," *Bulletin of the John Rylands Library* 68 (1985–86): 220–40.

(1656), and the other books that drew on the manuscript collections of the 1620s–1640s, should have transferred such work to print. *The Harmony of the Muses* (1654), for example, contains the first printed versions of the three elegies censored from the 1633 edition of Donne ("Going to Bed," "Loves Warre," and "Loves Progress")[13] as well as the old sixteenth-century poem quoted earlier ("Nay, phewe nay pishe?"—under the title "A Maids Denyall"). It did, however, take a relatively long time for the bawdy and obscene verse that was so popular in the manuscript system to reach print. It did so largely in the context of Royalist opposition during the Interregnum: it is, in such circumstances, not so much directly obscene as obliquely political.

## Manuscript Poetry and the Political World

There are a great number of explicitly political poems to be found in the manuscript collections of the sixteenth and seventeenth centuries. The surviving manuscript compilations of the period call attention to some of the most noteworthy issues and events of their day. Even when the interest seems to have been frivolous, more a matter of gossip and humorous satiric backbiting than of serious political analysis, these manuscripts nevertheless bring to light social and political relations and conflicts, even "constitutional" struggles as they manifested themselves in the times before, during, and after the English Civil War. Many manuscript miscellanies also contain prose pieces related to current events. For example, the Farmer-Chetham manuscript (Chetham's Lib., Manchester MS Mun. A.4.150) includes a description of the arraignment of the earls of Essex and Southampton (and others) for treason after the abortive 1601 insurrection, and subsequent letters by Essex, Lady Rich, and others. Political events, issues, and implications are widespread in the verse collected in manuscript throughout the period: poems highlight the centrality of patronage in the social system, the dynamics of political success and failure, the conflicts between the monarch and Parliament, and the political polarization of the English people (especially in the Civil War

---

[13] In *The Harmony of the Muses by Robert Chamberlain* (1654), a facsimile, ed. Ernest W. Sullivan II (Aldershot, U.K.: Scolar Press, 1990), p. xiii, Sullivan notes that this publication reproduces the first Donne poem in its entirety, but only lines 29–46 of the second and lines 1–48 and 53–96 of the third.

and Interregnum). Sixteenth- and seventeenth-century manuscript miscellanies and poetry anthologies were a barometer of political activity and conflicts, particularly as these affected the lives of aristocrats and individuals sheltered by their patronage.[14]

Carol Meale points out, in her study of John Colyns's commonplace book, that the anti-Wolsey poems of Skelton which Colyns transcribed (*Speke, Parrot* and *Colyn Cloute*) are evidence not only of the manuscript circulation of that poet's work, but also of support from "the citizenry of London" for his "rather subversive views on the Chancellor." Meale notes that "the majority of items in [BL MS] Harley [2252] which can be described as 'literary' . . . bear some relation to current affairs. Of the twelve lyrics present, eight deal with contemporary national figures or events, and Colyns' interest in them can best be explained by reference to the social and political climate in which he lived."[15] As noted earlier, the first surviving poem in John Finet's Elizabethan anthology (Bod. MS Rawl. Poet. 85) is the politically topical lyric "When I was fair and young and favor graced me," a poem associated with the last of the serious marriage negotiations in which Elizabeth engaged, the protracted dealings with the duke of Anjou. Another political poem that frequently appeared in the sixteenth-century manuscripts is "A pasquill of France" ("The State of France"), also called "The French Primero," which deals with political events in the years 1584–88.[16] Stephen Powle's commonplace

---

[14] Harold Love notes that much political prose was scribally transmitted before the mid-seventeenth century: "A large body of political documents circulated during the reigns of James I and Charles I, first as 'separates' and later as collections of greater or lesser degrees of comprehensiveness. Characteristically, these collections will include material relating to the Somerset scandal, the rise of Buckingham, the Spanish marriage negotiations, and the attempted impeachment of Buckingham, along with speeches from the parliaments of 1621–29, historical and political tracts, personal libels such as *Tom Tell-troth* and *The Forerunner of Revenge upon the Duke of Buckingham* and blatant political forgeries like *To the Father Rector at Brussels*" ("Scribal Publication," 132 [see Chap. 1, n. 38]).

[15] Meale, "Compiler at Work," pp. 96 and 101 (see Chap. 1, n. 145). See also the discussion of the anti-Wolsey poems in Alistair Fox, *Politics and Literature in the Reigns of Henry VII and Henry VIII* (Oxford: Basil Blackwell, 1989), pp. 134–35.

[16] Cummings, p. 702, cites, in addition to Finet's anthology, Marsh Lib. MS Z3.5.21, fol. 22; BL MSS Harl. 7392, fol. 62v, and 3787, fol. 112r, and Tanner 169, fol. 70v; Camb. MS Dd.5.75, fol. 29r; and Folger MS V.a.89, between interleaves 16 and 18. See Curt Bühler, "Four Elizabethan Poems," in *Joseph Quincy Adams Memorial Studies*, ed. James G. McManaway, Giles E. Dawson, and Edwin E. Willoughby (Washington, D.C.: Folger Shakespeare Library, 1948), pp. 700–701. Cummings argues (not very convincingly) that this poem, specifically, as Crum suggests, is about the treaty of Joinville and its attendant issues (1584–85), and that it might tentatively be ascribed to Sir Walter Ralegh (Cummings, p. 705; Crum, p. 887). Black, "Studies" (see Chap. 1, n. 39), devotes a whole chapter to this poem (1:83–118), which survives in four different versions.

book (Bod. MS Tanner 169) not only contains "The French Primero," but also items of political prose such as accounts of the deaths of individuals involved in the Essex conspiracy (fols. 71r–74v) and "Sr. Fran[cis] Bacons Argumentes against the Bill of Sheets 1605" (fols. 42r–43v) and a transcription of the infamous prose libel, "Leicester's Commonwealth" (fols. 92r–131v).[17]

Partly because it was a system associated with the lifestyle of an educated elite, partly because its persistence far into the Gutenberg era was a sign of its resistance to the democratizing forces of print, the manuscript system of literary transmission was largely a medium for socially and politically conservative individuals—although the political contents of manuscript collections vary considerably. In the period from the 1630s through the 1650s, especially during the Civil War and Interregnum, Royalists, especially at Oxford, but also in other social environments, found the relatively closed system of manuscript literary transmission especially congenial. BL MS Add. 37719 was, according to Brian Morris and Eleanor Withington, "The commonplace book of Sir John Gibson (1606–65) of Welburn, near Kirkby Moorside, Yorkshire, a Royalist prisoner in Durham Castle."[18] The two-part anthology kept by Peter Calfe and his son, BL MS Harl. 6917–18, is a classic Royalist collection: not unexpectedly, it contains such poets as King, Herrick, Cleveland, and Randolph, but also specifically Royalist exhortations as well as anti-Puritan and anti-Parliament pieces—for example, a poem to the Royalist general Prince Rupert (fols. 74v–77r) by Cleveland.[19]

Most manuscript collections of verse immerse political poems in a heterogeneous mass of poetic forms, including love lyrics, witty or satiric epigrams, funeral elegies and epitaphs, and encomiastic epistles. Some manuscript compilations, however, emphasize political

---

[17] Virginia F. Stern notes Powle wrote Lord Burghley from the continent about the popularity of the last of these items (*Sir Stephen Powle*, p. 62 [see Chap. 1, n. 46]). She claims that this copy of *Leicester's Commonwealth* was "written in the hand of Powle's current secretary-clerk" (p. 225 n.5; see also pp. 122–23).

[18] "The book is dedicated in a letter (f. 5b) dated March 1656 to his son, John Gibson" (*Poems of Cleveland*, ed. Morris and Withington, p. lii [see Chap. 1, n. 115]).

[19] It shares many poems with Bod. MS Eng. Poet. c.50, a manuscript that starts with a series of Jacobean political pieces, including "The Commons Petition" (fols. 8r–12v), poems on Francis Bacon (fols. 7v, 13r) and Lionel Cranfield (fol. 23r), and a piece on Buckingham's Isle of Rhé expedition (fol. 13v)—see Hobbs, "Early Seventeenth-Century Verse Miscellanies," p. 202 (cited in full at Chap. 1, n. 42). For a discussion of this manuscript, see also Margaret Crum, "An Unpublished Fragment of Verse by Herrick," *RES*, n.s., 11 (1960): 186–89.

pieces. Bod. MS Mal. 23, which looks like a presentation volume to a social superior, is a very interesting manuscript taken up almost entirely with political poetry dealing with events from the beginning of the reign of King James I through the assassination of the duke of Buckingham in 1628 in the early part of the reign of Charles I. It opens with a satiric poem directed at the earl of Northampton, "The great Archpapist Learned Curio" (p. 1A),[20] and includes the popular witty narrative poem "The Parliament Fart" (pp. 1B–4); an anti-Scots piece, "They begg our Lands" (p. 4); satiric epitaphs on Robert Cecil, "Here lyes little Robin that vainely was recked" (p. 4) and "Heere lyes Salisbury that little great commander" (p. 65), and the countess of Devonshire, "Heere lyes Penelopie the Ladie Rich" (p. 5); topical poems about the Carr-Howard marriage and murder of Sir Thomas Overbury (pp. 6–14); and poems about the falls of Sir Francis Bacon and Lionel Cranfield (pp. 23, 27). It also contains a short, politically dangerous satiric poem found in no other Bodleian or British Library manuscript:

> The king he hawkes, and hunts;
> The Lords they gather Coyne;
> The Judges doo as they weere wont;
> The Lawyers they purloyne.
> The Clergy lyes a dyeing;
> The Commons toll the Bell;
> The Scotts gott all by lying,
> And this is Englands knell.
>
> (P. 120)

Set in a section of the manuscript concerned with events of 1628, particularly with the duke of Buckingham's assassination, this political ditty expresses a deep cynicism.

This collection also contains the famous "Commons Petition," "The Coppie of a Libell put into the hand of Queene Elizabeths statue in Westminster by an unknowne person Anno domini <1619> 1621. ultimo Martii. 1623" ("If Saints in heaven cann either see, or

---

[20] Crum lists only this Bodleian manuscript for the poem (p. 854); it is found also in Hunt. MS HM 198, pt. 1, p. 164. It refers to Henry Howard, earl of Northampton (1540–1614), who switched back and forth between Catholicism and Protestantism; he was notoriously deceitful and dangerous. See Herford, Simpson, and Simpson, *Ben Jonson*, 1:166 (cited in full at Chap. 1, n. 35).

heare," pp. 32–34), preceded much earlier in the manuscript by the piece written as an answer poem to it, "A Gratious answere from that blessed Saint to her whilome Subjects, with a divine admonition and a prophetique conclusion" ("Your bold Petition Mortalls I have seen," pp. 14–16) and followed by "The most humble Petition of the nowe most miserable Commons of Long afflicted England" ("If bleeding harts dejected soules find grace," pp. 34–44 which is incomplete because of missing pages).[21] The first piece is a prologue to the second and the third is an answer to the first two. The "Commons Petition" is central to the phenomenon of Elizabethan nostalgia and anti-Stuart feeling that developed in the reign of James.[22] Poems such as "The states A game at Cards; the Counsell deale" (p. 119) and "Rex and Grex are of one sound" (p. 119) address the precarious political situation of the late 1620s. The pieces at the end of the collection attacking Puritans, lawyers, and Catholics (pp. 213–20,

---

[21] Crum lists many Bodleian manuscripts of these poems, indicating their political popularity (see pp. 419, 431, and 1186). The three poems are also found at pages 146–71 in the University of Texas "Herrick" MS, *Poems from a Seventeenth-Century Manuscript with the Hand of Robert Herrick*, ed. Norman K. Farmer Jr., *The Texas Quarterly* 16 (Winter 1973). With the relaxation of censorship in 1642, *The Commons Petition* (1642) was finally published (it was reprinted in *Fugitive Tracts . . . in Verse*, ed. Henry Huth, 1875, 2d ser, 15). Looking only at the printed version, Gerald MacLean discusses the poem as a manifestation of politically conservative nostalgia relevant to the events of 1641–42 (*Time's Witness: Historical Representation in English Poetry, 1603–1660* [Madison: University of Wisconsin Press, 1990], pp. 163–67), but it was composed almost two decades earlier (1623) out of opposition to James I and his policies. Coiro has a discussion of the "Commons Petition" and of the Texas manuscript, which she argues, was "the product of a group associated with Cambridge University who assembled it over a decade, from 1612–1623" ("Milton and Class Identity," p. 272 [see Chap. 1, n. 118]). Like Bod. MS Rawl. Poet. 26, this manuscript records in chronological order a series of politically topical poems—most of them dangerous to disseminate publicly: there are, for example, not only satiric pieces on the Somerset marriage scandal, but also on James's homosexual relationship with the duke of Buckingham. For example, the poem "Arme, arme in heaven, there is a faction" (pp. 129–33) criticizes the king for "loving . . . against nature" the "upstart" Buckingham/Ganymede. Similarly William Drummond's poem "The Senses" prays:

> . . . I crave,
> Thou wilt be pleas'd, great God, to save
> My soveraigne from a Ganymed,
> Whose whorish breath hath power to lead
> His excellencie which way it list,
> O let such lips be never kist.
>
> (pp. 139, 141)

[22] In *Puzzling Shakespeare: Local Reading and Its Discontents* (Berkeley and Los Angeles: University of California Press, 1988), p. 184, Leah Marcus states: "After her death . . . the image of the queen signified political difference from James: she stood for nationalism and 'local' identity."

221) are a sign of the more intense conflict to come, mirroring the struggles between Parliament and Crown, religious strife, and other conditions leading to the Civil War. The collection as a whole represents the kind of oppositionist critical perspective articulated throughout James's reign in the environments of the Inns of Court and in certain London political circles. Most of the work contained in this manuscript was necessarily withheld from print transmission.

Bod. MS Rawl. Poet. 26, compiled in sections by many different scribes between about 1615 and 1660, is, on the other hand, a collection of both verse and prose with clearly conservative biases.[23] It contains the following political poems: the oft-transcribed anti-Puritan pieces by Sir John Harington, "Sixe of the weakest sexe, but purest sect" (fol. 6r) and "A Puritan with one of her society" (fol. 8v); Corbett's poem on the Parliament's opposition to the duke of Buckingham, here called "Upon the breach between the King & the Subject, at the dissolution of the Parliament. March 1628" (fol. 8v); a poem against a Puritan minister, "Upon Master Cushion a Schoolmaster & Curate in Norwich; a Puritanicall non-conformist who (at the Bishops Visitation there, May 2. 1636.) was enjoyned to officiate service in the Cathedrall Church, at the high Altar, in a surplice and Cope" (fol. 15r); and "A Dialogue betweene 2 Zelots. concerning &c. in the New Oath" (by John Cleveland).[24] In the early part of the collection, there are some poems reflecting strong interest in late Elizabethan and Jacobean politics—for example, poems about the Essex conspiracy and Ralegh's fate; the popular comic political poem "The Parliament Fart";[25] pieces about the Robert Carr–Frances Howard marriage; and a poem allegedly written by King James on the 1623 voyage of Prince Charles and Buckingham to Spain (fols. 21r–21v), accompanied by poems written after their return from the politically disastrous adventure (fols. 22r–25r). There are memorial poems to Buckingham and the Protestant military hero, King Gustavus Adolphus of Sweden (whose exploits contrasted sharply with Stuart pacifist policies).[26]

[23] This manuscript was owned in the Restoration period by John Cooke of Bury St. Edmonds, Suffolk (Beal, 1.2.379).

[24] See *Poems of Cleveland*, ed. Morris and Withington, pp. 82–86, on the political context of this poem.

[25] See the discussion of this poem in "Crown against Parliament and Royalist against Puritan," this chapter.

[26] Largely because he was an activist Protestant hero, King Gustavus Adolphus of Sweden

The majority of the political poems in this collection, however, deal with the Caroline period, particularly the events of the 1640s, and most of these have strong Royalist, anti-Puritan, and anti-Parliamentary biases. The first of many poems on the period from 1640 on is a short piece unique in the Bodleian manuscripts:

> To the Parliament.
> Novemb:
> 1640
>
> The Stakes. 3. Crownes: 4. Nations, Gamesters are:
> These, 3. to one; and yet no man that dare
> Take those great Oddes. The cause is (as they say)
> The 4th. knowes, both or Stock & Cards wee play.
> This turnes the Oddes, & makes some Gamesters thinke,
> T'were but in jest, & play our Cards & winke.
> The Sett goes hard, when Gamesters think it best,
> Though 3. men vye't, the 4th setts up his Rest.
>
> (Fols. 95r–v)[27]

This poem, written at the start of the Long Parliament, is followed by others particularly concerned with crucial events of 1640–42.[28] The

---

was the subject of a fairly large number of elegies commemorating his heroic death in 1632. See the poems noted by Crum: A1377, B539, C40, G608, I180, I1113, L379, L580, O376, R71, S275, T541, T1580, T1734, T2833, T3385, U182, and W636.

[27] This is found also in BL MS Harl. 2127, fol. 75v. The political context of the poem is the beginning of the Long Parliament in November 1640 at a time the Scots had agreed to delay concluding a peace treaty to end the Bishops' War so Parliament might press its demands on Charles I, including the abolition of the episcopacy: see Conrad Russell, *The Crisis of Parliaments, English History 1509–1660* (London: Oxford University Press, 1971), pp. 329, and Derek Hirst, "The Crisis of the Three Kingdoms 1640–1642," in *Authority and Conflict: England, 1603–1658* (Cambridge: Harvard University Press, 1986), pp. 188–220, on the series of crises and events leading up to the Civil War.

[28] "To the Lower-House of Parliament" ("My Masters, you that undertake the Game," fol. 95v); "The Scottish Invasion. 1640" ("Scotts are no Rebells. Why? Th'are Conquerers," fol. 95v); "A Ballad; upon the Parliament, and Scotch-Business. Decemb: 1640" ("Let English-men sitt, & consult at theyr ease," fol. 96r–v)—a satire on the early proceedings of the Long Parliament; "A Ballet, upon the Parliament & Scottish-Army 1640" ("You wily Projectors, why hang your head") with an answer poem, "Let English-men sitt" (fol. 98r); a short poem on the Scots not found in any other Bodleian or British Library manuscript, "They may persuade us, to eate is a fault" (fol. 99v); "A Libell, upon Willyam Lord Archbishop of Canterbury in Parliament-tyme. 1640" ("U.R.I.C. poore Canterbury, in a tottring state," fol. 100v); "The distracted Puritan" ("Am I madd, o noble Festus," fol. 121r–v); "A Ballad from the English Camp in the North. 1640" ("Conductors come away," fol. 122r); "A Song or Ballad in Parliament-tyme. 1640" ("Come Weavers, come Coblers, come Butchers, come all," fols. 122v–23r); two other poems unique in Bodleian and British Library manuscripts, "Another Ballett at the Parliament 1640" ("Come merry Boyes, lett's

point of view expressed is strongly Royalist, anti-Parliament, and anti-Puritan.

On fol. 137v we encounter two striking pieces attacking Parliament and the leadership of Charles's political opposition:

Anagrammes of the.
PARLIAMENT.
1642.

A Pim al rent:
Paltrie man:
Am il Parent:
I part al men:
I trap al men.
An il rap ment.
Al men party.
Lay-men prate.
Il part. Amen.

On Cuckold, & 2 Bastards, & 5 Knaves;
Make Princes Subjects, & make Subjects slaves.
  A.1. the Earle of Essex
  B.1. the Earles of Warwick & Holland
  C.1. the 5 members of the House impeached
  by the King of Treason.

These pieces attack "King [John] Pym" and the other four opposition leaders in Parliament whom the king had tried to arrest in 1642 (John Hampden, Sir Arthur Haselrig, Denzil Holles, and William

---

sing a round," fols. 123v–24r) and "Upon the Scotts. 1641" ("The holy Brother-hood of zealous Scotts," fol. 124v); "Alderman Wooleston's speech upon that discreet Petition against Bishops, & Church-government, subscribed by him & Alderman Warner, together with some 15000 ingenious & understanding Crafts-men, and by them without feare or witting-faint-heart: adverse presented to the house of Commons. 1640" ("to you grave Speaker, and the rest beside," fols. 125r–26r); four poems about the fall of Thomas Wentworth, earl of Strafford, "Goe empty joyes," "Great Strafford! worthy of that name though al," "Heere rest's wise & valiant dust," and "Is noble Wentworth gone? (fols. 126v–27v, 131v); "Upon the Parliamentary occurrents, &c.. 1641" ("Wee fasted, & then pray'd, the warre might cease," fol. 132r); "Is there no God? the Fool sayes so by rote" (fol. 132r)—like the previous piece, an anti-Pym poem; "The Round-heads Race" ("Know then [my Brethren] heaven is cleer," fols. 133r–34r); "The Lord Say (a great Anti-episcopall man)" (fols. 135r); and "1642. A Song. of the Parliamentarian Occurrents of the tyme" ("To make Charles a great King, & give hym no power," fols. 136v–37r).

Strode),[29] the earl of Essex (that "impotent" former husband of Frances Howard) as lord general of the parliamentary army, and Puritan peers who sided with the opponents of Charles. In the early stages of the Civil War, the Royalist scribe looked on the conflict as one between loyalty and treason.

After three additional poems—the first a prologue to a comedy acted before Prince Charles at Cambridge (fol. 138r), the second a political poem labeled "1641" ("The upland people are full of thought," fol. 139r), the third "The New-Yeares-gift, or Prophecy, & Vote" ("Coblers, and Coopers, and the rest," fol. 139v)[30]—the manuscript contains an antiradical, anti-Pym prose tract (fols. 140v–41v), followed by other anti-Puritan, anti-Parliament poems and songs from the Civil War and its immediate aftermath, some of which were finally printed in the Restoration songbook, *A Collection of Loyal Songs Written against the Rump Parliament* (1660).[31] There are anti-Cromwell poems such as "What's a Protector he's a stately thing" (fol. 148v),[32] "It fell on a day when good people say" (fol. 153r), and a satiric epitaph toward the end of the manuscript:

Upon the Proctector Oliver Cromwell

Here lies the Body of My Lord Protector.
Who when hee was alive was as valiant as Hector.

[29] See Hirst, "Crisis," p. 216.

[30] This piece is attributed to J. Shirley in BL MS Harl. 6918, fol. 28 (Crum, p. 157).

[31] These include the following: Thomas Weever's "Zeale over-heated" ("Attend you brethren everyone," fol. 142r); "A New Ode" ("I meane to tell you of England's sad fate," fol. 142v); "1642" ("Up, up, wrong'd Charles friends: what, can you lye," fol. 143r); "Of the Parliament. 1642" ("No Pedigrees, no Progenies," fols. 143v–44r)—a piece called, as Crum, p. 610, notes, "The Generation of vipers"; three poems found in no other Bodleian or British Library manuscript—"The Irish Petition" ("Most sacred Majestie grant that wee may have," fol. 144v), "A Song of the Parliament. 1642 . . . to the tune of Tom a Bedlam" ("Regard our Proclamations," fol. 145r), and "Mr P's Lamentation. 1642" ("No Rout wee have, poore Westerne knave," fol. 145v); "Fight on brave souldiers for the cause feare not the cavaliers" (fols. 146v–47r), a lampoon on the Roundheads by Alexander Brome (Crum, p. 238); and two more poems found in no other Bodleian and British Library manuscript, "If this be a happy Parliament" (fol. 147r–v) and "On the received report of P[rince] Ruperts death to Ananias Simple a frequent auditor & zealous admirer of Obadiah . . . Love Pastor to the Regiment of Saints in Windsor Castle" ("Come, come you'd have it soe; sooner then I," fol. 147v).

[32] This piece was printed in the 1687 edition of John Cleveland's *Works* (Crum, p. 1054), and it also is found in three other Bodleian manuscripts. Ruth Nevo views it as a Royalist expression of "outraged hierarchical class-consciousness" (*The Dial of Virtue: A Study of Poems on Affairs of State in the Seventeenth Century* [Princeton: Princeton University, Press, 1963], p. 13).

Butt now hees gone where all shall be fed
There's no man alive can say but he's dead.
(Fol. 163v)[33]

This last part of the manuscript contains some anti-Scots pieces; a two-part satiric song against the Rump Parliament, "A newyeares Guifte for the Rumpe Sitting January. 1659 [1660]" ("You may Have heard of the Politique snout," fols. 158v–59v); and another poem found in no other Bodleian or British Library manuscript, "If Kings annoynted crowned & enstall'd," introduced by the following remarks on its context: "Charles the 2nd after he was crowned King of Scotland, was proclaimed Traytor, & all his Adherents Rebells: by the Rump-Parliament" (fol. 163r). Inserted also into this section of the manuscript is a poem on Clarendon dated 1667, "Ephetha' upon the Lord Chancelour Hide" ("Gude lust, ambition, and the peoples hate," fol. 160v), a piece also found in no other Bodleian or British Library manuscript.

A collection like Rawl. Poet. 26 is a vivid example of how the system of manuscript transmission was most receptive to political poems, many of which would have been difficult to bring out in printed form, except perhaps as broadside ballads. At the same time, interspersed in this largely political anthology, we find such poems as Herrick's "Welcome to Sack" (fol. 87r–v), Donne's "An Hymne to the Saints & to the Marques Hamilton" (fol. 112r–v), and the following two comic epitaphs:

A Scotch Cipitha

Here lies interred
In this Church yerd
Geeny Cuttberd
with her Coney upward.
(Fol. 148r)

Upon John Dodd a great Swearer

under this Clodd
Lies John Dodd
dead By god.
(Fol. 163r)

---

[33] Neither this nor the previously mentioned poem is found in any other Bodleian or British Library manuscript.

Very few of the manuscript miscellanies and poetical anthologies are as heavily political as Bod. MS Rawl. Poet. 26, for the politically topical poems are more typically scattered throughout collections that contain a great variety of other material. The Civil War and Interregnum, of course, intensified the production and collection of overtly political verse, but there were many directly and indirectly political pieces composed, transmitted, and collected from the mid-sixteenth century to the crisis period of the 1640s.[34]

Manuscript anthologies contain examples of a genre of poetry that although not always overtly political, was regarded as politically and socially dangerous, especially when in print, the poetical libel. Although most satiric political poetry dealing with public figures falls under the broad definition of the term "libel," I would like to concentrate here on those poems that actually use the word "libel" in their titles.[35] Such poems recur in the manuscript collections of the sixteenth and seventeenth centuries, texts that were not only sometimes politically hazardous, but also illegal. As Harold Love points out, "English law . . . insist[ed] that anyone encountering a libel had an obligation to destroy it."[36]

John Finet's anthology contains the libel against Edward Bashe (fols. 67r–72r), the victualler of the Navy who served in the government from the time of Henry VIII through that of Queen Elizabeth, a scabrous poem attacking Bashe's physical appearance, social ambition, and alleged dishonesty (Cummings, pp. 513–40).[37] This is fol-

---

[34] Another manuscript with a large number of political poems is Bod. MS Eng. Poet. c.50, which starts with poems about Bacon, "The Comons Petition," pieces on the Spanish match, Buckingham's expedition to the Isle of Rhé, and an epitaph on Queen Elizabeth. The University of Texas "Herrick" Manuscript also contains a number of poems and prose pieces about early seventeenth-century political events and personages (from about 1612–23). See the discussion of these in Farmer, *Seventeenth-Century Manuscript*, pp. 7–15.

[35] For a discussion of verse libeling, with a special emphasis on poems written about Sir Robert Cecil, see Pauline Croft, "The Reputation of Robert Cecil: Libels, Political Opinion and Popular Awareness in the Early Seventeenth Century," *Trans. Royal Historical Soc.*, 5th ser., 1 (1991): 43–69. Richard Firth Green notes the medieval custom of composing libelous rhymes to discredit one's political opponents or enemies (*Poets and Princepleasers*, pp. 178–79 [see Chap. 1, n. 53]).

[36] Love, "Scribal Publication," p. 137. Philip Hamburger notes that "until 1662 seditious libel was a term used exclusively for manuscript circulation" ("The Development of the Law of Seditious Libel and the Control of the Press," *Stanford Law Review* 37 [1985]: 661–765; cited in Coiro, "Milton and Class Identity," p. 268n).

[37] Cummings notes that the piece also appears in Henry Stanford's anthology (Camb. MS Dd.5.75) and BL MSS Add. 34064 and Lansdowne 740. It is also found in Rosenbach

lowed by "The Libell of Oxenforde" (fols. 72v–75v), a poem satirizing the amorous misadventures of academics, probably written in the 1560s by Thomas Bucklye (Cummings, p. 557).[38] Laurence Cummings observes: "Such scurrilous libels at Renaissance Oxford were not infrequent. John Fisher in 1573 was refused his MA at Oxford on account of popery and of publishing a libel called 'A Knack to Know a Knave.' In 1602 a Merton scholar named Darling was whipped in London and lost his ears in Oxford for libelling the vicechancellor and the Council, as Bucklye did" (p. 557). There are twenty-five leaves missing in Finet's manuscript following the two libels it contains, suggesting perhaps that some other poems of this kind were transcribed and then removed. Stephen Vallenger's analogous Cambridge Libel is found in Humphrey Coningsby's anthology, with identifications of the persons involved provided in the margins (BL MS Harl. 7392, fols. 54v–58v).[39]

Political libels are found in other nonacademic manuscript collections. Bod. MS Rawl. Poet. 26, for example, preserves a libel written against the enemies of the earl of Essex, "Admir-all weakeness wrong the right" (fol. 20v), as well as the later "Libell upon William Lord Archbishop of Canterbury, in Parliament-tyme, 1640" (fol. 100v).[40] In addition to the pro-Essex poem, Bod. MS Don. c.54, a manuscript connected with legal circles in London, contains several other libels: "A libell upon Master Edw[ard] Cooke, then Atturney general and sithance Cheife Justice of the Comon pleas upon some disagreement between him & his wife being widow of Sir Wm Hatton Kt. and daughter to the now Earle of EXETER then Sir Tho[mas] Cecill" ("Cocus the Pleader hath a Lady wedd," fol. 6v), followed by four more on same topic;[41] the "Libell against Robert Cecill" ("Proude and ambi-

---

MS 1083/15 and in the Arundel Harington Manuscript (see Hughey, 1:225–32 and 2:293–301) and the Dalhousie MS I, fols. 34r–36v (see Sullivan, *Dalhousie Manuscripts*, pp. 63–68 [cited in full at Chap. 1, n. 41]).

[38] The Arundel Harington Manuscript contains an incomplete version of this poem (Hughey, 1:223–25; see her notes, 2:276–93). Hughey points out that this poem is also found in Bod. MSS Rawl. Poet. 172, fols. 16r–18v, Tanner 465, fols. 105r–109r, and Rawl. Poet. 212, fols. 118r–23r.

[39] See poem 180 in the Arundel Harington Manuscript (Hughey, 1:216–23 and notes, 2:261–76).

[40] The former poem is also recorded in Bod. MS Don. c.54, fol. 7, and Eng. Hist. c.272, p. 41, as well as in BL MS Add. 5956, fol. 23 (dated 20 December 1599). The latter is found also in Bod. MS Douce 357, fol. 8r.

[41] This satiric poem has been ascribed to Sir John Davies (*Poems of Davies*, ed. Krueger, p. 171 [see Chap. 1, n. 126]).

tious writch that feedest on naught but faction," fol. 20r); "A libell against [Robert Carr, Earl of] Somerset" ("Poore Pilott thou art like to lose the Pinke," fol. 22v); and "A libell against Oxford upon their first entertainment of the kinge" ("When the king to Oxford came," fol. 25r). In addition to the Bashe and Oxford libels, Rosenbach MS 1083/15 includes other poems of this kind: "A libell against some Grayes Inn gentlemen and Revellers" (fols. 32v–33v); one against "Byshope Fletcher & my lady Baker" (fols. 38v–39r); and "Bastardes Libell" (fols. 45v–49r), another Oxford libel that lost Thomas Bastard his fellowship, according to Anthony à Wood.[42] Bod. MS Rawl. B.88 contains John Hollis's 1597 poem, "A lybell caste out agaynst John Markeham at Newarke" (Crum, p. 926).

Clearly, the universities and the Inns of Court were especially conducive to the production and transmission of libelous verse. The best targets were authority figures and rivals. The illegality of such texts not only made them unsuitable for print but also, not unexpectedly, made them desirable in the system of manuscript circulation and compilation of verse. Like political ballads, they were the medium for expressing resentments and criticisms outside the official discourses of the culture.

### Political Scandals and Political Falls

The falls of ambitious or highly placed individuals in the Elizabethan, Jacobean, and Caroline periods attracted much attention in the manuscript collections of the period, which contain poetry (and prose) related to the treason and execution of the earl of Essex; the trial, long imprisonment, and eventual execution of Sir Walter Ralegh; the political eclipse and death of Robert Cecil, earl of Salisbury; the murder trial and conviction of Robert Carr, earl of Somerset (and of his wife Frances Howard); the impeachments of Sir Francis Bacon and of Lionel Cranfield, earl of Middlesex; the career and assassination of George Villiers, duke of Buckingham; the political fall and execution of Thomas Wentworth, earl of Strafford; and the trial and execution of the earl of Castlehaven for sexual crimes.

---

[42] Sanderson, "An Edition," poems 180, 184, and 200, pp. 335–46, 377–82, and 440–70. He quotes Wood on p. 453, and on p. 451 points out that Bastard's libel also appears in Bod. MSS CCC 327, fols. 17v–21r, and Rawl. Poet. 212, fols. 123v–26v.

# SEX AND POLITICS

*Robert Devereux, Earl of Essex*

The political events that became the focus of the largest number of texts in Elizabethan manuscript collections were those having to do with the fall of Robert Devereux, earl of Essex, particularly his conspiracy, treason trial, and execution.[43] The Farmer-Chetham manuscript (Chetham's Lib., Manchester MS Mun. A.4.150) contains much prose on the trial of the earl of Essex. Rosenbach MS 184 is a collection of works by and about him: it contains letters and other prose, including Francis Bacon's "Appollogie of the Earle of Essex" (attributed to Anthony Bacon), as well as Essex's own "There was a tyme when seellye Bees could speake," the only poem in the manuscript. Bod. MS Don. c.54 has both verse and prose on the topic, including letters between Lord Keeper Egerton and Essex as well as between Lady Rich (Essex's sister) and the queen. It also has a transcription of an anonymous poem dealing with the fall of Essex, with prominent personages identified in the margin:

A dreame alludinge to my L. of Essex, and his adversaries

|  |  |
|---|---|
|  | Where Medwaye greetes old Thamesis silver streames |
|  | There did I sleepe, and then my thought did dreame |
|  | A stately Hart did grow on Northern shore |
| Earl of Essex | of Thamasis, and head full highe he bore |
|  | Of feature comelie, and of corradge bold |
|  | sterne was his Lookes, yet Lord of young and old. |
| The Queene | The LION helde him deere, and had cause whie |
|  | He did the Lions throne soe fortefie |
|  | That neither Romish wolfe nor Spanishe beare |
|  | The Lion cold hurte or one poore Lambkin beare. |
| Sr Rob: Cecill | Me thought I sawe a CAMMELS oglie broode |
| Crookbackt | That on the other side of Medwaie stood. |
|  | He could not relishe silver Medwaies foame |
| L. Cobham | A muddye BROOKE pleas'd better mixt with loame. |
|  | His meate blood RAWE his salletts all were REWE. |

---

[43] On the career of Essex, see Lacy Baldwin Smith, *Treason in Tudor England: Politics and Paranoia* (London: Jonathan Cape, 1986), pp. 192–276. For a discussion of Essex's 1601 insurrection as the last "honor revolt," see Mervyn James, "At a Crossroads of the Political Culture: The Essex Revolt, 1601," in *Society, Politics and Culture: Studies in Early Modern England* (Cambridge: Cambridge University Press, 1986), pp. 416–65.

| | |
|---|---|
| Sr Walt Rawleigh | Whose Wardes he swallowe could, and never chewe. |
| | The gorged Camell to the Lion came |
| | God shei'ld your Grace, and to your foes bring shame. |
| | The Hart is all to great, he boastes the swaye |
| | The peoples Love he hathe your Loves decay. |
| | If a preservative your Grace will take |
| | I'le make yow stronger; I'le make proud HARTE to quake |
| | Of Camels milke yow shall twoe spoonefulles take |
| | Treble as much from fleering Brooke his lake |
| | To this yow must ad a stalke of bitter REWE |
| | With sugred lies well altogether brewe |
| Sr. Ed: Coke: | A leafe wee'le have from Covake old his tree |
| Sr. Ro: Cecyll | That planted was of late in Cicelye. |
| | Should I quoth Lion thinke he meanes me ill |
| | [line missing] |
| | My banners he displaide in Gallian plane |
| | And Gerrion foil'd and did us glorie gaine |
| | O quoth the Cammell Hibernia let him swaye |
| | And tame the woolfes which on there foldes doe praie. |
| | Me thought he cheerelie went, yet scarce was there |
| | But home bredd wolves, our flockes at home did teare |
| | A thousand wolves he found and made them stoope |
| | And all he tam'd, who sicke and doth not droope |
| | He sicke retir'd, to him welcome was |
| | Till Camell brought a poison in a Glass |
| | which scarce had warm'd the Hart but night was daie |
| | And Lion roard, and th' Hart was sent awaye |
| | O that a Camell shoulde a Lion leade |
| | I saide, and thought I dream't yet did I dreade. |
| | Cammell for burthen is, and <not> for the waie |
| | And not for Kingdoms sterne and scepters swaye |
| | By sleight yet Camell swaies, and LION sleepes |
| | And noble Hart in dampie doungeon keepes. |
| | Wake noble Lion and this Cammell scorne |
| | And teare him that thy Noble Hart hath torne. |
| | Your Grace to Ireland should the Camell send |
| Char:Howard | His backe will beare Tirone, and never bend. |

L: Admirall
Or him or else where Liverd LION send
Poore Hart escape, this Lion soone will mend
To Ireland (generall) thrice renowned swaine
That bravelie triumpt on St. James his plane.
Goodlye thie feature is, thy stature talle
Thy couradge foli; thie witt God knowes is smalle.
Sterne yorke in Irish broiles sometimes did saye
Send Sommerset if yow will loose the daye
And send this Lion alwaies pale for dreade
Hee'le take the gold and bless himself from leade
Honor to wynne to Ireland he would faine
But that ould fathers ghost doeth him restrayne.
When on his Death bedd chardg'd him eaven so
To Ireland (sonne) see that thou never goe.
Or send him RAWE whose conscience now is seared
That knowes not Jove, nor Plato ever feared.
For he Pithagoras sowle doeth fast enclose
Within his [word missing] breast, by Metempsicose
But fie he waxeth penitent of Late.
And sinnes of former daies he now doeth hate
He will noe more in Court faire Ladies staine
Nor Chimney money beg to Comons paine
Nor cause to be one of the dampned Crewe
Nor paye to score for puddinges that is Due
Heele swere by God and worship Devill for gaine
Tobacco boye or sacke to swage his paine.
Then I awoke afrighted with the noise
And sawe my brightefull dreames were
dreaminge toies.
Finis.

(Fols. 6v–7r)[44]

This poem portrays Essex as a patriotic supporter of the queen, a military hero, and a popular leader brought low by his political enemies, among them Robert Cecil, who, determined to destroy the earl's political power, urged that Essex be sent on the disastrous Irish expedition. The context of this poem is important, following as it does the letters dealing with Essex's arrest and followed as it is by poems attacking Cecil and Cobham. Essex's partisans, many of whom were in the Inns of Court and who seem to have identified with both

[44] This poem is found in no other Bodleian or British Library manuscript.

his ambition and its frustration, no doubt circulated such pro-Essex literature. The manuscript of John Ramsey of the Middle Temple, for example, has a copy of a song on the fall of Essex subscribed "E: Essex Downe" (Bod. MS Douce 280, fol. 67r). In fact, the argument has been made by Lillian M. Ruff and D. Arnold Wilson that there was a direct connection between the decline and fall of Essex and the contemporary popularity of madrigals.[45]

Of course, not all poems dealing with Essex were sympathetic to him and to his fellow conspirators. Bod. MS Rawl. Poet. 26 contains a piece that jokes about the Essex circle:

> Essex prayes, Southampton playes;
> Rutland weepes, Sandes sleepes;
> Crumwell quaffs, Mounteagle laughs.
>     And amongst all this treachery,
>     they brought in L[ord] Pembroke for his lechery.
>                     (Fol. 2r)[46]

The reference to the lechery of William Herbert, earl of Pembroke, concerns his commitment to the Fleet in March 1601 (a month after Essex's failed coup) for fathering an illegitimate child by Mary Fitton.[47] "Essex prayes" is an allusion to the earl's repentance following his conviction for treason. The other figures mentioned were members of his inner circle—all of whom are portrayed satirically. Retrospectively, the mythology of honor that cloaked Essex and his cause is stripped away to reveal a group of fallible, self-absorbed men.

### Sir Walter Ralegh

The political fall of Sir Walter Ralegh was connected with a number of lyrics, many of them composed by or attributed to the protagonist himself. The poems by or attributed to Ralegh show up in an extraor-

---

[45] Lillian M. Ruff and D. Arnold Wilson, "The Madrigal, The Lute Song and Elizabethan Politics," *Past and Present*, no. 44 (August 1969): 3–51, on the relationship of the career and demise of Essex and the fashion for madrigals.

[46] This piece is also found in BL MS 10307, fol. 142v.

[47] See John Dover Wilson's biographical account of Pembroke in his edition of Shakespeare' *Sonnets*, 2d ed. (Cambridge: Cambridge University Press, 1966), p. cii. This material is discussed also by Gary Waller in *The Sidney Family Romance: Mary Wroth, William Herbert, and the Early Modern Construction of Gender* (Detroit: Wayne State University Press, 1993), pp. 78–79.

dinary number of manuscript collections of the seventeenth century because Ralegh was an example of spectacular political success and failure and, in the Jacobean and Caroline periods, a reference point for nostalgia for Elizabethan culture and government.[48] Initially, his work appears in manuscript collections in connection with his arrest, trial, and capital sentence; later, during his long imprisonment and after his execution, it is used to articulate political disaffection and disillusionment.

Bod. MS Rawl. Poet. 26 contains a poem addressed to Ralegh on the occasion of the publication (while he was in prison) of his *History of the World*, a poem that clearly served as a vehicle for criticizing the Court:

Master Thomas Scott sent these verses
by the hand of Doctor John White
to Sir Walter Raleigh; upon
the setting forth of his Booke
of the History of the World

Who doubts of Providence, or God denyes;
Let him thy booke read; & thy Life advise.
Thy book doth shew nothinge directly can
(Save grace infus'd from heaven) informe a man.
Thy Life doth likewise shew, that as the Devill
Drawes bad from good, God still drawes good from evill.
That at his set and fore-appointed tyme;
Hee to our good, t'his prayse, corrects each crime;
that 'ore the greatest favorites of Kings
The greatest danger hangs on smallest strings.
In greatnes thow art lost, as in a wood,
Treadinge the paths of flattery; falshood, blood.
The way to heaven neglected, thow dids't stray
As others now doe in thy Politick way.
But now thow'st found thy selfe; & wee have found
That sickness taught thee Art to make men sound.
For had'st thow never fall'ne, th'hadst never writt:
Nor hadst thow cleer'd, but clouded us with witt.

---

[48] On the important political phenomenon of nostalgia for the Elizabethan era, see Ann Barton, *Ben Jonson, Dramatist* (Cambridge: Cambridge University Press, 1984), pp. 300–320, and Martin Butler, *Theatre in Crisis, 1632–42* (Cambridge: Cambridge University Press, 1984), pp. 198–210.

But now thy falshood hath the truth so showne,
That a true World fore ^from^ a false World is knowne.

(Fol. 6v)[49]

Ralegh's ability to write a pragmatically wise historical work is rooted, paradoxically, in the sobering experience of political defeat. The manuscript in which this piece appears also contains three other items in which Ralegh is treated sympathetically after his execution: "Upon Sr Walter Raleigh his Execution & Death" ("Great hart, who taught the soe to dye," fol. 69r);[50] "His own Epitaph" ("Even such is time," fol. 69v, transcribed on fol. 2r as "Sir Walter Raleigh's Epitaph on his owne death"); and "Upon Sr Walter Raleigh" ("Fly fame, report that all the world may knowe," fol. 70r), a poem found in no other Bodleian or British Library manuscript. The second of these poems, "Even such is time," has a remarkable life in the system of manuscript transmission: it appears in some ninety-two surviving manuscripts, sometimes more than once in the same collection (Beal, 1.2.379–86). Identified in them as a poem Ralegh wrote either the night before or the morning of his execution in 1619, sometimes as a piece found transcribed in the Bible he left in the Gatehouse, this lyric was interpreted as a poem that brought moral closure to the life of an ambitious man who had played for high political stakes and lost, but it also was valued as a *contemptus mundi* piece that could be read as a protest poem indicting the Stuart power that crushed him.[51] This double function is certainly apparent in the popularity in the manuscript system of Ralegh's poem "The Lie," a work that, in whole or in part, accompanied or unaccompanied by answers, occurs in some thirty-two surviving documents (Beal, 1.2.390–92). This lyric is also related to another one of his moral poems with extensive manuscript circulation, "On the Life of Man" ("What is our life? a play of passion," Beal, 1.2.396–401). The love lyrics of Ralegh that recur in seventeenth-century manuscripts—particularly "The Excuse," "A Farewell to False Love," "Fortune hath taken thee away my love,"

---

[49] This piece appears in no other Bodleian or British Library manuscript.

[50] "Upon Sir Walter Raleigh his Execution & Death" was published in *Wits Recreations*, 1641, sig. S1, and appears also in Bod. MSS Eng. Hist. c.171, p. 51; Eng. Poet. e.14, fol. 98v rev.; Rawl. D. 954, fol. 35; Rawl. Poet. 209, fol. 10r; and Tanner 306, fol. 251r (Crum, p. 291). It is also found in BL MSS Harl. 791, fol. 49; Harl. 7332, fol. 215; Lansdowne 777, fol. 64; and Add. 33998, fol 96v.

[51] "Even such is time" was published in *The Good Wife* (1618) by Richard Brathwaite, *A Helpe to Memory and Discourse* (1620), and *Reliquiae Wottonianae* (1651).

and "Sir Walter Ralegh to the Queen" ("Our passions are most like to floods and streams," see Beal, 1.2.386–89, 404–6)—mark him as a figure who practiced the form of amorous/political courtship he helped to formulate for the Elizabethan era, but also call attention to the cultural and political differences between that time and that of the early Stuarts.

BL MS Add. 22601, an early Jacobean manuscript containing poems by Sir John Davies and King James himself,[52] is a court-centered document that contains not only "the Letter of Sir Walter Rawleigh to the Kinge, after his Arraignment" (fol. 17v), but also three anti-Ralegh poems written after his arrest and trial: "Wilye watt, wilie wat" (fol. 63r), "Water thy plaints with grace divine" (fol. 63v),[53] and "Watt I wot well thy overweeninge witt" (fol. 64r).[54] The contemporary treatment of Ralegh's fall in this manuscript is hostile, clearly an exception to how he is usually depicted in such collections.

*Robert Cecil, Earl of Salisbury*

The sudden death in 1612 of King James's chief minister, Robert Cecil, earl of Salisbury, was an event preceded by the secretary's political decline during the first Jacobean decade, largely because he could not push James's program through Parliament. It occasioned a number of libels and satiric political poems. Given Cecil's great power in the last years of Elizabeth's reign and in the first part of the reign of James, it is not surprising that he made a large number of political enemies and that his death should have inspired poems attacking everything from his Machiavellian ambition to his physical deformity and his alleged sexual voraciousness. He became one of the most ferociously libeled individuals in the early Stuart era.[55] Anti-Cecil poems are scattered through a large body of manuscript collections: they include "Here lies Salisburie or little great comaunder"

---

[52] Krueger and Nemser claim this manuscript "was written by or for someone at court, for it contains Davies's royal entertainments, letters and petitions to the King, tournament speeches by important peers, and notably . . . texts of many of King James's poems" (*Poems of Davies*, ed. Krueger, p. 435).

[53] This poem appears in Bod. MS Ash. 781, p. 163 (Crum, p. 1014).

[54] This Thomas Rogers poem is found in Bod. MSS Don. c.54, fol. 9v; Eng. Hist. c.272, fol. 46v; and Rawl. Poet. 172, fol. 14r (Crum, p. 1013). It also appears, according to William Ringler (Huntington notes) in Folger MS X.d.241 (fols. 1v–3) and five British Library manuscripts.

[55] Pauline Croft has examined this phenomenon in great detail, recovering a large number of anti-Cecil poems from the manuscript documents of the period, both those written while he was alive and those composed after his death ("Reputation of Robert Cecil").

(Hunt. MS 198, pt. 2, fol. 125v; also Bod. MS Mal. 23, p. 65); "In hatfield, nere Hartford there lies in a Coffin" (Hunt. MS HM 198, pt. 2, fol. 126r); "Upon Sr Robert Cecill, Earle of Salisbury" ("Heer Hobbinall lyes, or Sheapheard while," Bod. MSS Rawl. Poet. 26, fol. 78r; Eng. Poet. e.14, fol. 79 rev.; Tanner 299, fol. 12v);[56] "Here lyes little Robin that vainely was recked" (Bod. MS Eng. Poet. e.14, fol. 95v rev.).[57] Since Pauline Croft has extensively analyzed these pieces and their context, there is no need to examine them here in detail. What I would emphasize, however, is that the anti-Cecil poems are but one instance of a phenomenon that occurred when any major early-Stuart political figure fell from power or died. The negative evaluations of his life and career are unusual, perhaps, only in their ferocity.

### The Somerset-Howard Scandal

In the Jacobean period, perhaps the most spectacular and disgrace-ful political fall was that of Robert Carr, earl of Somerset. This fall and the scandal of the marriage to Frances Howard and the murder of Sir Thomas Overbury hold center stage, for example, in Anthony Weldon's critical account of the period.[58] Carr was the king's first erotic/political favorite, the most powerful man in England next to James after the political decline and death of Cecil. Carr's enemies found a young man to replace him in James's favors (George Villiers, later duke of Buckingham) in order to overthrow him; thereafter, he and his wife, Frances Howard, could be prosecuted for their part in the the murder of Sir Thomas Overbury, a crime connected with the circumstances of the countess's scandalous divorce from the third earl of Essex and with her politically arranged marriage to Somerset. The manuscript collections of the period are full of satiric squibs about Carr's fall and about the countess's loose morals.[59] Take, for example,

[56] Croft believes this was written by Ralegh, who was Cecil's bitter enemy (ibid., p. 62). Beal, 1.2.408–9, lists some nineteen manuscripts in which this appears.

[57] For a group of anti-Cecil poems, see Farmer, *Seventeenth-Century Manuscript*, pp. 41–51, for "Here lyes burried wormes meate," "Here lies Hobbinall our Shepheard whileare," "At Hatfield neere Hartford there lies in a coffin," and "Advance, advance my ill-disposed muse." The Farmer Chetham Manuscript has a complimentary epitaph on Cecil ("You that reade passing by") attributed to the earl of Pembroke (Grosart, *Dr. Farmer Chetham MS*, 2:188).

[58] Anthony Weldon, *The Court and Character of King James* (London, 1650).

[59] See the discussion of some of these in James L. Sanderson, "Poems on an Affair of State—The Marriage of Somerset and Lady Essex," *RES*, n.s., 17 (1966): 57–61. The first Dalhousie manuscript, which has been connected with the Essex family, not surprisingly, begins with two prose pieces related to the proceedings dealing with the annulment of the

the nasty piece that foregrounds Carr's political ascent and Frances Howard's moral descent, "Uppon Sr R. C. and the Lady F. H.":

> A page a knight a Vicount, and an Earle
> was matched lately to an Englishe girle
> But such A one as nere was seene before
> A mayde, a wife, a countess and A whore.
> (Bod. MS. Ash. 38, p. 116)[60]

An epigram attributed to Sir John Harington, "ICUR Good Mounsieur Carr," shows up in a large number of manuscripts.[61] It is interesting that Sir Henry Wotton's popular political poem, "Dazel'd thus, with height of place," originally written about Carr's fall, was subsequently applied by contemporaries to the falls of Bacon and Buckingham. It is clear that manuscript compilers of verse understood this lyric as applicable to almost any political fall and retitled it as needed to fit other circumstances.[62]

In the Skipwith family anthology (BL MS Add. 25707), there is a poem and answer set (found in no other British Library or Bodleian manuscript), evidently written at the time of the trial of the Somersets for Sir Thomas Overbury's murder, alternately pleading mercy and strict justice for Lady Somerset:

> Petitio.
> Looke, and lament, behould a face of Earth,
> In bewtie heavenly, great in place, & birth.
> Nor is her soule in bewtie less excellinge,
> In whome so manie vertues have their dwellinge.
> Much Noble Nature, bewtie, Charitie,

---

marriage of Frances Howard and the third earl of Essex. See Sullivan, *First and Second Dalhousie Manuscripts*, pp. 4–7. The University of Texas "Herrick" Manuscript contains a large number of anti-Somerset poems: see Farmer's discussion on pp. 12–14 and the poems on pp. 59–79 of his edition, *Seventeenth-Century Manuscript*.

[60] This also appears in the University of Texas "Herrick" Manuscript (Farmer, *Seventeenth-Century Manuscript*, p. 63); Bod. MSS Don. c.54, fol. 23; Mal. 19, p. 38; Rawl. D. 1048, fol. 64; Rawl. Poet. 160, fol. 163; and Tanner 465, fol. 96v; and BL MSS Sloane 1489, fol. 9v, and Egerton 2230, fol. 70v.

[61] Crum, p. 406, cites Bod. MSS Don. c.54, fol. 22v; Douce f.5, fol. 34v; Eng. Poet. e.14, fol. 49; Firth d.7, fol. 152; Rawl. D. 1048, fol. 64v; Rawl. Poet. 160, fol. 162v; and Sancroft 53, pp. 48 and 58. It also appears in BL MSS Sloane 1489, fol. 9v; Add. 15227, fol. 42v, and 30982, fol. 22; and Harl. 1221, fol. 91; 4955, fol. 81; and 7316, fol. 4v.

[62] See the discussion in Ted-Larry Pebworth, "Sir Henry Wotton's 'Dazel'd Thus, with Height of Place' and the Appropriation of Political Poetry in the Earlier Seventeenth Century," *PBSA* 71 (1977): 151–69.

Much in goodnes, witt, and pietie,
Nor is the fayrest peece without a staine,
In fayrest peeces spotts appeare most plaine.
Sence of dishonor, in best myndes most stronge,
Made her desire, t'avenge soe vile a wronge
By meanes unlawfull, which have given offence,
To Lawe, to God, to Kinge; In recompence
of one Soule lost, the Lawe hath taken fowre,
And this hath suffer'd much by Legall Powre.
   God doth shew mercie for the fowlest thinge
   to penitents. Doe thou so Mightie Kinge.

Respontio.
It's strange to se a face soe highe in birth,
And heavenly, to converse soe much with earth,
Naye more with hell; her soule noe less excellinge
In what? In Vice where all these had their dwellinge.
Much brybinge, breakinge, Pride, & Infamie,
Much of her Mother, new adulterie,
This ugly soule hath yet a fouler staine;
Though in foule soules, greate synns appeare least plaine.
Murther a Cryinge sin, in her more stronge,
For drawinge bosome frends, into the wronge.
Then blame not God, nor Kinge to take offence,
Nor yet our Lawes to take in recompence.
For owne soule lost, soe lost, wer't foure tymes foure,
And this of all deserves strict Legall power.
   To Livinge Lorde still suffers in this thinge
   Were't but for that. Proceede in Justice Kinge.

                                        (Fol. 46r)

The urging of justice rather than mercy in the second part of this poem expresses the outrage many contemporaries felt about the whole sordid business. When King James eventually pardoned the Somersets, his action cast suspicion on his own involvement in the divorce and marriage. Godfrey Davies remarks of this whole scandal: "Probably no single event, prior to the attempt to arrest the five members [of the House of Commons] in 1642, did more to lessen the general reverence with which royalty was regarded in England than this unsavory episode."[63]

[63] Godfrey Davies, *The Early Stuarts, 1603–1660*, 2d ed. (Oxford: Clarendon Press, 1959), p. 20.

One of the ironies of the Carr-Howard scandal is that the wronged former husband of the countess of Somerset, the third earl of Essex, became the first commander of the parliamentary forces in the Civil War. Frances Howard's politically engineered divorce from him was granted on the basis of his alleged impotence, a characteristic to which at least one later Royalist poet called attention in a satiric poem, "The Ladys Song" ("Why weare wee Maids made wives," Bod. MS Ash. 38, p. 50 [subscribed "Lady S[o]m[erse]t"]).[64]

### Sir Francis Bacon and Sir Lionel Cranfield

The impeachments of Francis Bacon and Lionel Cranfield in 1623 and 1624 generated several poems found in manuscript collections. The poems on the former include a much-transcribed piece in his defense by Dr. William Lewis of Oriel College, Oxford, "When you awake dull Brittons and behould,"[65] a long poem addressing the Commons as an unfair tribunal that condemned an intelligent and talented public servant whose few faults supposedly were far outweighed by his many virtues. A more cynical point of view, however, was expressed in an anonymous satiric epitaph:

> Within this sty heer now doth ly
> A hog wel fed with bribery
> A pig, a hog, a boare, a bacon
> whom God hath left, and the Divel taken.
> (Folger MS V.a.345, p. 25)[66]

Like the first of the royal servants offered to Parliament for impeachment, Sir Giles Momperson, Bacon was deliberately sacrificed by the

[64] This poem also appears in BL MS Add. 24665. For this information I am grateful to David Lindley of the University of Leeds, who deals with the Essex-Howard-Somerset affair in *The Trials of Frances Howard: Fact and Fiction at the Court of King James* (London: Routledge, 1993).

[65] See BL MS Add. 25303, fols. 83r–86r, in which the poem is titled "Doctor Lewis his foolish invective against the Parliament for proceedinge to censure his Lord Verulam." The poem also appears in BL MSS Sloane 826, fols. 4, 5, 8; Stowe 962, fol. 52v; Sloane 1792, fol. 109; Sloane 1489, fol. 46v; and Harl. 2127, fol. 27v and 77, and in Bodleian MSS Ash. 38, pp. 10–12; Eng. Poet. f.10, fol. 104; Rawl. B. 151, fol. 101; Rawl. Poet. 26, fol. 101r; Rawl. Poet. 84, fol. 64v; Rawl. Poet. 160, fol. 25; and Hunt. MS 198, pt. 1, pp. 37–40.

[66] This piece also appears in Bod. MS Douce f.5, fol. 16r, but is found in no British Library manuscript.

crown in the hope that some of the opposition to the royal policies might be dampened.[67]

Another important impeachment target was the talented lord treasurer, Lionel Cranfield, who was unpopular with powerful contemporaries because of his economizing reforms and was also resented by competitors for his extraordinary rise in power and status. After Cranfield opposed Buckingham's pro-war stance in 1623 (for sensible financial reasons) and made some effort to have Buckingham replaced as James's favorite, the duke retaliated by handing his client over to the Commons as a kind of political peace offering.[68] Like Bacon, Cranfield was the subject of manuscript-circulated poems: "On Sr Lyonell Cranfield Earle of Middlesex & Lo: Treasurer of England his fall. 1624" ("The base on which mans greatnes firmest stands");[69] "State Passages" ("There was some Policy as I believe," Hunt. MS HM 198, pt. 1, pp. 56–58), a piece dealing with the issues of the Parliament of 1624, which discussed money needed for a war with Spain (and during which Cranfield was impeached); and the satiric epitaph "Upon the late L. treasurer, Sir Lionel Cranfield earle of Middlesex: disgraced, imprisoned, and putt from his office by Parliament" ("There was a man, and he was semper idem," Bod. MS Don. c.54, fol. 29r).[70] The last piece was printed in *The Harmony of the Muses* (1654) with the more general title "Upon a Merchant":

> There was a man, and he was *semper idem*,
> And to be brief he was mercator *quidem*,
> He had a wife was neither tall nor *brevis*,
> Yet in her carriage was accounted *levis*,
> He to content her gave her all things *satis*,
> She to requite him made him Cuckold *gratis*.
>
> (P. 81)

[67] See Russell, *Crisis of Parliaments*, pp. 295–96. For a discussion of the various impeachment proceedings of the 1620s, see Linda Levy Peck, *Court Patronage and Corruption in Early Stuart England* (Boston: Unwin Hyman, 1990), pp. 185–96.

[68] See Russell, *Crisis of Parliaments*, p. 298, and Roger Lockyer, *The Early Stuarts: A Political History of England 1603–1642* (London: Longman, 1989), pp. 87–91, 212. For a discussion of Cranfield's whole career, see Menna Prestwich, *Cranfield: Politics and Profits under the Early Stuarts* (Oxford: Clarendon Press, 1966).

[69] This poem is found in Bod. MSS Mal. 23, p. 27; Ash. 781, p. 136; Eng. Poet. c.50, fol.23; and Rawl. D. 1100, fol. 89v, and in BL MSS Add. 28640, fol. 148, and Stowe 962, fol. 146.

[70] This piece is also found in Bod. MS Top. Oxon. f.39, fol. 24, and BL MS Add. 15227, fol. 42v.

Without the allusion to Cranfield, whose sociopolitical rise is criticized through the language of cuckoldry (a common means of attacking upstart members of the middle class), this poem is simply a piece of snobbish wittiness, which, transferred to the context of the Interregnum, expressed the social alienation of Royalist gentlemen.

### George Villiers, Duke of Buckingham

By far the largest number of topical political poems about a person other than a reigning monarch was associated with George Villiers, duke of Buckingham, whose relatively long career as a favorite of both King James and his son Charles was halted by an assassination that many contemporaries openly welcomed.[71] As a dispenser of patronage, of course, Buckingham attracted many encomiastic pieces, some of them concentrating on particular episodes within his period of service to the crown, such as the ill-conceived trip to Spain with Prince Charles to arrange a marriage with the Spanish Infanta[72] and the disastrous Isle of Rhé military expedition, but it was the assassination itself that evoked the largest body of sympathetic and unsympathetic poems, works assessing Buckingham's whole career and the meaning of his relationship with the two kings he served.

Several manuscripts have an unusual number of items concerned with Buckingham. Both BL MS Sloane 826 and Bod. MS Mal. 23 concentrate on Buckingham material. The Sloane manuscript, dealing mainly with political events from the period 1621 to 1628, opens, however, with a copy of a prose letter written in 1600 by the earl of Essex to Lord Keeper Egerton. It contains Lewis's poem about Bacon's fall ("When you awake, dull Brittons, and beholde," fols. 4r–

---

[71] Ted-Larry Pebworth and Claude J. Summers are working on a collection to be titled *Poems on the First Duke of Buckingham* (Pebworth, "Sir Henry Wotton's 'Dazel'd Thus with Height of Place,' " p. 158n). See also the chapter on the poems about Buckingham and Strafford in Gerald Hammond, *Fleeting Things: English Poets and Poems 1616–1660* (Cambridge: Harvard University Press, 1990), pp. 41–66.

[72] William Drummond of Hawthornden's poem, "The Five Sences" ("From such a fate whose excellence"), for instance, is a good example of the kind of verse that was written against the impending Spanish match. The poem was not printed until 1711 and is found in five Bodleian manuscripts (Crum, p. 261). It is also in Hunt. MS HM 198, pt. 1, pp. 30–32. Richard Corbett, a Buckingham client, wrote the complimentary "Letter to the duke of Buckingham, being with the Prince in Spaine" ("Sir:/ I've read of Ilands floating, and remov'd") along with at least two other poems to the duke, "A New-Yeares Gift to my Lorde Duke of Buckingham" ("When I can pay my Parents, or my King") and "Against the Opposing the Duke in Parliament, 1628" ("The wisest King did wonder when hee spy'd"). See the *Poems of Corbett*, ed. Bennett and Trevor-Roper, pp. 76–79, 70, and 82–83 (cited in full at Chap. 1, n. 70).

5v) as well as a 1621 speech by Bacon in Parliament (fols. 6r–8v) and another prose work, "The Commons Protestation concerning priviledges," dated "December 19, 1621" (fol. 8v), before turning to the preparations for the Spanish match and other Buckingham items: "His majesties Letter to the King of Spain," dated "1622" (fols. 9r–v); a long narrative of the journey of Prince Charles and Buckingham to Spain (fols. 10r–14v); "An Elegie upon the death of Mr Thomas Washington, who died at Madrid, while his Highness was there, 1623" ("Hast thou been lost a moneth and can I be," fols. 14v–15v) with "His Epitaph" (fol. 15v); a letter of George Abbot, archbishop of Canterbury, to the king (fol. 16r); and a piece on Buckingham's 1626 journey to Dover ("Why did the fond Plebians say," fols. 28v–29r). There is a narrative of Buckingham's Isle of Rhé expedition (fols. 30r–32r), accompanied by a poem on his return ("And art thou returnd again with all thy faults," fols. 32r–33v). This is followed by a 1627 prose work by Sir Robert Cotton on "The Daungers wherein the Kingdome now standeth, and the remidie" (fols. 34r–37v) and a long section of parliamentary diary entries with speeches by various M.P.'s from the 1628 Parliament, including "The Remonstrance" (fols. 121r–25v) and the king's reply, ending with the last business before this parliament's dissolution. After these items (and in a different hand), there is a collection of thirty-seven poems, all concerned with Buckingham and events associated with the 1628 Parliament (fols. 153r–97r), including the duke's assassination. This section concludes with the petition poem written from prison by the assassin, John Felton.

Bod. MS Mal. 23 contains over forty poems dealing with the duke and with Felton. What is unusual is that both pro- and anti-Buckingham works are gathered together in this late Jacobean and early Caroline political anthology, many, it would seem, in unique manuscript copies.[73] Although some of the poems were published in

___

[73] Crum lists only this Bodleian manuscript for the following pieces, but there is considerable overlap with BL MS Sloane 826: "Of Brittish beasts the Buck is king" (p. 103; BL MS Sloane 826, fol. 185v); "It makes me to muse, to heare of the newes" (pp. 104–5; BL Sloane 826, fol. 167v); "An Apologie, in memorie of the most illustrious Prince George Duke of Buckingham" ("I did not flatter thee Alive, and nowe," pp. 123–27; not in any British Library manuscript); "Thaelassiarchiae Manium Vindiciae" ("Yee snarling Satyrs, cease your horrid yells," p. 128; also found in BL MS Add. 15227, fol. 21); "A Contemplation over the Dukes grave" ("Heere lyes thy urne, O what A little blowe," pp. 128–32; not in any British Library manuscript), by "G. W. Hemmings"; "Who ever Lov'd Man vertuous" (pp. 140–41, not in any British Library manuscript); "Fortunes Darling Kings

seventeenth-century volumes—for example, three of the anti-Buckingham pieces (two addressed to the imprisoned Felton) appeared in *Wit Restor'd* (1658)[74]—most of them were confined to the manuscript tradition.[75] In Bod. Rawl. Poet. 26, a prose item following several anti-Buckingham poems suggests some of the reasons for the hostility to Buckingham and the sympathy for his assassin:

> Two Papers were found in the lining of the hatt of John Felton a Captain who stabbed George Villiers Duke of Buckingham at Portsmouth. about Aug. 26, 1628.
>
> 1. That Man is cowardly-base, and deserves not the name of a Gentleman nor Souldier, that is unwilling to sacrifice his life for his God, his King, & his Country.
>
> John Felton
>
> 2. Let no man <condemne> commend mee for doing of it: but rather discommend themselves, or the cause thereof. For if God had not taken away or harts for our sinnes, he could not have gone so along alive.
>
> John Felton<br>(Fol. 81v)

Obviously, the assassin looked like a patriot to many of his contemporaries.[76] Hostility to Buckingham, like that expressed toward other

---

Content" (p. 143; BL MS Sloane 826, fol. 184); "Epitaph" ("Great Buckinghams buried under a stone," p. 143; BL MS Sloane 826, fol. 183v); "Epitaph" ("Heere lyes A gratious graceless peere," p. 144; BL MSS Sloane 826, fol. 184, and Egerton 2725, fol. 82r–v); "Epitaph" ("This little Grave embraces," p. 145), "The Argument is cold, and senceles Clay" (pp. 145–57; BL MS Sloane 826, fol. 172); "The Pale Horse of the Revelation" (p. 197; BL MS Sloane 826, fol. 182v); "Upon his Funerall" ("Behold this obsequie: but without teares," p. 197; BL MS Sloane 826, fol. 182v); "Make haste I pray Launch out your shipps with speed" (pp. 201–3; BL MS Sloane 826, fol. 186v); "Why is our age turn'd Coward, that no penn" (pp. 205–7; BL MSS Sloane 826, fol. 191, and Add. 5832, fol. 197); and "Loe heere hee lyes, that with one Arme could more" (p. 211; BL MS Sloane 826, fol. 19v).

[74] The three anti-Buckingham poems that appear in *Wit Restor'd* are "Upon John Felton's hanging in Chaines at Ports-mouth, for killing the Duke of Buckingham" ("Here uninterd suspends [though not to save]," Bod. MS Mal. 23, p. 210), "To Felton in the Tower" ("Enjoy thy bondage, make thy prison know," p. 205), and "Some say, the Duke was vertuous, gratious, good" (p. 195). For the first Crum cites nine Oxford manuscripts (p. 357). See also BL MSS Add. 15226, fol. 28; Egerton 923, fol. 26v, and 1160, fol. 241v; Harl. 3511, fol. 18v, and 6057, fol. 6v; and Sloane 826, fol. 198. For the second Crum cites eight Oxford manuscripts (p. 214). See also BL MSS Egerton 2026, fol. 65, and Harl. 6931, fol. 48, and 7319, fol. 2. For the third Crum cites seven Oxford manuscripts (p. 794).

[75] In addition to BL MS Sloane 826, see the groups of poems on Buckingham found in Bod. MSS Rawl. Poet. 26, fols. 33r–34r, 37v–39v, 78v–80v; Ash. 38, pp. 13, 20, 44–45; Eng. Poet. e.14, fols. 9v, 12v, 13r, 14v, 15r–v; BL MS Add. 25707, fols. 70v–72v; and Hunt. MS HM 198, pt. 1, pp. 96, 156–59.

[76] See Christopher Hill, *Milton and the English Revolution* (Harmondsworth, U.K.: Penguin,

political figures, such as Robert Cecil and Robert Carr, was, of course, a way of criticizing the monarch(s) who entrusted such men with power.

### Thomas Wentworth, Earl of Strafford

The oblique attack on royalty is quite evident in the poems on Thomas Wentworth, earl of Strafford, who, with William Laud, helped Charles I govern during the long period of "prerogative rule." His execution for treason was a kind of dress rehearsal for the direct action against the king himself. To defend him was to defend the Stuart monarchy and its ideological underpinnings against its political opposition. Poems dealing with Strafford's execution include the following sympathetic pieces: "Upon my Lord Straford" ("Great Strafford, worthy of that name though all");[77] "An Ode or Meditation made by or upon the Earle of Strafford Lord Leiue-tenant of Ireland: when hee was Prisoner in the Tower. 1640" ("Goe empty joyes");[78] "An Epitaph upon the Earl of Strafford 1641" ("Heere rest's wise & valiant dust");[79] and a poem found in only one British Library manuscript and in no Bodleian one, "Is noble Wentworth gone?" (BL MS Egerton 2421, fol. 131v).

### Mervyn Touchet, Earl of Castlehaven

One other notorious figure was the subject of poems that show up in the contemporary manuscript collections. Although he was not a government official, his sexual crimes brought issues of class and gender together in a way that was threatening to social conservatives. Christopher Hill summarizes the bare facts of the situation: "A major

---

1979), p. 28, on the younger Alexander Gil's punishment for toasting the health of Felton at Oxford. On the danger of even copying out a pro-Felton poem, see Hammond, *Fleeting Things*, pp. 107–8. See also James Holstun's superb study of the Felton-Buckingham business, "'God Bless Thee, Little David': John Felton and His Allies," *ELH* 59 (1992): 513–52.

[77] "Upon my Lord Straford" is found in Bod. MSS Ash. 36, 37, fols. 33v and 214; Douce 357, fol. 2r; and Rawl. Poet. 26, fol. 127v; BL MSS Egerton 2421, fol. 39r rev., and 2725, fols. 78–78v. It was also printed in the 1668 edition of Denham's poems (Crum, p. 293).

[78] See Bod MSS Rawl. Poet. 26, fols. 126–27, and 117, fol. 2 rev.; Tanner 465, fol. 61r; Don. c.57, fol. 30v; and Douce 357, fol. 2r; BL MSS Harl. 4931, fol. 133v, and 6908, fols. 86–85 rev.; and Folger MS V.a.399, fols. 260v–61v (with the note "Written by Thomas Earle of Stratford").

[79] See Bod. MSS Douce 357, fol. 11v; Don. e.6, fol. 29v; Eng. Poet. c.50, fol. 127r, and e.97, p. 193; Rawl. D. 1099, fol. 190r rev.; Rawl. Poet. 26, fol. 131v, and 71, p. 146; and BL MS Egerton 2421, fol. 38v. It was printed in Cleveland's *Character of a London Diurnal* (1647). For other poems on Strafford, see those listed in MacLean, *Time's Witness*, p. 304.

scandal of the early thirties concerned Lord Castlehaven, who was executed for buggery, for conniving at the rape of his wife by a servant who was also his lover, and for prostitution of his daughter-in-law to another servant."[80] This is a limit-case of aristocratic licentiousness. Within the manuscript system one finds copies of a poem attributed to "Jo: R." that reflects the contemporary sense of outrage:

Upon Lord Audley Earle of Castlehaven,
his Conviction

Romes worst Philenis, & Pasyphae's dust
Are now chaste fictions, & noe longer lust.
This colder age hath monstred out a sin
Which vertues them, & saints an Aretine
Scorning to owe a studied vice to times
Examples burnes out with more noble crimes
This black EAnigma is so hardly scand,
That virtue hath not will to understand
How vice can bee soe Learned that man should know
To rape himselfe & make one rape prove two.
That lust should grow more barren then the Grave
It meritts: for to wife a man, a Slave
That soe high bloods should prompt soe base a spiritt
To gett an Heire his blood to disinheritt
If yet thy chaste beleife cannot discerne
That monster, know the King shall make thee learne,
Whose justice thus the riddle doth untie,
Tis such a Crime for which an Earle must dye,
And yet thy sin above dispaire may sitt
Since there's a higher King can pardon it.
                    (Bod. MS Eng. Poet. e.97, pp. 67–68)[81]

The king's justice condemns Castlehaven and thus (supposedly) dissociates the Stuart government and its aristocratic supporters from

---

[80] Hill, *Milton and the English Revolution*, p. 43. Cedric C. Brown argues the relevance of the Castlehaven scandal to the circumstances of the countess dowager of Derby's household and to Milton's *Arcades* (*John Milton's Aristocratic Entertainments* [Cambridge: Cambridge University Press, 1985], pp. 20–21). He cites the contemporary treatment of the scandal in *The Arraignment and Conviction of Mervin Lord Audley, Earl of Castlehaven* (1642) and the Miltonic scholarship on *Comus* that considers *Comus* in its context (p. 184, nn. 29, 30). See also Lawrence Stone, *The Crisis of the Aristocracy, 1558–1641* (Oxford: Clarendon Press, 1965), p. 668.

[81] This poem also appears in Bod. MS Ash. 47, fol. 88v, but it is not found in any British Library manuscript.

the earl's degeneracy. It was not often that a peer of the realm was severely punished for nontreasonous behavior, so it must have suited the government to make an example of him. Nevertheless, despite the outrageousness of Castlehaven's actions, there are also contemporary expressions of sympathy for him in two poems transcribed in some Royalist manuscript collections, which portray him simply as a husband burdened with an unfaithful wife. One of them, found in the first part of BL MS Sloane 1446, is reproduced in several other collections:

> On my Lord Castlehaven
> I neede no Trophies to addorne my hearse
> my wife exaltes my hornes in every verse
> and plac't them hath so fullie on my <head> tombe
> that for my Armes there is no vacant roome
> whoe will take such a Countess to his bedd
> that first gave hornes and then cutts of his head
>
> (Fol. 64v)[82]

It seems that the social elite needed to safeguard their own status by defending the seemingly indefensible behavior of one of their own. Given the later association during the era of the Civil War and Interregnum of sexual licentiousness or degeneracy with a Royalist aristocracy, the Castlehaven case looks to have been politically charged.

### Crown against Parliament and Royalist against Puritan

Although prominent national figures were the subject of most of the political poetry of the late sixteenth and early seventeenth centuries, growing tension between the crown and Parliament in the period leading up to the English Civil War and political divisions during the Civil War and Interregnum generated political poems that were preserved in manuscript collections.[83] From the first Jacobean

---

[82] See also Bod. MSS Eng. Poet. e.14, fol. 87v rev., CCC 327, fol. 32v, and 328, fol. 58., and BL MS Add. 22118, fol. 29. The poem found in Bod. MS Rawl. Poet. 26, fol. 21v, "Let none henceforth this wife for ever wedd," also takes the same approach.

[83] For a discussion of the circulation of prose news (and some poetry) in early Stuart England and of its relation to political "oppositionism," see Richard Cust, "News and Politics in Early Seventeenth-Century England," *Past and Present* 112 (1986): 60–90.

parliament (1604–10), which dealt with the difficult issues of subsidies and the union of the two kingdoms of England and Scotland, through the other irregularly convened Jacobean and Caroline parliaments, including the 1640 "Long Parliament," poets dealt with the continual conflicts between the monarch and Parliament from their own political and personal points of view.

The most elaborate and one of the most popular of these political poems was "The Parliament Fart," a piece whose first version was written in 1607 by a group of witty M.P.'s on the occasion of a fart let in the House of Commons by Henry Ludlow during a debate on the issue of Union, specifically while the members were listening to a message being read from the House of Lords. Discussed at length by Baird Whitlock in his book on John Hoskins, this poem survives in a surprisingly large number of manuscripts (as well as in some late printed forms) in various shorter or longer versions from 40 to 224 lines.[84] James Sanderson observes that it "was so popular that members of later parliaments kept adding to it."[85] Probably masterminded by the witty John Hoskins, whose free-speaking political remarks during the 1614 ("Addled") Parliament landed him briefly in the Tower, this poem was originally a coterie game played for the benefit of a group of rambunctious Commons members which included Richard Martin, Christopher Brooke and Henry Goodyer, Edward Phelips, Arthur Ingram, Robert Cotton, Henry Neville, Tobie Matthews, John Egerton and others, most of whom, incidentally, were friends and associates of John Donne.[86]

In its original political context, the politically overdramatized fart could be construed as a symbolic act of defiance toward both the more conservative House of Lords and a monarch who would bend

---

[84] Baird W. Whitlock, *John Hoskyns, Serjeant-at-Law* (Washington, D. C.: University Press of America, 1982), pp. 283–93. See also the annotations in Sanderson, "An Edition," pp. 535–54. Redding notes that this poem is found in versions of from 40 to 202 lines; the most complete version appears in *Le Prince D'Amour* (1660) and the shortest in *Wits Recreations* ("Robert Bishop's Commonplace Book," p. lvi). Sanderson notes, however, that the longest version of the piece is 224 lines ("An Edition," p. 256). He lists twenty-seven manuscripts in which this poem appears as well as versions in three printed texts: *Musarum Deliciae* (1655), *Le Prince d'Amour* (1660), and Thomas D'Urfey's *Wit and Mirth; or Pills to Purge Melancholy* (1699) (p. 536).

[85] Sanderson, "An Edition," p. 284.

[86] See Whitlock, *John Hoskyns*, p. 285. On this social and political circle, see also Shapiro, "Mermaid Club" (cited in full at Chap. 1, n. 127); Bald, *John Donne*. pp. 193–95 (cited in full at Chap. 1, n. 127); and Patterson, "All Donne," pp. 37–67 (cited in full at Chap. 1, n. 127).

the Lower House to his will. The poem refers to the "priviledges" (26)[87] of Parliament and "Englands Liberty" and "Lawes" (44) for which Sir Robert Cotton, "well read in old stories" (129), and the oppositionist members of the House of Commons stood in the face of Stuart assertions of royal authority.[88] It alludes to the controversial issue of the "Union" (50) of Scotland and England (which James I urged Parliament to facilitate) and to the problem of the differences between the legal systems of both countries—Scotland's being that of "Civil Law" (80), England's that of common law. In the version of the poem found in the Crawford Manuscript (Rosenbach MS 1083/15) the related issue of the citizenship status of the Scottish "post-nati" (62) is raised, those Scots born after James I ascended to the throne of England, for whom the king wanted English citizenship.[89] All of these questions were relevant to the debate being conducted at the time of the notorious fart. "The Parliament Fart" calls attention to the division in the House of Commons between more free-speaking oppositionist members such as Richard Martin and more conservative M.P.'s, who better served the king's wishes, such as Sir George More, John Donne's father-in-law; it alludes to one M.P., "Kit Pigot" (50), who was put in the Tower for attacking the Scottish people in his speeches.[90] "The Parliament Fart" alludes to the Jacobean unsettling of the Elizabethan religious settlement in the heightened conflicts between reformist Protestants and the more con-

---

[87] I cite the text from *Musarum Deliciae* (1655), pp. 65–71, but I have compared it with the version produced (from a collation of two main manuscripts) by Whitlock (*John Hoskyns*, pp. 288–92), and with that in the Crawford Manuscript edited by Sanderson ("An Edition," pp. 529–35).

[88] On this Parliament, see Wallace Notestein, *The House of Commons, 1604–1610* (New Haven: Yale University Press, 1971).

[89] Sanderson, "An Edition," p. 531. According to Notestein, "When [Sir Edwin] Sandys told the Lords that the Commons would not yield on the question of the difference between the *Post-Nati*, and the *Ante-Nati* he was presenting the peers with an ultimatum. It was the boldest refusal to cooperate with the Upper House that the Commons of that generation had ever made" (*House of Commons*, p. 236). King James himself intervened in the dispute with his famous "rex est lex" speech (Charles Howard McIlwain, ed., *The Political Works of James I* [Cambridge: Harvard University Press; London: Oxford University Press, 1918], 1:290–305).

[90] The version of the poem in the Crawford Manuscript has the following couplet: "then sir Christopher Pygott looking full sower / sayd sirs lettes us send this fart to the tower" (Sanderson, "An Edition," p. 533). Sanderson explains: "Sir Christopher Pigott (d. 1612) was M.P. for Buckinghamshire, 1604, until he was expelled in 1607....The reference to the 'tower' in line 132 probably is an allusion to Pigott's being imprisoned in the Tower of London for an abusive attack in parliament on the whole Scottish nation" (pp. 550–51). John Hoskins himself was imprisoned in the Tower along with some of his colleagues

servative Church establishment; it refers also to the Gunpowder Plot, which took place two years previously—"Quoth Sir Thomas Knevet, I fear here doth lurk / In this Hallow Vault, some more powder work" (139–40). The protracted power-struggle between Commons and crown lies behind this witty poem, the constraints on free speech in Parliament, for example, implicit not only in the reference to Pigott, but also in the mention of the potential "Tale-bearer" (102) M.P. who reported everything that transpired in the House to King James.

"The Parliament Fart" belongs to the period before the conflict between crown and Commons had reached the crisis point, and, as a witty recreation among an intellectual and social elite, it is a text similar to Donne's *Courtier's Library* in its iconoclastic attitudes. Its continued popularity, however, through the mid-seventeenth century among compilers of manuscript anthologies was probably related to Royalist political cynicism and distrust of Parliament as an institution: hence it is found at the beginning of the section of reverse transcription in Thomas Manne's anthology (BL MS Add. 58215, fols. 19v–189r rev.), and Smith and Mennes's Royalist anthology, *Musarum Deliciae* (1655) could print the poem without having it seem as antimonarchical as it did in its original circumstances of production and reception. It finally joined other (later) poems critical of Parliament: "The parliament sitts with a synode of witts" (Bod. MS Rawl. Poet. 172, fol. 79r);[91] "Upon the breach between the King & the Subject, at the dissolution of the Parliament, March 1628" ("The wisest King did wonder, when he spide," Bod. MS Rawl. Poet. 26, fol. 8v) "Made (as is reported) by Dr Corbet Bishope of Oxford"; and "Upon the dissolution of the Parliament, May 5, 1640" ("Two Parliaments dissolv'd? then let my Hart," Bod. MS Rawl. Poet. 26, fols. 90r–v).[92]

---

for his performance in the 1614 Parliament, an event that was joked about in a short ditty preserved in Bod. MS Rawl. Poet. 26:

> Hoskins the Lawyer is merrily sad:
> Sharpe the Devine is soberly mad.
> Cornwellis the Leiger, profanely precise:
> And Chute the Carver, foolishly wise.
> (Fol. 2r)

[91] Crum notes that this poem also appears in Bod. MS Mal. 19, p. 13 and suggests it was composed around 1624 (p. 874).

[92] This poem appears also in Bod. MSS Eng. Poet. c.25, fol. 38r, and e.97, p. 191; Mal.

Antagonism to Puritanism and to the rest of the parliamentary opposition lay behind many other poems that fill the largely Royalist seventeenth-century manuscript collections of poetry, especially those in which items were copied during the Civil War and Interregnum. The extraordinary popularity of Richard Corbett's long poem "Iter Boreale" was probably due to its politically conservative stance: it is the narrative of a journey taken by four Oxford dons, in the course of which they are morally revolted by the world outside the university because it is an environment of ugly economic, social, and religious conflict. Like the Elizabethan political poem, "A Journey into France," this work is in the tradition of "The Pilgrim's Tale." The particular targets of the satire are economic ambition, the behavior of the bourgeoisie, and the religious iconoclasm and other social disruptions associated with the Puritan movement. The idealized encounter of the protagonists with Fulke Greville at Warwick Castle celebrates the conservative aristocratic values Corbett believed were under attack by some of his contemporaries.[93] Despite its length (508 lines), this poem is found in a surprisingly large number of manuscript collections.[94]

Royalist ballads done in the popular style of such verse can be found in "elite" manuscript poetry collections. For example, Nicholas Burghe's manuscript (Bod. MS Ash. 38) contains the following ballad not only criticizing the contemporary social disruptions that were perceived by conservatives as a real threat to social order and hierarchy, but also suggesting upper-class complicity in a supposed moral and political corruption symbolized by sexual contact between the classes:

> Jockye would bee a gentleman
> And leave the plough alone A
> Tom Tinker hee a minister
> Though learning hee had none A

---

21, fol. 93r; Rawl. D. 361, fol. 68r (dated 1626 and attributed to Bishop Matthew Wren, according to Crum); Rawl. Poet. 117, fol. 150 rev.; and Tanner 306, fol. 290r (Crum, p. 994).

[93] In *Fulke Greville, Lord Brooke, 1554–1628, A Critical Biography* (Berkeley and Los Angeles: University of California Press, 1971), p. 20, Joan Rees describes Greville (as earl of Warwick) as a greedy, exploitative landlord who held to strongly conservative values.

[94] Peter Beal, 2.1.179–81, lists thirty-seven manuscripts. "Iter Boreale" is, for example, the opening poem in both Bod. MS Eng. Poet. e.14, fols. 2r–8v, and BL MS Sloane 1446, fols. 2r–9v.

# SEX AND POLITICS

And Madge our mayd would milke none
   nor butter would goe sell A
disorder in manye thinges
   god graunte all may bee well A


The sexton hee would bee a Clearke
   The Clerke a preest would be A
The preist a Miter hee would weare
   but that hee could not see, A
Such take small Care, for cure of soules
   to go to heaven or hell, A
disorder . . . [etc.]


The sergeant would a frier bee
   to arrest a man with speed A
And for his paynes hee was bescratct
   tell all his face did bleed A
The wife with distafe and her mayd
   did make his pate to swell A
disorder . . . [etc.]


The master smiles uppon the mayde
   The mistress frownes theratt A
When cattes a way the mouse may play
   Lett her take heed of that, A
But yf the mayd be well asayde
   This craftie knave will tell A
disorder . . . [etc.]


The paynter and the poulterers mayde
   thay went to Jopp and change A
& Sundrie birdes uppon her wombe
   he drewe in coulours strang A
But att the last on byrde hee drew
   Whear little mouse doth dwell A
disorder . . . [etc.]


What was the byrde then quoth the mayd
   the birde that you drew last A
it was a wag-tayle mayde he sayde
   That flyeth verye fast A

> Then make them wagtayles all quoth she
> The wag tayle doth excell A
> disorder . . . [etc.]

(P. 126)

The sexual joking and misogynistic tenor of the song undermine any serious effort at social criticism, but such a piece is typical of Royalist cynicism as expressed in much of the light verse in this period.

Anti-Puritan poems and ditties are found scattered through the manuscript collections of the period. Two poems by Sir John Harington, "A godly sister with one of her societie" and "Six of the weakest sex and purest sect," both satiric attacks on Puritanism for its supposed religious and sexual hypocrisy, are also found in a large number of manuscript collections.[95] Several documents contain a satiric poem titled in one version "A puritans character" ("Long hath it vext this learned age to scanne").[96] Many manuscripts and some printed texts reproduce an anti-Puritan piece attributed to Richard Corbett: "A godly exhortation to Mr John Haymond Minister of the word in the Parish of Beaully for the battering downe of those vanitys of the Gentiles, which are comprehended in a Maypole, written by a zealous Brother from the Blacke-Friers" ("The mightie zeale which thou has new put on"). In BL MS Add. 58215, this poem is subscribed "John Harris of Christchurch" (fols. 188v–86v rev.).[97]

Corbett's, Strode's, and Jeramiel Terrant's poems on the escape of the stained-glass windows of Fairford Church in Gloucestershire from the destruction by religious iconoclasts are found in several manuscripts. Corbett's popular poem ("Tell mee, you Anti-Saintes, why glasse"),[98] which precedes, but anticipates the violence of the Civil War, articulates a religiously conservative, anti-Puritan stance that persists through to the Restoration. In their edition of Cor-

---

[95] Beal, 1.2.142–46, cites twenty-six manuscripts for the first and twelve manuscripts for the second.

[96] BL MS Harl. 6917, fol. 14r–v; see also BL MSS Add. 21433, fol. 83r, and 25303, fols. 72v–73v; and Bod. MS Tanner 465, fol. 82r.

[97] Bennett and Trevor-Roper note that it was published in *Poetica Stromata* (1648) as Corbett's work, as well as in *Parnassus Biceps* (1656), *Poems Consisting of Epistles and Epigrams, Satyrs, Epitaphs, and Elegies etc.* (1658), and *J. Cleaveland revived* (1659) (*Poems of Corbett*, p. 130). See Beal, 2.1.174–76, for a list of the manuscripts in which it appears.

[98] *Poems of Corbett*, ed. Bennett and Trevor-Roper, p. 87. Bennett and Trevor-Roper note that Corbett's poem was printed in the 1648 edition of Corbett, in *Parnassus Biceps* (1656) and in *Westminster Drollery* (1651). It also appeared in a large number of manuscript collections: see Beal, 2.1.203–4.

bett's poems, Bennett and Trevor-Roper note that the church's stained-glass images of biblical scenes were later preserved from destruction during the Civil War by being removed and hidden.[99] Although Corbett's poem, as well as Strode's "I know no paynt of poetry" and Terrant's "I hope at this time 'tis no news"[100]—both on the same topic—refer to pre–Civil War Puritan iconoclasm, because of subsequent events, they continued to capture the attention of collectors of verse through the Civil War and Interregnum, when iconoclasm was at its height. Other anti-iconoclastic poems, such as Thomas Mottershed's "On Christ Church window and Magdalens wall" ("yee men of Gallilee why gaze yee soe")[101] and J. Gregorie's poem about the breaking of Christ Church Window, "In Iconoclaseum" ("Profane did not thy cursed hand waxe faint"),[102] also appear in manuscript collections.

In Folger MS V.a.262, a collection from the 1630s and 1640s probably associated with Oxford, the first poem is an anti-Puritan piece concerning the contemporary controversy over the Lord's Prayer:

A Divine Ode

Blesse us good Lord from that dull sect which say
Wee err in twice repeating when wee pray
          Our Father
They count themselves made of the purest clod
And give us lost: forbid it o my God
          which art in heaven
By them barnes stables and what roomes you see
More then our Churches are esteemed to bee
          Hallowed

[99] *Poems of Corbett,* ed. Bennett and Trevor-Roper, p. 156.

[100] Strode's poem is found, for example, in Bod. MSS CCC. 325, fol. 58v (an autograph manuscript); Eng. Poet. e.97, p. 32; and Mal. 21, fol. 1r; and BL MS Sloane 542, fol. 58r (idem.). It is also in BL MSS 542, fol. 58; Sloane 1446, fol. 51v; Harl. 6931, fol. 19v; Add. 33998, fols. 12v–13v; and Egerton 2421, fol. 32v. For the poem itself, see *The Poetical Works of William Strode,* ed. Bertram Dobell (London: Dobell, 1907), pp. 25–27. Terrant's poem is found in Bod. MS Eng. Poet. e.97, p. 33, and BL MS Sloane 542, fol. 59 (attributed to Corbett), and BL MS Sloane 1446, fol. 53. Another anti-iconoclastic poem by Strode, "You that prophane our windows with a tongue," appears with Corbett's in *Parnassus Biceps* along with other anti-Puritan pieces (sigs. B2r–B6v).

[101] Mothershed's poem is found in Nicholas Burghe's anthology (Bod. MS Ash. 38, pp. 46–48). Crum, p. 1166, also cites Bod. MS Eng. Poet. e.97, p. 37. It is not found in any British Library manuscript, but was printed in *Wit Restor'd* (1658).

[102] The author was Brian Duppa's chaplain (Crum, p. 723). The poem also appears in BL MS Harl. 6918, fol. 41v.

The word the word they say by them is teacht
But grant good God by better Schollers preacht
    bee thy name
The way next Faith I am addrest to goe
Is prayer surely which must bring me to
    thy Kingdome
Yett lett our bells ring out they are forgott
For to our Common prayers they will not
    Come
When I was blest from learn'd Armach to heare
And honourd Portter of the selfe same sheare
    Thy will
Howers were but minutes, but when these persever
In teadious Preachments, I thinke they will never
    be done
Doctrine and use men of a teadious rarity
Which both in Church and State require a parity
    In earth
These wee must heare by Inspiration raysd
Who most presumptious thinke thy name soe praysd
    As it is in heaven
But Lord unto thy Zion bee not cruel
Such men as Hoker Reignalds Whiteguift Jewell
    Give us
Wee have a Prideaux Collius and soe many
There sons more learnd noe Christian Church hath any
    This day
By whome if wee there guifts doe not abhore
Wee may bee well intrusted to pray for
    Our dayly bread
But these the sole elect long breathed men
For our sad patience doe prolong again
    And forgive us
That they speake not of Councell, Schoolemen Father
Is not there ignorance but rather
    Our trespasses
Which hindred us from things to be imparted
To none of foule, and soe poluted hearted
    As wee
Their Semigradiants, Pedants, who knowes who
Comes up to teach us, thus, and then wee doe
    forgive them

There first place, last place, 15 times said or'e
More over, and besides, and further more
$\qquad$ That trespasse
Upon all Christian patience, must be heard
Or else, next time a Sermon is prepard
$\qquad$ Against us
But if Episcopacy chance to bee put downe
A tradsman shall stop up in every towne
$\qquad$ And lead us
But where they know not: nor doe greatly care
Soe that they have there will: though Bishopps are
$\qquad$ Not
Good God rest ore them to there witts and call
Them home who leudly false opinions fall
$\qquad$ Into
And lett not thy true Church by such as these
Bee brought into through ignorance and ease
$\qquad$ Temptation
Lett Coblers weavers, madmen lead them still
In their AEgyptian darkenesse if they will:
$\qquad$ But deliver us
Who at thy footstoole prostrately fall bent
And blesse our King, and state, and Parliament
$\qquad$ From evil
And for the Jesuite Brownist and who pray
The contrary: Lett Tyborne be their way
$\qquad$ Amen $\qquad$ Finis.
$\qquad$ (Pp. 1–3)[103]

Obviously responding to the Puritan assault on High Church structures and practices, this piece, which reproduces the Lord's Prayer
in the Catholic version (without the "power and the glory" clause),
is followed in this manuscript by other poems addressing the events
of the Civil War era: "Gouldsmith hall Compounders" (pp. 3–4);
"On the demolishing of Charing Crosse" (pp. 4–5); "A Dismal Sum-
mons to Doctors Commons" (p. 6); "To the K[ing] Ch[arles] the
First att Holmeby" (pp. 6–7); then the anti-Cromwell poem, "Whats
a Protector hees a statly thing" (p. 7). A few pages later there is a

[103] This poem appears in Bod. MS Douce 357, fol. 31v, as "The Antibrownest" (Crum,
p. 121). It is not, however, found in any British Library manuscript.

poem titled "Upon May the 17 1653," which is introduced by a discursive title setting its topical context:

> On Tuesday last a gent[leman] came to the Exchange in a coach hee hang'd up Cromweels picture after 2 or 3 turnes tooke coach and away. The picture was carryed after to the Lord Mayers who carryed it to Cromwell on the picture was written It is I his armes sett on one side being an ould Lyon trampling on a Crowne.

>> Ascend 3 thrones great Captain and divine
>> In the will of God (oald Lyon) they are thine
>> Come preist of God bring oyle, bring robs, bring gould
>> Bring Crownes, bring Scepters, tis high time. unfould
>> Your cloystred baggs you state cheaters least the rod
>> Of steele and iron of your King and God
>> Pay you in's wrath with interest kneele and pray
>> To Oliver the toarch of Zion starr of day
>> Shout merchant Cittezen and gentry sing
>> And all bare headed cry God save the King.
>>                                    (Pp. 10–11)[104]

This is followed by the poem "Upon the dissolution of the Parliment by Cromwell" (1653):

>> Lett damned powder plotts amaze no more
>> Since one breath blowes the house out of the doare
>> I need not bid you wounder tymes to come
>> A souldier spake A Parliment was dumbe
>> Silenc'd it was brave Generall by thee
>> Well may'st thou boast of Christian Liberty
>> How sure Christs power did never more increase
>> Then when hee bid the divells hould their peace.
>>                                    (P. 11)[105]

These political poems are succeeded by love poems, epitaphs, epigrams, and complimentary pieces, as well as by other topical political pieces,[106] including poems by King, Corbett, and such older poets as Ralegh, Jonson, and Donne.

As noted earlier, Bod. MS Rawl. Poet. 26 contains a large number of both anti-Puritan and anti-Parliament poems.[107] The title page of

---

[104] This poem is also found in BL MS Harl. 3991, fol. 122.
[105] This poem is not found in any Bodleian or British Libarary manuscript.
[106] For example, "Upon the Lord Cheife Justice Sr Nicolas Hyde" (pp. 38–39).
[107] See, especially, the pieces on fols. 15r, 94r, 109r–10v, and 121r–48v.

Hunt. MS 16522 reads "A Collection of Poems & Ballads in ridicule of the Parliamentary Party during the Quarrel with Ch[arles] I." The manuscript collections assembled by Peter Calfe and his son (BL MS Harl. 6917–18) also have a large number of anti-Puritan and anti-Parliament pieces, one being the following echo poem, which satirizes Charles's opposition:

| | |
|---|---|
| Name Eccho who this new Religion grounded? | Roundhead |
| Who is professor most Considerable | Rabble |
| How doe they prove themselves the Godly | odly. |
| yet they are knowne in life to be most holy | o lye |
| Who are the common preachers men or women | women |
| Come they from any university | Citty |
| Ist not absurdity they then deliver | Ever |
| But still they ayme the godly to edifye | fye |
| What doe you call it then, to fructifye | I |
| What Churches have they, and what pulpits | pitts |
| But now in Chambers they do Conventicle | tickle |
| the holy Churches they are sure belyed | bellyed |
| the godly number then will soone descend | end |
| Our Churches in Zeale they doe embrace them | race them |
| What doe they make the Bishops Hierarchie | Archie |
| Are Crosses, Images, ornaments then Scandall | all |
| Nor will they leave us any Ceremonies | monies |
| Must even Religion downe for satisfaction | faction |
| nor stand they affected to the government Civill | evil |
| But to the King they say they are most loyall | lye all |
| God keepe the Church and state from these same men | Amen. |

(BL MS Harl. 6917, fol. 27v)

This poem attacks Puritans as an unlearned, hypocritical, iconoclastic rabble who falsely proclaim loyalty to the king, but who pose a great danger to both Church and state. This piece embodies the misogyny, class prejudice, and intellectual snobbery of Royalist conservatives responding to the threat from below posed by Puritan religious and political reformers.[108] It particularly responds to the attack on the Lord's Prayer as, in the words of one of the succeeding poems, "a popish thing" (fol. 36v).

BL MS Harl. 6918, the second Calfe collection, covering the period

---

[108] Crum notes that this echo poem is found in Bod. MSS Mal. 21, fol. 30r; Rawl. Poet. 62, fol. 50r; and Douce 357, fol. 41v; and that it was printed in *The Prologue and Epilogue* by Francis Cole [Abraham Cowley] in 1642.

of the Interregnum, also has some very bitter anti-Parliament pieces, including an apparently unique poem attacking John Pym:

On Master Pyms Counterfeit:

> Reader behold the Counterfeit of him
> who now orerules the state all daring Pym
> he who to feare the Divell now begins
> fearing to trust him with unprosperous sinnes,
> who now is wading through the crimson floud
> of Reverend Laud, and worthy Straffords bloud;
> striking too high as to pull Bishops downe
> and in the Myter to orethrow the crowne;
> The wretch hath mighty thoughts, and Entertaines
> Some glorious mischiefe in his active braines
> Which now is plotting to make England such
> as may outvye the Amsterdam oth' Dutch
> He scornes to goe to heaven, cause he doth feare
> to meete, and not pull downe the Bishops there;
> is it not strange that he should hatch a plott
> that may outvye the cunning of the Scott;
> is it not strange that in his subtle head
> three Kingdomes ruine should bee buried,
> nay and the party too a puritan,
> Reader tis true, behold and marke the man;
>> The picture's like him, it were very fitt
>> He had one likenesse more, and hangd like it.
>> (Harl. 6918, fols. 33r–v)

Written after the abolition of episcopacy and the overthrow of Archbishop Laud and the earl of Strafford, those two great pillars of Charles I's "prerogative rule" and policy of "Thorough," this piece takes aim at the parliamentary leader who most clearly represented the opposition to the Royalist ideology, but it obviously retained its interest as a forecast of political turmoil.[109] This poem is followed by one on the 1643 Kentish uprising, "Kents Invitation to take Armes" ("Bravely resolved, great hearts, I see some good," fol. 34r–v),[110] a

---

[109] For other anti-Pym poems, see Crum's items C154, I11761, N253, P454, R235, T33317, T3352, and W91.

[110] Crum, p. 129, cites three Bodleian manuscripts for this poem: Rawl. Poet. 62, fol. 43v; Rawl. Poet. 65, fol. 55r (attributed to "Guil: Taylor A: B: promus Joann."); and Rawl. Poet. 71, p. 64.

short "Epitaph" that, in some texts, accompanies the famous narrative of "The Parliament Fart" ("Reader I was borne and cryde," fol. 34v), and other Royalist and anti-Parliament poems and ballads, including a 1641 ballad by Francis Quarles ("Know then my brethren heaven is cleere," fols. 35r–36r).[111] This poem is succeeded by another political ballad (cited earlier) that begins "To make Charles a great King and give him no power" (fol. 36r–v), a protest against the "Nineteen Propositions" formulated by the Parliament and given to Charles I on June 1, 1642.[112] It, in turn, is followed by "A Game at Chesse" ("The pawnes have all the sport and beare the sway" (fol. 36v).[113] Such verse emerged from the manuscript system gradually in the latter half of the Interregnum in some of the poetical miscellanies and "drolleries" and in the Restoration era anthologies that featured political verse.[114]

Although in the Elizabethan and Jacobean periods political poetry in manuscript collections dealt largely with major figures and causes célèbres such as the Somerset marriage scandal, in the late Caroline era and during the Interregnum, such verse was largely conservative and partisan. It was written then, like some of the journalism of the

---

[111] This poem, "The Tryumph of the Round-heads," was printed in *Distractions of our Times* (1642), *Quarles's Shepherds Oracles* (1646), and *Rump Songs* (1662) (Crum, p. 498). It also appears in Bod MSS Ash. 36,37, fol. 81r; Don. c.57, fol. 27v; and Rawl. Poet. 26, fol. 133, but in no British Library manuscript.

[112] This poem was printed in *Rump* (1662) and is also found in Bod. MSS Ash. 36,37, fol. 67; Douce 357, fol. 25v; Rawl. D. 398, fol. 250r; and Rawl. Poet. 26, fol. 136v (Crum, p. 971). It is found as well in BL MSS Harl. 2127, fol. 19, and Add. 41996. On the "Nineteen Propositions," Crum cites *Lords Journals*, 1 June 1642. See also Godfrey Davies, *Early Stuarts*, p. 125, who quotes Edmund Ludlow's memoirs pointing to these as the "principal foundation of the ensuing war." Davies summarizes the demands as follows: "That privy councillors, the great officers of state, and the governors of fortifications should be appointed only with the approval of parliament; that the king's children should be educated by, and married to, those in whom parliament had confidence; that the laws against Roman Catholics should be strictly executed and popish peers excluded from the house of Lords; that the king should accept such a reformation of the church as parliament advised; that he should sign the militia ordinance; that he should abandon delinquents to the justice of parliament; and that peers created thereafter should not be admitted to the house of lords without the consent of both houses of parliament" (pp. 126–27).

[113] This piece is from "Prologue and Epilogue to the Game att Chesse by Pooley" acted before the Prince of Wales, March 1641/2, and is also found in Bod. MSS Don. d.58, fol. 59r, and Douce 357, fol. 40v (Crum, p. 874).

[114] There is a small section of the Hazlewood-Kingsborough Manuscript (Hunt. MS HM 198, pt. 1) with political poetry on confessional themes: "A Protestant is such another thing" (pp. 180–84); "A Papist" ("A Romanist is such another thing," p. 184); "Religion" ("Religion the most sacred power on earth," pp. 184–85); and "The True Puritan without disguise" ("A Puritan is such A monstrous thing / as loves Democraties & hates A King," pp. 185–89).

time, from a Royalist-oppositionist point of view, especially when Royalists were most threatened and imperiled during and just after the Civil War. Not coincidentally, the system of manuscript transmission—especially in the 1640s and early 1650s—was clearly the preferred medium of communication for politically forceful Royalist verse. In manuscript collections, explicitly and implicitly political lyrics declared the allegiances of members of an educated Royalist elite that, particularly after the fall of Oxford in 1645 to parliamentary forces, used such literature as a form of social and political bonding. It was as though the manuscript system of transmission itself had become politicized.

### Poems Popular in the Manuscript System

Sex and politics, of course, were not the only topics featured in manuscript poetry collections. If we look at the broad range of manuscript verse to find those poems which seem to recur with greatest frequency, we discover an interesting combination of texts that it would be difficult to anticipate from the printed volumes of the period or from the literary histories that are based on the products of print culture. In his study of sixteenth-century manuscript collections, L. G. Black has made a short list of poems that repeatedly appear in the miscellanies and poetical anthologies of that period:

Oxford's "When wert thou born desire," "My mind to me a kingdom is," and "Sitting alone upon my thought";

Dyer's "He that his mirth hath lost," "I would it were not as it is," and "As rare to fear, as seldom to be seen";

Ralegh's "Calling to mind mine eye long went about";

Breton's "In the merry month of May," "Some men will say there is a kind of Muse," and "The gentle season of the year";

Sidney's "If I could think how these my thoughts to leave," "Look up fair lids the treasure of my heart," "Ring out your bells," "The fire to see my wrongs for anger burneth," "What length of verse may serve," and "Who hath his fancy pleased";

the anonymous "When I was fair and young," "Her face, her tongue, her wit," and "Like to a hermit poor in place obscure."[115]

---

[115] Black, "Studies," 1:30.

One might possibly add to these Ralegh's poem "The Lie" ("Goe soule the bodies guest"; in thirty-two manuscripts, according to Beal, 1.2.390–92) and Essex's (?) "Buzzing Bee's Complaint," which appears in at least twenty-eight manuscripts: as a complaint about political disfavor, like Dyer's "He that his mirth hath lost," the latter spoke to a common experience of politically active courtiers.[116] Chidiock Tichborne's poem "My prime of youth is but a froste of cares," which appears in at least twenty-seven manuscripts, was also very popular: this lyric by an imprisoned recusant also articulated a human response to adversity in a memorable manner.[117] Not surprising for the Elizabethan period, most of poems mentioned were written in a politically coded amorous idiom: they thus spoke a peculiarly Elizabethan language that had a wide range of social and political uses.[118]

David Redding and Mary Hobbs have their own lists of poems that were popular in seventeenth-century manuscript transmission. Redding selects eighteen also found in Rosenbach MS 1083/16:

"A virtuous lady sitting in a muse" [Harington]
"As careful mothers in their beds"[119]
"Cock Lorell would needs have the devil his guest" [Jonson]
"Dawson the Butler's dead" [Corbett]
"Dearest thy tresses" [Carew]
"Down came grave ancient" [Hoskins et al., "The Parliament Fart"]
"Even such is time" [Ralegh]
"Fy schollers fie" [possibly by Strode]
"Four clearkes of Oxford" [Corbett's "Iter Boreale"]
"If shadows be a picture's excellence" [Walton Poole]
"It is not a full fortnight since" [Strode]
"Lawyers themselves maintain"[120]

[116] May includes this poem in a group of pieces "possibly" by Essex (*Elizabethan Courtier Poets*, pp. 266–69 [see Chap. 1, n. 19]). See the notes on the circumstances of this poem in Doughtie, *Lyrics from English Airs*, pp. 518–20 (see Chap. 1, n. 2): the only printed version is the publication of three of this poem's fifteen stanzas in Dowland's 1603 song book.

[117] See Hirsch, "Chidiock Tichborne," pp. 316–17 (cited in full at Chap. 1, n. 22), and the discussion of this poem in Chapter 1.

[118] See my discussion of this topic in " 'Love Is Not Love': Elizabethan Sonnet Sequences and the Social Order," *ELH* 49 (1982): 396–428.

[119] This poem was printed in the 1637 edition of Camden's *Remaines Concerning Britain* and in *Wits Recreations* (1640), and it appears in twelve Bodleian manuscripts, in one of which it is attributed to Sir John Davies (Crum, p. 73).

[120] This anonymous poem was printed in *Wit Restor'd* (1658) and is found in nine Bodleian manuscripts (Crum, p. 504).

"Nature waxing old" [William Juxon's elegy for Prince Henry]
"O heavenly powers" [anon., "On women"][121]
"What is our life" [Ralegh]
"Within a fleece of silent waters" [William Browne]
"Within this marble casket" ["On the Death of an Infante," possibly by George Morley][122]
"Wrong not dear Empresse" [Ayton][123]

To this list, Mary Hobbs adds the following:

"Ask me no more" [Carew]
"Ile tell you how the Rose did first grow Redd"[124]
"Accept, thou Shrine of my Dead Saint" [King's "Exequy"]
"Fair boy alas why fliest thou me" [Henry Reynolds's "A Black-more Maid Wooing a Fair Boy"]
"Black maid complain not that I fly" [King's answer poem to Reynolds's][125]

To the the poems in these lists certainly one might add Wotton's popular elegy "You meaner beauties of the night" (73 manuscripts, Beal, 1.2.569–75); Herrick's "Curse" ("Goe perjur'd man"; 58 manuscripts, Beal, 2.1.538–42), "Welcome to Sack" (23 manuscripts, Beal, 2.1.554–56), and "Farewell to Sack" (17 manuscripts, Beal, 2.1.542–44); Jonson's poem "The Houre-Glasse" ("Do but consider this small dust"; 38 manuscripts, Beal, 1.2.258–61), and two lyrics for Venetia Digby, "The Body" (45 manuscripts, Beal, 1.2.249–52) and "The Mind" (36 manuscripts, Beal, 1.2.252–55); and many of the poems of Donne. There are, of course, other pieces that deserve to be noted, especially the large number of witty epigrams and epitaphs

---

[121] See Crum, items O486, O484, O489.

[122] This poem was printed in Stowe's *Survey of London* (1618) and the 1623 edition of Camden's *Remaines* (Crum, p. 1152). It seems to have functioned as an all-purpose epitaph, for it is called "on the L. Mary daughter to K. James" in Bod. MS Eng. Poet. e.14, fol. 96v rev., and "on prince Henry" in Bod. MS Rawl. Poet. 31, fol. 2v.

[123] Redding, "Robert Bishop's Commonplace Book," pp. lii–liii.

[124] This anonymous poem was printed in *Wits Recreations* (1640), *Parnassus Biceps* (1656), and *Wit Restor'd* (1658) and appears in fourteen Bodleian manuscripts (Crum, p. 442).

[125] This list is from Mary Hobbs, "An Edition of the Stoughton Manuscript (An Early Seventeenth-Century Poetry Collection in Private Hands Connected with Henry King and Oxford Seen in Relation to Other Contemporary Poetry and Song Collections" (Ph.D. diss., University of London, 1973), p. 210.

that were copied over and over in student collections.[126] The point, however, is not simply to construct a list of popular poems in the manuscript system for its own sake, but rather to consider some of the reasons why particular poems are found in so many collections.

I divide the poems that recur frequently in manuscript collections into the following rough categories: (1) model epitaphs and elegies for either social superiors, equals, or inferiors; (2) poems that express general cultural beliefs or moral truisms or both; and (3) poems celebrating the lifestyle and shared values of a social or intellectual elite.

In the first category, there are some epitaphs and elegies that were repeated in the manuscript collections not only because they are especially eloquent expressions of their kind but also because they delineated social relations in a hierarchical system and clearly embodied attitudes that had widespread appeal. Manuscript compilers were extraordinarily preoccupied with death. They collected hundreds of serious elegies and epitaphs about both prominent and less well known adults and children as well as comic and satiric epitaphs and elegies about political enemies, social inferiors, and other figures of scorn. Like verse letters to social superiors, many elegies were designed to affirm or attempted to establish ties of social, political, or economic patronage; others were composed to declare in-group allegiances of various sorts—to family, to a network of friends or colleagues, to a political faction or program. In both serious and comical elegies and epitaphs the class issue was usually quite important. Despite the production of published volumes of commemorative verse and the appearance of elegies and epitaphs in both anthologies and editions of the work of particular authors, much of this verse was confined to the manuscript system, where the restriction of audience suited the social exclusiveness of much of this work.

These elegies and epitaphs include, for example, Juxon's epitaph on Prince Henry ("Nature waxing old"); William Browne of Tavistock's epitaphs for the countess of Pembroke ("Underneath this sable hearse"),[127] for six-year-old Anne Prideaux, "Nature in this small vol-

---

[126] In one of the four chapters appended to the 1623 edition of his *Remaines Concerning Britain* devoted to epitaphs as a poetic form, William Camden not only gave examples of serious funeral epitaphs (mostly from medieval verse), but also of "merry, and laughing Epitaphes" (*Remains Concerning Britain*, ed. R. D. Dunn [Toronto: University of Toronto Press, 1984], p. 355).
[127] Crum, p. 999, lists ten Bodleian manuscripts along with the printed version found

ume was about";[128] a beautiful epitaph on a dead infant, "Within this marble casket";[129] Henry King's elegy for his wife, "The Exequy," which celebrates the values of companionate marriage; Wotton's elegy for James I's daughter, Elizabeth, queen of Bohemia, "You meaner beauties of the night";[130] Francis Beaumont's elegies for the countess of Rutland ("Madame, so may my verses pleasing be") and Lady Markham ("As unthrifts groan in straw for their pawn'd beds");[131] and condescending comic epitaphs on two different men at Oxford named Prick.[132] The poems about social superiors accept the structure of the social hierarchy and the system of patronage it entails; the poems about deceased children permit their authors to express paternalistic sentimentality; the comic epitaphs are recreational trivia.

Poems that express general cultural beliefs include several lyrics written by or commonly attributed to Sir Walter Ralegh—"What is our life?" (in some 70 manuscripts Beal, 1.2.396–401), "Even such is time" (92 manuscripts, Beal, 1.2.379–86), and "The Lie." As noted earlier, the first two express the traditional attitude of *contemptus mundi*, but had currency because they were associated with Ralegh's fall and execution. The last takes a satiric point of view with which those whose sociopolitical ambitions were frustrated could identify. Sir Henry Wotton's poem "The Character of a Happy Life" (52 manuscripts, Beal, 1.2.565–68) articulates a stoic ideal that was especially attractive in times of political conflict, and the anonymous poem "Farewell, ye gilded follies" (39 manuscripts, Beal, 1.2.581–84) enacts a moral rejection of secular desires. Wotton's "O Faithless world" (24 manuscripts, Beal, 1.2.575–76) responds to betrayal in love from a male point of view.

---

in the 1623 edition of Camden's *Remaines*, p. 340. Beal, 1.1.131–34, lists fifty-one manuscript versions of this lyric.

[128] This poem appears in nine Bodleian manuscripts (Crum, p. 599). It also appears in BL MSS Add. 15227, fol. 89r, and 25303, fol. 163r; Harl. 2421, fol. 2v; Sloane 1446, fol. 65r, and 1867, fol. 32r; Stowe 962, fol. 151; and in Camden's *Remaines* (1623) and *Musarum Deliciae* (1656). Beal, 1.1.126–28, lists thirty-seven manuscripts of this poem.

[129] Crum, pp. 464 and 1152, lists nine Bodleian manuscripts for the two versions of this poem and printed texts in Stowe's *Survey of London* (1618), Camden's *Remaines* (1623), and *Recreation for Ingenious Head-pieces* (1663). It also is found, among other places, in BL MS Add. 58215, fol. 22v.

[130] Beal, 1.2.569–75, lists seventy-two manuscripts of this.

[131] Beal, 1.1.69–70, lists twenty-six manuscripts for the former and, on 1.1.72–74, twenty-nine manuscripts for the latter.

[132] See Crum, items A1362, O1094, S984, T607, T1445, and T1481.

## SEX AND POLITICS

In the third category of popular poems, I would place those (particularly early seventeenth-century pieces) that are witty trivia. These include Sir John Harington's bawdy epigram "A virtuous lady sitting in a muse" (37 manuscripts, Beal, 1.2.138–41); Randolph's "On a deformed Gentlewoman with a Sweet voyce" ("I chanced sweet Lesbias voice to hear"); Walton Poole's "If shadows be a picture's excellence";[133] Corbett's "To the Ladyes of the New Dresse" ("Ladyes that weare black cypresse vailes"; 35 manuscripts, Beal, 2.1.197–99); William Browne of Tavistock's "On one drowned in snow" ("Within a fleece of silent waters drowned"; 31 manuscripts, Beal, 1.1.129–31); Henry Reynolds's "Blackmore Mayd wooing a faire Boy" ("Stay lovely Boy, why fly'st thou mee") and Henry King's answer poem, "The Boy's answere to the Blackmore" ("Black Mayd, complayne not that I fly"; 70 manuscripts, Beal, 2.1.598–602);[134] the anonymous poem "Of a Lady with one eye which brought forth a Child with one" ("A one eyed boy born of a half blind mother");[135] and two enormously popular Carew poems, "A Flye that flew into my Mistris her eye" ("When this flye liv'd, she us'd to play"; 66 manuscripts, Beal, 2.1.60–64) and "Ask me no more whither do stray" (43 manuscripts, Beal 2.1.89–91), the second of which had an extraordinary life in the manuscript system of transmission, partly because it invited imitation.[136] Carew's "Secrecie Protested" ("Feare not [deare Love] that I'le reveale"; 39 manuscripts, Beal, 2.1.86–88) and "The Rapture" (29 manuscripts, Beal, 2.1.83–85), the second of which has been discussed as

[133] See Edwin Wolf II, " 'If Shadowes be a Picture's Excellence': An Experiment in Critical Bibliography," *PMLA* 68 (1948): 831–57, for a discussion of the transmission of this poem.

[134] See *Poems of Henry King*, ed. Crum, p. 151 (cited in full at Chap. 1, n. 56), for the texts of both poems. Crum notes that Reynolds's poem translates a Latin poem by George Herbert on the topic. Beal, 2.1.598–602, cites seventy manuscripts for the King poem. He notes that it was first published in *The Academy of Complements* (1646) and in the 1657 edition of King's *Poems*. See further discussion of these pieces in Chapter 3.

[135] See Crum, items A179, A324, F53, H142, and T2227, for the different versions of this found in Bodleian manuscripts. She points out that this poem was printed in Camden's *Remaines* (1637), p. 414, and in *Wits Recreations* (1640), sig. L1r. It also appears in Hunt. MS HM 198, pt. 1, p. 11. The different manuscript versions suggest variations created by processes of memorial transcription.

[136] It is found in ten Bodleian manuscripts and in a number of British Library Manuscripts (including Harl. 6918, fol. 41; Sloane 1446, fol. 35; Add. 30982, fol. 119 rev., with two answer poems: see Crum, p. 88). It was also printed in Benson's *Poems: by Wil. Shakespeare* (1640); Carew's *Poems* (1642), p. 180; *The Poems of Pembroke and Rudyerd* (1660), p. 92; John Playford's *Cheerful Ayres and Dialogues* (1660), p. 42; and *Wit Restor'd* (1658), p. 114.

a Royalist poem by Kevin Sharpe,[137] ought also to be mentioned. Herrick's "Welcome to Sack" and "Farewell to Sack" were popular partly because, as Lois Potter argues, drunkenness was used as a Royalist code during the Civil War and Interregnum.[138]

The Royalist printed anthology, *Parnassus Biceps* (1658), which draws on the manuscript tradition, prints many of its popular poems. Purporting to be *"Several Choice Pieces of Poetry, composed by the best Wits that were in both the Universities before their Dissolution,"* this collection contains such poems as Wotton's elegy for Princess Elizabeth of Bohemia (here titled "Sir Henry Wotton on Q[ueen] Elizabeth" and with the alternate first line "Ye glorious trifles of the East" instead of the more usual "You meaner beauties of the night," p. 34); Corbett's "You Ladies that wear Cypresse vailes" (p. 65) and its answer poem, "Black Cypresse vailes are shrowds of night" (p. 66); Walton Poole's "On a black Gentlewoman" ("If Shadowes be a Pictures excellence," pp. 75–77); Strode's "On a Gentlewoman walking in the Snow" ("I Saw faire *Cloris* walk alone," pp. 77–78); William Browne's "Upon one dead in the Snow" ("Within a fleece of silent waters drownd," p. 78); Henry Reynolds's "Black maid to the faire boy" ("Faire boy [alasse] why fliest thou me," pp. 91–92) and Henry King's answer poem, "Black girle complaine not that I fly" (pp. 91–92); and Herrick's "A welcome to Sack" (pp. 95–97).[139]

The popularity of some texts was due to their being part of larger collections of pieces that were passed on to a succession of transcribers. This was the case, for example, with the large number of manuscripts originating in Christ Church, Oxford, in the 1630s and early 1640s. Nevertheless, it is clear that the most popular poems had either topical or general cultural appeal that reached beyond the interests of an academic or specific social coterie. They spoke to the concerns, social attitudes, and political and moral values of many compilers, especially of those conservative or Royalist collectors who used the manuscript system as the more politically and socially congenial literary environment. Despite the repetition of certain poems that were often part of circulating groups of texts, the manuscript

[137] Kevin Sharpe, *Criticism and Compliment: The Politics of Literature in the England of Charles I* (Cambridge: Cambridge University Press, 1987), pp. 118–22.

[138] Lois Potter, *Secret Rites and Secret Writing: Royalist Literature, 1641–1660* (Cambridge: Cambridge University Press, 1989), pp. 134–40.

[139] See *Parnassus Biceps or Severall Choice Pieces of Poetry by Abraham Wright 1656*, facsimile, with an introduction and indexes by Peter Beal (Aldershot, U.K.: Scolar Press, 1990).

miscellanies and poetry anthologies still commonly reflected the personal tastes, interests, and situation of particular compilers. Highlighting, at the same time, many pieces whose popularity one might not expect from examining the printed books of the period and pieces that particular compilers chose for their own personal reasons, the manuscript collections of the sixteenth and seventeenth centuries comprise a mix of poems by major, minor, and anonymous authors that presents a picture of the literature of the period different from that presented by the body of printed texts, which, despite the persistence of anthologizing practices, came to emphasize individual authorship. These manuscript collections lay outside or on the periphery of an emerging literary institution shaped by print culture, one that valorized texts that escape their local, topical, coterie, and private circumstances, the very contexts that the manuscript system valued.

# CHAPTER THREE

# SOCIAL TEXTUALITY

## IN THE
## *MANUSCRIPT SYSTEM*

### Textual Instability and Malleability

In the system of manuscript transmission, it was normal for lyrics to elicit revisions, corrections, supplements, and answers, for they were part of an ongoing social discourse. In this environment texts were inherently malleable, escaping authorial control to enter a social world in which recipients both consciously and unconsciously altered what they received. Those who prepared poetry anthologies for publication were not usually composers of verse,[1] but compilers of manuscripts often added their own poems to the commonplace-book miscellanies or poetry anthologies they made. In the manuscript environment the roles of author, scribe, and reader overlapped: in a poem written in a lady's table book, Henry King, for example, invited her to be "both the Scribe and Authour."[2] What modern idealistic textual criticism, from an author-centered point of view, regards as "corruptions" we can view as interesting evidence of the social history of particular texts. The manuscript system was far less author-centered than print culture and not at all interested in correcting, perfecting, or fixing texts in authorially sanctioned forms.

---

[1] Hyder Rollins, however, notes that Thomas Proctor wrote verse for the miscellany he edited, pointing out that other editors felt free to do the same (*A Gorgeous Gallery of Gallant Inventions [1578]*, ed. Hyder E. Rollins [Cambridge: Harvard University Press, 1926], p. xix).

[2] Quoted in Crum, "Notes," p. 121 (see Chap. 1, n.34).

# MANUSCRIPT, PRINT, AND THE RENAISSANCE LYRIC

Commenting on late medieval social verse, Derek Pearsall has argued:

> It is important to realise how much these poems are intended to be used rather than read as we read them. They are no one's property and the whole notion of authorship is in a way irrelevant. Poems are borrowed and their allusions to date and circumstances changed so as to fit a new occasion. Verses are incorporated into love-letters. . . . Ascriptions to particular noble lords or ladies that we occasionally find in the manuscripts probably do no more than record a particular dignity once assigned to a piece from the general repertoire. . . . [S]tanzas from the common stock are interlaced and reworked; simple pieces, including popular songs, are adapted for more ostentatious purposes; famous opening stanzas and striking first lines are pressed into service again and again to launch new poems.[3]

Richard Leighton Greene similarly emphasizes the plasticity of the texts of carols: "To no form of poetry could verses be added more easily than the carol. . . . They offer a constant invitation to the versifiers to add, subtract, or transpose, and in the absence of a written copy it would be unusually easy to confuse the stanza-order. That faults of memory are responsible for some of the variations is shown by the fact that the first three or four stanzas of a carol are more usually preserved in the same order in variant versions than are later stanzas."[4] This medieval attitude was carried over into the Renaissance. In fact, some authors expected and even welcomed the changes that recipients of their works brought to them, acknowledging the possibility that modern textual scholarship has been reluctant to admit, that texts might (accidentally or deliberately) be improved by individuals other than the original writers.[5] J. W. Saunders notes, for example, that George Whetstone "left his poems dispersed among learned friends and expected them 'at theyr leasure to polish' the work, should he fail to return from abroad."[6] In a verse "letter of

[3] Pearsall, *Old and Middle English Poetry*, p. 221 (see Chap. 1, n. 10).

[4] Greene, *Early English Carols*, p. cxxxi (see Chap. 1, n. 54).

[5] According to Wolf, "The words of a poet were not sacrosanct in his own day; corruptions are common, but it may be that some . . . poetry was actually improved in the stream of transmission" "Textual Importance," p. 3 [see Chap. 1, n. 69]). Cheryl Greenberg points out that the fifteenth-century poet Richard Sellyng "wrote at the end of one of his poems that he sent it 'to John Shirley . . . For to amende where it is a misse' " ("John Shirley," p. 377 [see Chap. 1, n. 53]).

[6] Saunders, "From Manuscript to Print," p. 524 (see Chap. 1, n. 3).

the Author to J. C. concerning these Posies" prefaced to *A Poor Knight his Pallace of Private Pleasure* (1579), the young Cambridge student who was the anonymous writer sends his work to his friend with the assumption that it can be editorially improved: "And unto you gentle J. C. beeing pend I send the same, / To reade, to race, to blot, to burne, the faults that merit blame" (sig. Aiiv).

The issue of textual stability is a particularly interesting one, since, as Jerome McGann's challenging revisionist approach to textual scholarship suggests, the ontological status of texts is a function of their original sociocultural definition.[7] Although some postmodern conceptions of literature would have us view literary works as textually unstable, literary studies are still dominated by an idealism that privileges the best, latest, authorially sanctioned version of the text, the one reified in a modern edition that uses all the resources of sophisticated textual scholarship to produce the work in its "purest" form—that is, its printed version that supposedly realizes the author's final intentions (whether or not he or she was conscious of them). This is one legacy of the Gutenberg revolution that not only altered the status of writing but also, as Elizabeth Eisenstein has shown, wrought those religious, economic, social, and political changes that shaped the modern world.[8] But the idealism that governs both the practice of modern textual scholarship and of much literary criticism generally ill suits not only the literature of a manuscript culture but also much of the literature of the early era of print.

In the two different systems of transmission of literature, texts were treated differently, just as authors and readers had different roles. In the processes of manuscript transmission, texts were, of course, subject to copyist error, but they were also, by convention, open to reader emendation, supplementation, response, and parody. The text of a poem was malleable in a system of manuscript transmission. Even an authorial holograph was not immune to alteration: Wyatt's collection of his own verse in BL MS Egerton 2711, for example, contains not only that poet's own revisions of his work, but also the alterations introduced by Nicholas Grimald and other sixteenth-century correc-

---

[7] Jerome J. McGann, *A Critique of Modern Textual Criticism* (Chicago: University of Chicago Press, 1983), pp. 8, 44–45. Cf. Stephen Orgel, "What is a Text?" *Research Opportunities in Renaissance Drama* 24 (1981): 3–6.

[8] Elizabeth Eisenstein, *The Printing Press as an Agent of Change: Communications and Cultural Transformations in Early-Modern Europe*, 2 vols. (Cambridge: Cambridge University Press, 1979).

tors.[9] William Strode's ongoing revisions of his own poems are found in Oxford MS CCC 325.[10]

Sir Edward Dyer's lyric, "The lowest trees have topps," a poem arguing for a system of reward by merit, continued to mutate in the course of its transmission in both manuscript and print. Although it was published anonymously in Francis Davison's *Poetical Rhapsody* (1602), and in John Dowland's *Third and Last Booke of Songs or Airs* (1603), in the absence of those minimal controls that would have been exercised by the contemporary publication of this author's collected verse, the poem proliferated in manuscript, accumulating variants textual scholars regard as corruptions of an unavailable original text that the two printed versions are assumed to approximate. In Davison's volume, the last anthology of poetry printed in the Elizabethan era, the lyric appears as follows:

> The lowest Trees have tops, the Ante her gall,
>   The flie her splene, the little sparkes their heate:
> The slender haires cast shadowes, though but small,
> And Bees have stings, although they be not great:
>   Seas have their sourse, & so have shallow springs,
>   And love is love, in Beggars, as in Kings.
>
> Where rivers smoothest run, deepe are the foords,
> The Diall stirres, yet none perceives it moove:
> The firmest faith is in the fewest wordes,
> The Turtles cannot sing, and yet they love:
>   True Harts have eyes, & eares, no tongs to speake,
>   They heare, & see, and sigh, and then they breake.
>
>                                                   *Incerto*[11]

Since the poem, as Hyder Rollins has observed, "is made up almost entirely of proverbs and commonplaces,"[12] there were unusual pressures at work in manuscript transmission to change features of the

---

[9] See Hughey, 1:44–45. Richard Harrier says of one of the pieces in the Egerton Manuscript ("What rage is this?") that shows considerable revision that it is "a remarkable specimen of a poem in the process of being written" (*Canon of Wyatt's Poetry*, p. 3 [see Chap. 1, n. 65]).

[10] M. A. Forey observes that three-quarters of the Strode poems in this manuscript are corrected in the author's own hand ("William Strode," p. lxv [see Chap. 1, n. 70]).

[11] Hyder Rollins, ed., *A Poetical Rhapsody, 1602–1621,* 2 vols. (Cambridge: Harvard University Press, 1931), 1:186.

[12] Ibid., 2:168.

text as transcribers easily confused the lines of the lyric with their own store of familiar sayings. It is easy to see that this work presents an extreme case of textual malleability.

Variations found in the twenty manuscripts and three printed versions of this poem include the transposition of the two stanzas (BL MS Harl. 6910), the insertion of an additional stanza in the middle (Folger MS V.a.162; Bod. MS Mal. 19; and Bod. MS Tanner 169), and the addition of an eight-line supplement written by someone Ruth Hughey suggests "was making use of the poem for personal reasons" (2:308). Verbal variations include what look like misreadings of a transcribed source text—for example, "course" for "source" and "hollowes" for "shallowes" in line 5, as well as misremembered words or phrases possibly occurring in the process of memorial transcription, such as "smallest" for "lowest" and "shrubs" for "trees" in line 1, "rivers" for "waters" and "floods" for "fordes" in line 7, and "fairest" for "firmest," "love" for "fayth," and "clearest" or "sweetest" for "fewest" in line 9.[13] Although perhaps an editor's nightmare, this poem should be a social historian's delight—in its intertextual complexity and socioliterary vicissitudes, it is a collaborative social production, as open a text as one could imagine.

There is an interesting text of a poem in Humphrey Coningsby's manuscript (BL MS Harl. 7392) which reproduces, with some variants, the first six lines of a piece found in Camb. MS Dd.5.75 and Morley's *First Book of Airs* before continuing with a completely different twelve succeeding lines.[14] In Coningsby's manuscript, we find:

> Come Sorrow Com Sitte down & morne with mee,
> Enclyne thy head, upon the Balefull Breste,
> That careles pleasure may conceave and see,
> How heavy hartes, repose in little reste.
> Unfould thyne Armes and wring thy wretched handes,
> To show the state wherin poore Sorrow standes.
> For lo the Sequels of my lyfe & love,
> Ar sorrowes all enconmbred with myschaunce

[13] See the textual variants printed in Rollins, *Poetical Rhapsody*, 2:164–67; Hughey, 2:307–8; and Doughtie, *Lyrics from English Airs*, p. 520 (see Chap. 1, n. 2).
[14] For these differences, see May, *Henry Stanford's Anthology*, pp. 276–77 (cited in full at Chap. 1, n. 133); the Morley text is reproduced in Doughtie, *Lyrics from English Airs*, pp. 143–44.

My Hopes deceave: my purposes misprove,
   No trust in Time my fortune to advaunce.
Yet this I joy, although I lyve forlorne
   My Griefes (thoghe great) wer ever secret borne.
For most my griefes ar of so straunge a sorte
   As hould no meane unless they be conceald
Which makes me vow to kepe them from reporte
   Els with each care his Cause should be revealed,
I tell to much thoughe chiefest pointes I hyde
   And more He knowes, which hath like Sorrowes tryde
But sithe my lucke allowes no better happe,
   Wher grief & feare shall comfort shall exxell
Tyll lyef of love hath felt thextremest power,
   And love of lyfe hath seen the latest hower.
               fynys. quoth R.P.
                         (Fol. 32r)

The Cambridge manuscript text has the following:

Come sorrow comm sitte down & mourn with me
   Hang down thie head uppon thie balefull brest
that god & man & all the world may see
our hevy hartes doe lie at little rest
enfold thyn armes & wring thie wretched handes
to shew the state wherin poore sorow standes
Crye not outright for that is childrens guise
but let thie teares fall trickling down thie face
& weepe so long untill thie blubbred eyes
do shew in somnne the depthe of thie disgrace
o shake thie head but not a word but mumme
the heart once dead the tongue is stroken dumme
And let our fare be dishes of dispite
   to breake our hartes & not our fastes withall
& let us suppe with sorowes soppes at night
   a dish for death to make an end withall
thus let us lyve till heavens may rue to see
the doleful doome ordayned for the & me.[15]

The third from last line in Morley's version reads "And bitter sawce,
all of a broken gall"[16]—which seems to be an improvement on the

---

[15] May, *Henry Stanford's Anthology*, pp. 76–77.
[16] Doughtie, *Lyrics from English Airs*, p. 144.

Cambridge manuscript's line, which awkwardly repeats the rhyme word "withall"—but, otherwise the two versions are close textually. Given that one version of this poem was set to music, probably accounting for the references to it in Shakespeare's *Loves Labours Lost*,[17] it could have been used in whole or in part as poetic boilerplate to be rewritten or supplemented by anyone with an inclination to do so. The text in Coningsby's anthology may have taken off from the first six lines of the version found reproduced in Morley's song and Stanford's manuscripts.

A number of other poems by sixteenth- and seventeenth-century poets have similar histories. For example, the Nicholas Breton poem found in Bod. MS Rawl. Poet. 85, "Some men will saye there is a kynde of muse" (fol. 47r–v; Cummings, pp. 411–12), exists in different versions with different configurations of stanzas in several manuscripts.[18] Laurence Cummings notes that three stanzas of the poem appear in three different Breton poems (p. 416). Mary Hobbs suggests that a poem sometimes attributed to Thomas Carew, "Come thou gentle wind," may be that author's expansion of an eighteen-line poem by another author.[19]

One of the obvious ways that scribes exercised authorial functions was in adding lines or stanzas to the poems they were copying. Bod. MS Eng. Poet. e.14, for example, includes a supplement to Sir Henry Wotton's "You meaner beauties of the night" labeled "Two other Staves added by Another" (fol. 68v). The versions of Dyer's "He that his mirth hath lost" vary considerably in the six important manuscript collections in which it appears.[20] The most notorious case of this practice is probably the history of Ralegh's poem "The Lie."[21] This lyric, like Marlowe's "Passionate Shepherd," attracted answer poems that became part of the line of manuscript transmission.[22] Sir John Har-

---

[17] May refers to 4.3.[4], but the allusion also seems to be in 1.1.298 (*Henry Stanford's Anthology*, p. 277).

[18] Cf. BL MSS Add. 34064, fols. 20v–21v; and Harl. 6910, fols. 147v–48r, and 7392, fols. 76v–77r.

[19] Hobbs, *Stoughton Manuscript*, p. xviii (see Chap. 1, n. 36).

[20] Hughey remarks that "it is painfully evident that the versions differ considerably, indicating how much an Elizabethan poem might be changed as it was passed about from one collector to another. Unfortunately, it is very probable that no one of these versions presents the poem as the author wrote it" (2:206).

[21] See Rollins, *Poetical Rhapsody*, 2:218–21, and *The Poems of Sir Walter Ralegh*, edited with an introduction by Agnes M. C. Latham (1951; reprint, Cambridge: Harvard University Press, 1962), pp. 128–38.

[22] For an interesting treatment of Richard Latewar's interstanzaic answer poem to "The

ington's popular epigram about a husband's reproof to his wife for her inadvertant exposure of her genitals to the sight of others elicited responses. This poem was expanded by the addition of four new lines by John Davies of Hereford to include the woman's witty answer to her husband's metaphoric admonition.[23] Folger MS V.a.345 has this expanded version:

Of a Lady musing

A vertuous Lady sitting in a muse
As oftentimes fayre vertuous Ladyes use,
Leaning her elbow, on her knee so hard
The other distant from it halfe a yard,
Her knight to quip her by a secret token
Sayd, wife arise, your cabinet is open,
She rising blusht & smillingly did say
Sir lock it if you please you have the key.
Then he replyde & sayd good wife you mock
my key can open but not shut the lock,
Sith tis a spring, and keys in general
will doe't, if so it open ly to all.

(Pp. 29–30)

The earliest printed version of Harington's poem (without the four additional lines by Davies) is found in *Alcilia* (1613), but it is absent from both the 1615 and 1618 posthumous editions of his *Epigrams*.[24]

Sometimes in the course of their manuscript transmission, different poems were conflated in whole or in part to create new poetic units. In John Lilliat's anthology (Bod. MS Rawl. Poet. 148), Edward Doughtie notes, a poem attributed to Sir Henry Lee on his retirement is actually a conflation of three stanzas of a poem from Dowland's *Second Booke of Songs or Ayres* (1600) with the third stanza of a poem from

---

Lie," see Karl Josef Höltgen, "Richard Latewar, Elizabethan Poet and Divine," *Anglia* 89 (1971): 417–38.

[23] Beal, 1.2.140, notes four manuscripts in which this longer version of the poem is found, in one of which there is the marginal note: "A couplet or two fastened to Sr Jo: Harrington his epigram, to doe his Townes knight yeomans service" (Folger MS V.a.339, fol. 275r).

[24] See Beal, 1.2.138–41, who cites versions of the poem in thirty-seven manuscripts. The piece also appears anonymously in *Wit Restor'd* (1658), p. 81.

George Peele's *Polyhymnia* (1590).[25] John Finet, either accidentally or deliberately, merged excerpts from two Sidney poems in his poetical anthology to create a new poem.[26] Henry Stanford includes in his anthology a composite text made from parts of two poems found in *The Paradise of Dainty Devices*.[27] Another poem in this same anthology, "A dreame" ("In pescodd tyme when hound to horne," fols. 51r–53r) represents a expansion of a Thomas Churchyard poem by another writer.[28]

Another important cause of textual change in the course of extended manuscript transmission was the practice of transcribing from memory, a widespread phenomenon in an era much closer than our own to the workings of an oral culture. This resulted in (sometimes interesting) unconscious alterations in the production of variant texts of poems. J. B. Leishman has argued that this process accounts for many of the unusual textual changes that occured in manuscript transmission, most of which have traditionally been mistakenly attributed to copyist errors. He defines the process as follows:

> The author was not accustomed, either with his own hand or with his secretary's, to write out copy after copy [of a poem] at the request of friends, each time incorporating some small revision and correction, but . . . after one or two authentic versions, perhaps with not inconsiderable variants between them, had been circulated, the author's (or the poem's) friends got the poem by heart, unconsciously modified it in their memories, repeated it or wrote it out for *their* friends, and . . . the various versions in commonplace-books and miscellanies have, in varying degrees, a rela-

[25] *Liber Lilliati*, ed. Doughtie, p. 165 and the text of the poem on p. 77 (see Chap. 1, n. 8).

[26] See Cummings, pp. 504–8. Sidney's "My earthly mould doth melt in watry teares" is merged in Rawl. Poet. 85 with his "Thus do I fall to ryse thus."

[27] See May, *Henry Stanford's Anthology*, pp. 155 and 369: the combined poems are no. 71, lines 1–6, and no. 95, lines 7–18, of *The Paradise of Dainty Devices*.

[28] This piece is also found in BL MS Harl. 7392, fols. 51–53, attributed to the earl of Oxford and in *England's Helicon* (1600), sigs. z3r–z4v. May identifies it as Churchyard's poem, first published in *Churchyard's Chance* (1580) and later revised for *England's Helicon*, where it is signed "Ignoto" (*Poems of DeVere and of Devereux*, p. 82 [see Chap. 1, n. 19]). May notes that Bod. MS Rawl. Poet. 85 "preserves a second manuscript version of Churchyard's poem which is anonymous and complete except for lines 61–72." There is evidence, by absence of internal rhyme, that someone other than Churchyard did the section after line 32. Since Churchyard was Oxford's client, May suggests that there might have been "some sort of competition or collaboration between patron and protege" in the production of the poem (p. 83).

tionship to the original similar to that of the various versions of traditional ballads.[29]

For example, Bod. MS Mal. 23 contains a poem written against Lady Lake beginning "Here lyes the breife of badnes vices nurse," a piece that, in other manuscript versions has the words "breast," "prize," or "bride" as alternatives to "breife."[30] It would appear that the variants were more likely to have been caused by alterations of texts in the minds of those who memorized the poem before setting it down on paper than by simple copyist error. Transcription from memory was an essential part of the social history of texts in a manuscript system, and we should not simply, from the point of view of textual idealism, dismiss its effects as unwanted corruptions of authorial originals.

Though within the publication process, sloppy editorial practices, compositorial inconsistences, and poor proofreading created still new variants of received texts, print worked to stabilize or fix texts that were constantly changing in manuscript transmission. Nevertheless, some of the habits that produced textual changes in the manuscript system carried over into print culture, as owners of books felt free to change the texts they read. Hyder Rollins remarks about the Bodleian copy of the 1587 edition of *Tottel's Miscellany* that "two or three hands of different dates" made "elaborate manuscript notes . . . in the text and margins":

> These notes often show an utter disregard for what the poets may have written, a sublime confidence in individual powers of emendation. . . .In literally dozens of . . . emendations the annotators of this copy proceeded exactly as did the editor (or editors) [of the first three editions], changing words or phrases wherever they believed the rhythm or the sense, or both, could be improved. . . . Occasionally the annotators had consulted some earlier edition from which . . . they supplied lines dropped in [this one]; but more often they depended on their own ingenuity rather than on any printed text.[31]

---

[29] J. B. Leishman, " 'You Meaner Beauties of the Night,' A Study in Transmission and Transmogrification," *The Library*, 4th ser., 26 (1945): 101. Cf. Suzanne Woods, " 'The Passionate Sheepheard' and 'The Nymphs Reply,' A Study of Transmission," *HLQ* 34 (1970): 25–33.

[30] See Crum, pp. 346, 348, 352, and 359.

[31] *Tottel's Miscellany (1557–1587)*, ed. Hyder Rollins, 2 vols., 2d ed. (Cambridge: Harvard University Press, 1927), 2:100.

Clearly literary reception was not so passive a matter as it became in a more developed print culture.

Some authors were, of course, more drastically altered than others in the course of the manuscript and print transmission of their work. Take, for example, the case of Ralegh. Ralegh's poems passed into the system of manuscript transmission and were subjected to radical revision and supplementation. The poem beginning "Farewell falce love, thou oracle of lies," for instance, survives in eighteen-, twenty-four-, and thirty-line versions, the longest of which first appears in print posthumously in Thomas Deloney's *Garland of Good Will* (1631). By conservative textual standards, the 1631 text is a particularly corrupt version of the poem, but in addition to preserving what are probably scribal errors and deliberate changes and additions to an original authorial version, it does contain compositor "errors" that produce some interesting readings—for example, in line thirteen, "fortlesse field" for "fortress foiled" of the text in the Dobell Manuscript (Harv. fMS 1285, fol. 72v), which has the sole surviving eighteen-line version of the poem.[32] As the second printed version of the poem (the earlier one consisting of twenty-four lines—in William Byrd's *Psalmes, Sonets, & Songs,* [1588]), this text had an undeniable historical impact, and, after all, the third printing of the poem, in the 1660 collection, *Le Prince d'Amour,* reproduces the longest version. Because Ralegh's most recent editor, Michael Rudick, cannot find any evidence that Ralegh himself produced either the twenty-four-line or thirty-line version of the poem, as a conservative textual editor he has little interest in them, though he does quote the two "spurious" stanzas in his notes. But if we consider that the "purest," eighteen-line version of the poem survived only in a single manuscript, and the twenty-four- and thirty-line versions of the poem were *historically* more important, what is the sense of editing "Ralegh" in a way that denigrates nonauthorial variants or that encourages historical erasure in the name of rescuing an authorial archetype that is allegedly prior to historical vicissitude? The "Ralegh" that emerged within the trans-

[32] For Ralegh's poetry, in the absence of an adequate published standard edition, I have used Michael Rudick's "Poems of Ralegh" (see Chap. 1, n. 99). Rudick points out that two additional stanzas came to be attached to Ralegh's original in the course of manuscript transmission (pp. 25–26). The twenty-four line version of the poem is found in the Arundel Harington Manuscript, Nat'l Lib. Wales MS 473B, and PRO MS SP.46/126; the thirty-line version is found in John Finet's anthology (Bod. MS Rawl. Poet. 85) and Humphrey Coningsby's anthology (BL MS Harl. 7392) (see Beal, 1.2.387–88, and Hughey, 2:383–86).

mission and reception of a body of verse that was a mixture of authorially sanctioned work, additions and revisions to these texts, and the incorporation of texts by other writers is, finally, an authorship sign that makes sense historically in terms other than those of verifiable canon.

Many individual poems existed in both manuscript and printed collections in their own time: in some cases publishers only reproduced one form of a text that continued to be changed and rewritten in a still-vital manuscript tradition in which no one version assumed primacy. Although one might expect that the appearance of a printed edition of the verse of a particular author would have established his or her texts, the lines of manuscript transmission, in the cases of such poets as Donne and Herrick, retained variant versions of their work (as though the printed texts had no especial authority or, more to the point, as though the issue of authoritative texts meant little). For example, in Hunt. MS HM 198, pt. 2, fol. 118v, there is an alternate version of Ben Jonson's eleventh epigram, which may be an earlier draft of the poem that appeared in the 1616 folio (variant readings in boldface):

### of Somewhat I mett somewhere

**In** Courte I mett it in cloths brave enough
to be a courtier, and looks grave enough
to seeme a Statesman **and towards me it came.**
It made me a great face I ask'd the name.
A Lord (it cride) **clothed** in flesh & bloud
and such **a one from whom expect no** good
for I will doe none, and as little ill
for I will dare none **Lorde walke great there** still.

The folio version as edited by Herford, Simpson, and Simpson reads:

### ON SOME-THING, THAT WALKES SOME-WHERE.

At court I met it, in clothes brave enough,
To be a courtier; and lookes grave enough,

To seeme a statesman: as I neere it came,
  It made me a great face, I ask'd the name.
A lord, it cryed, buried in flesh, and blood,
  And such from whom let no man hope least good,
For I will doe none: and as little ill,
  For I will dare none. Good Lord, walke dead still.[33]

Four of the poem's eight lines are revised, the last line of the piece most drastically in order to increase the force of the satiric condemnation. But in all probability the Huntington manuscript version *postdates* the revised printed version.[34] As F. W. Moorman has pointed out, in compiling his verse for print Robert Herrick also revised earlier drafts of poems that had been in manuscript circulation, but these older texts continued to be reproduced in both the manuscript system and in print.[35] There were, of course, Herrick poems circulating in the manuscript system that never made it into print.[36]

## Corrupting Donne

Perhaps the most striking case of textual malleability is that of John Donne's poetry. In his magisterial *Index of English Literary Manuscripts*, Peter Beal notes that "probably more transcripts of Donne's poems were made than of the verse of any other British poet of the sixteenth and seventeenth centuries. The large number of extant transcripts . . . are . . . a reminder that his verse belonged essentially to a manuscript culture" (1.1.245). Scholars have identified some 250 manuscripts containing Donne poems, and as the search continues, more will doubtless surface.[37] Only a very small number of these have been collated in the standard Oxford editions of the verse by Grierson,

---

[33] Herford, Simpson, and Simpson, *Ben Jonson,* 8:30 (see Chap. 1, n. 35).

[34] See the discussion of this manuscript in Armitage, "Donne's Poems," pp. 697–707 (cited in full at Chap. 1, n. 79).

[35] F. W. Moorman, *The Poetical Works of Robert Herrick* (Oxford: Clarendon, 1915), p. xvi. Wolf suggests that Herrick, like Donne (or Sir John Davies), might not even have had the originals of his poems when he was assembling *Hesperides* and was forced to use textually corrupted copies he obtained ("Textual Importance," p. 7).

[36] See, for example, the poems cited in *The Complete Poetry of Robert Herrick,* ed. J. Max Patrick (Garden City, N.Y. Doubleday, 1963), pp. 537–57.

[37] See Pebworth, "Manuscript Poems and Print Assumptions," pp. 1–21 (cited in full at Chap. 1, n. 37).

Gardner, and Milgate:[38] most of these documents are rejected because of the corrupt or allegedly corrupt texts they contain. Although Beal has suggested that some of the versions of Donne's poems found in the manuscript miscellanies may represent "independent early copies of particular poems" (1.1.249) and thus be legitimate alternate versions or stages of revision of individual texts, textual scholars have not yet systematically approached the whole field of documentary evidence with this possibility in mind—though, apparently, scholars working on the *Donne Variorum* are making a serious effort to do so.

Allegedly corrupt texts, however, do *not* have to be justified as alternate authorial versions of works to merit our attention—that is, we need not, in examining literary production, transmission, and reception, take the idealistic, author-centered approach of traditional textual scholarship. An author such as Donne could control somewhat the form in which his poems were first received in manuscript by coterie readers, but, both before and after his death, others accidentally or deliberately altered those texts in an unfolding process of literary transmission. What happened to Donne's poems historically, especially in the manuscript system, deserves study—for the Donne poems people actually read, transcribed, and modified are part of a fascinating social history of literature that idealistic textual scholarship has largely ignored.

Textual editors have divided the manuscripts containing Donne's poetry into three basic groups. Group I was associated by Helen Gardner and others with the collection Donne himself supposedly began to compile when he was contemplating publishing his poetry in 1614 before entering the ministry.[39] Group II has been connected with a later collecting effort—which as Margaret Crum has argued, originally constituted a gathering of separate smaller booklets of poems between 1619 and 1625.[40] Both groups shaped the text found in the 1633 edition of the poetry. The recent study by Ernest Sullivan II of

---

[38] See the *Divine Poems of John Donne,* ed. Gardner (cited in full at Chap. 1, n. 74); also see *The Elegies and Songs and Sonnets,* ed. Helen Gardner (Oxford: Clarendon Press, 1965); *The Epithalamions, Anniversaries and Epicedes,* ed. W. Milgate (Oxford: Clarendon Press, 1978); and *The Satires, Epigrams and Verse Letters,* ed. W. Milgate (Oxford: Clarendon Press, 1967).

[39] See the analysis of the groups of manuscripts in *Divine Poems of John Donne,* ed. Gardner, pp. lxvi–lxxxii. Gardner, however, relies heavily on Grierson's original analysis.

[40] See Crum, "Notes," pp. 121–32.

the two Dalhousie manuscripts in relation to the development of the Group II manuscripts, however, challenges the assumption that Donne himself *ever* collected his verse.[41] Sullivan concludes (and I agree) that "Donne's patrons and poetical coterie, rather than Donne himself, may lie behind the major manuscript collections of his poems";[42] and, of course, once beyond the coterie, the transformation and compilation of the poems were even farther away from authorial control. This is especially evident in the case of the Group III manuscripts, of the large number of manuscripts loosely connected with them, and of the miscellaneous collections in which Donne's verse is found. It is understandable that Grierson, Gardner, and Milgate would want to see the hand of the author, wherever possible, in the establishment of texts and in the assembling of various generic groups into large collections of verse, but it has become more and more apparent that the authorially sanctioned texts and collections are not going to be found. As far as the poetry is concerned, with the exception of an authorial holograph of one verse epistle, we have no documentary remains of Donne's Donne.

What we do have is a massive amount of documentary evidence of the manuscript transmission of Donne's poems through the first two-thirds of the seventeenth century, both before and after the production of printed collections of his work. These manuscripts constitute separate collections of Donne's poems; Donne collections intermixed with, sometimes confused with, or supplemented by the verse of other poets; poetry anthologies in which a large block or blocks of Donne's poems are included or in which Donne's poems are scattered; and miscellanies in which Donne's poems are found along with the work of other poets as well as with such prose texts as medical recipes, sermon notes, and personal diaries. The Group I manuscript BL MS Harl. 4064, for example, includes a large business diary and models of legal and financial documents as well as ninety-five numbered poems, forty-seven of them by Donne.

The manuscripts containing Donne's poems were associated with a variety of social environments, but especially with (1) aristocratic households; (2) the universities; and (3) the Inns of Court (and City). Although the first of these deserves much attention—Donne collec-

---

[41] Sullivan, *Dalhousie Manuscripts*, p. 10 (see Chap. 1, n. 41).
[42] Ibid., p. vii.

tions were assembled for or connected with the earls of Westmoreland, Northumberland, Bedford, Newcastle, Bridgewater, Norwich, Denbigh, Essex, and Dalhousie,[43] I am more interested in the vicissitudes of Donne's texts in the universities and the Inns of Court, where his poems were absorbed into particular social environments through the activities of scribes and compilers within them, for these manuscripts reveal more clearly their social-historical determinants.

In various interesting ways, Donne's texts were "corrupted" in the process of their manuscript transmission—not only by small-scale verbal changes that appeared in due course but also in the more deliberate efforts to rewrite his texts. There were three kinds of changes: (1) the titling, retitling, and discursive ascription of particular poems, (2) the excerpting of parts of whole poems to create new pieces, and (3) the wholesale revision of particular texts or the plagiaristic imitation of them.

Especially since so many of Donne's poems probably originally lacked titles and compilers of poetry anthologies always felt free to title or describe particular items according to their personal whim, there are many examples of the first practice. Take, for example, Donne's verse epistle to Sir Henry Wotton ("Here's no more newes, then virtue"), a poem written in 1598 while the addressee was away from court after Queen Elizabeth had boxed the ears of his patron, the earl of Essex. This piece appears in the miscellany compiled by Richard Roberts with the following elaborate ascription that not only identifies the author but also sketches some of his biography: "By Mr JOHN DUN once secretary to the lord Keeper Egerton, disgraced by him for marrying with his wives neece: since proceeded doctor of Divinitie one of the kings chaplens: and now the paste Moneth of Aprill 1624 Deane of Powles" (Bod. MS Don. c.54, fol. 9r). These comments, in effect, locate the political gossiping and attitudinizing of the poem itself in a brief career sketch that takes Donne from the status of a young political outsider to that of a mature, successful churchman in royal favor. It replaces the immediate sociopolitical context of the verse letter with that of the poet's extended public life.

[43] See Alan MacColl, "The Circulation of Donne's Poems in Manuscript," in *John Donne: Essays in Celebration,* ed. A. J. Smith (London: Methuen, 1972), pp. 28–46; Beal, 1.1.244–61; and Sullivan, *Dalhousie Manuscripts,* pp. 4–7. Peter Beal notes the existence of a miscellany compiled by Francis Russell, fourth earl of Bedford (1593–1641) with "extracts from some 18 poems by Donne, headed 'Dunse verses' (ff. 50–4v)" ("More Donne Manuscripts," *John Donne Journal* 6 [1987]: 213).

In the same manuscript Donne's elegy "The Bracelet" is transcribed without an ascription and with the title: "A gent[leman] having lost a bracelet of a gent[l]ew[oman] being enjoyned by hir to cause an other to be made of vi angells writes as followeth" (fol. 24v)—a thematic title that generalizes the action of the poem to any love relationship. By contrast, Rosenbach MS 239/22, from the fourth and fifth decade of the seventeenth-century, pointedly associates the poem with Donne by (comically) titling it "To a Lady whose Chaine was lost by D.D.D.P. [Doctor Donne, Dean of St. Paul's]" (fol. 44r).

As the literary institution evolved in the early modern era and practices of collecting and anthologizing verse developed in both manuscript and print culture, the excerpting of parts of authors' works became more common and Donne's verse was subjected to this treatment. For example, in the first part of the Haslewood-Kingsborough Manuscript, which contains many Donne poems within a large anthology, one of the scribes used part of Donne's lyric "The Paradox" as a two-column poetic coda to a run of eight poems and answer poems attributed to William Herbert, earl of Pembroke, and Sir Benjamin Rudyerd:

No lover sayeth I love     he thinks that els none can
nor anny other     nor will agree
can Judg a perfect lover     that anny loves butt hee
(Hunt. MS HM 198, pt. 1, p. 147)

Since the Rudyerd poem that precedes this ends with a line that recalls Donne's original "Each lover thinks none ever lov'd but he," it was apparently deemed appropriate to cite the original that Rudyerd had imitated.

In the second part of the Haslewood-Kingsborough Manuscript, which also contains many identified Donne poems, there is an abridged version of Donne's "Song: sweetest love I doe not goe" that not only includes some obvious textual corruptions but also reproduces the poem in a form that alters the lineation of the original:

Sweetest love I doe not goe for wearines of thee
nor in hope the world can shew a fitter love for me
but since that wee must dy at last tis best
to use our selves in Jest thus by fained deathes to dy

> Yesterday the sunne went hence & yet is here to day
> he hath noe desire nor sence nor halfe soe short a way
> Then feare not me
> Since I doe make speedier Jorneys & doe take
> more wings & spurres then he
> Oh how feeble is manes powre that if good fortune fall
> Cannot add another hower nor a lost hower recall
> but comme badd chance
> And wee add to it our strength & teach it art at length
> It self over us to advance
> (Hunt. MS HM 198, pt.2, fol. 46r)

It is not unusual to find versions of songs that comprise only portions of the originals, so this case is not an atypical one. The unusual lineation, moreover, may have been the result of transcribing from memory rather than of copying from a written original.

The Lingard-Guthrie family manuscript miscellany contains a shortened, eighteen-line version of Donne's "Love's Diet" (Bod. MS Eng. Poet. c.53, fol. 9v). Bod. MS Eng. Poet. c.50, fol. 32v, has the first stanza only of this same poem, with an unusual alternate reading for the last word of the first line: "To what a combersome unrulines" (instead of "unwieldiness"). Rosenbach MS 1083/16 not only records lines 53–62 of the elegy "The Perfume" as a separate poem titled "One proving false" (pp. 303–4), but also lines 35–40 of "Farewell to Love" as a separate poem titled "Beauty" (p. 303). Compilers felt free to transcribe whatever parts of poems suited their fancies.

The most radical form of altering poetic texts was wholesale rewriting. For Donne, the case of "A Valediction: forbidding mourning" is particularly instructive. This lyric was rewritten by one "Simon Butteris" (or "Butterix"). It is found in a large mid-seventeenth-century poetry anthology with the label "Song the 21[st]" in a section of numbered songs:

> As dying saintes who sweetly pass away
> & whisper to their faynting soules to goe
> & some of theire circumstant frinds do say
> the breath now goes, others replye with noe
> So let us parte, that our disjoyned love
> no teares floods rayse /2/ nor loud sighs tempest move

Dull sublunary lovers sensuall love
whose soule is fed by th'eye cannot admitt
the least of absence, cause it Doth remove
those objects which at first Ingendred it
but wee by Constant love soe much refinde,
remayne assured of /2/ Interchayned mynes


Our two soules therfore, which by Love are one
Though I be gone from the, Indure not yet
A reall breach, but an expansion
Like finest gould to ayerye thynneys bett
This forced absence may Constrayne a two
Disdayne perhaps /2/ but noe disjunction shew


If it [that] our soules bee two they are two soe
as stiffe twin Compasses of brasse are two
Thy soule the fixt foote is, which makes me show
to stirr or move, but Doth if th'other dooe
thoughe it stand fast, when th'other farr Doth come
it Leanes and growes /2/ erect as it Comes home


So must you doe with me, poor me who must
Like to the other foot Obliquely runn
thy Constancye Dothe make my Circle Just
thy firmness makes me end wheare I begunne
Be Loyall in thy Actions, as for mee
my hart is wax, /2/ steele my Integritye
finis S Butterris
(Bod. MS Ash. 38, p. 121)

This is more than simply a "version" of Donne's famous "Valediction," as Margaret Crum has called it in her first-line index of Bodleian manuscripts (p. 74); it is a major reworking—one done with the creative freedom that collectors and imitators in the system of manuscript transmission felt free to exercise. Butteris converted Donne's nine tetrameter quatrains into five pentameter six-line stanzas, each ending in a rhymed couplet after the first four lines replicated the alternating rhymes of the "original." The conversion of tetrameter to pentameter lines necessitated the addition of words or syllables to some lines.[44] It also allowed for the compression of two-line units of the original to single lines, as is the case in the couplet at the end of Butteris's fourth stanza, which condenses one of Donne's quatrains. In fact, all the couplets in the new poem forced significant changes. The first, for the sake of rhyme and closure, revises the first line of Donne's second stanza and leads to the omission of six lines of the original. The second stanza's couplet picks up on Donne's first cross-rhyme and omits the second and fourth lines of the fifth stanza of Donne's poem. The couplet at the end of stanza four compresses four of Donne's lines to two, retaining the second cross-rhyme. The couplets of the third and fifth stanzas of Butteris's poem are his own invention.

This kind of revision of Donne's "A Valediction: forbidding mourning" is similar to the rewritings of Shakespeare sonnets or other famous lyrics as songs by seventeenth-century composers.[45] Revision of the poem for singing might explain the omission of the intellectually difficult third stanza of Donne's poem and the use of such simple adjectives and adverbs as "sweetly," "faynting," "loud," "sensuall," "Constant," and "finest." Songwriters felt free to appropriate and change the texts they wanted to adapt, and Butteris was no exception.

Butteris's adaptation of Donne's poem is found in Nicholas Burghe's poetry anthology, a large folio compiled in the mid-seventeenth century. It is interesting that the first two poems in this anthology were originally ascribed to Donne: "Doctor Donns valediction to the worlde" ("Farewell yea guilded follies, pleasing troubles," p. 1), which was probably written by either Sir Henry Wotton or Sir Kenelm Digby, and "On mans Moralitie by Sir Francis Bacon" ("The worlds a A buble and the Lyfe of man," p. 2). The first authenticatable Donne poem in this collection is "A Hymne to God the Father" (p. 14)—identified here by the simple title "To Christ." Burghe also transcribed Donne's poem "The Curse" under the heading "A Cominction wrighten by D. Donne" (pp. 49–50), following it with an

---

[44] Thus, "sweetly" (1), "faynting" (2), "circumstant" for "sad" in line 3, "sensuall" (7), "Constant" (11), "remayne" (12), "by Love" (13), "from the" (14), "reall" (15), "finest" (16), "of brasse" (20), "is, which" (21), "stirr or move" (22), "poor me" (25), "to the" (26), "Constancye Dothe make" (27) for "firmnes makes."

[45] See Mary Hobbs, "Shakespeare's Sonnet II—'A Sugred Sonnet'?" *Notes and Queries* 26 (April 1979): 112–13. In *Verse Miscellany Manuscripts*, pp. 50–61 and passim, Hobbs discusses the relationship of poetical anthologies to manuscript and printed songbooks (see Chap. 1, n. 60).

anonymous poem on the same theme possibly written by himself ("He that would my mistress knowe," p. 49) and "The answer by him that was suspected," a lyric by William Browne of Tavistock. Page 61 of the manuscript has a poem labeled "Doctor Donn verses" ("I know as well as you, she'is not faire")—a piece published in the 1658 edition of the popular anthology, *Wits Recreations* (p. 109)[46] in a version that lacks several of the lines found in Burghe's text. This is followed, two poems later, by a fourteen-line love poem ascribed to Donne ("When I doe love, my Mistris must be faire," p. 62), transcribed as though its seven rhymed couplets constituted a sonnet. The next piece is Donne's famous Elegy 19, "To his Mistris Going to Bed," a very popular poem in seventeenth-century manuscript anthologies, especially those compiled at Oxford or Cambridge—it is the first poem in the miscellany compiled by Nathaniel Highmore while at Oxford (BL MS Sloane 542). Thus, apart from the Butteris song version of "A Valediction: forbidding mourning" and three poems undoubtedly by Donne ("A Hymne to God the Father," "The Curse," and "Elegy 19"), Burghe's anthology contains three poems *misattributed* to Donne. In the context of a personal anthology of several hundred poems, which contains, incidentally, many poems composed by the compiler himself, Donne's texts become part of a mid-century literary and political environment dominated by such Cavalier and Royalist authors as Carew, Randolph, King, Herrick, and Corbett: in effect his idiom is dissolved into theirs.

The final permutation of "A Valediction: forbidding mourning" I would like to consider is what might be regarded as a plagiaristic imitation of the poem in large poetical anthology associated with Christ Church, Oxford. In this volume, there is a poem that was obviously inspired by the compass image of Donne's lyric, prefaced by a drawing of a seventeenth-century compass meant to illustrate the poem's central metaphor (see figure 1):

> The man and wife that kinde and loving are
> <The> I fitly may to compasses compare,
> The compasses are two conjoynd at the head,
> So man and wife in Christ are coup<i>led,
> One part steps forth & doth the circle trace

---

[46] See Crum, p. 396; Ringler (in his Huntington notes) records a twenty-line version of this in Trinity Col. Dublin MS 877, fol. 174v.

44

The Clergy ~ Lawyers they are sick
~~[crossed out]~~ are il at ease
But poor men they are drunk
Yet al is one disease.

The man and wife that kinde and louing are
~~The~~ fitly may to compasses compare
The compasses are two conioynd at the head,
So man and wife in Christ are coupiled,
One pt steps forth & doth y circle trace,
The other firmly keeps y center'd place,
So while the man doth trauel from to gain
The wife at home doth to it yet maintaine,
They being in pt disioynd by circle-wide,
Do yet in pt united stil abide,
And when y circle'd drawne, & figure done
They are conioynd againe at twere emon
So though far busied the man and wife do
They are together stil in loue and hart
And when y man returneth to his place
They both at one doe louingly embrace
Nothing but force can separate those twain

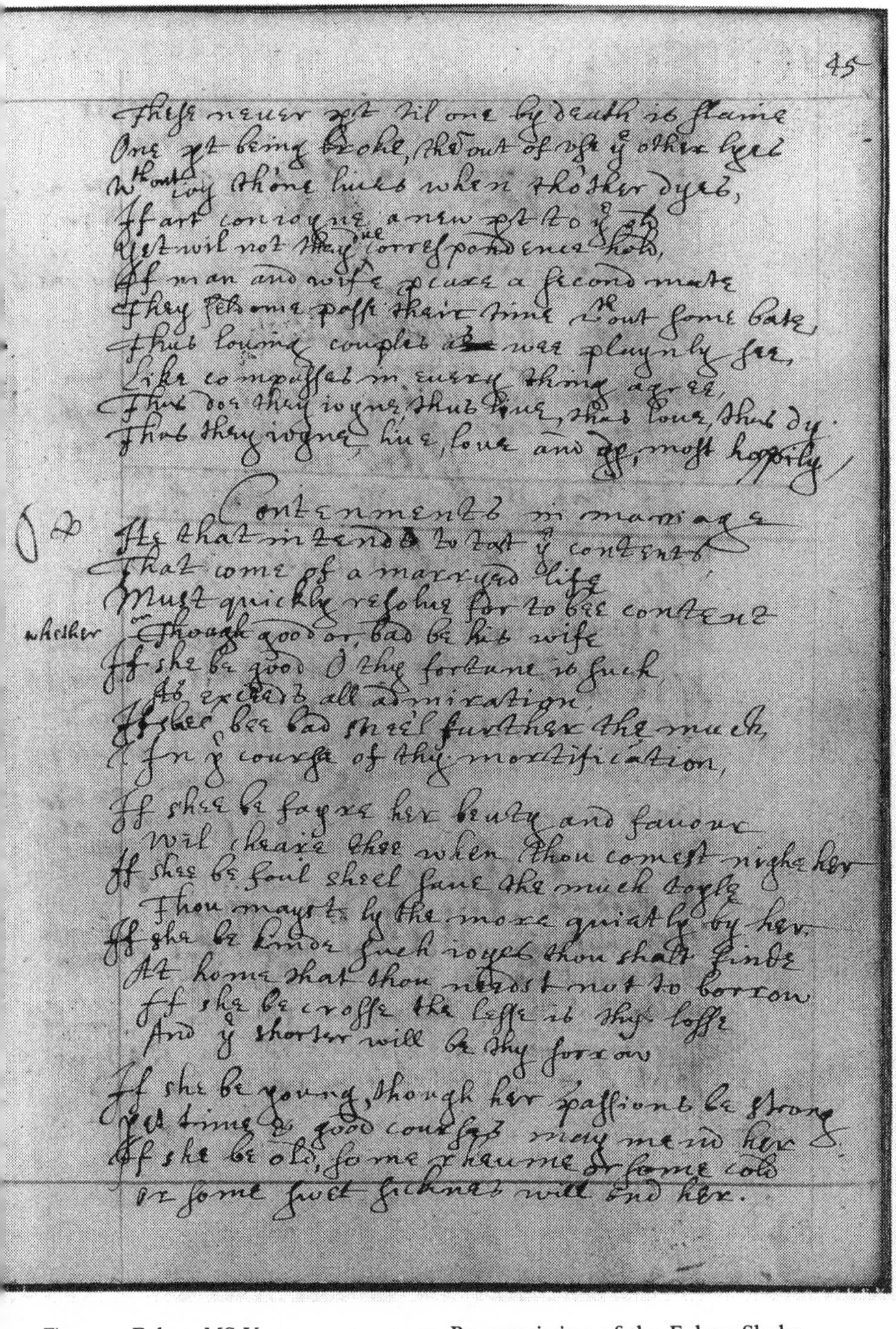

These neuer yet til one by death is slaine
One yt being broke, the out of vse is other lyel
Wthout ioy thone liues when thother dyes,
If art contioyne a new ptt to y oth
Yet wil not they correspondences hold,
If man and wife procure a second mate
They selome passe their time wout some bate,
Thus louing couples as wee playnly see,
Like compassed in euery thing agree,
Thus doe they ioyne thus liue, thus loue, thus dy.
That they ioyne liue, loue and dy, most happily

### Contenmentb in marriage

He that intends to tast y contents
That come of a married life
Must quickly resolue for to bee content
whether Though good or, bad be his wife
If she be good o thy fortune is such,
As exceeds all admiration
If shee bee bad sheel further thee much,
In y course of thy mortification,
If shee be fayre her beuty and fauour
Wil cheare thee when thou comest nighe her
If shee be foul sheel saue thee much toyle
Thou mayst by the more quiatly by her.
If she be kinde such ioyes thou shalt finde
At home that thou needst not to borrow
If she be crosse the lesse is thy losse
And y shorter will be thy sorrow

If she be young, though her passions be strong
Yet time & good counsel may me... her
If she be old, some rheume or some cold
Or some such sicknes will end her.

*Figure 1.* Folger MS V.a.345, pp. 44–45. By permission of the Folger Shakespeare Library.

> The other firmly keep the centers place,
> So while the man doth travel fr^o^<om> his gaine,
> The wife at home doth what is got maintaine.
> They being in part dis[j]oynd <with> by circles wide,
> Do yet in part united stil abide,
> And when the circles drawne, & figure done
> They are conjoynd againe as twere in one
> So though for busines the man and wife do part
> They are together stil in love and hart
> And when the man returneth to his place
> They both as one doe lovingly embrace
> Nothing, but force can separate those twaine
> These never part til one by death is slaine
> One part being broke, then out of use the other lyes
> Without joy th'one lives when th'other dyes,
> If art conjoyne a new part to the old
> Yet wil not they ^due^ correspondence hold,
> If man and wife procure a second mate
> They seldome passe their time without some bate,
> Thus loving couples a^s^<> wee playnly see,
> Like compasses in every thing agree,
> Thus doe they joyne, thus live, thus love, thus dy.
> Thus they joyne, live, love and dy, most happily/
> (Folger MS V.a.345, pp. 44–45)

Although, as John Freccero long ago pointed out,[47] Donne did not himself invent the compass conceit as a metaphor for the relationship of a married couple, in the particular literary tradition in which this derivative poem is found, this poem clearly develops out of Donne's valediction. In a system of literary transmission full of answer poetry, parodies, and other forms of poetic competition, this piece presents itself as an amateur's response to a famous lyric.

More poems are misattributed to Donne than to any other English Renaissance poet. Grierson prints a large number of these in appendices to his edition, but many more are found in seventeenth-century manuscripts. Rosenbach MS 243/7, for example, has five poems misattributed to Donne: "Deepe are the woundes which strike a vertuous name," "Absence, heare thou my protestation" (by John Hos-

---

[47] John Freccero, "Donne's 'Valediction: Forbidding Mourning,' " *ELH* 30 (1963): 335–76.

kins), "Come you swarmes of thoughts & bringe" (by John Grange), "What is our life? a play of passion" (by Ralegh), and "Dearest Mira, since thou hast." Bod. MS Eng. Poe. e.97 has a poem misattributed to Donne: "On the word Jape in Chaucer" ("My Mistress could not be content," pp. 103–4). Folger MS V.a.345 ascribes William Browne's poem "Her for a mistress faine would I injoy" (pp. 82–83) to Donne.

The paradoxical effect of the extended transmission of Donne's poetry in manuscript through the seventeenth century is that it both reinforced his importance as an eminent "author" and immersed his work, often without ascription, in a large body of poetic writing whose textual instability and vulnerability to appropriation as literary property worked against the isolation of individual authorship and the fixing of authorized texts (two marks of the modern institution of literature). On the one hand, Donne's name centripetally attracted the works of many other authors whose poems were ascribed to him; and on the other, Donne's own poems continued to be "corrupted" by virtue of their immersion in the social history of manuscript transmission. The irony is that although modern textual scholars have assumed they were doing the appropriate thing in trying to recover Donnean texts purged of their alleged corruptions, it is the mutable environment of manuscript transmission that Donne himself chose for his writing, releasing his poems into a world in which he had to have known they would have their own independent histories.

### Answer Poetry

Given the socially dialogic context of the manuscript miscellanies and poetry anthologies of the sixteenth and seventeenth centuries, it is no surprise to discover in such an environment various forms of verse exchange, including large numbers of answer poems, not only by recognized poets but also by others. Broadly defining "answer" poetry, E. F. Hart distinguishes four different sorts of verse in this category: "the answer proper, in which the theme of arguments of a poem are criticized as a whole, or (more usually) refuted one by one," "imitations," "extension poems [that] develop or amplify some idea, image, or characteristic feature of rhythm or style of the original poem," and "mock-songs."[48] Such verse foregrounds the so-

---

[48] E. F. Hart, "The Answer-Poem of the Early Seventeenth Century," *RES*, n.s., 7 (1956):

cial and occasional character of poetic composition, marking poetic discourse less as the product of isolated artistic geniuses than as continuous with other forms of communication.

Sometimes answer poems indicate the processes of transmission of verse that led up to the collection of groups of poems in miscellanies and poetry anthologies. At the simplest level, this is reflected in those pieces which look like direct exchanges between individuals who used verse either as a medium of epistolary communication or as part of a competitive social game. BL MS Add. 15227, for example, preserves a witty exchange between two friends, Thomas Roberts and William Bond, concerning an unreturned borrowed cloak. Bond answered Roberts's prose letter demanding the cloak back with a poem in which every line ends with the word "cloak" (fol. 19r–v). On a higher intellectual and aesthetic level are epistolary exchanges between such poets as John Donne and Sir Henry Wotton or the earl of Pembroke and Sir Benjamin Rudyerd. Donne's verse letter to Sir Henry Wotton beginning "Sir, more then kisses, letters mingle Soules" is answered by Wotton's own epistle, "Tis not a coate of gray or Shepheardes life," both poems apparently, in Wesley Milgate's words, "part of a literary debate among some of the wits associated with [the earl of] Essex."[49] The most elaborate set of exchange verse is that associated with Pembroke and Rudyerd, who were both friends and political allies. Unfortunately, John Donne Jr.'s printed edition of their work is actually an anthology of verse by a number of authors, despite its misleading title, *Poems Written by the Right Honorable William Earl of Pembroke, Lord Steward of his Majesties Houshold. Whereof Many of which are answered by way of Repartee, by Sr Benjamin Ruddier, Knight. With several Distinct Poems, Written by them Occasionally, and Apart.*[50] This collection does, however, contain a number of poems that were competitively

---

19–29. Panofsky relates sixteenth-century answer poetry, including verse of this sort written by Googe, Turbervile, and Howell to "the school exercise called *thesis*, the writing on a given issue either favoring or denying a given position. Here the school's ideals of using poetic composition as a means of social exchange carried over into the writerly recreations of the young men of a literary circle" ("English Mid-Tudor Short Poetry," p. 127 [see Chap. 1, n. 56]).

[49] Donne, *Satires, Epigrams, and Verse Letters*, ed. Milgate, p. 225; Milgate refers to Herbert Grierson's article on the topic, "Bacon's Poem, 'The World': Its Date and Relation to Certain Other Poems," *MLR* 6 (1911): 145–56. See also Ted-Larry Pebworth and Claude J. Summers, " 'Thus Friends Absent Speake': The Exchange Verse Letters Between John Donne and Henry Wotton," *MP* 81 (1984): 361–77.

[50] See the discussion of this collection in Chapter 4.

composed by these writers, including some that appear repeatedly in the seventeenth-century manuscript collections—most notably those two poems that were published in the 1635–69 editions of John Donne's poetry, Pembroke's "If her disdain least change in you can move" and Rudyerd's answer poem, "'Tis Love breeds Love in me, and cold disdain."[51] These very lyrics begin a run of eight Pembroke and Rudyerd poems in the Haslewood-Kingsborough Manuscript (Hunt. MS HM 198, pt. 1, pp. 138–47).[52]

Various forms of competitive versifying are preserved in the manuscript collections—for example, poems on the same topic or theme. There is an interesting poem and answer set in the Arundel Harington Manuscript concerning the situation of Mary, Queen of Scots, in the early 1570s, the first poem by Sir Henry Goodyer pleading for mercy for her and the second, by the more radical Protestant Thomas Norton arguing for harsher treatment (see Hughey, 1:179–82 and 2: 193–201). Steven May argues that early in his career Sir Walter Ralegh wrote his "Sweet are the thoughts" as a variation on some lines by his friend George Whetstone and later another of his lyrics, "Farewell false love, thow oracle of lyes," was answered by a poem composed by his court rival Sir Thomas Heneage, "Most welcome love, thow mortall foe to lies."[53] As noted earlier, Lady Mary Cheke wrote an answer poem to Sir John Harington's epigram "Thear was, not serten when, a certayne preacher" ("That no man yet could in the bible finde"), and Queen Elizabeth composed an answer poem to Ralegh's "Fortune hath taken thee away, my Love" ("Ah silly pugg, wert thou so sore afrayd?).[54]

Sidney and the other poets in his circle, particularly Greville and Spenser, engaged in poetic competition; for that matter, members of

---

[51] The 1660 volume surprisingly conflates these two lyrics, pp. 3–4; Crum, p. 424, notes that, among the Bodleian manuscripts in which these poems appear, are some that attribute them to Sir Henry Wotton and John Donne (Rawl. Poet. 117, fol. 199v, and 147, p. 81). Rosenbach MS 240/2, pp. 13–17, also ascribes these poems to Donne and Wotton as well as the poems "Yee heavenly powers why did you bring to light" and "Blest bee yee heavenly powers that brought in sight" (pp. 17–19): these last two anonymous lyrics are found by Crum, pp. 122–23, 655, in different forms in several Bodleian manuscripts, the former poem more common than the latter. In only one manuscript is there an ascription: Rawl. Poet. 214, fol. 81 rev., attributes "Oh heavenly powers, why did you bring to light," a poem also found in BL MS Sloane 1446, fol. 29v, to "Mr Guilford."

[52] This group of Pembroke and Rudyerd poems is the largest one I have found in manuscript collections.

[53] Steven W. May, "Companion Poems in the Ralegh Canon," *ELR* 13 (1983): 260–73.

[54] See May, *Elizabethan Courtier Poets*, pp. 246, 319 (cited in full at Chap. 1, n. 19).

the extended social circle surrounding the countess of Pembroke and the Sidney family seem to have been attracted to answer poetry.[55] *Certain Sonnets* 16 answers Dyer's "Prometheus when first from heaven hie," and Spenser's "More than most fair, full of the living fire" (*Amoretti* 8) appears to have also been part of the friendly poetic competition.[56] There is also an obvious connection between Greville's *Caelica* 74 and 75 and the eighth song of Sidney's *Astrophil and Stella*.[57]

Leweston Fitzjames's commonplace book (Bod. MS Add. B.97) contains three related anonymous sonnets (unique among the Bodleian manuscripts) that were probably originally the product of a coterie game: "Read in my face the fortunes of my youth", "Another dependinge on this" ("Never more deuly on his Cynthias grace"), and "An other on this" ("The Rocke wher youth made shipwrack of my lyfe," fols. 19v–20r). Corbett's, Strode's, and Terrant's poems on the windows of the Fairford Church are the product of competitive versifying within an academic social circle at Oxford.[58] The University of Texas "Herrick" manuscript contains two poems written on a set theme or the specific "question" recorded after the first of them, "The Question is, whether affection to his mistris, or shee hirself, gives man most delight": "for affection" ("Betwixt two jewels, such as she") and "for hir person" ("Twixt gemmes so pretious as the Lass").[59]

Some poetic exchanges, however, were originally quite hostile—for example, the poem and answer set attributed to the earl of Oxford

---

[55] Lamb, "Three Unpublished Holograph Poems," pp. 305–6 (see Chap. 1, n. 87), points out in her discussion of the Bright Manuscript that much answer poetry was written in the Sidney circle. She also notes that "the large number of 'Aunsweres' written to or by friends in *Howell His Devises* (1581), a volume of poems written by a family retainer at Wilton, shows the prevalence of writing verses as replies on the Countess of Pembroke's estate. Perhaps the practice was common among the Sidneys in general."

[56] See *Poems of Sidney*, ed. Ringler, pp. 396–97 (cited in full at Chap. 1, n. 207), for a discussion of Sidney's participation in the composition of answer poetry. On these poems, see Ringler's discussion on pp. 144–45. Black thinks all three poems were written at Leicester House in 1579–80 ("Studies," 1:35 [see Chap. 1, n. 39]). Sidney seems to have turned the matter of Dyer's poem, which suggests the hyperbolic praise of Elizabeth as an overwhelmingly beloved "Angell from above" into the specific situation of Sidney's own disgrace with the queen for speaking out on the Alençon match, a political context that might account for the popularity of this poem and answer set with the miscellany compilers of the time.

[57] See *Poems and Dramas of Greville*, ed. Bullough, 1:267–68 (cited in full at Chap. 1, n. 68), and *Poems of Sidney*, ed. Ringler, p. 486.

[58] See the discussion of these in Chapter 2.

[59] Farmer, *Seventeenth-Century Manuscript*, pp. 97–103 (see Chap. 1, n. 21).

and Sir Philip Sidney preserved in the Farmer-Chetham manuscript (along with two additional answer-poems)

By the Earle of Oxforde.

Were I a kinge I coulde commaunde content,
　　Were I obscure hidden shoulde be my cares,
or were I deade no cares shoulde me torment,
nor hopes, nor hates, nor loves nor greifes nor feares:
　　A doubtfull choice of these three which to crave,
　　a Kingdom or a Cottage or a Grave.

Answered thus by Sir P.S.

Wert thou a Kinge, yet not commaunde content
　　Seth Empire none thy minde could yet suffice:
Wert thou obscure, still cares woulde thee torment,
but wert thou deade, all care & sorrowe dies:
　　An easy choice of these three which to crave
　　No kingdome, nor a Cottage but a grave.[60]

Sidney's answer takes direct aim at the egotistical pretensions of the socially superior peer. Class antagonism surfaces, as it did in their famous Tennis Court quarrel.[61] The class issue also figures in Dyer's popular lyric "The lowest trees have tops" and in the several poetic answers to it.[62]

It should come as no surprise that many of the situations dramatized in poem and answer sets have to do with heterosexual love. The poems and answers that survive either represent actual verse exchanges between lovers or, more typically, fictionalized exchanges, although not always between fictional lovers. In the Blage Manuscript, which contains poems from the Wyatt circle, there is a poem and answer combination that characteristically portrays male importunity

---

[60] Grosart, *Dr. Farmer Chetham MS*, pp. 93–94 (see Chap. 1, n. 125). Steven May includes the first piece in his edition of Oxford and Essex and discusses it in "The Authorship of 'My Mind to Me a Kingdom Is,'" *RES*, n.s., 26 (1975): 388–89.

[61] On this political and social confrontation, see Katherine Duncan-Jones, *Sir Philip Sidney, Courtier Poet* (New Haven: Yale University Press, 1991), pp. 23, 163–67.

[62] See *Liber Lilliati*, ed. Doughtie, pp. 191–94. In *Elizabethan Courtier Poets*, pp. 307–9, May examines the textual vicissitudes of Dyer's poem. See also Hughey, 2:306–9; Rollins, *Poetical Rhapsody*, 2:164–69; and Doughtie, *Lyrics from English Airs*, pp. 520–21.

and female resistance—"Madame, I you requyre / No longer tyme detrack" and "Your Folyshe fayned hast / Full small effecte shall tak."[63] The Arundel Harington Manuscript has a wife's answer poem to a piece written by Sir John Harington of Stepney, "Husband, yf you will be my deare" (see Hughey, 1:95–96 and notes, 2:30–33).

Ann Cornwallis's short anthology (Folger MS V.a.89) contains mainly love poetry, including a dialogue poem associated with the notorious love affair between the earl of Oxford and Anne Vavasour, "Sittinge alone upon my thought in melancholye moode" and " 'O heavens,' quothe she, 'who was the first that bred in me this fevere?' "[64] In the Arundel Harington Manuscript, "Sitting alone" is noted as "The best verse that ever th'autor made" (Hughey, 1:215). The Cornwallis Manuscript ascribes the answer poem to Anne Vavasour: it is possible, despite the piece's flattering portrayal of the earl, that she actually did write it.[65] Even if both pieces were composed by the earl himself, the dialogic character of the set points to the connection between lyric verse and social intercourse in both subject matter and literary transmission. The poem and answer set attributed to Sir Walter Ralegh and Queen Elizabeth (Ralegh's "Fortune hath taken away my love" and the queen's reply, "Ah silly pugge wert thou so sore afraid")[66] reverses the male-female power relationship of the Oxford-Vavasour exchange. The queen exercises the full measure of her control in the politically coded game of amorous courtship, and it is Ralegh who works under severe restraints. On a somewhat lower social level, the answer-poem exchange attributed to Sir George Radney and the countess of Hertford also highlights the questions of status and class (here in relation to the clash between free choice in love and the exigencies of familial marriage arrangements). Radney's suicide-note poem sometimes stands alone in the manuscript collections, although at least one anthology, BL MS Sloane 1446, prefaces it with a love poem of his and the countess of Hertford's reply: "Sr

---

[63] Muir, *Wyatt and His Circle*, pp. 41–42 (see Chap. 1, n. 59). See also the answer poem spoken by a woman to her lover, "Evyn when you lust ye may refrayne" (pp. 23–24). Since these poems appear only in the Blage Manuscript, their authorship is quite doubtful.

[64] They are both reproduced in May, *Poems of Oxford and Essex* in the category of "Poems Possibly By Oxford," p. 38 (see Chap. 1, n. 19). See May's notes on pp. 79–81.

[65] Black believes this ascription should be taken seriously ("Studies," 1:197).

[66] See Black, "Lost Poem," p. 535 (cited in full at Chap. 1, n. 27), and May, *Elizabethan Courtier Poets*, pp. 317–21.

George Radney to the Countess of Hertford" ("From one that languisheth in discontent"), "The Countesse Answere" ("Divided in your sorrowes, I have strove"), and "Sr George Radney beefore hee killd himselfe" ("What shall I doe that am undone?" fols.30r–34v).[67] A lyric beginning "Oh love whose powre & might nor ever yet withstood," usually attributed to Master Polden of New College, Oxford, is accompanied in manuscripts by an answer poem by "Lady Jacob" ("Yor letter I receivd bedeckt with flourishinge quarters" (BL MS Add 25303, fols. 70v–71r).[68] The courtship poems of Herbert Aston and Katherine Thimelby preserved in Hunt. MS HM 904 are a much happier example of the poem and answer.[69] They married.

---

[67] The first poem also appears in Bod. MSS Ash. 38, p. 32, and 781, p. 581, and Rawl. Poet. 160, fol. 117v, and the third in Bod. MSS CCC 328, fol. 90r, and Rawl. Poet. 172, fol. 11v (Crum, p. 259). Radney committed suicide after the woman he loved married the earl of Hertford. Crum refers to *Complete Peerage*, 6:506. One manuscript dates the last poem December 1600. Radney's verse suicide note, as found in Sloane 1446, is as follows:

> Sir George Radney beefore hee killd
> himselfe
> What Shall I doe that am undone?
> where shall I flie my selfe to shunne
> Ah mee my selfe my selfe must kill
> And yett I die against my will
> In Starry letters I behold
> my death in the heavens inroll'd
> there finde I wrytt in Skyes above
> that I (poore I) must die for love
> T'was not my love deserved to die
> O no it was unworthie I.
> I for her love should not have dy'de
> but that I had no worth beside.
> Ah mee that love such woe procures
> for without her no love endures
> I for her vertues, her <send> serve
> doth such a love a death deserve.
> (Fol. 34v)

[68] Crum, p. 1188, cites also Bod. MSS Rawl. Poet. 26, fol. 5r, and Jones 58, fol. 65v. The Polden poem appears in many manuscripts as well as in a printed version in *Wit and Drollery* (1656), p. 32 (Crum, p. 664). See this poem and answer in Sanderson, "An Edition," pp. 220–36 (cited in full at Chap. 1, n. 121). The answer poem appears in *Le Prince d'Amour* (1660), and thus may have been part of the Inner Temple Revels (p. 235). Some manuscripts attribute the poem to "Master Lawson of St. Johns College" (Bod. MS Rawl. Poet. 26, fol. 5r) and to John Hoskins (BL MS Add. 25303, fol. 70v) (Crum, p. 664). Osborn prints the poem from BL MS Add. 25303 among the "Doubtful Verses" of Hoskins, noting also that the piece appears in BL MSS Add. 22601 and 24665 (*John Hoskyns*, p. 301 [see Chap. 1, n. 18]).

[69] La Belle, "Huntington Aston Manuscript," pp. 542–67 (see Chap. 1, n. 158).

More ordinary social intercourse between the sexes provided the frame for the following exchange preserved in a collection associated with Cambridge University, BL MS Add. 15227:

One of the Feminine kind, in a morning I lying
in bed sent me these two verses written on
a Trencher for my breakfast.

> Thy love that thou to one hast lent
> In labour lost thy time was spent.

To which perusing presently
replyed these ensuing Distichs.

> If time in love most men doe loose & spend
> I to my selfe my time & Love will lend.

> Aliud.
> If time in Love bee lost & spent
> My love's mine owne, which once was lent.

> Aliud
> I [ ] in vaine love, lovers their time doe I

> Aliud
> Love is a labour. Have I Labour loste
> Ile love my labour, though my love be crost.
> (Fol. 28r)

The jilted lover is portrayed as trying out several appropriately witty responses to the poetic brush-off by his mistress: the last of these is followed by the note, "These verses as an answere to the former, which I had com[posed] I sent backe to their Patronesse."

Although the answer poetry and verse exchanges preserved in manuscript collections were signs of the social embeddedness of verse, such works gradually took on a higher degree of literary self-consciousness within the manuscript system, partly in response to the strengthening of the institution of literature brought about by print culture. Poetic imitations and parodies, in particular, foregrounded the literary medium as much as its messages. This is not to say that practitioners of imitation and parody were merely engaged in formal exercises—for there were still obvious ideological, political, social, and (sometimes) personal issues at stake in such verse—but rather that as the status of the author was strengthened within the literary system and as mastery of literary modes, conventions, and language became more socially prestigious, imitations and parodies left the realm of the aesthetically ephemeral to take their place within the emerging literary canon. Of course, examples of literary imitation and parody go back to the ancients. Particularly in translating the work of others, poets demonstrated their awareness of the sphere of the literary into which they self-consciously entered: hence Chaucer, Wyatt, Gascoigne, Spenser, and others who translated and imitated foreign authors were not only following a literary tradition, but also extending it into new national territory.

Famous poems by respected poets stimulated answers, imitations, and parodies. Marlowe's poem "The Passionate Shepherd to his love" elicited not only Ralegh's famous "Nimphs Reply," and Donne's imitative "Baite," but also other responses over the half-century following its composition, including Herrick's "To Phillis to love, and live with him," the anonymous "Come live with me and be my deare," and Pembroke's (?) "Dear leave thy home and come with me."[70] Southwell turned Dyer's "He that his mirth hath lost" from a secular to a religious complaint, but Fulke Greville, James Murray, and King James himself also imitated the poem.[71] George Herbert converted Sir Edward Herbert's love lyric, "Soules joy, now I am gone," into a sacred poem in "A Parodie."

Ben Jonson's much-transcribed lyric "Still to be neat" lies behind an anonymous poem in BL MS Harl. 6917, "A motion to pleasure":

> Still to affect, still to admire
> yet never satisfy desire
> with touch of hand, or lyp, or that

---

[70] This poem is found in Hunt. MS HM 198, pt. 2, fols. 53v–54r, and is printed in the *Poems of Pembroke and Rudyerd* (1660), pp. 38–39. See Woods, " 'The Passionate Sheepheard' and 'The Nimphs Reply,' " pp. 25–33, and Hart, "Answer-Poem," pp. 24–25.

[71] On the imitations of Dyer's poem, see May, *Elizabethan Courtier Poets*, p. 292: in addition to Southwell's "Dyer's Phancy Turned to a Sinner's Complaint," May cites Greville's *Caelica* 83; James Murray's imitation, "Murrayis Dyer" (following his transcription of Dyer's poem in Camb. MS Kk 5.30, fol. 5r–v); and King James's "If mourning might amend."

> which pleaseth best, I know not what
> like Tantalus I pining dye
> taking Loves dainties at the eye:
>
> Nature made nothing but for use
> and fairest twere a grosse abuse
> to her best worke, if you it hold
> un-used, like misers ill gott gold,
> or keepe it in a virgin scorne
> like rich Roabes that are seldome worne.
>
> (Fol. 41r)

This persuasion-to-love only uses the well-known Jonson lyric for its opening and its style of aristocratic refinement. That poet's imposing presence as an author in both print and manuscript in the seventeenth century helps to explain the popularity of the epigram criticizing the publication of his plays as monumental "Workes." In BL MS Egerton 2421, fol. 29r, the often-copied poem mocking Jonson for publishing what was considered ephemeral in the prestigious folio format is followed by an answer poem written in Jonson's defense:

> On Ben: Johnsons booke in folio
>
> Methinkes in this a mystery then lurkes
> Why Johnsons playes are not cal'd Johnsons works.
>
> Reply
>
> A friend of his this for the authour sayes
> His playes are workes when thy best workes be playes.[72]

Thomas Randolph wrote "Come leave the loathed stage" as an answer to Jonson's "Ode on Himself."[73]

Donne's lyric "The Apparition" inspired the imitation or supplementary lyric found in both the O'Flaherty Manuscript (Harv. MS

---

[72] Crum, pp. 7, 564, cites two other Bodleian manuscripts of the original poem and one of the reply.

[73] See Bod. MS Firth e.4., pp. 30–35. See the version of the poem in *The Poems of Thomas Randolph*, ed. G. Thorn-Drury (London: Etchells & Macdonald, 1929), pp. 82–84. Hunt. MS HM 198, pt. 1, contains "Ben Johnsons Ode to himselfe," "Randolph's answer to Benn Johnsons Ode," and Carew's related answer-poem, "Tis true deare Benn: thy Just Chastizing hand" (pp. 114–17).

Eng. 966/5) and the Bridgewater Manuscript (Hunt. MS EL 6893), "Cruell since that thou doest not feare the curse" (see Grierson, 1: 446). In the former manuscript it is appropriately placed in the context of a collection that mixes Donne's poems with works by such members of his coterie as Sir John Roe, Ben Jonson, and Sir Edward Herbert. The poem is introduced by the comment "This hath relation to 'when by thy scorne O Murdresse &c' " (fol. 115r). In his article on the answer poem, Hart cites William Habington's "Against them who lay unchastity to the sex of Women" as a response to Donne's "Goe and catche a falling starre."[74]

Many of the poets well represented in the Oxford (especially the Christ Church) anthologies of the second quarter of the seventeenth century had their poems supplemented, answered, and imitated. Hart points out that William Strode's lyric "I saw faire Cloris walke alone" and Herrick's "Gather ye Rosebuds while ye may" were both imitated.[75] As noted previously, Henry Reynold's poem "A Blackmore Mayd wooing a faire Boy" ("Stay lovely Boy, why fly'st thou mee") and Henry King's reply, "The Boy's answere to the Blackmore" ("Black Mayd, complayne not that I fly"), were reproduced in a large number of manuscript collections.[76] Richard Corbett's poem "To the Ladyes of the New Dresse" ("Ladyes that weare black cypresse vailes"), a poem wittily teasing the women of a courtly social elite which was quite popular in manuscript collections,[77] elicited an answer poem (probably by John Grange) titled "Ladyes Answer" ("Black Cypresse vales are shrouds of night"), a piece to which Corbett himself responded with a "Replye to the Answere" ("Yff nought but love-charmes power have").[78]

Thomas Carew's lyric "Ask me no more whither do stray" was not only one of the most popular poems in both manuscript and print, but also editors, scribes, and writers other than the original author felt free to rearrange the order of the stanzas, to add new stanzas, and to answer the lyric with poems of their own. Furthermore, ac-

---

[74] Hart, "Answer-Poem," p. 20.
[75] Ibid., pp. 23–23, 25.
[76] See the discussion of these poems in Chapter 2.
[77] Beal, 2.1.179–81, lists thirty-seven manuscripts containing this poem.
[78] See the texts of these pieces in *Poems of Corbett*, ed. Bennett and Trevor-Roper, pp. 90–92 (cited in full at Chap. 1, n. 70); Beal, 2.1.197–99, lists thirty-five manuscripts of the first poem. Bennett and Trevor-Roper note that the piece appeared in *Wits Recreations* (1640), *Parnassus Biceps* (1656), and *Wit and Drollery* (1663) as well as in the 1648 posthumous edition of Corbett's poems, *Poetica Stromata* (*Poems of Corbett*, p. 159).

cording to Rhodes Dunlap, an early draft of the piece circulated in the manuscript system (see, for example, BL MS Add. 23229). In BL MS Add. 30982, Dunlap notes, the poem is accompanied by an answer poem, "I'le tell you true whereon doth light," and "A Moderating Answeare to both" ("Ile tell you of another sun").[79]

Competitive Cavalier verse, such as John Mennes's "Upon Sir John Sucklings hundred horse" ("I tell the Jack t'hast given the king")[80] and Suckling's answer, "I tell the foole who ere thow bee," are found together in some manuscripts—for example, in Hunt. MS HM 198, pt. 1, p. 160, where they are transcribed in parallel columns for ease of comparison.

The Haselwood-Kingsborough Manuscript (Hunt. MS HM 198, pt. 1) contains three poems in which a member of Gray's Inn objects to the satirization of lawyers in a play performed at Cambridge before the king, a Cambridge student answers the objections, and the Gray's Inn poet answers the academic writer: "To the Comedieans of Cambridg who in theyr Acts before the King, abused the lawyers with false imposed ignorance, in two rediculous persons Ignoramus the master and Dulman the Clarke, John A Stiles Student of the Coman Lawes wisheth A sounder judgment, and A more reverent oppinion of theyr betters from Greys Inne" ("Faith Gentlemen I doe not blame your witt"); "Dulman the Clearke to John of Stile of Greyes Inn sendeth greeting" ("Reverend John Stiles, for stile wee will not jarr"); "The Replication of John A Stile, unto the Comedians answere after whose rejoinder he will demurr in lawe for the insufficiency of the Plea" ("Wee are your betters in A better sense") (pp. 46–51).[81] Answer poetry, in these circumstances reinforced institutional or professional rivalry and social contacts.

Throughout the period in which manuscript collections were made, despite what Hart describes as the decline of true answer poem and its replacement by the "mock-song" favored by political balladeers in the 1640s and 1650s, poets and compilers involved in the

---

[79] In *Poems of Carew*, p. 264 (see Chap. 1, n. 31), Dunlap observes that "parodies and satirical adaptations (some of them including the cancelled sixth stanza, thus suggesting that it must have attained wide currency) appeared from time to time throughout the century." Hart calls this poem "One of the most frequently imitated poems of the age" ("Answer-Poem," p. 25).

[80] This was printed in *Wit and Drollery* (1656), p. 44. It is found in three Bodleian manuscripts and in BL MS Harl. 6917, fols. 56v–57.

[81] Crum, p. 228, notes five Bodleian manuscripts of these poems.

system of manuscript transmission and collection of verse were attracted to different sorts of answer verse: blank manuscript pages were an open invitation for people to compose and transcribe all sorts of texts, and the medium itself laid less emphasis on single-author collections of verse than did the culture of the book. Of course, one of the most striking features of the system of manuscript transmission was its openness to the poetry composed by compilers of collections—in the most general sense, their "answer" or response to the kinds of texts they were reading and gathering. This topic, especially since the work of minor and anonymous writers has been neglected by a literary history based on print culture, deserves considerable attention.

## Compiler Poetry

One of the most important features of the system of manuscript transmission is the inclusion of verse composed by those who owned or transcribed texts in collections. Compilers, owners, and other individuals who put their own poetry in manuscripts did so for various reasons: to introduce collections (sometimes as part of the ritual of offering a presentation copy to a social superior); to record their autographs as the owners or borrowers of the documents;[82] to imitate, answer, or parody the work of others; to translate verse from Latin or one of the modern languages; to take part in poetic competition or other forms of poetic exchange; or to pass on the manuscript to another or to thank someone for the loan of such a document.

Often the flyleaf or cover page of a manuscript was used not only to display the name of the document's owner or compiler, but also to preface the collection with a poem or poems composed by that person. For example, on the verso of the first surviving folio of Humphrey Coningsby's collection (BL MS Harl. 7392), there are two English poems and one Latin poem by the compiler—the first a couplet about wasted youth, the second a short misogynistic piece about the faithlessness of women, and the third a Latin couplet with an English title "My nativytye," followed by a couplet from Martial. Such trivial pieces contrast with the more elaborate compositions he attempted. On the verso of the first folio of the second Dalhousie manuscript,

---

[82] See Boffey, *Manuscripts*, p. 25 (cited in full at Chap. 1, n. 10).

someone twice signing his name "andreae RAmsey" and "Andrae RAmsey" began what appears to be a simple verse prayer, but then drifted into prose:

> In my defenc god me defend and bring
> my soull to ane good end guhen I am sick and
> Lyk to the father of heavens heavie mynd amene
> andreae RAmsey     Andrae RAmsey finis amene
> god
> seave and defend thy /chosen/ flok
> floke which now [the rest is incomplete][83]

Ernest Sullivan speculates that this member of the family of the earls of Dalhousie was a child who died young but who obviously had access to the manuscript in which he transcribed his words ahead of the work of the professional scribes who copied the anthology of poems found in this document.[84]

In one of the three prefatory poems addressed to the readers of Folger MS V.a.345, the compiler defends the recreational character of his collection against possible criticisms of those hostile to the kind of pleasurable wittiness represented by so many of the items in the anthology:

Ad Lectorem

> Some may perchance account my time mispent
> And mee unwise to write such things as these
> But let them know my deed Ile ne're repent
> Twas not for profit but my selfe to please
> For though most profit gaines most commendation
> Yet some time must be spent in recreation.
> He that most busied is, somtime will finde
> As interims freed from serious affayres
> Wherein to recreate his dulled minde
> Not able to endure continual cares
> The vilest miser he that never spares
> To search and scrape for gold, hath in his fashion
> Seasons selected for his recreation

---

[83] Sullivan, *Dalhousie Manuscripts*, p. 131.
[84] Ibid., p. 195.

Then let no any this as idle deeme
Whose only end was idlenes to shun
Lest being more busy they most idle seeme
Condemning, never thinking why twas don[ne]
But if such Momists hither needs wil come
   This is my answere to such peevish elves
   I laugh to see themselves displease themselv[es].

This declaration illustrates well the point made by Peter Beal, who compares the utilitarian commonplace book with the verse miscellany, calling the latter "the 'pleasurable' rather than strictly 'useful' side of the genre."[85]

Blank pages or blank spaces at the bottoms of pages invited compilers as well as others into whose hands manuscripts fell to insert their own poems. The fifteenth-century compiler Humfrey Newton apparently used such spaces for writing and revising his own verse.[86] In a collection kept by Thomas Manne, Henry King's amanuensis, (BL Add. MS 58215), someone who subscribed his initials "F V" inserted the following at the foot of one of the pages:

        Nature abhorres Vacuitie
          And so doe I
        For i am Natures pride, and will
          This voyd page fill.
        Leafe thou before wast but a blanke
          now thou maist thanke
        my pen, but doe not; for unless
          thou this expresse
        I serve your Mistress still there's emptines
                (Fol. 72v)

The Scots complier of the Bannatyne manuscript included several of his own compositions in the collection by way of address to the potential readers of the huge collection he transcribed over some three months in 1568.[87]

The manuscript environment was especially receptive to occasional

---

[85] Beal, "Notions in Garrison," p. 143 (see Chap. 1, n. 56).

[86] See Boffey, *Manuscripts*, p. 24. See also Rossell Hope Robbins, "The Poems of Humfrey Newton, Esquire, 1466–1536," *PMLA* 65 (1950): 249–81.

[87] See *The Bannatyne Manuscript: National Library of Scotland Advocates' MS. 1.1.6*, with an introduction by Denton Fox and William A. Ringler (London: Scolar Press, 1980). See especially the poems on p. 59, and fols. 211v, 298v, and 375.

poetry, especially to elegies and epitaphs about members of one's family or social circle. For example, the seventeenth-century owner of the Cosens Manuscript (BL Add MS 34064) did two separate drafts of poems commemorating his sister's death: "An Elegye upon the death of my deare Sister M: W: who died of a feavour the 7th of January An: Do: 1653." The second of these pieces is an acrostic poem spelling out her name, "Margaret Wyseman," in the initial letters of the lines of the poem:

> M ay th' stranger know that this tombe hides from's site
> A glorious, rare, illustrious margarite;
> R ak't up in dust by death, who gaster'd stands
> G asinge o'th' horrid worke of's barb'rous hands.
> A lmost asham'd this monument to see
> R ear'd as a trophy of his crueltie.
> E nvie could not finde any thinge whereby
> T o soile her credit with foule calumny.
> V ertu's Elixar! natur's pride is fled
> V anish't and gone now thou (deare soule!) art dead.
> I t greeves <that> th'whole universe, which mourns to see
> S oe great a share of'ts glory lost in ye.
> E ach grace and vertue'n the did jointly meete
> M akinge thy minds sweete sumetry compleate,
> A nd perfect, yet alas! all these wont save
> N or free thy body from the noisome grave.
>           Her epitaph
> natur's bright starr has cast her gellie heere
> That she i'th' heaven of heaven may shine moore cleare.
>                               (Fol. 59r)[88]

Acrostic verse of this sort had been used earlier in complimentary poems that found their way into such printed anthologies as *Brittons Bowre of Delights* (1591) and *The Arbor of Amorous Devices* (1597). In transferring the practice from the hierarchical environment of the court and of patronage relations to the family, Wiseman performed an act of sociocultural appropriation typical of those who collected and composed poetry in their personal manuscripts. Similarly, in the thirteen folios bound into BL Add. MS 28253, Edward Bannister, a Catholic acquainted with Sir Philip Sidney, not only collected poems

---

[88] This poem is preceded by a two-page elegy on fols. 56v–57r.

by Sidney and Sir John Davies but also recorded two of his own poems composed on the occasion of the death of his wife, Mary, the sister of the Jesuit poet Robert Southwell. The first is titled: "A tragicall Rememberance of the death of Mrs. Marye Banystere who dyed atte Putteny in Bury uppon Ester daye in Anno Dm. 1587 of the small poxe: writen by her husbande . . . July Anno 1587":[89]

> In Mortem Mariae Banister qua fuit Uxor Edwardi Banister
> & filia Jacobi Gage qua obiit in festo Pascha in Anno domini 1587

My penne ys broken quyll Rawght frome the wynges of Deathe
my Standyshe dead mans skull newe diggid frome the grave
my Incke harte bluddde that drops by pantynge breathe
a balefull theame that so greate dole moste have
my trembellinge hande my penne lete fall before
And faythe wannghte Rage for I cann sturre no more

I sawe the tomes of vertue over Rowlde
with furye torne and throwne unto the grownde
Gastelye in sighte and uglye to behoulde
where vertue fledde for feare of mortall wounde
And cawghte her crosse and cartayne foloyd she
that murderid was uponn tormentinge tree

Then Tyrantes flwe with Rigowre in my face
And frome my bosome wolde my harte have Rente
Rage deathe furye and Rigor ware in place
All mercyles on me theire gleamynge Eyes were bent
Because I wepte her vertues dedd had I be
had not the helpe of helpeles sucoryd me

Shorte Rowghe and violente was the Rage
and marcye durste not cume into the presse
Marye a thinge mortall she cawght in Gage
and flede with yt unto the throne of blesse
which Baynshte to the stars most still remayne
To taste of Joye in steade of Endles payne

Loe troye ys burnte and yet I stande agaste
and trembell still althoughe the storme be paste

---

[89] See *Poems of Sidney*, ed. Ringler, p. 555.

Edward Banystere//
her poore and desolete//
husbande for her Remembrance
(Fol. 4r–4v)

It is interesting that this elegy begins with some reflections on the physical act of writing, metaphorizing the quill pen, ink, and inkwell for Bannister's elegaic purposes. The act of composing his own verse is portrayed as an extension of the writer's other transcribing activities in his manuscript.

The university students and the members of the Inns of Court who collected verse as individual and group activities exercised skills in translation and composition they had been taught or took the opportunity to imitate the work of the contemporary poets whose verse they had encountered in both manuscript and print. For example, John Finet included a few of his own compositions in his late Elizabethan anthology (Bod. MS Rawl. Poet. 85), subscribing them with his initials (see Cummings, pp. 104–5). These include two translations of Latin couplets, a longer poem only surviving in a fragment because some pages were torn from the manuscript and a short piece of misogynistic doggerel:

Are Women so namde
As creatures framde
To be a woe to man?
My Mistress sayes no.—
Should I saye so?
Beshrowe me than:
(Fol. 84r; Cummings, p. 609)

The youth who composed these lines later became King James's master of ceremonies and had a reputation at court for composing obscene verse.[90]

Sir Humphrey Coningsby also apparently composed verse for his anthology (BL MS Harl. 7392). Since many of the poems in this document are unique, anonymous productions, since the whole man-

[90] See the discussion of Finet in Chapter 1. Dale B. J. Randall mentions Finet's having composed bawdy jests and songs to amuse King James (*Jonson's Gypsies Unmasked: Background and Theme of "The Gypsies Metamorphos'd"* [Durham: Duke University Press, 1975], p. 166). See also Albert J. Loomie, S.J., ed., *Ceremonies of Charles I: The Note Books of John Finet, 1628–1641* (New York: Fordham University Press, 1987).

uscript seems to speak a common culture-specific language of desire, frustration, and moralizing, and, finally, since Coningsby's initials have been deleted under a number of pieces, it is difficult to identify what poems he actually wrote himself.[91] There are, however, at least a few pieces we might assign to him as representative of his related collecting and composing efforts. An apparently unique unascribed love poem on fol. 32v of this manuscript looks like it might be his, especially since the envoy marks the poem as a personal gift and, to the left of the first four stanzas, there are marginal summaries of their contents: "myne Eye hath fownd thee"; "My harte hath chese thee"; "To thee Love hath bound mee"; "From the, Death Shall loose mee" (see fig. 2):

> my curious Eyes (whose wary sight
>   Surveyes each comly vyrgins face)
> Hath thee (in whom they most delyght)
>   Found out by vyew of seemely grace
>
> My Harte to whom is given the choise
>   A thing which curious eye doth finde)
> Hath thee (in whom it doth rejoyce)
>   Chosen my chyef: prove not unkinde.
>
> And Love whom choyse and sight of Eye
>   Do cause to knytte the loyall knotte)
> To thee (in whom I lyve and Dye)
>   Hath bownd me fast: refuse me not.
>
> Tyll Death whose cruell parte it is
>   To frustrate Hope and finishe Love)
> Shall Loose (or losse of worldly blysse)
>   My lyfe from thine: loth to remove.
>
> Disdayne me not for Daungers sake,
>   Deride me not, for my good wyll
> Deprave me not, milde answere make
>   Delude me not, with scornful skyll.

[91] Black claims that some of the poems in this manuscript are marked with "HC" either because he admired them or in order to distinguish them from those obtained from Robert Allot, whose name is recorded after other poems ("Studies," 1:47). The simplest explanation, however, is that he wrote them.

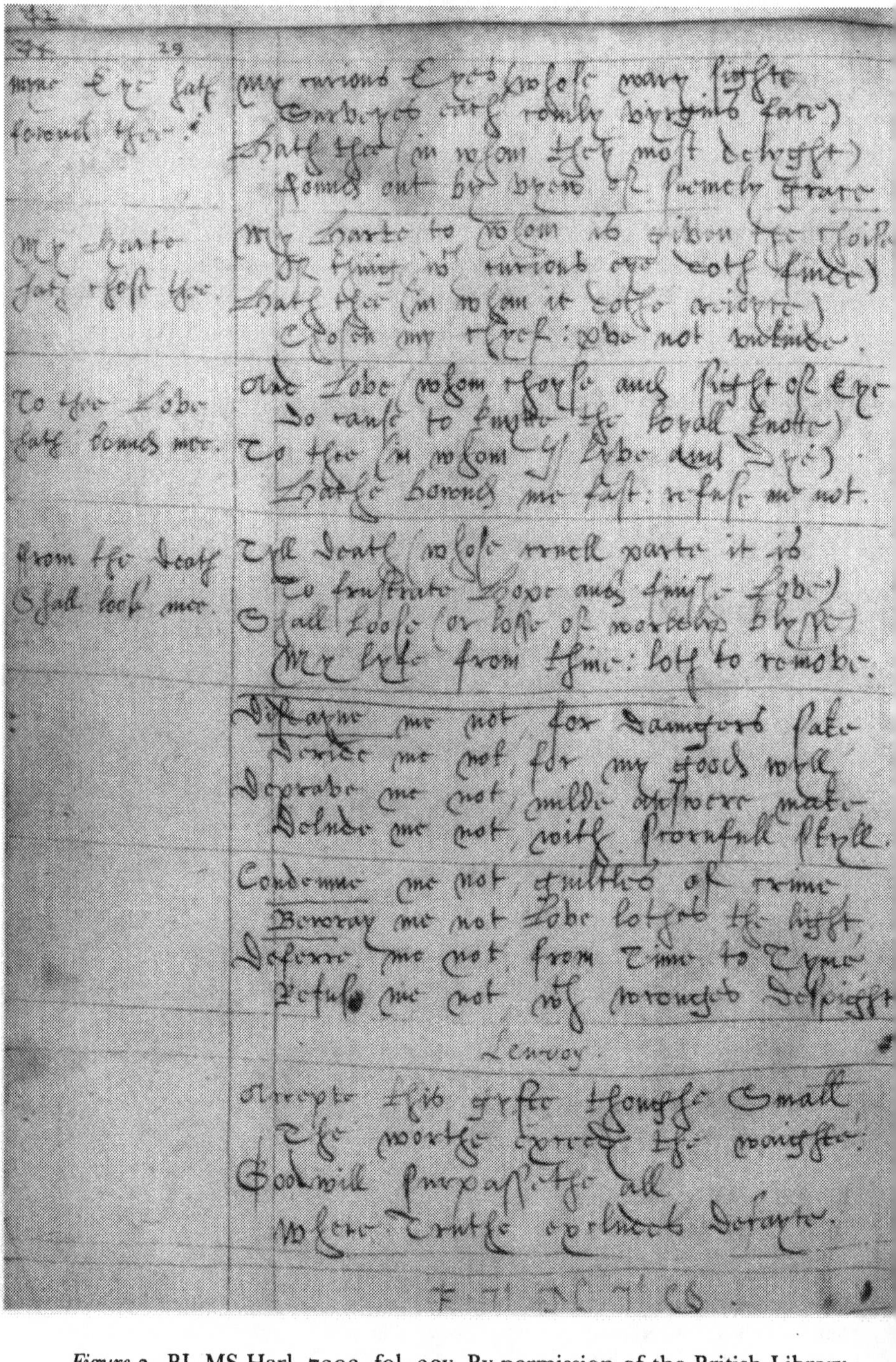

*Figure 2.* BL MS Harl. 7392, fol. 32v. By permission of the British Library.

Condemne me not, guiltles of crime,
  Bewray me not, Love lothes the light,
Deferre me not, from Time to Tyme,
  Refuse me not, with wronges Despight.

Lenvoy
Accept this gyfte though Small,
  The worthe exceedes the waighte:
Goodwill surpassethe all
  Where Truthe excludes Defayte.

This epistolary proposal of love looks like a private gesture of communication, most likely by Coningsby himself. Significantly, the next
poem, about the frustration of delaying love ("Myne eye Bewrayes /
My Harte Desires," fol. 33r), is followed by the compiler's deleted
initials.

Late in the manuscript, in a section that probably contains pieces
transcribed in an Inns of Court environment, poem 86 (of the 127
numbered poems in this collection) is a palinode Coningsby appears
to have addressed to someone with the initials "Q.R.":

Being asked how he lyked, he wrote.

86 To lodge Delight on Fancies single sight
    Or builde my Hope on Bewties synking Sandes
  Were to submit my Mynde to Fortunes spight
    And snare my selfe with Cares in Cupids bandes,
  And what althoghe dame Bewty bid do soe?
    Vertu forbyds, & bids suche baytes forgoe.

  Let Venus vawnt of all hyr gallant Gloze:
    Hir fairest Face, hyr Grace and semely Shape.
  Yea hyr on whom Dan Paris did repose
    Hys Hope and Hart, & made at laste his Rape,
  Helen of hew was fayre I must confesse,
    A hoorishe Hart she bare yet naytheles.

  Wheron but vayne can Venus make her Vaunt?
    Allurying lookes ar all but triflying toyes.
  Suche symple Showes no wyse mans Hart can daunt
    Bables for Fooles & Mayegames made for Boyes.

anNot every one that lyst to loke doth Lyke,
Some smile to see that bredes theyr most mislyke.

Forme Nulla Fides.

(Fol. 53v)

Written in the early Tudor idiom best suited to complaint and to
moral verse, this poem uses its simple classical allusions in a didactic,
medieval manner. It is followed in the manuscript by a plaintive piece
titled "In Passione Melancholia":

87 Care is the Gate that openeth to my Hart,
    And gives me Gryefes, but gives my griefes no end,
My thoughtes lyke Woundes, that never cease to smart,
    Encrease my Cares but no relyef will lend.
Consumed thus with Cares in careful stryfe,
    In Feares and Teares I leade my loathed lyfe.

Not Lyfe, but Death; nor yet desired Death,
    And yet suche Deathe as dauntes to Death my Joyes,
As kils my Hart, but can not stop my Breath,
    Wyth endles Cares augmentinge myne Annoyes.
So have the Fates Long to (I feare) fore-sworne,
    My self to suche mysfortune to be borne.

I can not pen, that can not be expreste
    I neede not fayne I feele my Griefes to greate,
I caste of woes and wishe they were redreste
    But thats but Wynde, & cannot coole such heate.
I tast the worst, and styll do hope the best,
    And so wythe Cares concent perforce I rest.

Contra fatum niti fatuum.
<H C to C G>        RDTFOF

(Fol. 54r)[92]

In the ambiguous idiom adopted by Coningsby, the poem's subject
may be either frustration in love or worldly misfortune. Both this
poem and the previous one represent the kind of verse found in a
printed verse miscellany such as *The Paradise of Dainty Devices,* from

[92] In his notes preserved in the Huntington Library, William Ringler reads "Grace" for
"Gate" in line 1.

which Coningsby seems to have copied some selections.[93] The impression created by the compiler's probable and possible contributions is that first as university student and then as more mature young man, Coningsby responded to the literary language of his contemporaries and predecessors, wished to appropriate and imitate their writing, and encouraged by the medium in which he was transcribing verse, immersed himself and his own compositions in a shared literary language.

In a miscellany of verse and prose associated with an Inns of Court environment (Bod. MS Add. B.97), a collection that contains a large number of Sir John Davies's manuscript poems, Leweston Fitzjames probably composed some of the anonymous, apparently unique pieces himself. He put his initials to an English translation of a Latin poem on justice copied "out of Mistress Grimestons Miscellanea" (fol. 47v) and he followed this with another one of his translations, of a Latin poem on the theme of the impermanence of worldly glory ("transitio gloria mundi") (fol. 48r). In this miscellany of verse and prose, the first poem is a lyric by Campion, but this is followed by two poems addressed to the same person, the second of which is signed with the compiler's initials:

In Calvum Poetam.

Well didst thou prayse the noble high conceit
of that Arcadian knight & Collin swayne.
For hadst thou toucht their palmes with toungs desceit
who would not blame thy too ambitious nayme.

But why didst thou disprayse the meaner witts,
of modern Poets in these Later tymes,
Is it so envie? for we use those fitts,
When wee disprayse who pass us in or rimes.

It seemeth so, sith thou so far dost rest
Behind the worst, as moest behind the best.
(Fol. 17r)

---

[93] Both poems are crossed out in the manuscript, possibly to signal that they should not be transcribed further in another collection.

In eundem

Calvus is pleasd with none but <best & worst> with the best.
To those his pen affords some mishell <paines> prayes
he nought esteemes of any of the rest
but on their idle witts his witt displayes.
  Fye Calvus, fye man hate thou not thy selfe
  Thou art not best, make not thy eye accurst
  Thus may thy words be true sayd folly selfe
  thou art in love with none but lest & worst.
So Calvus maye be lov'd amongst the rest,
For he is worst, who even prove the best.

            LF

There are obvious similarities between this sort of verse and the satiric lyrics of someone like Sir John Davies. In the Inns environment, to which the poetry of Davies that Fitzjames transcribes belongs, literary self-consciousness was very high, amateur poetic composition and translation were encouraged, and, thus, Fitzjames found it easy to write and insert his own verse in the collection of prose and poetry he was compiling.[94] For Richard Roberts, however, who was largely responsible for the compilation of another collection in the same setting (Bod. MS Don. c.54) (one that contains, like Finet's anthology, the work of Richard Mills and of other university versifiers), the Inns environment was also one in which Latin epistolary communication could take place. In particular, the compiler recorded poems that he and his friend George Baughe exchanged.

As noted earlier, several sixteenth- and seventeenth-century Catholic miscellanies and poetry anthologies contain compiler poetry. In a manuscript owned in 1601 by Thomas Wenman (BL MS Egerton 2403), there is a series of religious poems by the compiler, which appear to have been written in prison. One, for example, is a prayer (in fourteeners or psalm measures) for the welfare of Queen Elizabeth, a politic gesture by a persecuted member of a religious minority:

---

[94] Other poems probably composed by him are "Kisse me sweete now we are heere" (fol. 17v), "Read in my face the fortunes of my youth" (fol. 19v), "Never more deuly on his Cynthia's grace" (fols. 19v–20r), and "The Rocke wher youth made shipwrack of my lyfe" (fol. 20r). After "Calvus is pleased" the subscription "LF" is superimposed. None of these poems is found in any British Library or any other Bodleian manuscript.

Bowe downe thie heavenlye eyes o Lorde
bowe downe thie eare alsoe
and harken to the voice of them
whose sinnes do overflowe

With humble hartes we wretched wightes
in wofull state do crave
to pardon this our sinful life
and spotted soules to save.

And for the persone of our Prince
Elizabeth by name
preserve longe time in perfecte health
her subjects crave the same

In quiet peace to triumphe stil
with honour and renowne
in prosperous state to governe us
and longe to weare the Crowne

O Lorde graunte this our juste requeste
most happie subjects then
all Englishe hartes for this do praye
and saye amen amen      finis: quoth: Tho[mas]: Wen[man]:

(Fol. 33v)

Despite Wenman's protestation of patriotism in this piece, there are clear signs in this manuscript of Catholic opposition to the queen. On the verso of the first folio, we find the following political advice:

| In the lives of | 1. Cover theire secret vices |
| princes | 2. Mildely interprete theire doubtfull faultes |
| we should always | 3. With patience beare their knowen evills |

provided
That they doe not by them
bringe utter destruction to
the common wealthe

(Fol. 1v)

This statement is followed immediately by the transcription of a long religious/political poem, "The sad Complaint of mary Queen of

[ 183 ]

Scotts who was beheaded in England in the reign of Queen Elizabeth" ("Baldwyn awake thie penn hathe slept to longe," fols. 2r–
33v). Thus, there is a charged political context for the compiler's
own religious verse that follows. A copy of the earl of Essex's elaborate
farewell poem ("The Passion of a Discontented Mind") follows the
section of compiler poetry, reinforcing the connection between political oppositionalism and religious verse.

In a poem in which he retrospectively examines his own life, Wenman falls into composing in an old-fashioned poulter's measure, re-
producing the style of verse with which he might have been familiar
in his youth:

> Alacke when I looke backe
> uppon my youthe thats paste
> and depely ponder youthes offence
> and youthes rewarde at laste
> with sighes and teares I saye
> o god I not denye
> my youthese withe follye hathe deserved
> with follye for to dye
> But yet if ever sinfull man
> mighte mercye move to ruthe
> good Lorde with mercye doe forgeve
> the follies of my youthe
> In youthe I ranged the feildes
> wheare vices all did growe
> in youthe I wanted grace
> suche vice to overthrowe
> In youthe what I thoughte sweet
> most bitter nowe doe finde
> this hathe the follies of my youthe
> with follie kepte me blinde
> yet as the eagle cast her bill
> whereby her age renneth [reneweth]
> so Lorde with mercye do forgeve
> the follies of my youthe
>      Amen        Tho[mas] Wenman
>                     (Fol. 35r)

If poetry was one of the follies of the author's youth, it is here re-
deemed by being put to religious and moral uses.

At the opposite end of the religio-political spectrum, there are a few instances of Puritan participation in the manuscript system, despite the largely Royalist character, during the seventeenth century, of manuscript verse, especially from the mid-1630s to the Restoration. For example, in BL MS Harl. 7332, a manuscript in which loose sheets and fascicular collections are bound, including a verse miscellany used for writing practice, Feargod Barbon, whom Peter Beal associates with the Anabaptist politician Praisegod Barbon, a zealous relative whose name was facetiously used in references to the 1649 Commonwealth assembly as "Barebone's Parliament" (Beal, 1.2.139 and 1.1.209), included a poem of his own at the start of the verse collection, a piece in which he expressed his thanks for the loan of the book from a friend:

> This Booke was given me by A frende
>   To Reade And overlooke
> Because she often Did Commende
>   The pleasure that shee tooke
>
> By Reading it I needes would Crave
>   This gistore At her hande
> Which shee Did grante I straight should have
>   To be At my Comande
>
> I tooke it then being ofte Desired
>   To read it for her sake
> I have performed what she required
>   And Did sutch pleasure take
>
> That twice or thrice I red it over
>   And plainely there Did Finde
> I received good that did before
>   Comend the same in minde
>
> Wherefore to shew my thankefulnes
>   Unto my frend so kinde
> I wish that shee all happynes
>   for evar more may Fynd
>                 Finis
>                         per me Fearegod Barbon
>                         (Fol. 40r)

This Puritan reader/transcriber, however, had misgivings about some of the texts in the anthology, for he wrote the following shortly after copying the bawdy poem that begins "Sweete harte lett me feele thy cunny" (fol. 46v): "Fearegod Barbon of Daventry in the County of Northhampton beinge at many times Idle and wanting Employment Beestood his time with his penn & Incke wrighting thease sonnets songes And epigrammes thinks—that it weare bettar so to doe for the mendinge of his hand in wrighting then worse to bestow his time" (fol. 48r). His work ethic thus excused his indulging in the morally dubious literary practices he probably associated with religiously misguided Royalist men and women of leisure.

Both ecclesiastical and secular professionals compiled manuscript anthologies in which the contexts of their employment are visible. Bod. MS Rawl. Poet. 148, the commonplace book of John Lilliat, an Elizabethan cathedral musician,[95] contains works by Sidney, Essex, Dyer, Davies, Watson, Campion, and other late sixteenth-century authors as well as poems by Lilliat's academic and ecclesiastical associates. It also has a fairly large number of poems written by the compiler himself. The main collection opens with two of Lilliat's compositions, "A welcome to Cupid" and an elegy on William Goldingham. His other poems are quite varied: elegies for Thomas Lewkner, "Mary Nevill," and "Dulcebell Porter, my scholler," pious or religious verse, translations of passages from classical authors, epigrammatic pieces, complaints dealing with both moral and social abuses (some apparently arising from personal experiences of injustice and unfairness),[96] and two poems connected with his marriage, one about strife, the other about reconciliation.[97] Despite his condemnation of the contemporary ascendency of secular over religious love (for example, "Against cold devotion"),[98] Lilliat did allow himself to compose some courtly amorous verse, including two poems inspired by Marlowe's "Passionate Shepherd" and Ralegh's famous "Reply" (versions of which he includes in the collection). The first, "Upon a kisse given," is a persuasion to love, the second, "*The S[h]epperdisse her Replie,*" is a pastoral (rather than an antipastoral) rejection of the offer.[99]

In his miscellany, Robert Commaundre, who was, according to William Ringler, "Rector of Tarporley (Cheshire) and Chaplain to the

[95] See *Liber Lilliati,* ed. Doughtie, pp. 15, 24.
[96] It contains for example, poems on how the law persecutes the weak and lets the powerful go free—see poems 89, 91, and 106 in Doughtie's edition.
[97] See Ibid., poems 122 and 131.
[98] Ibid., pp. 77–78.
[99] Ibid., poems 115 and 119.

Lord President and Council of the Marches of Wales in Henry Sidney's time,"[100] transcribed some of his own pieces among the 135 poems. These include "Who Listes to speake of Emperours fame" (fols. 222r–25r), a poem evidently written against someone named "Hugo Shadwell" ("You Shade not well, your glorious pryed within your puffed Breaste," fol. 235), "Fyrste Learne to Honour god a right" (fols. 248v–49r), "This Thing to me I Accounpte for a Prayse" (fol. 258v, which is a translation of a passage from Terence on the nature of harlots), an answer poem to someone else's lyric ("Your twanting Letters your Apishe toyes") and the following moral quatrain:

> Speake the treweth and spare not
> Crye owte a Lowde and feare not
> Leave halting and do well
> Doble dealing deserveth Hell
> R[obert] C[omaundre]

In his anthology (Camb. MS Dd.5.75), Henry Stanford not only recorded some of the best manuscript-circulated and printed verse of such poets as Sidney, Breton, Spenser, Gorges and Ralegh but also set aside sections of his anthology both for the poetry he taught his young pupils to compose and for his own verse.[101] His poems include many examples of commendatory verse meant to accompany New Year's gifts of books to his patroness-employers: for example he wrote sonnets for the presentation of such volumes as a 1581 translation of Voisin's history of France, the 1596 edition of books 4 through 6 of Spenser's *Faerie Queene*, a 1597 selection and translation of Margaret of Navarre's *Heptameron*,[102] the 1609 edition of *The Faerie Queene*,

---

[100] This information is found in Ringler's notes at the Huntington Library. Black says "Commaundre or Commander was apparently born in London c. 1532, fifth son of William, a brewer. Educated at Eton (c. 1544–8) and King's College, Cambridge (1548–50), he left the latter without taking a degree, having 'destroyed many good books in the College library.' He seems to have been a keen Puritan, and was Rector of Tarporley from 1571 till his death in 1613" ("Studies," 1:104).

[101] See May's analysis of the organization of the manuscript in his edition (*Henry Stanford's Anthology*, pp. xx–xxvii and xxxviii–xlii). May says Stanford probably wrote the Nativity hymns 281–83 (p. xxi): "He wrote sonnets almost exclusively after 1596, and is even responsible, I think, for a tediously conceived 'Sonnet sequence' (Items 284–89, 291–93)." See also Black, "Some Renaissance Children's Verse," pp. 1–16 (cited in full at Chap. 1, n. 216).

[102] For these, see May, *Henry Stanford's Anthology*, p. 255, items 58–60.

Chapman's *Homer*, Philomen Holland's translation of Camden's *Brittania*, and an edition of some of DuBartas's poetry.[103] Some of these texts fit the reading interests attributed by contemporaries and by modern scholars to Renaissance aristocratic women, some obviously, and significantly, did not (Chapman's *Homer* and Camden's *Brittania*, in particular). Stanford's choice of the sonnet form was not an unusual one, given the widespread use of this form for such a purpose. Since the sonnet was associated not only with amorous lyricism but also with complimentary and commendatory verse, it was well suited to the context of Stanford's clientage and to the situation of New Year's gift-giving that was a traditional occasion for the demonstration of gratitude within the patronage system. One sonnet, for example, was written to accompany Stanford's gift to Lady Hunsdon of Heywood's *Troia Brittanica*, "To the lady Hunsdon. 1612 [1613]. Brittaines Troy sent" ("A newyeares gift receave thrice honourd dame").[104] In this piece, he simultaneously instructs and offers homage to his patroness-employer, but in alluding to King James's wish to redefine England, Scotland, and Wales as Britain, he also glances at the larger sociopolitical context of the reigning monarch's campaign for Union.

Stanford's other efforts in the sonnet form suggest that he was responding to the popularity the sonnet had enjoyed toward the end of the Elizabethan era. Late in the collection, he includes nine sonnets on the theme of constancy in love probably addressed to one of the women he served, all variations on a Petrarchan original.[105] In them, however, pedantic allusions all but overwhelm the complimentary rhetoric. In most of them classical references abound, but in one Stanford used a different strategy, accumulating exotic geographical place names that reflect the contemporary desire for exploration and expansion ("Place me in Japan Zeilan Barbarie").[106] Employed by aristocratic families to tutor their children, the domestically restricted Stanford indulged, in the narrow confines of this complimentary lyric, in global fantasy.

Despite his wish to compose in the fashionable sonnet form, however, in his four religious hymns, Stanford fell into the old-fashioned

---

[103] For these, see ibid. p. 249, items 62–66, 84–85, 93.
[104] Ibid., pp. 57–58, item 68.
[105] Ibid., items 284–93; see May's comments on pp. 375–77.
[106] Ibid., pp. 198–99, item 289.

reproduced the kind of verse he probably learned in his youth and thus adopted an anachronistic poetic style that contrasted with that of the contemporary poetry he transcribed. He does, however, complicate the poetic forms somewhat—for example, by inserting tetrameter couplets in among fourteeners, as in the following passage:

> O golden birthe of pereles babe, a mayd a mother is
> & being inspired by holy ghost to us salvation gyves
> this sacred imp from mothers wombe as this day shewes his face
> which is to be our saviour by his mercie & his grace
>     as long as sonne shall gyve his light
>     or phebe use to shine by night.[107]

Stanford obviously had a strong affection for the poetic rhythms and idioms he knew from childhood, despite his attraction to the newer poetic modes of the late Elizabethan era.

Some compilers, however, were more insistent about imitating what were for them the most up-to-date poetic models. This was the case with John Ramsey, the compiler of Bod. MS Douce 280, a miscellany of verse and prose.[108] After Ramsey transcribed Spenser's "Mother Hubbards Tale," he inserted his own imitation/paraphrase of the sixty-fourth sonnet of that poet's *Amoretti:*

> To the Fayrest. A Sonnet.
> In Eandem dominae suae.
> A: B: E. E: D

> Survayinge with a curious serchinge eye
>     my loves sweete feature & her comly grace
>     me seemde a garden was her Majestye
>     where many fragrant flowers decke the place

---

[107] Ibid., p. 192, item 282.

[108] May states "Douce MS. 280 was compiled from about 1596 to 1633 by John Ramsey, 'who was admitted into Peterhouse Cam 1601' (f.i)" (*Poems of Oxford and Essex*, p. 92). In the *Register of Admissions to the Honourable Society of the Middle Temple: From the Fifteenth Century to the Year 1944*, comp. Sir Henry F. MacGeagh and H.A.C. Sturgess (London: Butterworth, 1949), p. 86, there is the following listing for March 23, 1605/6: "John Ramsey, son and heir of William R., of Charlwood, Surrey, gent., decd." See also Doughtie, "John Ramsey's Manuscript," pp. 281–88 (cited in full at Chap. 1, n. 61). See also the discussion of this manuscript in Chapter 1.

Her lipps like Gillyflowers in a race
 her ruddy cheeks like roses sweet did smell
 her snowey browes like Bellamours enchact
 her lovlye eyes like Pinkes becomes her well
The bosomes like a Strawberrye bedd in smell
 her Ivorye necke like Cullambines in showe
 her brestes like lillyes eare their leaves be fell
 her nipples like younge Jessamynes in rowe
These dayntye flowers give a pleasant sent
But her sweet selfe above them all outwent.


 O therefore blest & treble blest weare hee
 that might enjoye so faire a soule as shee.


  by him that must love
   or not live. Poore, J. R.
     (Fol. 35r)[109]


Ramsey's imitation of Spenser's lyric for his own uses, closest in his handling of the second and third quatrains, is a good example of how literary property might be appropriated within the world of manuscript collection and transmission. In this case, a printed source stimulated a private individual to write a love poem to his own beloved in a way that a later age might have judged as plagiarizing.

 Ramsey's imitative sonnet is followed by two more poems in which

---

[109] The closeness of the two poems is obvious. The following is *Amoretti* 64, in *Spenser's Minor Poems*, ed. Ernest De Selincourt (Oxford: Clarendon Press, 1910), p. 403:

 Comming to kisse her lyps, (such grace I found)
  Me seemd I smelt a gardin of sweet flowres:
  that dainty odours from them threw around
  for damzels fit to decke their lovers bowres.
 Her lips did smell lyke unto Gillyflowers,
  Her ruddy cheekes lyke unto Roses red:
  her snowy browes lyke budded Bellamoures,
  her lovely eyes lyke Pincks but newly spred.
 Her goodly bosome lyke a Strawberry bed,
  her neck lyke to a bounch of Cullambynes:
  her brest lyke lillyes, ere theyr leaves be shed,
  her nipples lyke yong blossomd Jessemynes.
 Such fragrant flowres doe give most odorous smell,
  but her sweet odour did them all excell.

he adopts a Spenserian pastoral persona, "Sheephearde Montanus," the second of which reads:[110]

### An Excellent Pastorall Dittye

Mated with griefe a faithfull sheephearde sate,
  in shadye groves (fitt place for sorrowes guest)
And thus him playned still, earlye and late,
  with pipe in hande payntinge out his unrest.
    when havinge sob'd & sigh'd & mourn'd his fill:
    He tunes this Dittye to his Oaten Quill.


O all yee Sheepheardes swaines which on these downes,
  soe many thousande milke white heardes doe feede:
If ever you have bene in these sad stoundes,
  lett pittye move to lende some teares att neede.
    For love forsaken cannot chuse but weepe:
    When woe, which woe doth thus uppon him creepe.


O dreadfull god of love which nowe doest lye,
  carelesly smilinge att my sore mischance:
Doth it befitt soe greate a Dyetye,
    Thus in a wretches miserye to Daunce.
      Thy fire it was (before your hurte I spide)
      which through mine eyes into my breast did glide.


And there o there such life & spirite it bredd
  Such joye of harte such stirringe of my blood:
As everye thought with pleasure still it fedd,
    to reape the fruite of my desiered good.
      But shee whose memorye my very soule doth vexe,
      Basely forsooke me vilefinge her sexe


Thus in my mournefull songe I playne of love,
  for love hath broke me of my wonted sleepe:
And sleepe is hindred by the paines I prove,
    and paine doth force me piteouslye to weepe.

---

[110] Doughtie connects Ramsey with Mount Surrey, which would account for this pseudonym ("John Ramsey's Manuscript," p. 283).

> then farewell loue, sleepe, paine, & every sore:
> And farewell weepinge I can waile no more.

Sheepheard Montanus.

(Fol. 36r–v)

This surprisingly good Spenserian piece is followed by a transcription of Spenser's "Tears of the Muses," then another of Ramsey's own pastoral lyrics, "Sheepheardes confesse with me" (fol. 43v), Spenser's "Visions of Petrarch," and a final pastoral poem:

Montanus the Sheephearde his love to Flora.

> I serve sweete Flora brighter then Cinthias light,
> More plesant then the feilde that lyllyes breedes:
> Clearer then Phoebus, or the Crystall bright,
> Finer then tripping Roe on Violetts feedes.
>   More joyfull to my harte & to my eyes,
>   Then all the good in this earthes paradise.

> Straighter then Cedar, statelyer then the Pine,
> More sweete then roses, Fresher then the Maye:
> Softer then downe, more fruictfull then the vine,
> More beawtifull then Marble or more gaye.
>   More faire in shewe then is the fairest swan,
>   Wonder of wonders, smaller then my Span.

> And can it be that she more curst should be,
> Then is the Tyger & the Beare by kinde:
> Harder then flint, tougher then Oaken tree,
> More glibe then Oyle, more fickle then the winde.
>   Yea, thus my service is a lastinge sore,
>   Yet will I serve although I dye therfore.

Sheepheard Montanus./
Shepheard Montanus. [in a different hand]

(Fol. 45v)

Ramsey, then, chose both to record and to imitate the matter and the manner of a well-known poet in his own personal collection: his imitations of Spenser are one early register of the literary impact of that poet on individuals for whom verse was only an occasional indulgence. It is interesting that the final poem Ramsey seems to have composed for the collection, a retelling of the story of Arion of Lesbos, implies his clear identification with the poet's role. The piece is subscribed with his own name rather than with his pastoral persona and dated 1597:

### Arion of Lesbos

The farthest fett is best for ladies eyes,
    The dearest bought is fittest for a kinge:
    The Jewells that are common noe man buyes,
    for fewe regard the vertue of the thinge:
    wee chuse the dearest not the newest hand,
    a profet is noe profett in his land.

Which made Arion loth his native soyle,
    of Lesbos towne where he was borne & bred:
    he goes to Rome and tarryes there a whyle,
    where he so much delights the princes hed;
    that with greate wealth he paid him for his paine,
    with which he goes to Lesbos back againe.

And beinge shipt among his cuntrye kinde,
    which shapt their homeward course uppon the floods,
    the heape of goulde so peirct the saylors minde,
    as they would kill the owner for his goods:
    while he was tryinge if his things were true
    to singe both Rome & Romaines their adue.

But when their swords invirond him each where,
    he leaps into the raginge seas straight waye:
    to singe the rest unto the fishes there,
    which swome about to here his plesaunt laye:
    A gallant Dolphin takes him one his backe,
    and saves the poet both from sword and wracke.

        Et solo & salo
        Jo: Ramsey
        1597.

                     (Fol. 181r)

Accompanying this piece is Ramsey's elaborate pen-and-ink drawing of the figure of Arion. Followed only by a short Latin piece by the

compiler, described by him as "This shewes wee noe where are es-
teemd than among our owne," this illustrated composition is the last
English verse in the miscellany. By exercising the freedom to add his
own compositions to the contents of his miscellany of verse and prose,
Ramsey assumed the poetic identity in a context conducive to literary
appropriation.

The compiler of Bod. MS Ash. 38, Nicholas Burghe, placed some
of his own verse in his compendious collection, signing his work in
a fairly transparent cipher.[111] His four poems represent various seventeenth-century poetic styles and idioms, resembling several kinds
of verse he collected in his anthology. For example, his first piece is
a love poem that pretends to criticize his resistant mistress but ends
up elaborately praising her by detailing the features of her beauty:

> You sayd that I would Rayle, I vowe tis true,
> Nay more that I would rayle; dear sweet att you
> Well you shall keep your worde; now Ile begine
> and Never feare Loves Punyshment for this synn
> For from thy Globe-like heade unto thy foote
> I will defeate the; and lay bare that Roote
> From which Springs all my Sorrowes, make the know
> How much to thy rare bewtye I dare owe
> And tell the world, thy heade, that Glorious Mound
> In which two starrs are fixt, which peirce and wound
> The most Obdurate harte with such a sight
> Making men blynd, that veywes thy purer light
> The Forhead with Joves Frontispice Ile Compare
> Glorious Ariadne neer Could match thy heayr
> Thy bewtiows Cheeckes, whear Cupid doth Repose
> Is Mixt with Lillies and the blushing Rose
> And Is more lovely then that white and redd
> that Irus shutts In when hur Curtaynes spread
> Thy Crymson Lipp None ever ytt Could taynte
> Currall Compard with ytt growes pale and faynte
> That Ivorye pillar, which this Globe upbeares
> that often Courted by thy more softer heayrs
> Uppon two Mylke whyte Mountaynes Comlye fixt

[111] "83CH461S B59GH2." In this cipher, the vowels *A, E, I, O,* and *U* are numbered 1,
2, 3, 4, and 5; the consonants *L, N,* and *R* are numbered 6, 7, and 8. Burghe used both
the cipher and a personal conflated form of his initials—a practice Mary Hobbs has shown
was becoming a common one in the seventeenth century ("W. S. Manuscript," p. 647 [see
Chap. 1, n. 142]).

Whear Azure veynes lyke Rivletts Runn betwixt
two snowye Alpes; the which Exceed as farr
Praysed Ledas swans, as sol the meanest starr
Thy softe sleecke Belle's a pillow for the head
of that great God of love, when Tytan spreads
his sable Curtaynes over the universe
Wheare pleasures dwell, noe tongue Could ere rehearse
Or yf on should presume the same to paynt
hee'd streight Adore and Take the for a saint
To which night morne and Noone, hee still would praye
and never sighe but when thou art a way
Those payre of Cullums spread with Saffyer vaynes
On which the Fabriques buylt, the which Contaynes
All Earthly pleasures; stands on those daynte feet
which Flora<'s> proud to kyss A myd'st the streett
But staye thou wandring Infante of my brayne
wheather dost flye, why this is nott the strayne
thy Muse should runn, for I did bidd the Rayle
on this Rare Creature, why then didst thou fayle
for to perform my will; for thou shoul[d]st tell
how that In Cruellty she Doth excell
that nyght and Day shee keeps the from thy rest
and that she hates hym that Dothe Love hur best
Tell hur thes twentye yeares thou hast byne hur slave
Yett for thy love on kyss she ner the gave
Tell hur <thy> hur voyce Doth soe Inchant thyne eares
Thou thynkest thou hearst the musick of the spheares
Tell hur hur eyes hath so Inflamed thy harte
thou find'st A scortching fier In every parte
of all thy bodye; And how that each Nerve
strive with each other which hur best should serve
Tell hur shes growne so fixed In thy sight
Thou thinks in hur the world Intombes Delight
Since nought but Death, or she can eare release the
Butt styll I am out; Oh then great god I see
Tis Constant Love which thus ^doth^ governe
Nay lett hur Rypp my hart I'le kyss the knyffe
And Bless that Arme which tooke a way my Lyfe
And when my Vitall sperritts begines to fayle
Styll kyss hur hand and gaynst hur thus would rayle.

(Pp. 22–23)

This self-consciously derivative piece—a hybrid of complaint and at-
tenuated poetic blazon—evidently provoked from its addressee a

charge of plagiarism, if we can judge by the quatrain added to the page sideways in the margin:

> You cal'd me Theefe, when I presumed to Raise
> Thes few rude Lynes thy bewtye for to Prayse
> Thou stol'st my hart; why then tis past beliefe
> ytt tis not I; but Thou that arte the theefe.
>
> (P. 23)

Authorial originality is not the point in Burghe's imitative versifying; rather composition accompanies transcription of the work of others as a way of participating in a wider literary institution and reinforcing upper-class ownership of poetic texts. In this spirit, Burghe composed a prison poem: "Being In prison and his Mistress fearing hee would dye then by reason of the plague being Amongst them he wrights thus to hur" ("Seing I am Incased by death," p. 24). In this *contemptus mundi* piece, he professes to reject the worldly values of "Bewtye, Honor, wealth" as well as the distinctions of social and political status. Burghe exercises himself poetically in a familiar literary (sub)genre, adding his effort to the similar work of poets such as Wyatt, Ralegh, Essex, Hoskins, and Lovelace.

The last of Burghe's poems, however, is in a very different mode, a satiric attack "On that famous (Infamous) whore Grace Coocke" ("Hells porter and A bawde on tyme being meet," p. 37). It reproduces the misogynistic rhetoric of similar pieces by Sir John Davies, Ben Jonson, and others. Burghe's poems, then, demonstrate his familiarity with a variety of amorous and satiric poetic modes and forms; they assert his desire to incorporate his own compositions in the larger body of literary discourse, a large selection of which forms the body of his rich collection.

In a manuscript associated with the Skipwiths, a family connected with that of Donne's close friend Henry Goodyer, William, Henry, and Thomas Skipwith transcribed some of their own verse in an anthology that contains sixty of Donne's poems along with the work of such other poets as Jonson, Carew, Beaumont, Wotton, King, and Herrick.[112] The manuscript, which was transcribed in sections by sev-

[112] Beal, 1.1.252, has the following note on this manuscript: "composite volume of MS verse belonging to the Skipwith family of Cotes, Leicestershire, including . . . 60 poems by Donne and . . . one Problem; in numerous hands, written over an extended period; some poems by William Skipwith (? Sir William Skipwith [d. 1610] or his grandson, William, or

eral hands over several decades, represents the extended coterie circulation of the poems of Donne and of a number of poets who were highly valued in Royalist circles. In such a context, the compilers' work is a sign of class and kinship ties, shared political sympathies and sophisticated tastes. It is revealing that Henry Skipwith signs his name to "An Elegie on the Death of my never enough Lamented master King Charles the first" ("Weepe, weepe even mankinde weepe, soe much is dead," fol. 40r).[113] Several of William Skipwith's poems have intertextual affinities with the love poetry of Donne, Jonson and the Cavalier poets who developed Donne's and Jonson's complimentary rhetoric and amorous realism. Skipwith writes in the social idiom of the seventeenth-century verse that bears the imprint of both Donne's and Jonson's styles—for example, in a piece entitled "A Woemen":

---

possibly a cousin, William Skipwith of Ketsby, Lincolnshire [fl. 1633]), Sir Henry Skipwith (fl. 1609–52), and Thomas Skipwith; several poems also by Sir Henry Goodyer (1571–1627) (to whom one branch of the Skipwith family was related by marriage); c. 1620–50." See Hobbs, *Verse Miscellany Manuscripts*, pp. 62–67, for a description of this manuscript. James Knowles, "WS MS," *TLS*, April 29–May 5, 1988, pp. 472, 485, and Mary Hobbs, "W.S. Manuscript," p. 647, identify the compiler-author, whose initials "W:Sk:" are found under several compositions in the manuscript, as William Skipwith (c. 1564–1610) of Leicestershire, a neighbor and friend of the Hastings family, the dedicatee of Fletcher's The *Faithful Shepherdess* (1608) and the object of an elegy by Sir John Beaumont. There is evidence that this Skipwith, the father of Sir Henry Skipwith, has used the same mark of authorship in some other documents found in the Public Record Office, and "Fuller, in his *Worthies*, described him as 'a person of much Valor, Judgement, and Wisedome, dextrous at the making fit and acute *Epigrams, Poesies, Mottoes,* and *Devices* ... neither so apparent that every rustic might understand them, nor so obscure that they needed an Oedipus to interpret them" (Knowles, p. 485). Despite this, one should note that the hands in which the poems of William, Henry, and Thomas Skipwith are transcribed look quite late and that there are two sons of Sir Henry, William and Henry Skipwith, who matriculated at University College, Oxford, April 27, 1632, and thus were educated in an environment especially conducive to the related activities of collecting and composing verse for manuscript anthologies. See the account of Skipwith family in *The English Baronetage* 3 (1741), p. 532. There may have been some connection between the Skipwiths and the Astons of Tixall: On fol. 91r there is a poem by Thomas Aston and the poem on fol. 40r by Henry Skipwith has been attributed to Sir W[alter] A[ston] in Bod. MS Eng. Poet. e.37. See also my discussion of the Skipwith manuscript in Chapter 1.
   In this manuscript, Skipwith poems are found, for example, on fol. 40r; fols. 135r–36r (three poems, one of which, "If anie bee content with woordes; tis I," fol. 135v, appears also in *The Harmony of the Muses* [1654], p. 90); fol. 137r (two poems); between fols. 148r and 186r (e.g., Henry Skipwith's two poems on 176r–v, William Skipwith's five poems on 179r–8or, and another four by him on fols. 181v–83r).
   [113] Crum cites another copy of this poem in Bod. Eng. Poet. e.37, p. 47, subscribed "Sr. W. A."; since Sir Walter Aston died in 1639, perhaps this refers to another member of that family. No other British Library manuscript contains this poem.

Hee's jug'd, and damb'd that saith thou art noe more
such things as those these eyes have seene before,
Yet neaver were they scourge unto my harte;
eyther with mortall bewtie, or with arte;
Noe sure thou art some pure Coelestiall thinge,
sent from above good messages to bringe.
Tell us then faire one; tell us sure you can
tell us more newes then anie mortal man
and truly, tell us (as you love your mother)
for thats a greater charm then anie other
What shall become of us poore, wretched soules
Whose foule contempt that face of yours controules,
and makes me see my sencelesse sinfull error
that thought your heavenly bewtie was no <wonder> mirror
Though I have heard my master often saye
that I would one daye curse the houre, & daye
that ever I <was> poor wretched I was borne
to hould such glorious bewtie in such scorne
forgive it mee; and give him his dew praise
that with such zeale your vertuous name doth raise.
O God how ofte his pipe sounds dolefull thinges
And syghinge Eccoe still Eliza: singes
When my accursed pipe mockinge his passion
did Joley playe thinges of a lighter fashion.
But thou ill taught misguided idle whistle
that knew'st not such sweete roses from a Thistle
Ly there, & rott, and let noe lyienge thinge
Delight to heare thee; or thy Master singe.
But faire one since you see how I repent mee
Let not my sinnes dishonor him, that sent mee.
Accept from the trew Lover of <of> your vertue
this token too too far unworthy of you:
And when he leaves with reverence to adore you,
or to prefer weake flesh & bloud before you
Then let this knife your favour cut a sunder,
And kill him with a <thought> frowne as sharp as thunder.
      W: Sk:/

                    (Fol. 135r)

This poem seems to have been written to accompany the gift of a
knife, perhaps on behalf of someone else for whom the poet acted
as a spokesperson. Skipwith was able to compose witty compliments
and love complaints, but he also shows an interest in the rhetoric of

misogynistic invective, which became a popular Cavalier mode—in, for example, a poem that attacks a woman as a diabolical corrupter of men ("O thou that art the Tigar of this age," fol. 137r). He imitates the manner of Donne's poems "The Comparison" and "The Anagram" in this piece, one instance among many of the Skipwiths' attraction to Donne's poetic style. The early part of the manuscript, after all, contains not only Donne's satires (fols. 48r–54v) and several elegies, including "The Anagram" (fol. 12r–v), but also some two dozen of the *Songs and Sonnets* and a generous sampling of the epistolary, occasional, and religious verse.

Robert Codrington, an Oxford author, inserted a number of his own poems in his personal collection of verse (Bod. MS Eng. Poet. f.27).[114] These include "An Epitaph on C. Seymour" ("Seeke further for a Monument," pp. 236–37); "On the Death of the Right Hounourable Charles Lorde Herbert who died in Italy &c." ("Avaunt you toung-tyde Mourners whose ambition," pp. 237–38); and "Uppon the untimely fate of John Barlow Master of Arts and Scholler of C[orpus] C[hristi] C[ollege] By R[obert] C[ordington] [of] C[orpus] C[hristi] C[ollege]" ("O the prodigious vanity," pp. 238–39).[115] These commemorative pieces are followed by two contiguous patronage poems. The first is "To my Lady C. on the report of her being with childe. The joyes and wishes of a friend" ("Madame, Some callt the fate of Poetry to finde," pp. 239–44). The second, also to the same addressee on the same topic, wishes her a safe delivery of her baby:

> Madame.
> What in a Poet's style is Prophecy
> Is in a freinds, Desire: the message I
> Did humbly bring, is now my pray'r become,
> That you enjoy the blessing of your wombe
> Perfect as heav'n can frame it, to bee found

---

[114] Joseph Foster, *Alumni Oxonienses, 1500–1714,* 4 vols. (Oxford: Parker, 1891), 1:298, contains the following biographical information: "Codrington, Robert, of co. Gloucester, gent. MAGDALEN COLL., matric. 26 June, 1621, aged 19; demy 1619–27, B.A. 18 Feb. 1622–3, M.A. 27 June 1626 (2s.Robert, of Codrington, co. Gloucester), settled on a property in Norfolk, died of the plague in London 1665." Cf. *DNB*, 1:665–66. Since Codrington signs himself "R.C.C.C.C.," it would seem that he identified himself as a member of Corpus Christi College.

[115] Foster associates a "John Barloe" with Corpus Christi College; he received a B.A. 19 February 1631 and an M.A. 18 March, 1634 (*Alumni* 1:73).

In all degrees of happinesse beyond
Your wishes; that your Goodnesse, Sweetnesse, Worth
May long survive in that you now bring forth.
                    So prayes
                        Madame
                    Your humble servant
                        R.C.
                                (Pp. 244–45)

After recording the poem about the ducheess of Chevereux's swimming in the Thames ("Twas calme and yet the Thames toucht
Heaven today," pp. 245–46), Codrington continued with several
other pieces he himself wrote, the first probably meant to accompany
a gift to a beloved:

On a Ringe give to
his Mistrisse
By R.C.C.C.C.

Goe gentle Ring and shew a heart
Of him that gives thee which no part
Of Zeuxes skill can pourtray, see
The heart thou shew'st a wounded bee.
Goe tell my Sweet the givers heart
Is bottomless ev'n as thou art.
Then thus bespeake her Mistrisse prove
The depth and measure of his Love
And when you see 'tis infinite
Bee not too cruell but requite
His love with yours, unlesse that hee
May in his love ingulphed bee.

Goe gentle Ring and represent
A circle if by it bee meant
A magick one 'tis best, but soe
Take heed by it my Love thou show
Tell her a circle hath no end
Then thus bespeake her, Sweet, your friend
Beares such a Love as neither date
Of yeares nor chance can expiate
Then charme her to a pitty, and
By force of Loves sweet spells command
Her heart to meet mee in the way

In which Loves magicke made mee stray:
O let her not my soule confine
To wander in an endlesse Line.

  Goe gentle Ring gently embrace
Her finger, tell her that a place
Within her heart would fitt mee best;
And if so bee soe kind a guest,
Shall, as hee would, bee entertain'd
Goe for her favour kisse her hand.
                (Pp. 249–51)

This light poem is followed by an anacreontic piece, "On Xanthus that dyed with Love" ("Unwellcome news! Cupid agen," pp. 251–52), then by one of Codrington's longest poems, "An Elegie sacred to the immortall memorie of the truely noble, and most accomplished FRANCIS Countesse of Bridgewater on of the daughters and coheirs of the illustrious FERDINAND, Earle of Derby. Dedicated to the true mirrour of her sexe and this age the righthonourable ALICE Countesse of Derby, Lady Stanley Strange of Knocking Vicecountesse Kinton and Queene in the Ile of Man. Composed by her most humble and devoted Servant Robert Codrington Master of Arts" ("These teares on blest Bridgwaters Death we doe," pp. 252–64).[116] Another elegy, "On the death of Master Rich[ard] Feild Bach[elor] of Divinitie and fellow of C[orpus] C[hristi] C[ollege]" ("When even now I meant to pay Feilds name," pp. 269–70)[117] completes the selection of poems by this academic compiler. Codrington thus engaged in a widespread practice in composing occasional poems for friends, patrons, and a beloved, incorporating them in his personal anthology. His case is unusual, perhaps, only in the number and length of the pieces he chose to transcribe.

In a commonplace book containing meditations, sermon notes, and apothegms as well as the poems of other authors (Hunt. MS HM 1338),[118] Thomas Parsons, whose signature appears at the end of a letter on fol. 92v, inserted ten poems signed with his initials.

---

[116] This is followed by a Latin poem that ends on p. 269.

[117] Foster associates Richard Feild with Corpus Christi College. He matriculated 17 October 1615 at the age of thirteen and received a B.A. 8 February 1620, an M.A. 24 April 1623, and a B.D. 21 June 1632. He died 24 November 1638 (*Alumni*, 1:489).

[118] In notes to this manuscript at the Huntington Library, A. R. Braunmuller notes that Parsons included excerpts from Bacon's *Essays* and Overbury's *Characters* in his miscellany.

Among them is a socially realistic palinode "To his Mistrisse who (though lately married to another) would notwithstanding have her old servant continue his wonted familiaritie" ("I lov'd thee then I hate thee now," fol. 85v). Among his other poems is an interesting libertine epistle obviously influenced by the style of both Jonson and Donne:

A gentlewoman in London having lately removed her lodging had her freend come to visit her whom shee entreated to salute her new land-lady, which he refusing, shee expostulated that busines with him; & why he had not writt to her more than once shee having writt to him often. and all so why he had punished her for a little dog & would not make good his vowe. he breaking his promise for the next visitation salutes her thus.

> (Besse) I confess I am no neat
> observer of a woman; yet
> not so slavish to my will
> nor in bluntnes halfe so ill
> but that I can with small a-doo
> salute and that with letters too,
> this and more than this may be
> without straying courtesie
> with mine owne humour; for just now
> I write and know not why nor how:
> Suppose a dog you do expect
> and thinke him lost through my neglect
> can you not a-while suspend
> though I nether come nor sent?
> Put-case I promis'd you ere this
> purposely to come and kisse?
> <[line deleted]>
> <[line deleted]>
> breach of promise in this kind
> quickens a dull lovers mind
> whilst absence doth our fancie prove
> and set on edge our keenest love.
> Yf it be true as lovrs sing
> that in love is everie thing?
> Why should not wee do this or that
> without making matter what?

## SOCIAL TEXTUALITY

Sometime loath and sometime love
as <[word(s) deleted]> ^meere fancie^ shall us move?
I hate a formall constant freend
who makes fondnes all his end
I must waver up and downe
and in a breath both smile and frowne
What ere you thinke what eyre you say
just when I list Ile come or stay
I will be silent I must speake
allthough my verie girdle breake,
I must with hony mixe some gall
or else I cannot love at all
I must be wonn I must be lost
and have my humour though it cost
the losse of her whom I love best
and value more than all the rest
assured hope is nothing rare
give me love with some dispaire
I cannot with delight go to-it
when I easilie may do-it
nor can I find sure pleasure out
unlesse the way be full of doubt;
And yet for all this will wee do
as much in love as any two
a Dramme of our love shall weigh more
than the love of halfe-a-score.
our shortest minute farr more deere
then a fondlings whole sev'n yeyre,
and when wee list for to endite
our loves Character shall write
upon a Nut-shell more and better
than ere yet was in love letter
But why do I miselfe expresse
being so wellknown to Besse?
or why do I apologize
since I know thee to be wise?
Therefore in a word or two
farewell without more adoo
If I come I come if not
do not thinke your'selfe forgot
but let mee still reputed be
your verie loving freend T.P.

(Fols. 86v–87v)

Parsons opposes the conventions of love politeness that would constrain behavior and prescribe forms of amorous courtesy, but he assumes the addressee of the poem can value his rhetoric of honesty, even though he uses it to tease her and justify his neglect of her. This antisentimental or anti-Petrarchan love epistle is characteristic seventeenth-century verse, infused with the sexual realism that developed out of both Donne's and Jonson's amorous poetry. It is not surprising that the author of such a poem should have transcribed in his manuscript selections of the pragmatic wisdom found in Bacon's *Essays* and Overbury's *Characters*.

At the end of a two-part mid-seventeenth-century manuscript anthology (BL MS Harley 6917–18), there is a group of poems by Peter Calfe, beginning with an elegy for a deceased friend who was a member of the same social circle. Speaking on behalf of their common friends, Calfe uses the occasion to rationalize his decision to compose verse:

An Elegy:
On the much Lamented Death of his
Ever honourd friend Gerard Gore Esquire

Since thou art fledd, nere more for to appeare
within the Compasse of our Hemi-spheare;
Suffer a friend, though farre unfitt, to bee
thy passionate mourner in an Elegie;
And for sweet flowers to adorne thy Hearse,
accept this prime-Rose of my mayden verse;
Love makes a poet, and hath power t'infuse
that, which by nature was deny'd his Muse;
Deare Losse, but I doe ill to call it soe
Thou art not lost, for thou didst only goe
before, and ledd'st the vann 'gainst Tyrant Death,
who to our griefe depriv'ed thee of thy breath;
Thy grieved Comfort lost a friend, but wee
shall want the Soule of our Societie;
Our meetings will be dull, and flatt, for hee
was the true Genius of our Company;
Yet our losse proves thy gaine, it was to thee
A happy Entrance to faelicity;
for thou hast quitt this Orbe, ascended higher
To singe sweet Anthems in an Angels Quire.
                                        P.C.
                                    (Fol. 96r)

This poem seems to have belonged to a restricted environment in which the literary transmission of elegies and epitaphs affirmed social bonds.[119] Calfe put eight more poems of this sort at the end of his manuscript, including an elegy on his own wife:

> To his matchlesse never to be forgotten friend
> Elegye
>
> Love'd Relique of my deare departed Saint,
> could I my Sorrow's to the life but paint,
> I then would offer at thy honourd shrine
> these weeping verses, that are steept in brine.
> Thou art my Saint, for thou art all Divine;
> If Saints can heare, to me your Eare Encline;
> Since thou'rt departed to thy sadder Urne,
> how can I chuse but like a Turtle mourne;
> Could I but give my troubled passions vent,
> I should esteeme it noe great punishment;
> Light triviall greifes, good language may become,
> But greater Sorrowes Strike the Sufferers Dumbe;
> Now thou art gone, Deare Comfort, I doe see
> A Symptome of mine owne Mortalitye,
> for how can he that loves, live long alone,
> when that his Soule, which gave him life, is gone?
> Thou wert my Second Selfe, my better part;
> Soule of my body, and of that the heart;
> farewell thou partner of my Joyes, thou'lt nere
> Be folded more within these armes thy spheare;
> Farewell those nuptiall sweets, wee did Enjoy
> for many yeeres without the least annoy;
> farewell those Sweet Embraces wee have had
> able to make the Saddest heart turne gladd;
> farewell that Orient Beauty, fresher farre
> then Roses, or the whiter Lillies are;
> farewell thy kinder Language, which to mee

[119] In his verse anthology, for example, Thomas Manne included an elegy commemorating the death (on 11 June 1638) of the young Lord Bayning ("Wert thou an ancient Coarse of a gray head") (BL MS Add. 58215, fols. 37r–39r rev.). Stone, in *Crisis of the Aristocracy* (see Chap. 2, n. 80), identifies Viscount Bayning as from a *nouveau riche* family (p. 498) and points out that he took the grand tour of the Continent after his marriage (p. 659). Bayning, born in 1615, died quite young. Manne's poem, which employs the familiar econmiastic gestures appropriate to the occasion, suggests, perhaps, both a prior academic and personal relationship between the two, if not also Manne's hopes for patronage support from the wealthy family of the deceased.

did farre exceed soft musicks Harmonye;
Thy kisses were Ambrosia to my taste;
wherein all Happiness Justly may be place'd;
Thy breath unto my scent doth call to minde
the fragrant spices, or th'Arabian winde;
my Touch was ravishd with thy softer skinne,
But the best Beauty was conteyn'd within;
How can I then Expresse my losse, to mee
She was the soule of Amabilitye;
now must I bidd Adieu to all content
my Taske is now to grieve since hence you went,
for Death hath robd me of my greatest wealth
A Nurse in sicknes, and my Joy in health

P.C.

(Fols. 100r–v)

Imitating Henry King's popular marital elegy, "An Exequy" (the full title of which reads "An Exequy To his Matchlesse never to be forgotten Freind") Calfe expresses the contemporary ethos of companionate marriage in this poem.[120] Since Calfe transcribed seventeen of Henry King's poems along with thirty-one other poems connected with the King family (including pieces by John King and Henry's younger brothers William and Philip) in his collection, this imitation is not surprising. Calfe does, however, have trouble with the rhetoric of this elegy when, in referring to his spouse, he shifts momentarily in the fifth line from the end of the poem to the third person. The confusion might have been caused, in part, by the instability of the rhetorical situation of a poem that is, in effect, part soliloquy, part apostrophe to the deceased, part address to an imagined sympathetic audience.

Many of the apparently unique copies of epitaphs and elegies that survive in sixteenth- and seventeenth-century manuscript miscellanies and poetry anthologies were, no doubt, composed by the compilers. But this raises the larger issue having to do with the mass of anonymous and unidentified verse one finds in these documents. In the absence, however, of a broad-based first-line index of the poetry found in the manuscripts of this period, it is difficult to separate out those poems that cannot be attributed to particular authors from the

---

[120] See Lawrence Stone, *The Family, Sex and Marriage in England 1500–1800* (New York: Harper & Row, 1977), pp. 325–404 and passim.

numerous anonymous productions. Compiler poetry is a much greater phenomenon than this brief, partial survey can hope to suggest. Most of those individuals who were assembling miscellanies and poetry anthologies probably could not resist trying their hands at the literary forms whose examples they were transcribing.

This leaves a vast field for investigation, hundreds of poems from the manuscripts of the period, an impressive record of ordinary readers' and collectors' full participation in a system of amateur versifying and manuscript transmission. In that literary environment the specialized roles of producer and consumer that characterize print culture and the modern literary institution were nearly meaningless: their involvement in the system of production and reproduction of texts has left a rich body of evidence that is interesting in its own right, but is also an invaluable resource for a social-historical understanding of the literature of the early modern period. As a group of writers, the selective compiler-poets discussed in this chapter have been almost invisible in literary history, unknown except to those very few scholars who happen to have familiarized themselves with the manuscripts in which their poetry appears. This is the case for a number of reasons: first, because the modern literary institution and the kind of literary history it has fostered have largely been shaped by print culture, those poets whose work exists primarily or wholly in manuscript documents have either been ignored or judged unworthy of much notice; second, because the manuscripts in which the poems of these writers are found have been examined, for the most part, only by scholars producing critical editions of major poets, the presence in these documents of aesthetically less valued work has evoked little interest; third, because scholars have not been especially interested in examining literary documents (in manuscript or print) from a social-historical point of view, the verse of poetic compilers or collectors has been pushed well beyond the margins of literary history. Though some of these writer-compilers are identifiable historically, as far as literary history is concerned, they might as well be anonymous.

The presence of answer poetry, compiler verse, and a large body of anonymous work in the manuscript system tells us that the conceptions of authorship, literary reception, and literature itself appropriate to the world of print simply do not apply to this medium of transmission. I have discussed a relatively small number of manuscript documents and dealt with a few aspects of the subject of manuscript transmission, but it is clear from even a cursory survey that this whole field of investigation is vast, complex, and full of undiscovered riches. It is clear also that the history of manuscript transmission should be incorporated in a more systematic way into the histories we continue to write about the literature of the early modern period and the texts we find in this nonprint environment should be taken more seriously in the editions of individual authors we produce, even though such texts will complicate the attainment of some of the traditional author-centered goals of scholarly editing.

CHAPTER FOUR

# PRINT
## AND THE
## LYRIC

IN EARLY modern England, vernacular lyric poetry, like drama, only gradually came to be incorporated in the literary institution shaped by print culture.[1] On the Continent, of course, lyrics had a secure place in the world of print—partly because of the prestige of the work of Petrarch and his imitators, partly because of the connection between "academic" writing, scholarly editing, and print technology. In Italy and France, by the mid-sixteenth century, editions of lyric verse had a cultural centrality they did not achieve in England until much later.[2] In England, there were at least five factors inhib-

---

[1] In my discussion of the impact of print culture, especially on literature, I am indebted to Eisenstein, *Printing Press* (see Chap. 3, n. 8); Lucien Febvre and Henri-Jean Martin, *The Coming of the Book: The Impact of Printing 1450–1800*, trans. David Gerard, ed. Geoffrey Nowell-Smith and David Wootton (London: NLB; Atlantic Highlands, N.J.: Humanities Press, 1976); Richard Helgerson, *Self-Crowned Laureates: Spenser, Milton, and the Literary System* (Berkeley and Los Angeles: University of California Press, 1983); Chartier, *Cultural Uses of Print* (see Chap. 1, n. 2) and "Texts, Printing, Reading," pp. 154–75 (see preface, n. 1); and Richard Newton, "Making Books from Leaves: Poets Become Editors," in *Print and Culture in the Renaissance*, ed. Gerald P. Tyson and Sylvia S. Wagonheim (Newark: University of Delaware Press; London: Associated University Presses, 1986), pp. 246–64. In her study of the relationship of poetry to print in Renaissance England, *Imprint of Gender* (see preface, n. 2), Wendy Wall highlights the gender politics involved in the production and reception of texts within that medium and in the formation of conceptions of authorship and literary authority. See her articles: "Isabella Whitney and the Female Legacy," *ELH* 58 (1991): 35–62 and "Disclosures in Print: The 'Violent Enlargement' of the Renaissance Voyeuristic Text," *SEL* 29 (1990): 35–59.

[2] In her study of the transmission of courtly love lyrics in late medieval manuscripts, Julia Boffey remarks: "The advent of printing had less effect on the circulation and transmission of courtly lyrics in England than might have been supposed. No collections of English lyrics (of any kind) on their own survive from the years before 1500, and none of those which appeared after this date, until the mid-sixteenth century, and the advent of publishers like Tottel, can rival the full-scale French collections such as Antoine Ve'rard's

iting the printing of lyrics. The first was the absence of a clear and strong tradition of vernacular literature into which such publications could be incorporated. English literature, like English nationhood, was a developing entity in the sixteenth century, and it took the achievements of a series of extraordinary writers as well as the growth of some sense of English literary history to put English vernacular literature on an equal footing both with other European traditions and with classical literature.[3] The second factor was a class issue sharpened by print culture, related to what J. W. Saunders discusses as the "stigma of print":[4] aristocratic or "gentle" men and women, or lower-class individuals with social aspirations, were reluctant to print their poetry because they felt threatened by the commercializing and democratizing features of the print medium. A third factor had to do with the perception of love poetry as immature, not intellectually serious writing—morally suspect from a traditional Christian point of view, an attitude captured in the derogatory reference on the title page of the much-reprinted Sternhold and Hopkins translation of Psalms to "ungodly Songs and Ballads, which tend onely to the nourishment of vice, and corrupting of youth." Such verse was also regarded as frivolous and wasteful from the point of view of Renaissance civic humanism (Lord Burghley carried about with him a copy of Cicero's *De Officiis*, not Petrarch's *Rime Sparse*). A fourth factor was the association of love lyrics with privacy, and therefore the belief that it was inappropriate to expose such writing to general public scrutiny. A fifth, and related factor, was the association of lyrics with specific social occasions: people perceived such pieces as ephemeral artifacts, rather than as enduring literary monuments to be preserved in print.

There were many prejudices to overcome before lyric poetry could settle into print as its normal medium of transmission: a whole mindset had to change, lyric poets had to be granted a measure of literary and cultural authority, and educated and socially elite readers had to accept print as the proper environment for lyric verse. Although the

---

*Le Jardin de plaisance* (1502), *Le Vergier d'honneur* (n.d.), and *La Chasse et le depart d'amours* (1509)" (*Manuscripts*, p. 29 [see Chap 1, n. 10]).

[3] For a recent, masterful examination of the development of English nationhood and of the place of vernacular literature in the process, see Richard Helgerson, *Forms of Nationhood: The Elizabethan Writing of England* (Chicago: University of Chicago Press, 1992).

[4] Saunders, "Stigma of Print," pp. 139–64 (see Chap. 1, n. 3).

# PRINT AND THE LYRIC

Renaissance editions of Chaucer set the precedent for sheltering lyric verse within a large, prestigious collection,[5] it took a relatively long time for poetry anthologies and single-author editions of lyric poetry to become an established feature of print culture in England, as the manuscript system of transmission continued to have a remarkable strength and durability through the first two centuries of English printing. First, just before the start of the Elizabethan era, poetry anthologies began to be printed, extending the circulation of those poems that were already being disseminated through manuscript transmission, then, in the last third of the sixteenth century, single-author editions of poems came on the market, as writers and publishers started to claim a new respect for literary authorship and print came to be regarded less as a "stigma" than as a sign of sociocultural prestige.[6]

In the long process of incorporating lyric poetry into print culture, there were (at least) four important moments in English publication history that deserve special attention, the appearance of *Tottel's Miscellany* in 1557; the 1591 and 1592 publication of Sidney's *Astrophil and Stella* and Ponsonby's 1598 folio of that author's collected works; Ben Jonson's 1616 *Workes;* and the 1633 editions of the poems of John Donne and George Herbert. There are, of course, other publications that might be highlighted, such as the 1579 publication of Spenser's work *The Shepheardes Calendar,* which Paul Alpers has discussed as a landmark "lyric" collection,[7] but I would like to emphasize how these other publishing events, spread over some seventy-five years, each had a marked influence on the relationship of lyric poetry to print culture and together worked to make print the normal and preferred medium for such verse.

[5] See Alice S. Miskimin, *The Renaissance Chaucer* (New Haven: Yale University Press, 1975), for a discussion of the important editions and of their relation to the development of an English vernacular literary tradition. She argues that "Thynne's edition of 1532 established the Renaissance 'Chaucer' " (p. 245).

[6] As H. S. Bennett's studies of English books published from 1475 to 1640 have shown, literary works comprised only a small percentage of the books printed in that period, with poetry constituting only a portion of that total: see *English Books and Readers 1475–1557,* 2d ed. (Cambridge: Cambridge University Press, 1969); *English Books and Readers 1558–1603* (Cambridge: Cambridge University Press, 1965); *English Books and Readers 1603–1640* (Cambridge: Cambridge University Press, 1970). J. W. Saunders calls "poetry and works of imagination . . . the poor orphans of the printed book market" ("From Manuscript to Print," p. 527 [see Chap. 1, n. 3]).

[7] Paul Alpers, "Pastoral and the Domain of Lyric in Spenser's *Shepheardes Calendar,*" *Representations* 12 (Fall 1985): 83–100.

# MANUSCRIPT, PRINT, AND THE RENAISSANCE LYRIC

## Richard Tottel and the Appropriation of Poems by Print Culture

Despite the printing of John Skelton's collected works in 1568 and the appearance of those pamphlets constituting the largely lost anthology *The Court of Venus*,[8] the story of the literary institutionalizing of English lyric poetry in print culture really begins in 1557 with *Songes and Sonettes, written by the ryght honorable Lorde Henry Haward late Earle of Surrey, and other* (see figure 3), a book that has come to be known as *Tottel's Miscellany*.[9] This publication not only inaugurated the fashion for publishing anthologies that disseminated privately circulated, mostly courtly, poetry to a wider public, but it also demonstrated some of the sociocultural implications of print as a medium. Works of individual writers such as Chaucer had already been printed, but lyric poems were left to the vagaries of manuscript transmission. Richard Tottel's collection, which went through at least nine editions (and more printings) in thirty years, led to the publication of other poetry collections in the Elizabethan period—including *The Paradise of Dainty Devices* (1576), *A Gorgeous Gallery of Gallant Inventions* (1578), *A Handful of Pleasant Delights* (1566), *Brittons Bowre of Delights* (1591), *The Phoenix Nest* (1593), *The Arbor of Amorous Devices* (1597), *England's Helicon* (1600), *Belvedere: or the Garden of the Muses* (1600), *Englands Parnassus* (1600), and *A Poetical Rhapsody* (1602), many appearing in several editions and printings.[10] It also led to the printing of regular and "augmented" editions of the poetry of individual authors.

Tottel's collection diverted poetry from the relatively closed system of manuscript transmission to present it to a larger public through print: the verse of Wyatt, Surrey, Grimald, and other early Tudor poets, which had been confined previously to manuscript circulation, made its debut in the print medium in this volume. Tottel's anthology and its successors in many ways resemble such surviving manuscript

---

[8] Boffey does not consider *The Count of Venus* a significant anthology of love lyrics (*Manuscripts*, p. 32n). The surviving fragments of *The Court of Venus* have been edited by Russell Fraser (Durham: Duke University Press, 1955). John King argues that the "badly fragmented state of these editions suggests great popularity" (*English Reformation Literature*, p. 226 [see Chap. 1, n. 136]).

[9] I used H. E. Rollins's revised edition of *Tottel's Miscellany* (see Chap. 3, n. 31), which henceforth I cite in the text by volume and page number.

[10] For a discussion of the published miscellanies, see Hyder Rollins's editions of individual sixteenth-century collections as well as Elizabeth Pomeroy, *The Elizabethan Miscellanies: Their Development and Conventions* (Berkeley and Los Angeles: University of California Press, 1973). The exact count of the number of editions of these works is uncertain because of their poor survival rate.

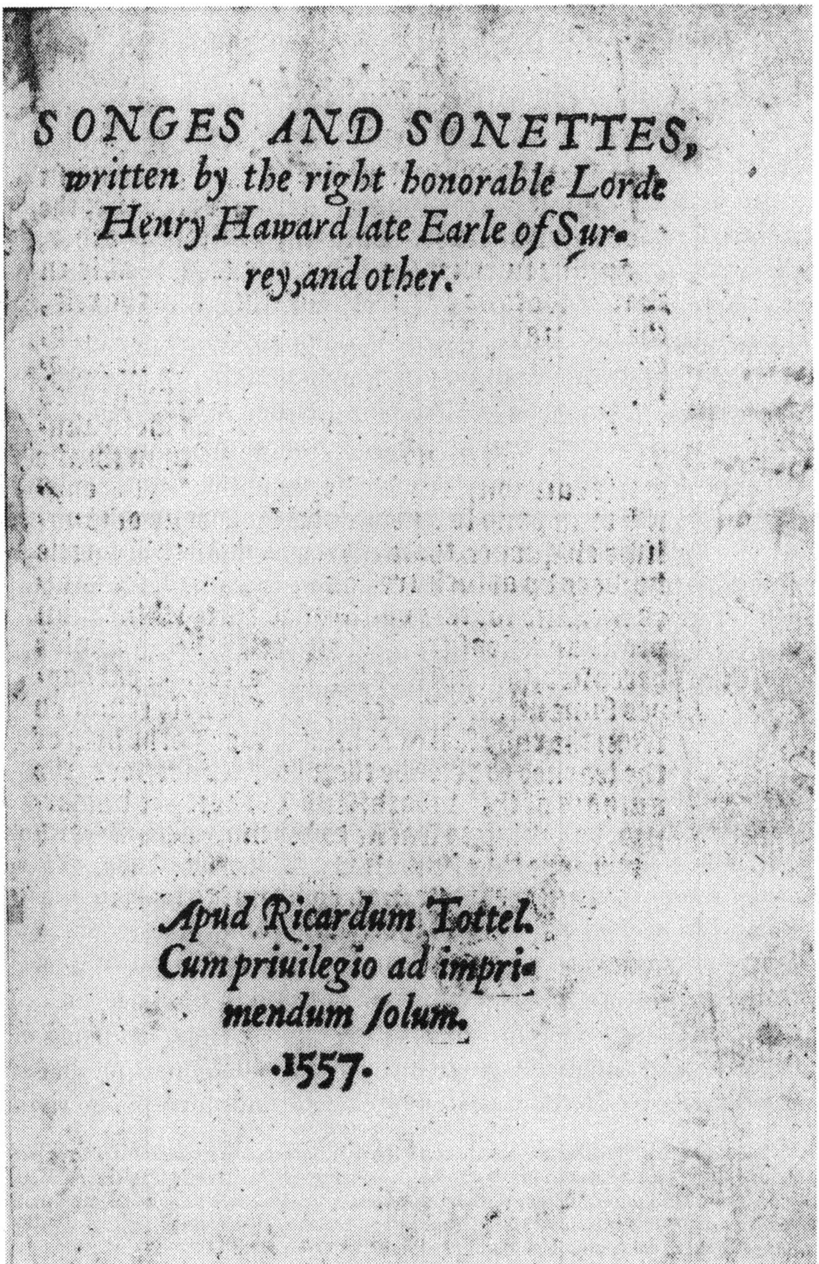

SONGES AND SONETTES,
written by the right honorable Lorde
Henry Haward late Earle of Surrey,and other.

Apud Ricardum Tottel.
Cum priuilegio ad impri-
mendum solum.
·1557·

*Figure 3. Tottel's Miscellany* (1557), title page. Courtesy of the Huntington
Library.

collections as the Arundel Harington Manuscript, Bod. MS Rawl. Poet. 85, and BL MS Harl. 7392:[11] largely courtly poems dealing with love, the vicissitudes of fortune, death and loss, ceremonial social occasions, the relationships of patronage and clientage, and so on—the sorts of verse that someone in contact with the political and social elite might include in a private compilation. We know, for example, that *The Paradise of Dainty Devices* (1576) was based on the personal commonplace-book collection of Richard Edwards, the dramatist who was Queen Elizabeth's Master of the Children of the Chapel Royal;[12] in *A Gorgeous Gallery of Gallant Inventions,* Hyder Rollins claims, the editor Thomas Proctor "simply collected from various sources poems that appealed to him, perhaps changing or supplying words and lines at his fancy, and to the whole adding original compositions of his own";[13] *The Phoenix Nest* (1593) is a gentleman editor's collection that includes poems, Rollins argues, by "authors whom he knew personally";[14] Francis Davison's *Poetical Rhapsody* (1602) (before any possible additions made by the publisher, John Bailey) was a young gentleman's anthology of his own and his brother's poetry along with selected verse by contemporary Elizabethan writers;[15] *England's Helicon* was also the product of a gentleman's editing, not a project initiated by a publisher.[16]

The published anthologies, like the manuscript collections, came to contain both old-fashioned moral verse of the mid-Tudor variety and the newer courtly, "aureate" verse that largely supplanted it in the late Elizabethan period. Courtly, Inns of Court, academic, and aristocratic family coteries circulated and collected poems in manuscripts and manuscript commonplace-book anthologies or in miscellanies containing different kinds of writing. A larger audience of educated and fashionable gentlemen and gentlewomen purchased printed poetry collections and pamphlets of individual poets' work

[11] Richard Harrier has suggested that the original editor of the collection Tottel published in 1557 was the same man responsible for beginning the Arundel Harington Manuscript, John Harington of Stepney. Both texts have a close relationship to the important manuscript of Wyatt's work, BL MS Egerton 2711 (*Canon of Wyatt's Poetry*, pp. 19–20 [see Chap. 1, n. 65]). This point is made in Chapter 1.

[12] Rollins, *Paradise of Dainty Devices*, p. xiii (see Chap. 1, n. 132).

[13] Rollins, *Gorgeous Gallery*, p. xxi (see Chap. 3, n. 1).

[14] Hyder Rollins, ed., *The Phoenix Nest, 1593* (Cambridge: Harvard University Press, 1931), p. xxxii. References to the poems contained in this edition are inserted in the text.

[15] Rollins, *Poetical Rhapsody*, 2:71–81 (see Chap. 3, n. 11). References to the poems in this edition are inserted in the text.

[16] See Rollins, *England's Helicon*, 2:63 (cited in full at Chap. 1, n. 209).

partly to gain access to such socially restricted literary communications. Some later Elizabethan anthologies, especially those associated with John Bodenham (notably *England's Helicon* and *Belvedere*), were more obviously the product of editorial design and further from the manuscript anthologies that served as the sources for many printed texts. The former is a collection of verse in the pastoral mode, the latter a collection of poetical excerpts. The editor of *Belvedere,* in explaining the sources of his selections, says that some were obtained "out of the privat Poems, Sonnets, Ditties, and other wittie conceits, given to [the Queen's] Honourable Ladies, and vertuous Maids of Honour; according as they could be obtained by sight, or favour of copying" (sig. A4r).[17] By and large, the relationship between manuscript and printed miscellanies in the sixteenth century was close and the coexistence of the two forms of publication explainable as an effect of the transition from an old medium of communication to a new.

Tottel's address to the reader of his anthology asserts the public's right to the legitimate "profit and pleasure" derivable from texts that had been socially restricted by "ungentle horders up of such treasures": he reverses the received notions of gentle and ungentle in this formulation. Since the demonstration and learning of "English eloquence" (1:2) made possible through the print medium are part of a program of nationalistic self-assertion (a great country has a great literature), he claims that printing the work of such courtly writers as Wyatt and Surrey is a patriotic act. By prominently featuring the aristocrat Surrey, however, in a frontispiece portrait and on the title page, he seems to be contradicting his more democratic arguments. Tottel characterizes print as fostering a civilizing process that reaches down to the lowest strata of society. He implicitly accepts a model of intellectual and moral self-improvement that is basic to print culture and to developing notions of social progress: he not only offers his book to the "learned," but also states "I exhort the unlearned, by reding to learne to be more skilfull, and to purge that swinelike grosseness, that maketh the swete majerome not to smell to their delight" (1:2).

[17] This passage is quoted in Saunders, "From Manuscript to Print," pp. 523–24. There are, of course, some manuscript collections in which the poems and excerpts from poems are arranged in alphabetical order. Siegfried Wenzel discusses the medieval handbook of Friar John of Grimestone, which contains 240 poems in English "arranged in 232 alphabetical articles, which run from *Abstinencia* to *Vestris*," many of which "consist of only one or two couplets" (*Preachers,* pp. 102, 106 [see Chap. 1, n. 57]).

Tottel condescendingly uses a metaphor that later appears in pictorial form on the title page of the 1593 edition of Sidney's *Arcadia*, which shows a swine and a marjoram bush, with the inscription "Spiro non tibi" ("I breathe forth [sweetness] but not for you").[18] But, of course, the messages of Tottel and of the Sidney edition are contradictory: Tottel's more democratic attitude toward print assumes the less refined can become more refined, whereas the inventor of the 1593 *Arcadia* frontispiece reinforces the class boundaries affirmed by the romance itself. In any event, it is clear that by translating lyric poetry from courtly manuscript circulation to the more public environment of print, Tottel was attempting to market his book to a general readership. In such circumstances, the noble status of Surrey and the aristocratic social origins of the anthology dignified the print medium (and the publishers who controlled the flow of texts within it).

Tottel knew that the perceived value of a collection of lyrics could be enhanced by association with a figure whose life held some special interest to potential readers, and the earl of Surrey's high rank and death by execution assured him a certain romantic notoriety. Social and political preeminence was a better advertisement for printed works, at least for printed anthologies of lyrics, than was literary reputation. Hence the gentleman editor of the miscellany *The Phoenix Nest* followed the title of his book with: "*Built up with the most rare and refined workes of Noble men, woorthy Knights, gallant Gentlemen, Masters of Arts, and brave Schollers.*" The educational and social affiliations of authors were foregrounded in two earlier collections, Timothe Kendall's *Flowers of Epigrammes* (1577) and the anonymous *A Poor Knight his Pallace of Private Pleasure* (1579). The first indicates on the title page that its author was "late of the Universitie of Oxford: now student of Staple Inne in London," and the second identifies its author as a "student in Cambridge" and is introduced by "J.C.," who writes the reader-epistle "from my Chamber in Grayes Inn" (sig. Aiir). The movement of verse from the universities to the Inns of Court that was common in the course of manuscript transmission is highlighted in the print medium. The printer of *The Arbor of Amorous Devices* (1597)

---

[18] In their study of frontispieces, Margery Corbett and Ronald Lightbown have traced this emblem to its Continental sources (*The Comely Frontispiece: The Emblematic Title-Page in England 1550–1660* [London: Henley; Boston: Routledge, 1979], pp. 62–65). They cite an emblem from Camerarius, which they translate as follows: "Wholesome teaching is poison to corrupt minds; so the filthy pig flies from the smell of marjoram" (p. 62).

assured his "Gentlemen Readers" that of the "excellent Poets" represented in the collection, "most" were "not the meanest in estate and degree."[19] The editor of *Belvedere* (1600) listed the authors included in his collection in order of social rank, beginning with the earl of Surrey, the marquis of Winchester, the countess of Pembroke, and Sir Philip Sidney, descending finally to writers regarded as virtual professionals—such as Francis Kinwelmarsh and George Whetstone.

By transferring the anthology model from manuscript to print, Tottel's collection set the precedent for the publication of miscellaneous social verse in other poetry anthologies as well as in single-author editions. The history of poetical anthologies from *Tottel's Miscellany* through Davison's *Poetical Rhapsody* (1602) is well known, but one ought also to note that the editors of single-author collections of such poets as George Turbervile, Barnabe Googe, and George Gascoigne assume, as Tottel does, a close relationship between a published collection of verse and the social circumstances that generated the poetry. Turbervile's *Epitaphes, Epigrams, Songs and Sonets* (1567), for example, as Richard Panofsky has pointed out, contains short poems that "are frankly occasional and social, the *nugae* of a young literary gentleman with court connections."[20]

Tottel was not, however, simply a transporter of texts from the restricted social circulation of manuscript transmission to the more public environment of print. He took an active role in the enterprise. He felt free, for example, to rearrange the syntax of some of Wyatt's poems in order to regularize the meter and to title (or retitle) the poems in the anthology.[21] Similarly, Richard Jones, the printer of *A Handful of Pleasant Delights* (1566), *A Gorgeous Gallery of Gallant Inventions* (1578), and *A Smale handfull of fragrant Flowers* (1575), not only compiled and edited verse for his collections, but also altered texts. In his misadvertised *Brittons Bowre of Delights* (1591), which appropriated a number of poems by Nicholas Breton, using that author's name to help sell what was, in reality, a miscellaneous collection, he

---

[19] Hyder Rollins, ed., *The Arbor of Amorous Devices* (1936; reprint, New York: Russell & Russell, 1968), p. 3.

[20] George Turbervile, *Epitaphes, Epigrams, Songs and Sonets (1567) and Epitaphes and Sonnettes (1576)*, facsimile, with an introduction by Richard J. Panofsky (Delmar, N.Y.: Scholars' Facsimiles & Reprints, 1977), p. vi.

[21] Rollins discusses Tottel's activities as "editor-printer-publisher" (*Tottel's Miscellany*, 2: 93–101). For an interesting analysis of the depoliticizing effects of Tottel's titles for Wyatt's poems, see Jonathan Kamholtz, "Thomas Wyatt's Poetry: The Politics of Love," *Criticism* 20 (1978): 349–65.

called his readers' attention to fact that the poems were "wel com-piled," highlighting their quality, but also calling attention to his own role as compiler-editor.[22] The several anthologies associated with the name of John Bodenham represent the activities of connoisseurs who elevated personal taste and interests into aesthetic prominence.[23] But, of course, anthologists and editors were only extending into print culture the freedom enjoyed by collectors and compilers in a manu-script culture.

Tottel's practice of providing special titles for the poems in his collection signals the recoding of social verse as primarily *literary* texts in the print medium. When the poems themselves were cut off from the contexts of their production and initial reception, a recontex-tualizing process began in which the works lost their vivid particularity of meaning and began to speak a language whose general and ab-stract terms were a hybrid of poetic conventionality and culture-specific code words.[24] Although sometimes manuscript copies of poems indicate the (imagined or actual) circumstances in which the works were written and read, it was not until lyrics were committed to print that titles or introductory comments were necessary to allow readers to perceive the poems' connection either to an actual social world or to the traditional fictional world of love experience. Al-though titles trace their origin as far back as the *vidas* and *razos* at-tached to troubadour verse (those biographical and explanatory/interpretive comments framing individual lyrics cut off from their enabling social conditions,),[25] titles for lyric poems were institution-

---

[22] Hyder Rollins, ed., *Brittons Bowre of Delights 1591* (Cambridge: Harvard University Press, 1933), p. 3. The words "compile" and "compiler" had at least two significantly different meanings in the Renaissance. To "compile" verse could mean to compose it or to collect and edit it. Elizabeth Eisenstein quotes Bonaventure on the four functions that might be performed by those who produced manuscript collections: "A man might write the works of others, adding and changing nothing, in which case he is simply called a 'scribe' (*scriptor*). Another writes the work of others with additions which are not his own; and he is called a 'compiler' (*compilator*). Another writes both others' work and his own, but with others' work in principal place, adding his own for purposes of explanation; and he is called a 'commentator' (*commentator*). . . . Another writes both his own work and others' but with his own work in principal place adding others' for purposes of confirmation; and such a man should be called an 'author' (*auctor*)" (*Printing Press*, 1:121–22).

[23] See Hyder Rollins's discussion of John Bodenham, Nicholas Ling, and the literary/social coterie connected with *England's Helicon, Belvedere, Wit's Theater* and *Politeuphuia* (*England's Helicon*, 2:41–71).

[24] See Corti's discussion of "desemiotization" in *Literary Semiotics*, p. 19 (cited in full at preface, n. 1).

[25] See Maurice Valency, *In Praise of Love: An Introduction to the Love-Poetry of the Renaissance* (New York: Macmillan, 1958), pp. 90–91.

alized in certain ways by the practices of collecting verse, first, in manuscript anthologies, then, in printed volumes. Sometimes compilers tried to identify the actual conditions of composition and reception. Sometimes they invented contexts for works whose original authors, recipients, and/or circumstances of composition and reception were lost or unknown.

The situations defined in the titles or explanatory introductions to lyrics might either be presented as real-world occasions or, with more literary self-consciousness, as conventional ones associated with the experiences of the poetic "lover." Tottel has both kinds of "titles": for example, "A song written by the earle of Surrey by [for] a lady that refused to daunce with him" (1:207-9) and "Upon sir James wilfordes death" (1:135-36) illustrate the first type, whereas "A Complaint by night of the lover not beloved" (1:10) and "The aged lover renounceth love" (1:165) illustrate the second. The first sort of titling assumes that print is a latecomer in a process of transmission that moves progressively farther away from the social world to which lyric poems belong and therefore must make special (usually flawed) efforts to recreate the text's social context; the second sort treats the individual text as an instance of "literature," as a work liberated from some of the constraints that affected its original function and meaning, interpretable through the medium of a reader's historical and literary imagination. One practice, of course, shades into the other, as original elements of a poem's social context are fictionalized to make them conform to romantic expectations. John Stevens, in his fine study of early Tudor verse, traces such processes back to the fifteenth-century collector John Shirley, whose annotations in his manuscript poetical anthologies point to a social world behind the lyrics, and to Charles d'Orleans's simultaneous creation of fictional and social environments in his collection of courtly love lyrics.[26] To a certain extent, Sir John Harington's title for Sidney's sonnet sequence in the Arundel Harington Manuscript, "Sonnettes of Sir Phillip Sydneys *uppon* to the Lady Ritche" (Hughey, 1:254), both identifies and romanticizes the social matrix of the sonnet sequence.

In print, titles became standard for lyrics, but the prose surrounding intercalated verse in narratives such as George Gascoigne's "Ad-

---

[26] John Stevens, *Music and Poetry in the Early Tudor Court* (Lincoln: University of Nebraska Press, 1961), p. 208. Cf. Boffey, *Manuscripts*, p. 66 and passim.

ventures of Master F. J.," Thomas Whythorne's *Autobiography*,[27] and Sir Philip Sidney's *Arcadia* perform a similar contextualizing function. Tottel and the manuscript tradition both encouraged the model of the miscellaneous poetry collection. The other major model was that of the lyric narrative sequence (going back to Petrarch's *Rime Sparse* and Dante's *La Vita Nuova*); the first kept verse close to the unpredictability of social life and social occasions; the second highlighted the constructive activity of the poet and the fictional and literary character of poetic collection. Both models coexisted within Gascoigne's, Whythorne's, and Sidney's prose narratives as well as, more generally, in the poetry collections published in the period covered in this book.

Gascoigne's novella, for example, is itself presented as part of a (counterfeit) miscellany of "divers discourses & verses, invented uppon sundrie occasions, by sundrie gentlemen" that the fictional editor, "G.T.," has "confusedly gathered together."[28] "The Adventures of Master F.J." itself contains fourteen poems whose circumstances of composition and transmission the narrator is careful to define, even as he intrudes his own, often inept, literary and moral observations. The first lyric, for example, composed in response to falling in love with Dame Elinor, F.J. "thought not best to commit . . . willingly into hir custodie, but privily lost them in hir chamber, written in counterfeit" (p. 53). The third poem, a sonnet the narrator identifies as having "borrowed th'invention of an *Italian*" (p. 60), F.J. gives directly to his mistress, explaining that it is a trivial piece "such as I might be ashamed to publish in this company" (p. 59). The eighth poem, which praises his mistress as a "Hellen" (p. 75) for beauty, is one of the hubristic pieces composed after F.J. has entered a sexual relationship with Elinor. It gets into general circulation "by the negligence of his Mistresse dispersed into sundry hands, and so at last to the reading of a Courtier" (p. 76). The editor-narrator notes that "this and divers other of his most notable Poems, have come to view of the world, although altogether without his consent. And some have attributed this prayse unto a *Hellen*, who deserved not so well as this dame *Elynor*" (p. 76).

Referring to the poems composed at the stage of the affair in

---

[27] See *The Autobiography of Thomas Whythorne*, Modern Spelling Edition, ed. James M. Osborn (London: Oxford University Press, 1962).

[28] *George Gascoigne's "A Hundreth Sundrie Flowers,"* ed. Prouty, pp. 49, 51 (see Chap. 1, n. 4). Henceforth cited in the text by page number.

which F.J. feels fulfilled both sexually and emotionally, the narrator remarks:

> These two Lovers passed many dayes in exceeding contentation, & more than speakeable pleasures, in which time *F. J.* did compyle very many verses according to sundrie occasions proffred, whereof I have not obteyned the most at his handes, and the reason that he denied me the same, was that (as he alleged) they were for the most part sauced with a taste of glory, as you know that in such cases a lover being charged with inexprimable joyes, and therewith enjoyned both by dutie and discretion to kepe the same covert, can by no meanes devise a greater consolation, than to commit it into some cyphred wordes and figures speeches in verse, whereby he feeleth his harte halfe (or more than halfe) eased of swelling. (P. 77)

The poetry of fruition is thus identified as the most private kind of amorous verse. This is a convenient excuse in the narrative, for F.J.'s poems do not simply seem "sauced with glory"; they are insensitively arrogant, the worst being a nasty sonnet about the cuckolding of Elinor's husband that F.J. hands over to his mistress. After this, the tenth poem, the narrator says "I will surcease to rehearse any more of his verses, untill I have expressed how that his joyes being now exalted to the highest degree, began to bend towardes declination" (p. 79). When the relationship sours as a direct result of F.J.'s charging his mistress with having betrayed him by resuming her affair with her secretary and F.J. has raped her in an attempt to recover the control he knew he'd lost, the poems return to the more dignified plaintive mode of frustrated love—the twelfth composed as an answer to Elinor's curt letter of rejection, but the thirteenth converting Petrarchan complaint into inelegant moral-satiric attack. This last piece seems to conflate sonnet and epigram, becoming a poem with a "sharpe conclusion" of the sort found often in Shakespeare's *Sonnets*. It is transmitted to the mistress in much the same way as the first poem in the sequence: "He lost it where his Mistresse found it, and she immediately emparted the same unto Dame *Pergo,* and Dame *Pergo* unto others: so that it quickely became common in the house" (p. 104). The final poem is a farewell-to-love lyric composed in solitude.

Taken together, the poems in this comically ironic narrative constitute an anthology of genres in various styles—plain to aureate. They include sonnets, ballads, pieces composed to preexistent music, complaints, a formal blazon of beauty, a version of a section of Ariosto's *Orlando Furioso* and other translations and imitations of Italian texts, native and popular verse, even a short (three-poem) sonnet sequence. They are tied to the changing situations associated with a love affair that begins conventionally with falling in love at first sight, runs through an ironically easy stage of fruition, and is destroyed both by jealousy and by treachery. The lyrics are transmitted for the most part to the mistress, thence to a wider audience in the castle that serves as the scene of the tale, and, in at least one case, to the larger world of polite courtly society. The publication of the narrative and of the supposed courtly anthology of verse of which it is a part enlarges the audience still further. In a fictional frame, then, Gascoigne has replicated the circumstances of the production, transmission, and preservation or collection of social verse, calling attention to the social and the biographical circumstances in which lyrics were typically written, while making straightforward social and biographical interpretation quite problematic.[29]

One of the things to remember when examining the components of the printed book in the early modern period, for example, the frontispiece, the title page, the dedicatory epistles to patrons, the addresses to readers, and the commendatory poems, is that each was a site of contestation and negotiation among authors, publisher/printers, and readership(s).[30] In the format of printed publications, despite the illusion of stability created by some published texts, the ideological and social assumptions of various restricted socioliterary environments often clashed with the democratizing force of print and the commercial commodification of texts in print culture. Every party

[29] Wendy Wall points out that Isabella Whitney similarly signals the processes of manuscript transmission in her second published work, *A Sweet Nosgay* (1573). By combining poetry and letters, prose and verse epistles exchanged with friends, "The *Nosgay* counters the anxieties of print publication by presenting a book that replicates private textual circulation. By including letters sent between family members and friends and by referring to the text's place in a gift/patronage cycle, Whitney sets up a textual exchange system within the work. Through these devices, she informs the print commodity with the reciprocity of social exchange at the very moment that she bewails her exclusion from prestigious circles in London. . . .Whitney creates a textual artifact that imitates the practices of those in more elite coteries" ("Isabella Whitney and the Female Legacy," p. 47).

[30] One of the crucial factors in the shift from manuscript culture to print culture was the place of patronage in the social relationship of authors, publishers, and readers. I discuss this topic separately in Chapter 5, since I wish to highlight its dynamics apart from those of the (undoubtedly related) issues I deal with in this chapter.

to the literary transaction—author, publisher, printer, dedicatee, reader—had to be positioned. At stake was the sociocultural authority of writers and patrons; the property rights to texts to be claimed variously by authors, publishers, and consumers; the control of interpretation by authors or readers; the relationship of classes and subgroups in the society in which printed books transported texts over social boundaries; and the stability or instability of the literary institution being shaped by the print medium. Given this situation, we should pay special attention to the "front matter" of early printed books, since such features as frontispieces, title pages, dedications, epistles, and commendary verse historically mediated texts in revealing ways.

There is, for example, an interesting set of differences between the title pages of the 1573 and 1575 editions of George Gascoigne's collected works. The first is presented as a miscellany of works by ancient and modern Continental writers and contemporary English authors: *A Hundreth sundrie Flowres bounde up in one small Poesie. Gathered partely (by translation) in the fyne outlandish Gardins of Euripides, Ovid, Petrarke, Ariosto, and others: and partly by invention, out of our owne fruitefull Orchardes in Englande: Yelding sundrie sweete savours of Tragical, Comical, and Morall Discourses, both pleasaunt and profitable to the well smellying noses of learned Readers.* No swine are invited to smell this posy (or read this poesy). Although Gascoigne's name appears in the table of contents, he is conspicuously and misleadingly absent from the title page of this putative literary florilegium. The personal motto, however, *"Meritum petere, gravé"* ("To seek reward is a weighty business"), suggests the author's pursuit of status and preferment. Apart from the classical authors mentioned, only the name of the publisher, Richard Smith, appears.

The slightly revised edition of the anthology two years later has a title-page that advertises a very different kind of publication. An "architectural" frontispiece[31] enshrining the work as a literary monument encloses the following: *The Posies of George Gascoigne Esquire. Corrected, perfected, and augmented by the Authour. 1575. Tan Marti, quam Mercurio. Imprinted at London by H. Bynneman for Richard Smith* (see Figure 4). The same author, the same publisher (accompanied now by

---

[31] For a discussion of this type of title page, see Corbett and Lightbrown, *Comely Frontispiece,* pp. 6–9 and passim.

The Posies of
*George Gascoigne*
Esquire.

*Corrected, perfected,*
and augmented by the
Authour. 1575.

*Tam Marti, quàm Mercurio.*

❡ IMPRINTED AT
London by H. Bynneman
for Richard Smith.

These Bookes are to be solde at the North-
west dore of Paules Church.

*Figure 4.* George Gascoigne, *The Posies* (1575), title page. Courtesy of the Huntington Library.

the printer), and (basically) the same collection of works here stand in a very different relation to one another. The writer's name is printed in a type size larger than the printer's, which is itself printed in slightly larger type than the publisher's. Gascoigne is identified simultaneously as an "Esquire" and an "Authour" as though there were no conflict between genteel status and professional authorship. His well-known motto calls attention to his accomplishments as a soldier and scholar-writer. The text of the work is encoded in a significant way, advertised as the "Corrected, perfected, and augmented" version: the first two adjectives associate the writing with print culture's tendency to fix texts, which were more malleable in the system of manuscript transmission, and the last adjective, "augmented," signals the author's alleged revision and expansion of a body of works over which he exercised proprietary care. He gave the appearance of having produced a new and improved version that was more commercially attractive to book buyers than the previous publication. Although the earlier book was supposedly more casual in its arrangement, the "Posies" ("Poesies") of this version, as indicated by the division of the works into "Flowers," "Hearbes," and "Weedes," is more deliberate (the product, therefore, of another act of authorial control). Whereas the presentation of *A Hundreth Sundrie Flowres* foregrounds the reader's convenience and use, this second edition of Gascoigne's work is designed to dignify, even monumentalize, its author, a purpose also served by the newly added commendatory verse.[32] Richard Newton distinguishes three types of poetry collection in the printed books of the English Renaissance: "the sequence, the 'gathering' or miscellany, and the 'critical' collection."[33] These two collected editions of Gascoigne's works represent the second and third types—though *The Posies* has nothing like the structural meticulousness of a later work such as Ben Jonson's *Forrest.*

Partly because amorous writing was generally considered frivolous, embarrassing if made public, and the sign of an inability to accept moral and civic responsibility, publishing did not secure for Gas-

---

[32] See Newton, "Making Books from Leaves," pp. 254–55, on Gascoigne's two editions. Newton argues that "the ostentatious promotion in the second edition of the garden image as structural principle and his trite preface to the volume . . . in which he at once acknowledges the poems to be his and systematically reaffirms his amateur standing" along with the information that he wrote many pieces "for other men" were an attempt to keep the work from being read as a record of personal experience.

[33] Ibid., pp. 247–48.

coigne the respect he sought. Clearly, through the first two decades of Queen Elizabeth's reign, it was hazardous for a gentleman to print verse, especially amorous lyrics. And so Edmund Spenser took a different tack in 1579 when he published *The Shepheardes Calendar*. Paul Alpers has argued that "by writing a book of eclogues, conceived as the performance of pastoral roles, Spenser created . . . a 'domain of lyric,' " an "aesthetic space" that freed him from some of the constraints under which poets like Gascoigne, Googe, and Turbervile operated, because he had "a certain distance from courtly and social accountability." Seeking "*literary* authority," Spenser found the medium of print suited to his needs, using it a a way of "staking out his claim in the world of European letters." Alpers attributes to *The Shepheardes Calendar* "lyric authority," by which he means that "the work itself is a complete and substantial book of short poems that stands on its own terms."[34]

Spenser's self-authorizing publication, however, which was printed with some of the paraphernalia of classical texts and annotated "modern" classics such as Dante's *Divina Commedia* and Petrarch's *Rime Sparse*, did not exactly open the floodgates for gentlemen to print their love-poetry collections. The old prejudices against such work were still strong. When, in 1593, that mediocre, but prolific, writer, Thomas Churchyard, published the newest in a long list of printed works, *Churchyards Challenge*, he felt it necessary to advertise his prominence in the system of manuscript literary transmission as well as in the world of print by prefacing his work with two lists. The first, "The bookes that I can call to memorie alreadie *Printed*" (sig. *v), consists of thirty-one titles from the time of Edward VI and Mary through the reign of Elizabeth, and Churchyard mentions all the prestigious individuals to whom they were dedicated.[35] The second list of "workes . . . gotten from me of some such noble freends as I am loath to offend" includes a translation of "*Aeneas* tale to *Dydo*," "A book of the oath of a Judge and the honor of Law" (sig. **r), a Shrovetide entertainment celebrating the earl of Leicester's accomplishments, a translation of some of the works of Dubartas, and "an infinite num-

---

[34] Alpers, "Pastoral," pp. 94–96. Alpers has invited us to read *The Shepheardes Calendar* as "a mid-Tudor collection of short poems" in which "the fictions and conventions of pastoral resolve problems of motivating lyric utterance" (pp. 84, 91).

[35] He takes credit not only for works published under his name but also for the pieces included in Tottel's collection: "Many things in the booke of songs and Sonets, printed then, were of my making."

ber of other Songes and Sonets, given where they cannot be recovered, nor purchase any favour when they are craved" (sig. **v). Clearly Churchyard desperately wanted to claim a place of respect for himself in the more socially prestigious environment of manuscript transmission, despite his less-than-eminent reputation as a professional writer.

Although we associate print with the preservation of texts that, if confined to the system of manuscript transmission, faced the danger of being lost, it is important to recognize that many printed works were conceived of or treated as ephemeral. Especially when published in short octavos and quartos, poetry anthologies and small editions of individual authors had small chance of surviving given how they were treated by contemporary readers. Hence, many printed texts (in some cases, entire editions) have disappeared—some, as Hyder Rollins has suggested, having been "literally read out of existence."[36] The treatment of lyric poems as ephemera, encouraged by the circumstances of their original production and reception as well as by their transmission in loose papers by writers who did not necessarily even keep copies of what they had written, carried over into the cultural situation of printed texts as well. In the disingenuous letter "To the Gentlemen Readers" of *Euphues*, John Lyly points to this fact when he compares the book he is publishing to another perishable object: "A new work should not endure but six months. Gentlemen use books as gentlewomen handle their flowers, who in the morning stick them in their heads and at night strew them at their heels. . . .[A] fashion is but a day's wearing and a book but an hour's reading."[37] He might have been arguing ironically that a printed literary work should be treated as an artifact worthy of preservation, but Lyly knew that entertaining "pamphlets" (to use the term printers often used to describe the prose and poetry they produced for young fashionable gentlemen) were apt to be treated as disposable objects. After all, this evidently was the attitude of writers *and* readers toward recreational productions in an era before such works had been securely incorporated in a body of institutionalized literature as

[36] Rollins, *Brittons Bowre of Delights*, pp. xxiv–xxv. King also notes, with reference to Edwardian literary works, that "English readers wore out their pamphlets, proclamations, ballads, broadsides, and other ephemera" (*English Reformation Literature*, p. 104).

[37] John Lyly, *Euphues: The Anatomy of Wit*, in *Elizabethan Prose Fiction*, ed. Merritt Lawlis (New York: Odyssey Press, 1967), p. 123.

aesthetically sacred texts. William Lambarde voiced a not-uncommon objection to such ephemeral material in complaining about the "sundrie bookes, pamfletes, Poesies, ditties, songs, and other woorkes . . . serving to let in a mayne Sea of wickednesse . . . and to no small or sufferable wast[e] of the treasure of this Realme which is thearby consumed and spent in paper, being of it selfe a forrein and chargeable commoditie."[38]

## Sidney and the Legitimizing of Printed Lyric Verse

Through most of the sixteenth century (and much of the seventeenth), because of the "stigma of print," men of rank and others who pretended to gentility either deliberately avoided print or, usually with the cooperation of a publisher, tried to maintain the illusion that they had only reluctantly allowed their work to be printed. John Selden's comment in his *Table-Talk* expresses the typical attitude: "'Tis ridiculous for a Lord to print Verses; 'tis well enough to make them to please himself, but to make them public, is foolish. If a Man in a private Chamber twirls his Band-strings, or plays with a Rush to please himself, 'tis well enough; but if he should go into *Fleet-street*, and sit upon a Stall, and twirl a Band-string, or play with a Rush, then all the Boys in the Street would laugh at him."[39] When Thomas Watson published his Petrarchan collection of love poetry in 1582, he protected himself somewhat against the stigma of print not only by dedicating the work to the earl of Oxford but also by asserting his gentility and alluding to an educated coterie of supporters: the book's title page states that it was "Composed by Thomas Watson Gentleman; and published at the request of certaine Gentlemen his very frendes." Nevertheless, Watson still apologized for poems as "idle toyes proceedinge from a youngling frenzie" (sig. A4r), aware, as Gascoigne was, of the Protestant humanist prejudice against amorous verse as well as of the embarrassment of making one's work available to the general public through print.

It took the landmark posthumous publication in the early 1590s of Sir Philip Sidney's *Astrophil and Stella*, a collection of sonnets contem-

---

[38] Quoted in Marjorie Plant, *The English Book Trade: An Economic History of the Making and Sale of Books*, 2d ed. (London: Allen & Unwin, 1965), p. 48.
[39] Quoted in Sanderson, "An Edition," p. 116 (see Chap. 1, n. 121).

porary with Watson's, to begin to provide the necessary sociocultural legitimation for printing of lyric verse.[40] As William Ringler and others have noted, Thomas Newman's two 1591 quartos of Sidney's *Astrophil and Stella*, despite the poor and incomplete state of their texts, were enormously important publishing events.[41] They were part of a process in the 1590s in which the work of this author was posthumously made available to a public beyond the closed circle of the Sidney-Herbert family and those who were connected with it through friendship and/or clientage. Newman's two quartos and Lownes's 1592 quarto of *Astrophil and Stella*, Ponsonby's 1590 and 1593 *Arcadia* texts, that same publisher's 1595 *Defence of Poesie*, and his great 1598 folio of Sidney's collected works together had a remarkable impact.[42] From one end of the decade to the other, the influence of Sidney on the printing of literary texts was pervasive: not only did the publication of *Astrophil and Stella* as the love sonnets of a national hero who was portrayed as a Protestant martyr[43] elevate the sociocultural status of lyric poetry and of literary authorship, stimulating the production *and publication* of many other sonnet collections, but also it fundamentally changed the culture's attitudes toward the printing of the secular lyrics of individual writers, lessening the social disapproval of such texts and helping to incorporate what had essentially been regarded as literary ephemera into the body of durable canonical

[40] I make this argument in "Love Is Not Love" (see Chap. 2, n. 118).

[41] See, for example, W. A. Ringler Jr., "Sir Philip Sidney: The Myth and the Man," in *Sir Philip Sidney: 1586 and the Creation of a Legend*, ed. Jan van Dorsten, Dominic Baker-Smith, and Arthur Kinney (Leiden: E. J. Brill/Leiden University Press for the Sir Thomas Browne Institute, 1986), pp. 3–15. Ringler points out that before the publication of his writing, "Sidney was . . . first known and praised primarily as a learned soldier and an accomplished courtier" (p. 11), but that after his major works were published in the 1590s, "allusions to Sidney changed from praising him primarily as a hero to praising him as a man of letters, and he was hailed as the foremost literary artist of his century" (p. 12).

[42] The 1598 folio, *The Countesse of Pembrokes Arcadia. Written by Sir Philip Sidney Knight. Now the Third Time published, with sundry new additions of the same Author*, is an elaborate production of some 292 leaves: it contains the *Arcadia* and the *Defence*, the full text of *Astrophil and Stella*, and the first published versions of *Certain Sonets* and the Wanstead entertainment. It had thirteen printings between 1599 and 1674 alone. See the *Poems of Sidney*, ed. Ringler, p. 535 (cited in full at Chap. 1, n. 207). For a discussion of Ponsonby's publications and of his relationship to the Sidney-Herbert circle, see Michael Brennan, "William Ponsonby: Elizabethan Stationer," *Analytical & Enumerative Bibliography* 7 (1983): 91–110.

[43] For an interesting discussion of how the four Latin commemorative collections of poems mythologize and politicize the death of Sidney, see Dominic Baker-Smith, " 'Great Expectation': Sidney's Death and the Poets," in van Dorsten, Baker-Smith, and Kinney, *Sir Philip Sidney: 1586 and the Creation of a Legend*, pp. 83–103.

texts. Sidney made both poetry pamphlets and collected literary works more socially acceptable and thus paved the way for such poets as Daniel, Drayton, and Jonson to print their poems.

In the 1591 quartos of *Astrophil and Stella*, Newman claims to have been editorially conscientious in establishing the text of Sidney's sonnet sequence: "For my part, I have beene very careful in the Printing of it, and where as being spred abroade in written Coppies, it had gathered much corruption by ill Writers: I have used their helpe and advice in correcting and restoring it to his first dignitie, that I knowe were of skill and experience in those matters."[44] Whether or not Newman actually did this is not really the issue: the important thing about his statement is not whether it is true (after all this first quarto descends from the worst of the manuscript traditions, according to Ringler),[45] but rather that he conceives of clearing texts of alleged corruption as part of the editorial process at all. Of course, there is evidence that in producing the second quarto several months after the first, Newman corrected many of the textual errors of his first edition in this improved text of *Astrophil and Stella*—which appears to have been extensively (if sloppily) revised through sonnet 95 with the help of a manuscript text from a textually superior tradition.[46]

In print, texts were typographically fixed as objects within a set of publishing conventions and printing-house practices: their final form was often the result of such authorial and/or editorial "perfecting" or "correcting." Print cultivated the notion of an "authorized" text—with or without the cooperation of authors.[47] Both publishers and authors began to express concern for the correctness of the texts being printed—a contrast to the more casual attitude toward texts in the manuscript system. For example, in their address "To the great Variety of Readers" of the first folio of Shakespeare (1623), John Heminge and Henry Condell make the claim that their publication corrects and fixes the texts of the plays: "Where (before) you were

---

[44] *The Complete Works of Sir Philip Sidney*, ed. Albert Feuillerat (Cambridge: Cambridge University Press, 1922), 3:369.

[45] See Ringler's discussion of "Z" in *Poems of Sidney*, pp. 451–53.

[46] The manuscript line designated "Y" by Ringler (ibid., p. 545). Warkentin suggests that Samuel Daniel, who wanted to wrest his own work from Newman to publish it in carefully revised form, probably helped the publisher to correct the first quarto ("Sidney's *Certain Sonnets*," pp. 484–85 [see Chap. 1, n. 38]).

[47] Robert Herrick wrote in "His Request to Julia" that he would rather have his poems burned than printed in texts that were "not perfected" (*Hesperides* 59, in *Complete Poetry of Herrick*, ed. Patrick, p. 32 [see Chap. 3, n. 36]).

abus'd with diverse stolne, and surreptitious copies, maimed, and deformed by the frauds and stealthes of injurious impostors, that expos'd them: even those, are now offer'd to your view cur'd, and perfect of their limbes; and all the rest, absolute in their numbers, as he conceived them."[48] When he published the full edition of his *Delia* (1592), Samuel Daniel partly justified his enterprise by asserting that the "uncorrected" (sig. A2r) texts of his own poems that Newman printed along with Sidney's in the first quarto of *Astrophil and Stella* needed fixing.

Newman had augmented his edition of Sidney's sonnets with "Poems and Sonets of sundrie other Noble men and Gentlemen" (sig. I3r), printing twenty-eight of Daniel's sonnets, five musical cantos (some or all of which were written by Thomas Campion), a Greville poem ascribed to the earl of Oxford, "Faction that ever dwells in court" (*Caelica* 28),[49] and an anonymous two-stanza piece that appeared in later songbooks, "If fluds of teares could cleanse my follies past" (sig. L4v).[50] Partly because of the popularity of poetry anthologies, partly because the publisher wanted to fill out a short quarto with other work, much of which could be associated with the Sidney-Pembroke circle, Newman thus made the first edition of *Astrophil and Stella* an "augmented" one. Practices of gathering the work of many authors in manuscripts, then, carried over into print culture not only in the production of poetry anthologies, but also in the presentation of single-author editions. Such an augmentation of an individual author's work was imitated—for example, in the 1594 edition of Constable's *Diana* and in the 1640 edition of Carew's poetry.[51] In one

---

[48] *The Norton Facsimile of the First Folio of Shakespeare,* prepared by Charlton Hinman (New York: Norton, 1968), p. 7.

[49] This poem (at sig. L4v) is signed with the initials "E. D." Newman probably wanted the social prestige of having at least one poem by a major aristocrat in his edition.

[50] See the discussion of authorship of all these poems in Christopher R. Wilson, "*Astrophil and Stella*: A Tangled Editorial Web," *The Library,* 6th ser., 1 (1979): 336–46.

[51] Grundy argues that forty-one of the poems in the second edition of *Diana* (1594) are by poets other than Constable and that of the seventy-six sonnets in that edition only twenty-seven can be shown to be his (*Poems of Constable,* p. 51 [see Chap. 1, n. 160]). Dunlap confirms this, adding that the poems on pp. 168–206 of the 1640 edition of Carew constitute a little anthology of work by such writers as Herrick, Waller, Shirley, Constable, Strode, and Henry Blount (*Poems of Carew,* p. lxii [see Chap. 1, n. 31]). A (deceptive) practice related to that of augmenting editions of individual authors was, conversely, the presentation of miscellaneous work as though it were the product of one popular or respected author—for example, the miscellany *Britton's Bowre of Delights* (1591), Jaggard's *Passionate Pilgrim by William Shakespeare* (1599 and 1612), and *The Poems of Francis Beaumont* (1640 and 1653). William Ringler, for example, believes only four poems of the combined

sense, Newman's edition delivers a double message: Sidney is a great author and his unpublished verse deserves to be published and respected as great literature; but also Sidney is one of a number of coterie writers whose work should be liberated into print. The first message is obvious, and it is connected with the Sidney cult, which began at that author's death in 1586 and flourished through the 1590s. The second message is, perhaps, more important, since by it Newman argues, as Tottel had, for a more general transfer of literature from restricted manuscript circulation to public availability through print. After all, this publication marks the first appearance in print of Daniel's, Campion's, and Greville's poetry.[52] Partly through the instrumentality of Newman's and Lownes's quartos, some of the "stigma of print" associated especially with the publication of lyric poetry was lessened and the publication of lyric collections became a regular feature of print culture in England, as it had become on the Continent.

After the printing of Sidney's works in the 1590s, both publishers and writers alluded to the authorizing example of Sidney as the decade following the publication of Newman's quartos of *Astrophil and Stella* witnessed an extraordinary increase in the number of poetry pamphlets and anthologies: Sidney became, as Gabriel Harvey put it, the "Paragon of Excellency in Print."[53] With Sidney's sonnets in print, Samuel Daniel, for example, felt free to publish his *Delia* in 1592, dedicating it to Sidney's sister, the countess of Pembroke. Daniel explained: "Although I rather desired to keep in the private passions of my youth, from the multitude, as things uttered to my selfe, and consecrated to silence: yet seeing I was betraide by the indiscretion of a greedie Printer, and had some of my secrets bewraide to

---

total of 132 items in the 1640 and 1653 "editions" of Beaumont's work are actually by Beaumont ("The 1640 and 1653 *Poems: By Francis Beaumont, Gent.* and the Canon of Beaumont's Nondramatic Verse," *Studies in Bibliography* 40 [1987]: 140).

[52] *Poems of Sidney*, ed. Ringler, p. 543.

[53] In praising the *Arcadia* Gabriel Harvey refers to Sidney with a chain of epithets, this last of which points to his status as an authorizer of printed literature: "the Secretary of Eloquence, the breath of the Muses, the hoony-bee of the dayntiest flowers of Witt and Arte, the Pith of moral & intellectual Vertues, the arme of Bellona in the field, the toung of Suada in the chamber, the spirite of Practise in esse, and the Paragon of Excellency in Print" (*Pierce's Supererogation* [1593], in *Elizabethan Critical Essays*, edited with an introduction by G. Gregory Smith, 2 vols. [1904; reprint, Oxford University Press, 1959], 2:264–65).

the world, uncorrected: doubting the like of the rest, I am forced to publish that which I never ment."[54] While bemoaning the "greedie" printer's violation of his privacy and the integrity of both Sidney's texts and his own, Daniel calls Sidney's poems "holy Reliques,"[55] not only using the hagiographic language associated with the cult of the Protestant martyr canonized by his contemporaries, but also suggesting that his texts, as well as Sidney's, had a sacred status and merited special treatment. Despite his protestations of humility and dependency, Daniel was asserting authorial authority and defining poetic texts in ways proper to print culture. Daniel took miscellaneous poems belonging to various earlier social occasions, some addressed to particular individuals, and immersed them in the new context of the printed sonnet sequence. He thus brought texts that had passed out of his possession back under authorial control and, erasing their original social coordinates, re-presented them in the medium of print as self-consciously literary work. Sidney's friend, Fulke Greville, did something quite similar when he assembled the poems he had written in various social situations into his collection *Caelica,* which he planned to publish.

In *Ideas Mirrour* (1954), Michael Drayton invoked the example of Sidney to assert his own literary originality: "Divine Syr *Phillip,* I avouch thy writ, / I am no Pickpurse of anothers wit" (Unsig. 2v). It is interesting that the title page of Spenser's *Amoretti* highlights the author's name, and the printer's dedicatory letter praises the poet more than the patron; combined with the argument in two commendatory poems that Spenser should be brought home from "foreign" (Irish) service because of his intellectual and literary abilities, these features indicate that, thanks largely to Sidney's example, a pamphlet of poetry could be used to bestow both literary and cultural authority on the poet. When Giles Fletcher published his sonnet collection *Licia* in 1593, he defended his writing of love poems by pointing out that "in other countryes, as *Italie,* and *France,* men of learning and great partes . . . have written Poems and Sonnets of Love; but even amongst us, men of best nobilitie, and chiefest families, to be the greatest Schollers and most renowned in this kind." It is not surpris-

---

[54] Samuel Daniel, *Poems and A Defence of Ryme,* ed. Arthur Colby Sprague (Chicago: University of Chicago Press, 1930), p. 9.
[55] Idem.

ing, in this context, that he should mention the name of "that wor-thie *Sidney*"[56] in a passage dealing with the affinity of scholarship with gentility: Sidney served Fletcher's purpose as an example of how so-cial status, learning, patriotism, and amorous writing might be com-bined.

Two verse miscellanies published in the last years of Elizabeth's reign, *The Phoenix Nest* (1593) and *A Poetical Rhapsody* (1602), explic-itly invoked the memory of Sidney and benefited from the increased social prestige with which he invested printed lyric poetry. *The Phoenix Nest* is the first such anthology since Tottel to emphasize gentility and to highlight the sonnet as a lyric form,[57] neither feature of which is surprising, given its date and Sidney's example. Presented as a kind of memorial to the deceased poet-statesman, *The Phoenix Nest* (1593) begins with prose and poetry associated with Sidney and his circle: the first piece in the book is a prose apology for Sidney's uncle, the (deceased) earl of Leicester, who had been libeled in the influential pamphlet that came to be known as *Leicester's Commonwealth* (1641) and whom the poet himself had defended in a prose rejoinder.[58] As Hyder Rollins has pointed out, however, "The signature-marks and page-numbers indicate a first intention of beginning the collection with the three elegies on Sidney, an appropriate opening, since that dead poet himself was in 1593, and earlier, recognized as 'the Pe-trarch of the age.' "[59] The editor, in effect, presented the collection under Sidney's auspices, making available to gentlemen readers the kind of coterie verse whose print publication the Sidney precedent had legitimated.

The poems collected in *The Phoenix Nest* are an interesting combi-nation of older and newer kinds and styles: complaints, dream-vision verse, moral allegory, on the one hand, and complimentary, Ovidian, Anacreontic, and anti-courtly writing, on the other—pieces in old-fashioned meters such as fourteeners and poulter's measure, with heavy alliteration and strong caesuras, as well as sonnets, sixains, tro-

---

[56] *The English Works of Giles Fletcher, the Elder,* ed. Lloyd E. Berry (Madison: University of Wisconsin Press, 1964), p. 75.

[57] See Rollins, *Phoenix Nest,* pp. xvii, xxxviii.

[58] See *Miscellaneous Prose of Sir Philip Sidney,* ed. Katherine Duncan-Jones and Jan van Dorsten (Oxford: Clarendon Press, 1973), pp. 128–41. See the discussion of this book and of the Sidney patronage in Margaret Hannay, *Philip's Phoenix: Mary Sidney, Countess of Pem-broke* (New York: Oxford University Press, 1990), pp. 260, 267–68.

[59] Rollins, *Phoenix Nest,* p. xxv.

chaics, madrigals, and even an experimental quantitative lyric in Sapphic meter.[60] Courtly in its orientation to Queen Elizabeth, whose motto, "Semper eadem," was symbolized by the mythical bird, *The Phoenix Nest* contains many poems composed in the political/amorous idiom that Sidney himself had mastered, especially those poems found in the so-called "Ralegh group."[61] But the collection also has a strong component of anti-courtly bawdy and Ovidian verse—for example, Robert Greene's erotic dream-poem (pp. 39–51), a piece with affinities to the fashionable epyllia of the 1590s, and an anonymous instructions-to-a-painter lyric, which might be described as an example of mannerist prurience (pp. 109–10).

By connecting his verse miscellany with a prestigious, aristocratic name, the gentleman editor of *The Phoenix Nest*, like Tottel, gave a certain legitimacy to the published writings of lower-born poets. Authors, editors, and publishers were willing to exploit for their own benefit Sidney's raising of the cultural value of both the printed verse miscellany and the poetry pamphlet. In the last of the great Elizabethan miscellanies, *A Poetical Rhapsody*, the editor, Francis Davison, inserted a long epistle "To the Reader" that cloaks the anthology in the Sidney legend and example, using it to authorize not only the printing of his own and his brother's poems but also the act of publishing a collection of occasional lyrics. In defending the writing of verse as an activity worthy of a serious man of affairs, Davison anticipated some of the old prejudices against lyric poetry: "If liking other kindes, thou mislike the Lyricall, because the chiefest subject is Love; I reply, that Love being virtuously intended, & worthily placed, is the Whetstone of witt, and Spurre to all generous actions: and that many excellent spirits with great fame of witt, and no staine of judgement, have written excellently in this kind, and specially the ever-praise worthy *Sidney*" (1:5). Though obviously using the precedent of Sidney to his own advantage, however, he blamed the printer for exploiting the Sidney name, in effect, ceding to his agency the final editing of the miscellany: "If any except against the mixing (both at the beginning and ende of this booke) of diverse thinges written by great and learned Personages, with our meane and worthles Scriblings, I utterly disclaime it, as being done by the Printer, either to grace the fore-

---

[60] See Lodge's poem "The fatall starre that at my birthday shined" (ibid., pp. 63–64).
[61] See the discussion of this section of the anthology by Michael Rudick, "The 'Ralegh Group' in *The Phoenix Nest*," *Studies in Bibliography* 24 (1971): 131–37.

front with Sir *Ph. Sidneys,* and others names, or to make the booke grow to a competent volume" (1:5). Despite his dismissal of his and his brother's poems as the indulgences of their youth, Davison obviously wished to associate his work with that of the Sidney/Dyer/Greville circle and with the myth of the martyred shepherd-knight. The collection proper opens with "Two Pastoralls, made by *Sir Philip Sidney,* never yet published," poems explicitly naming Dyer and Greville, and after an anonymous third poem, continues with the first publication of a pastoral poem by the countess of Pembroke, before turning to the pastoral verse of the Davisons and others.[62]

The 1598 folio of Sidney's collected works published by William Ponsonby was a model for the incorporation of a writer's lyric poems in a comprehensive, monumentalizing edition that celebrated his or her total achievements (see figure 5). This edition of Sidney's works, and the subsequent editions, which continued to appear into the next century, both memorialized this author and helped establish the authority of printed literature, especially of collected editions in the prestigious folio format. Certainly the sixteenth-century folio editions of Chaucer (and their reprints) by Pynson (1526), Thynne (1532), and Speght (1598) contributed to this process: the last was issued in the same year as the Sidney Folio. It is significant that Speght's 1598 Chaucer edition contains a prefatory pedigree and life of Chaucer, a sign of the growing importance of authorship.[63] The Sidney model, however, was more significant, the realization of the possibility of canonizing contemporary or recently deceased writers: folio editions of such authors as Spenser (1611, 1617), Jonson (1616, 1640–41), Shakespeare (1623, 1632), Daniel (1601), Drayton (1619), and Beaumont and Fletcher (1647) were, in a real sense, made possible by the printing of Sidney's *oeuvres,* as was the planned, but posthumous, publication of the collected works of his friend Fulke Greville, *Certaine Learned and Elegant Workes of the Right Honorable Fulke Lord Brooke, Written in his Youth, and familiar Exercise with Sir Philip Sidney* (1633), a work introduced by a long account of Sidney's life and of Greville's relationship with him.

---

[62] It should be noted that *England's Helicon* also makes use of Sidney's authorizing model by beginning its collection with several poems lifted from the 1598 Sidney folio (nos. 1, 3, and 5). Also, *Spensers Colin Clouts Come Home Again* (1595) ends with three elegies for Sidney.

[63] Miskimin says that in his 1598 edition of Chaucer, "Speght presents our *Antient and Learned English Poet* with more grandeur, apparatus, and annotations than he had ever before received" (*Renaissance Chaucer,* p. 251).

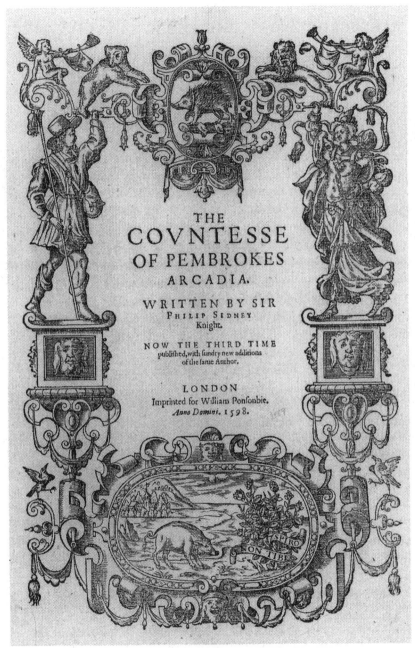

*Figure 5.* [Sir Philip Sidney], *The Countess of Pembrokes Arcadia* (1598), title page. Courtesy of the Huntington Library.

The Sidney example not only provided the precedent for Sidney's niece, Lady Mary Wroth, to publish in folio her romance, *Urania*, in 1621 along with her own sonnet sequence,[64] but it also encouraged a Scots aristocrat, William Alexander, earl of Stirling, to publish his poetic juvenilia, *Aurora. Containing the First Fancies of the Authors Youth* (1604), in a volume also containing *The Monarchick Tragedies* and *A Paraenesis to the Prince* (the latter two works being more prestigious, public, and political texts). An admirer of Sidney, Alexander had written the link between the revised sections of the *Arcadia* and that portion of the *Old Arcadia* that completed the version known as *The Countess of Pembrokes Arcadia* (1593), which appeared from 1621 onward. He was self-conscious about making the transition from the manuscript environment, to which such poems rightly belonged, to the medium of print, in which the private would become public. Thus, in the initial poem he not only made excuses for the verse as youthful "trifling toyes," but also apologized for taking them out of the private "cabinet" in which such "scroles" (sig. A3r) should rest.

## Jonson, Authorship, and Print

Ben Jonson obviously benefited from the precedents of the publication of Sidney's lyrics in quarto and of his collected works in folio. Certainly, in publishing plays, masques, and two collections of poetry (*Epigrammes* and *The Forrest*) in folio in 1616 as *The Workes of Benjamin Jonson* (see Figure 6), Jonson advertised his ownership of a body of work and his status as a writer laying claim to cultural authority.[65] In recent years scholars have focused on this monumental folio and on Jonson's use of the print medium to establish sociocultural authority both for himself and for his writing and authorial ownership of texts. Joseph Loewenstein calls the 1616 folio "a major event in the history

[64] Although Jeff Masten states that "Wroth's class position and illustrious family precursors served as an authorization to write and to be read," he argues that she was reluctant to submit herself to the male-controlled circulation system of print: "Wroth, as a woman-writer, must resist publication as a form of male trafficking, yet that resistance can only register if it is made public. . . .Paradoxically, the published texts must announce their resistance to publication, in the multiple senses of the word; they stage their own privatization" ("Mary Wroth's Sonnets," pp. 81, 83 [see Chap. 1, n. 185]).

[65] Elizabeth Eisenstein has argued that in print culture "possessive individualism began to characterize the attitude of writers to their work. . . .[B]oth the eponymous inventor and personal authorship appeared at the same time and as a consequence of the same process" (1:121). Cf. Febvre and Martin, *Coming of the Book*, pp. 159–66.

*Figure 6.* Ben Jonson, *Workes* (1616), title page. Courtesy of the Huntington Library.

of what one might call the bibliographic ego."[66] He considers the issue of the "expansion of authorial rights" as part of the institution-alizing of the literary in the Renaissance: "As Jonson intruded himself on the mechanisms of print publication—revising, annotating, cor-recting print runs—in the course of all this, he strengthened his con-ception both of the abstraction of the work of art and of his own proprietary interest in that abstraction."[67]

The 1616 folio includes a frontispiece portrait of Jonson himself, a common means in print culture for elevating the sociocultural status of authorship. George Gascoigne's portrait is placed before his posthumous, collected edition, *The Whole Woorkes of George Gascoigne Esquire. Newlye compyled into one Volume* (1587).[68] The frontispiece im-age of the author of a book was a normal feature of posthumous editions—for example, it was used for the editions of Chaucer (1598), Shakespeare (1623), Donne (1635), and Cartwright (1651), but it also became, with such publications as Jonson's *Workes*, Wither's *Juvenilia* (1622), and Milton's *Poems* (1645), a gesture of claiming authorial authority for a living writer.[69]

Jonson's incorporation of lyric poetry in his *Workes* is a function of his conception of such work as ethically serious production. By em-phasizing didactic, satiric, and encomiastic verse, however, Jonson went against the literary current of his times, which had seen a de-velopment, in the sixteenth century, from moral-didactic to aureate recreational verse—that is, the divorce of lyric poetry from utility and moral education and the creation of a leisure commodity whose use-value was suspect or denied. This development, of course, was one

[66] Joseph Loewenstein, "The Script in the Marketplace," *Representations* 12 (Fall 1985): 101. See also Timothy Murray, *Theatrical Legitimation: Allegories of Genius in Seventeenth-Century England and France* (New York: Oxford University Press, 1987), pp. 39–93; Helgerson, *Self-Crowned Laureates*, pp. 101–84; Richard C. Newton, "Jonson and the (Re-)Invention of the Book," in *Classic and Cavalier: Essays on Jonson and the Sons of Ben*, ed. Claude J. Summers and Ted-Larry Pebworth (Pittsburgh: University of Pittsburgh Press, 1982), pp. 31–55; Don E. Wayne, "Jonson's Sidney: Legacy and Legitimation in *The Forrest*," in *Sir Philip Sidney's Achievements*, ed. M.J.B. Allen, Dominic Baker-Smith, and Arthur F. Kinney, with Margaret M. Sullivan (New York: AMS Press, 1990), pp. 227–50; and *Ben Jonson's 1616 Folio*, ed. Jennifer Brady and W. H. Herendeen (Newark: University of Delaware Press; London: Associated University Presses, 1991).

[67] Loewenstein, "Script in the Marketplace," pp. 102, 108.

[68] See the discussion of printing and portraiture in Leo Braudy, *The Frenzy of Renown: Fame & Its History* (New York: Oxford University Press, 1986), pp. 264–312. See also Corbett and Lightbown's *Comely Frontispiece*, on this topic.

[69] The frontispiece portrait was quite rare for a female author: but see the engraved image of the duchess of Newcastle included in the third edition of her poems (1668).

stage in the institutionalizing of literature, running from Sidney and the sixteenth-century courtier poets through the Inns of Court verse of Donne and his contemporaries, to Cavalier poetry and Royalist or loyalist witty verse. Milton later objected to such a development from his radical Protestant point of view and from the vantage of his claims to authority and seriousness. Like Milton, Jonson wanted to fuse moral and literary authority: hence he felt that his epigrams, which he called "the ripest of my studies," and the didactic and encomiastic verse of *The Forrest* supported, rather than impeded, his efforts to win high sociocultural status as an author in a folio published in the very year that the king's own collected works were produced in the same format as *The Workes of the Most High and Mighty Prince, James . . . Kinge of Great Brittaine, France & Ireland.*

Jonson, however, evidently contemplated publishing his book of epigrams *before* deciding to include them in his 1616 folio.[70] The prefatory and introductory material to the epigram collection we find in the folio were obviously designed for a separate volume, the kind of work that in the light of the 1599 bishops' order against such publications and the mixed reception of Jonson's own satiric drama, left the poet especially vulnerable both to the condemnation of his social and political superiors and to the hostility of malicious or offended readers. In using print for his own purposes, Jonson characteristically heaped scorn on the commercial enterprise with which he has associated himself, criticizing not only printers and booksellers, but also the usual purchasers of literary texts. In the brief epigram addressed to his reader, Jonson is both defensive and condescending: "PRay thee, take care, that tak'st my booke in hand, / To reade it well: that is, to understand."[71] The second epigram, "To my Booke" assumes, however, that most readers would be ill disposed to what he has written and misinterpret it. Given his usual attitude toward the general public, it is not surprising that Jonson objects to the stationer's desire to reach a broad readership. Contemptuously addressing the bookseller in the third epigram as "THou that mak'st gaine thy end," he expresses a belligerantly anticommercial attitude, ob-

[70] The *Epigrammes* were entered separately on May 15, 1612, in the Stationers' Register: this fact is mentioned in Hoyt Hudson's bibliographical note to *Epigrams, The Forest, Underwoods by Ben Jonson* (New York: Facsimile Text Society and Columbia University Press, 1936), p. iii.
[71] *Complete Poetry of Ben Jonson,* ed. Hunter, p. 4 (see Chap. 1, n. 35). Further references to this edition are included in the text.

jecting to the normal ways of advertising books, instructing the stationer *not* to

> ... have my title-leafe on posts, or walls,
> Or in cleft-sticks, advanced to make calls
> For termers, or some clarke-like serving-man,
> Who scarse can spell th'hard names. . . .
>
> (P. 5)

Scorning those who might be induced to lay out the relatively small sums necessary to purchase a pamphlet of poetry, he singles out two of the major segments of the book-buying public, fashionable "termers" (both gentlemen and lawyers in town during sessions of the law courts) who had a taste for contemporary amorous and satiric literature and the middle-class readers who wished to improve themselves by imitating the language and behavior of their social superiors. In desiring that only the wise seek out his work (presumably aware of it by word of mouth), he imagines, in effect, a worst-seller, a publication whose remaindered copies might serve as grocers' wrapping paper. But, of course, this epigram refers not to the folio edition of Jonson's *Workes,* of which *Epigrammes* is only a part, a major joint commercial venture for both publisher and author, but rather to a slighter pamphlet anticipated in the 1612 registration. Had this separate edition of the *Epigrammes* been published, its fate would probably have been similar to that of other ephemeral productions, as the many lost copies of drama and poetry quartos suggest.

When Ben Jonson tried to assume control over the reception and interpretation of his writings, he was was encouraged to do so by the new conditions of literature in a print culture that made possible what was virtually impossible in a system of manuscript transmission, where the uses and interpretation of texts were more obviously under reader control. In print, authorial authority applied not only to property rights over corrected texts but also to issues of meaning and interpretation. In the rhetorically slippery preface to *The Posies,* George Gascoigne, who suffered from the supposed misinterpretation of the prose and poetry of *A Hundreth Sundrie Flowres,* accused some readers of not having understood "the meaning of the Authour, nor the sense of the figurative speeches."[72] Whatever the degrees of seriousness or facetiousness, the exegetical notes of "E.K." printed with Spenser's work *The Shepheardes Calendar* are an obvious device to control interpretation from the author's end of the author-reader axis of communication. Giles Fletcher's preface to his sonnet sequence *Licia* teases the reader with the knowledge that the coordinates of the meaning of the collection are in the possession of the author: "If thou muse what my *LICIA* is, take her to be some *Diana,* at the least chaste; or some *Minerva,* no *Venus,* fairer farre. It may be shee is Learnings Image, or some heavenlie woonder, which the Precisest may not mislike: perhaps under that name I have shadowed [The Holy] *Discipline.* It may be, I meane that kinde courtesie which I found at the Patroneese of these Poems; it may bee some Colledge; it may bee my conceit, and portende nothing: whatsoever it be, if thou like it, take it."[73] Despite the "as you like it" gesture and the subsequent profuse praise of his patroness, it is clear that, in the midst of his deconstructive mischievousness, Fletcher exploits this developing position of authority for authors in a print medium. Print, of course, has been seen as strengthening reader control as well as authorial control. As Richard Helgerson has observed, "Intended to represent the power of the authorial self, print ends by empowering the consumers of that representation. Print makes readers kings."[74] This is one of the major points Elizabeth Eisenstein makes in her book *The Printing Press as an Agent of Change.*

When the 1598 folio of Sidney's works was published, Sidney had been dead some dozen years, but when the 1616 folio of Jonson was published Jonson was a living author, and this monumental publication in mid-career had an ironically damaging effect on him.[75] After its appearance, as Jennifer Brady argues, "Jonson is held endlessly accountable to his authoritarian classic" for the remaining two decades of his life. "By the last decade of Jonson's life," she argues, "the

[72] George Gascoigne, *The Posies,* ed. J. W. Cunliffe (Cambridge: Cambridge University Press, 1907), p. 11. On the problem of literary authority, see McGann, *Critique of Modern Textual Criticism,* pp. 48, 81–94 (cited in full at Chap. 3, n. 7).

[73] *Works of Fletcher,* ed. Berry, pp. 79–80.

[74] Richard Helgerson, "Milton Reads the King's Book: Print, Performance, and the Making of a Bourgeois Idol," *Criticism* 29 (1987): 6.

[75] See Jennifer Brady, " 'Noe fault, but Life': Jonson's Folio as Monument and Barrier," in Brady and Herendeen, *Ben Jonson's 1616 Folio,* pp. 192–216.

Folio had gained a canonical life independent of its author and maker. The *Workes* supplanted Jonson as the authority that co-erced."[76] Sidney did not have to live under the burden of being a (self-promoted) contemporary classic. Jonson, however, did and he responded by returning to the socioliterary environment of manuscript transmission for the poems that were finally printed in the posthumous 1640–41 folio as *Under-wood*. As Brady has put it, "For Jonson, longevity meant lasting long enough to witness a partial fragmentation of the *corpus* he had labored to construct."[77]

Jonson's old mentor William Camden, in his one of the literary-historical chapters added in 1623 to his *Remaines Concerning Britain*, not only referred to Chaucer as "our English *Homer*" and named Surrey as the one who "first refined our homly English Poesy," but also suggested that if he wanted to give examples of fine contemporary verse he could present work by "Sir *Phillip Sidney, Ed. Spencer, John Owen, Samuel Daniel, Hugh Holland, Ben: Johnson, Th. Campion, Mich. Drayton, George Chapman, John Marston, William Shakespeare,* & other most pregnant witts of these our times, whom succeeding ages may justly admire."[78] Camden thus canonized Jonson's works along with those of a number of his contemporaries. After Jonson's death, the memorial volume for him also signaled the new sociocultural status of authorship Jonson desired in his literary career: *Jonsonus Virbius, or the Memorie of Ben: Jonson Revived by the Friends of the Muses* (1638) is the kind of publication that was usually produced to commemorate deceased royalty or major aristocrats. In it Jonson is celebrated as an author who, as the reader address has it, is "left . . . to your posteritie" (sig. A2v). Not only did poets such as King, Waller, Mayne, Cartwright, Felltham, Marmion, and Ford pay tribute to Jonson, but also prominent academics and titled aristocrats added their praise to this chorus.[79] The extraordinary outpouring of elegies after the death of Sir Philip Sidney, no doubt, was the most notable model for such a volume,[80] but Sidney was celebrated as much for his sociopolitical

---

[76] Ibid., pp. 193–94.

[77] Ibid., p. 205.

[78] Camden, *Remains Concerning Britain*, pp. 293, 344, 294 (see Chap. 2, n. 126).

[79] Helgerson calls this anthology "a general gathering place for the choicer wits of the new generation" (*Self-Crowned Laureates*, p. 190). Helgerson, however, associates the generation of the Cavalier poets with a "decline in literary autonomy" (p. 201).

[80] This point is made by G. W. Pigman III, *Grief and English Renaissance Elegy* (Cambridge: Cambridge University Press, 1985), p. 53.

status as for his intellectual and literary achievement; Jonson, on the other hand, like the Shakespeare of the 1623 folio, was being celebrated entirely for his literary merits.[81]

After the publication of his folio, Jonson's return to the system of coterie manuscript circulation for his lyric verse is a sign both of the continuing strength of that system and of the lowered prestige of lyric verse in the Jacobean period. Despite the outpouring of lyric poetry in the late Elizabethan period and the strong impact of Sidney's work, the older tradition that defined lyrics as occasional verse belonging to social intercourse and the system of manuscript transmission was still strong. Thus, for example, the 1613 publication *Alcilia. Philoparthens Loving Folly* explains, "These Sonnets following, were written by the Author, (who giveth himselfe this fained name of Philoparthen, as his accidental attribute) at divers times, and upon divers occasions, and therefore in the forme and matter they differ, and sometimes are quite contrary one to another, considering the natures and qualities of Love, which is a Passion full of varietie, and contrarietie in it selfe" (sig. B2r). The poems appended to the ninth impression of Sir Thomas Overbury's poem *The Wife* create the impression of a literary coterie exchanging verses. Addressed to a social in-group, this publication refers to "our easie conversations of wit by printing" (sig. ¶ 3v) as though print were only an extension of manuscript practices. The title page announces that to the text of Overbury's poem are added "many new Elegies upon his untimely and much lamented death, as also New Newes, and divers more Characters, (never before annexed) written by himselfe and other learned Gentlemen."[82] The Huntington Library copy of this book has two contemporary handwritten items added, presumably by an earlier owner, the first a misogynistic stanza about wives:

> Some give there wives those tytles
> good, faire sweete.
> as they find beautie love or honesty
> but for to call them deare wives
> were more meete,

---

[81] See ibid., pp. 63–64.

[82] These were primarily elegies for Overbury and commendatory poems for "The Wife," but they also included elegies for Lord William Howard, baron of Effingham, and for the countess of Rutland ("I may forget to eat, to drink, to sleepe"), and Wotton's popular "The Character of a Happy Life" ("How happy is he borne or taught").

though in the word be ambiguity
for they bring men to troble cost & care
then deare they are, be they good swet or faire.

The second is a satiric prose character about "A Parveiour of tobacco." In effect, the book's owner extended the coterie recreations
of the authors represented in the collection, treating the printed
book like a poetry manuscript.

On the whole, the Jacobean era was not a good time to publish
secular lyric poetry. No new substantial anthology appeared in this
period and the rate of publication of single-author editions of lyrics
dropped considerably: the latter includes Drayton's *Poems* (1605,
1608, 1610, 1613, 1619) and *Poems Lyrick and Pastorall* (1606), John
Davies of Hereford's *Witts Pilgrimage through a World of Amorous Sonnets*
(1605), Shakespeare's *Sonnets* (1609), and Harington's *Epigrams*
(1613, 1615, 1618). And, of course, earlier single-author editions and
poetry anthologies were reissued—for example, Daniel's *Delia* (in
1611 and 1623), *England's Helicon* (in 1614), and *A Poetical Rhapsody*
(in 1608, 1611, and 1621).[83]

Many poets restricted their lyric writing to coterie audiences and
to the system of manuscript transmission, especially since in the Jacobean period, secular lyric poetry declined somewhat in importance,
partly due to King James I's preference for other kinds of writing.
Such works as Wither's *Juvenilia* (1622), *The Golden Garland of Princely
Pleasures and Delicate Delights* (1620), and *A Description of Love* (1621?)[84]
were published in this period, but compared, for example, to the
previous fifteen or so years, there was clearly a drop in the production
of editions of lyric poetry, as very few new titles came on the market.
Particularly, from the mid-Jacobean period through the first seven

[83] David Norbrook, *Poetry and Politics in the English Renaissance* (London: Routledge,
1984), p. 207, has argued that the reissuing of *England's Helicon* in 1614 was a political act
in which pastoralism signaled an aversion to *Jacobean* rule and nostalgia for the *Elizabethan*
era. He argues elsewhere that during the era of the English Revolution, George Wither
used the sonnet form in his political poems, *Campo-Musae* and *Vox Pacifica*, for "conjuring
up the associations of the Elizabethan political as well as poetic world, a world Parliamen-
tarians looked back to as one of lost purity before Stuart corruption" ("Levelling Poetry:
George Wither and the English Revolution, 1642–1649," *ELR* 21 [1991]: 237).
[84] The *Short Title Catalogue (1485–1640)* identifies the 1625 edition of this work as the
fifth edition, and counts nine editions through 1638. Though it claims to contain "Epigrams, Elegies, and Sonnets" in addition to the long title poem, its "sonnets" are songs
(the seventeenth-century meaning of the term), its epigrams are witty trifles, and its love
elegies are old-fashioned.

years of the reign of Charles I, lyric verse tended to remain within the system of manuscript circulation: poems by such contemporary authors as Richard Corbett, William Strode, Thomas Carew, and Robert Herrick were confined to manuscript transmission along with the work of older poets such as Donne and Ralegh. In his book of satires dedicated to William Herbert, earl of Pembroke, *Vices Anotimie, Scourged and Corrected in New Satirs* (1617), Robert Anton of Magdalen College, Cambridge, expressed contempt for "obsceane and shallow Poetry" and the young university graduate who "murders the Presse with fellonious Pamphlets stolne from the imperfections of their deerest friends, nay, purloined from their own scabbed dispositions, and ulcerous inclinations" (sig. Bir): he is typical in his opinion that occasional, amorous, recreational verse should not be printed.

## Donne, Herbert, and the Lyric Collection

The virtually simultaneous, posthumous publication of John Donne's *Poems* and George Herbert's *Temple* in 1633 however, was a watershed event that changed the relationship of lyric poetry to the print medium, helping to normalize within print culture the publication of poetry collections by individual authors (see figures 7 and 8). As successive editions of both Donne's and Herbert's verse continued to appear through the pre–Civil War and Civil War periods and the Interregnum, they became part of a process by which courtly and Royalist poets were installed in the literary institution taking shape within print culture. After the publication of Donne's and Herbert's poems, and certainly after the appearance of the numerous single-author collections whose publication was partly authorized by the Donne and Herbert editions, lyric poems themselves were perceived less as occasional and ephemeral and more as valuable artifacts worth preserving in those monumentalizing editions that were among the most prestigious products of print culture.

Donne's and Herbert's posthumous poems, however, were quite different productions. Herbert's masterfully shaped collection of religious verse, whose individual pieces were models of lyric virtuosity, encouraged imitation of the work as a whole. It spawned, for example, not only Richard Crashaw's imitative *Steps to the Temple* (1646), which appeared in the same duodecimo format, and the editions of Henry Vaughan's religious lyrics, but also Christopher Harvey's work, *The*

# POEMS,

*By* J. D.

## WITH

## ELEGIES
## ON THE AUTHORS
### DEATH.

LONDON.
Printed by *M. F.* for IOHN MARRIOT,
and are to be fold at his fhop in St *Dunftans*
Church-yard in *Fleet-ftreet.* 1 6 3 3.

*Figure 7.* John Donne, *Poems* (1633), title page. Courtesy of the Huntington Library.

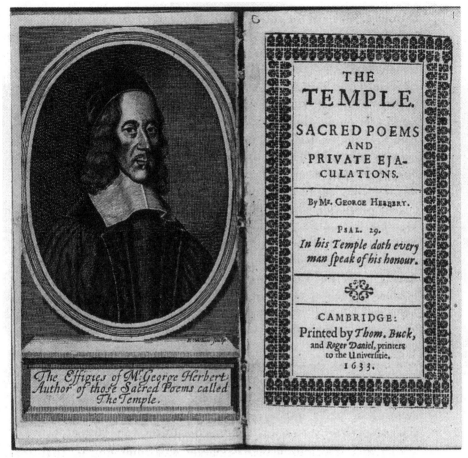

Figure 8. George Herbert, *The Temple* (1633), frontispiece and title page.
Courtesy of the Huntington Library.

*Synagogue* (1647), a duodecimo pamphlet Philemon Stephens sold
bound with Herbert's collection,[85] and, perhaps also, An Collins's *Divine Songs and Meditacions* (1653), a work the author tells the reader
is "set forth . . . for the benefit, and comfort of others" (sig. A2v).[86]

---

[85] See T. A. Birrell, "The Influence of Seventeenth-Century Publishers on the Presentation of English Literature," in *Historical & Editorial Studies in Medieval and Early Modern English*, ed. Mary-Jo Arn and Hanneke Wirtjes (Groningen: Wolters-Noordhoff, 1985), p. 164.

[86] See Helen Wilcox, "Exploring the Language of Devotion in the English Revolution," in *Literature and the English Civil War*, ed. Thomas Healy and Jonathan Sawday (Cambridge: Cambridge University Press, 1990), pp. 76–77, 84–87.

Donne's *Poems*, on the other hand, were valued as the collected miscellaneous pieces of a deceased ecclesiastical figure whose prominence in Stuart culture contrasted with the relative privacy of his verse, a body of work formerly available only through the various lines of manuscript transmission. What was important is that such coterie poetry was finally transferred to a different medium, which encouraged the publication of similar work. The series of editions of Donne's poetry beginning in 1633 not only effectively canonized Donne within the literary institution emerging within print culture, but also helped to reinforce the prestige of single-author collections through the rest of the century.

The posthumous 1633 edition of Donne's poetry began the process that led to Donne's conversion from coterie poet to English author. Before its publication the Donne poems that were most widely known were the *Satires*, selected songs such as "Goe and catche a falling starre," and the *Anniversaries* (Donne's only deliberately published poems, appearing originally in 1611 and 1612, then reprinted in 1621 and 1625).[87] The other verse, especially the amorous and religious lyrics, had reached a more restricted audience. Along with the other seventeenth-century editions of Donne, however, the 1633 edition lay in the shadow of Donne's identity as "Doctor Donne, Dean of St. Paul's." Donne had published individual sermons, the *Devotions*, and earlier religious polemics, but he was known primarily as the dean of St. Paul's and by reputation as an eloquent preacher.[88] His ecclesiastical role, however, conflicted with the role of poet in interesting ways. Ben Jonson had remarked to Drummond in 1619 that Donne "now since he was made Doctor repenteth highlie and seeketh to destroy all his poems"[89]—a statement that indicates the potential embarrassment posed by some of them. The 1633 edition

---

[87] See, for example, the early references to and imitations of Donne's poetry gathered in *John Donne: The Critical Heritage*, ed. A. J. Smith (London: Routledge, 1975), pp. 33–45, 64–83.

[88] Although only Donne's initials appear on the title pages of the 1633, 1635, 1639, 1649, 1650, and 1654 editions and printings of the poems, some of Donne's other published works (such as the editions of individual sermons and small groups of sermons published before 1633) and the elegies on the author appended to the editions of the poetry both foreground his ecclesiastical identity. The editions of the popular sermon *Deaths Duell* identify its author as "that late learned and Reverend Divine, John Donne, D[octo]r. in Divinity, & Deane of S. Pauls, London" (Geoffrey Keynes, *A Bibliography of Dr. John Donne Dean of St. Paul's*, 4th ed. [Oxford: Clarendon Press, 1973], p. 51).

[89] Ben Jonson, "Conversations with William Drummond of Hawthornden," quoted in Smith, *John Donne: The Critical Heritage*, p. 69.

highlights the awkwardness of publishing the secular along with the religious poetry of the lately deceased dean. The image that Donne himself wished at the close of his career was the one he fabricated for the sermon *Death's Duel*, whose printing in 1632 was accompanied by the figure of the clergyman in his funeral shroud (for which he posed in his terminal illness) and by two of the elegies that were also carried over into Marriot's edition of the poetry.[90]

The unusual order of poems in the 1633 edition is the product not only of the arrangement of verse in the manuscripts used by the editor but also of the desire to locate relatively late in the collection those amorous lyrics that could damage Dean Donne's reputation.[91] We encounter the satiric *Metempsychòsis* first in the collection under the title "The Progresse of the Soule." This is followed, in turn, by the *La Corona* sonnets and twelve other holy sonnets. It is no surprise that the collected verse of the recently deceased dean of St. Paul's would begin with poems signaling their author's interest in the spiritual life. One of the most noteworthy features of the compilation is that the first amorous lyric is the ninety-fourth poem in the book: this looks like deliberate postponement, since such love poetry posed the greatest risk of scandal. The epigrams and elegies that follow the religious poems at the start of the collection, since they could be taken as exercises in classical form, did not pose this kind of threat, especially after the licenser of the publication censored such bawdy pieces as "To his Mistris going to Bed," "Love's Progresse," and "Love's Warre,"[92] poems that were by that time circulating freely in manuscript and were especially popular in university students' manuscript anthologies. In fact, the inclusion in this edition, of the letter Donne wrote in 1625 to his friend Sir Robert Ker underscores the problem raised by printing the secular love poems of the man who had won great respect as an eloquent preacher and religious authority. Although it follows the memorial poem on the Marquis Hamilton that Donne composed at Ker's request, the self-protective comment Donne made from his position as a respected clergyman is obviously meant to extend to his other poetry: "You know my uttermost when

[90] Henry King's "An elegie, On Dr. Donne, Deane of Pauls" and Edward Hyde's "An Epitaph on Dr. Donne."

[91] For a list of the contents of this edition, see Keynes, *Bibliography of Donne*, pp. 190–96.

[92] Keynes quotes the Stationer's Register entry that excepts "the first, second, Tenth, Eleventh, and Thirteenth *Elegies*" from the approval to publish the verse (ibid., p. 188).

it was best, and even then I did best when I had least truth for my subjects."[93] Helen Gardner uses this quotation to distance Donne from the erotic behavior dramatized in the amorous verse,[94] but in its way, her assertion only continues the process generated not only by Walton's hagiographical model of Donne's life but also by the editorial frame in which the verse was first presented. The Ker letter, coming as it does shortly before the appearance of the first love lyrics in the 1633 edition, argues for a fictive rather than an autobiographical basis for poems that might have been perceived as scandalous. Of course, the problem is faced directly by Sir Thomas Browne's elegy on Donne appearing toward the end of the book, "To the deceased Author, Upon the *Promiscuous* printing of his Poems, the *Looser sort,* with the *Religious*"—a poem that suggests that the "*Wanton Story*" represented in the amorous verse can be read as the "*Confession*" of the divine whose religious verse and prose are morally exemplary.[95] As a group, the thirteen elegies and epitaphs on Donne positioned at the end of the 1633 edition define for him the composite role of poet/priest. Thus, in the movement of Donne's coterie verse from its original social and biographical matrices and extended manuscript circulation to the context of printed literature, the need to protect the reputation of Dean Donne from moral taint affected the presentation of the texts to the public.

The 1633 edition had an important place in the history of printed verse—a context that ultimately wrought the transformation of Donne from a literary amateur into a canonical English author, from someone writing for manuscript circulation for coterie readers, sometimes within the framework of social and political patronage, into an "author" in the modern institution of literature. When Donne's verse was published posthumously in a form that indicated that the book was a prestigious collection rather than a slight pamphlet, the sociocultural significance of such a text was set by some of the printed literature (especially poetry) that had appeared in the previous four decades—the 1598 and 1602 folio editions of Chaucer, the 1598, 1599, and 1604 Sidney folios, the 1611 and 1617 folios of Spenser's collected poetry, the 1616 Jonson folio, the 1623 and 1632 folios of

---

[93] See the whole text printed in *The Life and Letters of John Donne,* ed. Edmund Gosse, 2 vols. (1899; reprint, Gloucester, Mass.: Peter Smith, 1959), 2:215.

[94] Donne, *The Elegies and Songs and Sonnets,* ed. Gardner, p. xviii (see Chap. 3, n. 38).

[95] See the text of this poem in Grierson, 1:372–73.

Shakespeare's Plays, and the 1623 edition of Daniel's collected works.[96] The following decade and a half yielded the second (1640–41) folio of Jonson, Benson's 1640 edition of Shakespeare's poems, the posthumous edition of Thomas Carew's *Poems* (1640), John Milton's 1645 *Poems*, the edition of the verse of Donne's contemporary Richard Corbett, *Certain Elegant Poems, written by Dr. Corbet, Bishop of Norwich* (1647) edited by John Donne Jr., Robert Herrick's *Hesperides* (1648), and the collections of religious verse influenced by Herbert's *Temple*. The boundaries between private aristocratic or courtly amateur verse and professional literature were becoming blurred; it was no longer necessarily a public disgrace for the lyric poetry of a private gentleman to be printed. The prestige of Sidney and the "Renaissance Chaucer" and the examples of Spenser, Jonson, and Milton combined to change the cultural position of printed literature from what it had been a century before—even though it was not until the end of the eighteenth century that the full effects of this transformation could be felt. The 1633 edition of Donne is a crucial part of the process by which Donne's hybrid identity as a poet/priest was established after his death by the printing of his works and by Walton's influential myth of his career. But it is important to note the place of the 1633 and subsequent editions of Donne's verse in the history of published poetry—especially of those landmark publications that helped establish printed verse as serious cultural artifacts.

The 1633 edition of Donne, then, was presented as a prestigious publication making accessible to a wide readership the writings of a respected author and churchman. In his address to the readers, Marriot indicated that the book was not like "ordinary" publications, and that the verse collection was "the best in this kinde, that ever this Kingdome hath yet seen" and that, like Tottel earlier, he was doing a kind of public service in "making so much good common." Since Donne himself had a position of social eminence secured by the "best warrant that can bee, publique authority, and private friends" (that is, the approval of the monarch and the social elite), Marriot explains that he puts the elegies on Donne at the end of the book rather than at the beginning (as commendatory poems) since "encomiums of the

---

[96] The fashion for prestigious folio editions of authors' collected works was parodied on the level of popular literature with the 1630 printing of *All the Workes of John Taylor the Water-poet, being sixty and three in number.*

Author (as is usual in other workes, where perhaps there is need of it)''[97] are not necessary in Donne's case. He uses Donne's social prestige to validate the importance of the 1633 edition, but, in fact, the prestige of the collected edition of the works of the great man or great writer also enabled this text to take its place in the company of similar important publications.

Two changes in the presentation of the collection of Donne's poetry from the first (1633) to the second (1635) and subsequent editions deserve comment. First of all, in contrast to the 1633 edition, which prints Donne's verse in the kind of order one might find in a manuscript collection, the 1635 edition arranges the verse in strict generic groupings. John Shawcross has pointed out the importance of this early example of generic arrangement in English publication history[98]—though, of course, such organization can be found in some manuscript collections of Donne and of other poets (in the Westmoreland Manuscript, for example). In this edition, Donne's lyrics, called for the first time by that Petrarchan title *Songs and Sonnets,* begin the collection—perhaps in order to appeal to the interests of readers for whom they would have been among the least available of his poems. But, of course, this placement made it necessary to do something in this edition to cope with the general problem posed by the nonedifying love poetry written by Dean Donne in his earlier years. Thus, the second significant change, the inclusion of Marshall's frontispiece engraving of Donne, an illustration based on the 1591 painting of the poet as an eighteen-year-old dressed in military garb. Purchasers of the 1635 volume knew that the "J.D." of the title page was Doctor Donne, dean of St. Paul's; they were invited to adjust their point of view to see the poetry, at least the potentially scandalous verse, as the work of a very young man. Similarly, the *Poetical Blossoms* of Abraham Cowley printed in 1633 are presented as the juvenilia of a poet whose boyish image faces the title page of that short pamphlet.[99] Lest they miss the point, Marriot placed some verses by Isaac Walton beneath the illustration, a short poem that established the

---

[97] John Donne, *Poems* (London, 1633), in Smith, *John Donne: The Critical Heritage,* pp. 84–85.

[98] John Shawcross, "The Arrangement and Order of John Donne's Poems," in *Poems in Their Place: The Intertextuality and Order of Poetic Collections,* ed. Neil Fraistat (Chapel Hill: University of North Carolina Press, 1986), pp. 119–63.

[99] See also the image of the eighteen-year-old Hugh Crompton facing the title page of the *Poems by Hugh Crompton* (1657).

hagiographical career model for Donne later elaborated in Walton's short biography:

> This was for youth, Strength, Mirth, and wit that Time
> Most count their golden Age; but t'was not thine.
>    Thine was thy later yeares, so much refind
>    From youths Drosse, Mirth, & wit; as thy pure mind
>    Thought (like the Angels) nothing but the Praise
>       Of thy Creator, in those last, best Dayes.
>    Witnes this Booke, (thy Embleme) which begins
>    With Love; but endes, with Sighes, & Teares for sins.[100]

Once Donne's life was presented as an example of that of a reformed prodigal, or of a sinner turned saint, the love lyrics could be put in a context that did not threaten the esteem in which Donne was held: they could be perceived as the "Dross, Mirth, & wit" of his immaturity. Of course, this did not keep the opportunistic John Donne Jr. from complaining in his 1637 petition to the archbishop of Canterbury about the unauthorized printing of his father's works that their publication was "scandalous," a consequence that the younger Donne did not seem to fear when he himself brought out the 1650 and 1654 editions of that same verse.[101]

Through the 1635, 1639, 1649, 1650, 1654, 1669, and 1719 editions of the poetry, Donne's identity as Doctor Donne, dean of St. Paul's, was foregrounded. Of course, the 1634, 1640, 1649, and 1660 collections of the sermons of "that Learned and Reverend divine, John Donne, Doctor in Divinity, Late Dean of the Cathedral Church of St. Paul's London" kept this image before the public. And, incidentally, it was not until the 1669 edition of the poetry that Donne's full name appeared on the title page. In order for the poet Donne to be installed in literary history as an author in the modern sense of the term, his identity had to be secularized: he had to be extricated from the immediate sociocultural contexts in which he had functioned and which his verse was received during his lifetime and in the extended period after his death and to be relocated in the newly emerging institution of literature in which texts and authors were

---

[100] Keynes, *Bibliography of Donne*, p. 198.
[101] See the discussion of John Donne Jr.'s activities in ibid., pp. 245–49.

defined differently. This process was not really completed until the late eighteenth century.[102]

Although many volumes of devotional poetry had been published earlier, from William Hunnis's much-reprinted collection, *Seven Sobs of a Sorrowful Soule for Sinne* (1583), to Henry Lok's *Sundry Christian Passions Contained in Two Hundred Sonnets* (1593), and Robert Southwell's various poetry pamphlets, clearly Herbert's *Temple* (1633) gave to such published work a prominence and prestige it lacked before. The Cambridge University Press edition of this work was presented to the public in an unusual way.[103] Nicholas Ferrar's preface, disguised as the printers' epistle to the readers, presents the text of Herbert's verse "in that naked simplicitie, with which he left it, without any addition either of support or ornament, more then is included in it self." This formulation puts Herbert's verse in the same relation to any possible illustrations that scripture has to visual religious symbolism—the Protestant assumption being that the plain words suffice. But, of course, this suits the tendency in print culture to spatialize, iconize, and fix the verbal. Most of Nicholas Ferrar's prefatory epistle is given over to a short biography of the poet, which is justified in the following way: "Onely for the clearing of some passages, we have thought it not unfit to make the common Reader privie to some few particularities of the condition and position of the Person [of the poet]." The author's life matters as an index to meaning, but also because the "author-function" has become important in printed literature, a locus of authority communicable in the print medium. Apart from this epistle, the only addition to Herbert's sacred text is an index of titles at the end that facilitates the book's use as a devotional work. Justified, then, as serious religious writing by a saintly, learned parson whose exemplary life could edify readers, presented by the press of the university with which he was formerly affiliated,

---

[102] See, for example, my discussion of Bell's late-eighteenth-century reprint series, *The Poets of Great Britain* in "John Donne, Author," *Journal of Medieval and Renaissance Literature* 19 (1989): 80–81.

[103] For a discussion of this edition in the context of the economic rivalry between the Cambridge University Press and the London Stationers, see M. H. Black, *Cambridge University Press 1584–1984* (Cambridge: Cambridge University Press, 1984), pp. 68–86. The Cambridge Press also published, in 1633, Phineas Fletcher's *Purple Island*, which, according to David McKitterick, *Four Hundred Years of University Printing in Cambridge 1584–1984* (Cambridge: Cambridge University Press, 1984), p. 45, "had circulated for some years in manuscript" while Fletcher was a fellow of King's College. Referring to the 1634 edition of John Donne's *Six Sermons*, McKitterick points out that Humphrey Moseley "commissioned the book from the Cambridge press" (p. 47).

published in the handy portable form of the duodecimo, "*The Temple. Sacred Poems and Private Ejaculations. By Mr. George Herbert*" had no need for apology as a printed volume of lyrics. Posthumously glorifying its humble author through the print medium, it offered a model other religious writers of lyric verse could, and did, follow. After Herbert, at least as far as the religious lyric is concerned, print was the proper medium for its dissemination—one sign of how print culture paradoxically both made the private public and demarcated private life itself more clearly as a social space.

The Donne and Herbert editions paved the way for the publication of the work of other poet-ecclesiasts such as Richard Corbett (1647 and 1648), Robert Herrick (1648), William Cartwright (1651), and Henry King (1657). King, as Donne's literary executor, probably served as the original editor of the 1633 *Poems,* and this might have helped him to overcome any reluctance to see his own verse published in 1657. When Owen Felltham appended his own poems to the eighth impression of his *Resolves* (1661), however, in a section headed "Lusoria," he excused them as "sports; that rather improve a man by preserving him from *worse,* then by bringing otherwise any considerable *profit*" (sig. A2v). He assumed that secular lyric verse was still socially stigmatized.

As posthumous editions, the 1633 Donne and Herbert volumes continued a tradition of posthumous collected editions of writers' works: the 1568 Skelton, *The Whole Woorkes of G. Gascoigne: Compyled into one Volume* (1587), the 1598 Sidney folio, the 1611 collected Spenser, the 1623 first folio of Shakespeare, and Daniel's 1623 *Whole Workes* are all memorials to esteemed authors as well as compilations of their works. The collected editions of living authors—the 1605 Daniel, 1616 Jonson folio, the 1619 Drayton *Poems*—are the exceptions rather than the rule. Greville's 1633 collected works, though prepared by the author, appeared posthumously. Many of the editions of poets that appeared over the two decades following the first Donne and Herbert editions were also posthumous publications: the 1638 Randolph (prepared by his brother and printed by the university press at Oxford), the 1640 *Poems* of Thomas Carew, two editions of Suckling's works, *Fragmenta Aurea* (1646) and *The Last Remains* (1659), the two (poorly produced) collections of Richard Corbett's poetry in 1647 and 1648. Although the 1660 edition of Richard Lovelace's book of poetry is titled *Lucasta, Posthume Poems* (1660), the

1649 edition of *Lucasta* was not a posthumous publication, but an authorially produced one. In the preface to his selected and collected *Poems* (1656), Cowley seems to present the book as a "posthumous" volume.[104] In that interesting and far-reaching document, he considers, among other topics, the question of the posthumous character of fame and suggests that "the *Reader* . . . may look upon me as a *Dead*, or at least a *Dying Person*" (sig. a2r). He presents himself as engaging in a preemptive act of publication, preventing the unauthorized printing of his work by opportunistic publishers and anticipating the posthumous collection meant to gather an author's poetic remains. Robert Herrick's *Hesperides* (1648) is also presented as a kind of pre-posthumous collection.[105]

In a period of political conflict, however, posthumous poetry, like funeral elegies, offered the opportunity to reinforce the political partisanship of poets, publishers, and readers. In particular, from the mid-1640s through the 1650s collected editions of poets' works as well as poetry anthologies were largely a manifestation of Royalism. Whereas, especially during the Interregnum, the published religious lyrics of "poetical deans," versifying ministers, and devout laymen could, as Lois Potter suggests, be valued for their authors' association with High Church Anglicanism and Royalist politics, printed secular lyrics were also a sign of Royalist partisanship. Referring to Donne and Herbert and the other "writers most frequently quoted after 1642," Potter remarks that "it is difficult to separate admiration for an author and what he stood for."[106] In effect the aristocratic and conservative associations of poetry within the manuscript system carried over into the medium of print when, in the middle third of the seventeenth century, lyric texts moved from one medium to the other.

Donne and Herbert, then, were influential not simply because of the aesthetic impact of their printed work but also because they came to be associated with the publication of Royalist and High Church authors in the period of the Civil War and Interregnum. In an era in which conservative authors and readers felt embattled, print could

---

[104] Helgerson makes this point, explaining that "though the man is not yet dead, the poet is" (*Self-Crowned Laureates,* p. 222).

[105] Warren Chernaik argues that Herrick's *Hesperides* (1648) "is designed by the author as his own funeral monument, an old man's book" ("Books as Memorials: The Politics of Consolation," *Yearbook of English Studies* 21 [1991]: 208).

[106] Potter, *Secret Rites and Secret Writing,* pp. 115–16 (see Chap. 1, n. 23).

have an antidemocratic function (and thus lose some of its social stigma for members of the upper classes). This may account for the willingness of someone like Dudley, Baron North to publish his occasional writings (*A Forest of Varieties*, 1645). He indicates that despite what he calls the "prostitution of the Presse," he found it necessary to overcome his scruples in publishing private writings: "Meeting with this plundering age, if they venture not to undergoe the Presse, they are obnoxious to a sodain destruction" (sig. A3r). Margaret Cavendish, duchess of Newcastle, also found it desirable and possible to print her own verse and prose in 1653. The medium of print was converted from a potential embarrassment to Royalist writers to a safe haven for their work and a sign of political resistance to the authority of those who had defeated the king's forces. In the hands of a Royalist satirist like John Cleveland, a collection of poems could be associated with Royalist journalism—*The Character of a London Diurnal: With severall select Poems By the same Author* (1647)—some six editions of which appeared in its year of publication. The nineteen or so editions of Cleveland's verse that were published before the Restoration are an obvious example of Royalist poets' free resort to the print medium.

### Humphrey Moseley, Single-Author Editions, and the Anthologizing of Verse

The Donne and Herbert editions remained a potent force through this period, but one publisher in particular, Humphrey Moseley, exploited the potential Royalist market for such publications by producing more collections of lyric poetry than any of his competitors. It is interesting to note the categories Moseley used to advertise his publications in one of his catalogs: "Various Histories, with curious Discourses in humane Learning, &c," "Books in Humanity lately Printed," "Severall Sermons, with other excellent Tracts in Divinity," "Books in Divinity Lately Printed," "Choyce Poems with excellent Translations, by the most eminent wits of this age," "Poems lately Printed," "Incomparable Comedies and Tragedies," and "New and Excellent Romances." The prominence given literary works, poetry in particular, is unusual.[107] The number of poets Moseley published

---

[107] This catalogue is printed in Edmund Waller, *Poems 1645, together with Poems from Bodleian MS Don D 55* (Menston, U.K.: Scolar Press, 1971), sigs. A1r–B8v.

is extraordinary. He was responsible for printing the poems of Quarles (1642), Milton (1645), Waller (1645), Crashaw (1646 and 1648), Shirley (1646), Suckling (1646, 1648, and 1658), Cowley (1647 and 1655), Carew (1651),[108] Cartwright (1651), Stanley (1651), and Vaughan (1651 and 1654). He also produced the famous 1647 folio of Beaumont and Fletcher and many quartos of plays.[109] In a commendatory poem to Moseley's edition of Cartwright's *Comedies, Tragedies and Other Poems* (1651) John Leigh praises the publisher for having brought before the public the "high Atchievments" of "Noble Souls" that "wrote Wit," urging him to "gather up all / Those precious Lines which brave Wits have let fall" (including the poems of Cleveland and Cowley), "For times approach wherein Wit will be dear" (Reed, pp. 65–66). In the midst of the austere Commonwealth/Protectorate period, Moseley served to preserve the courtly and Royalist aesthetic. In the preface to his edition of Beaumont and Fletcher, he portrays himself as the preserver of the scattered dramatic texts that had "escaped these Publick Troubles, free and unmangled" (p. 80)—that is, the social disruption of the English Civil War. In his 1651 preface to his edition of Cartwright, an Oxford scholar-author, he yearns for "those daies [when] Oxford was a University" (p. 87), that is, for an Oxford undamaged by Parliament.[110]

As someone with a strong professional, commercial investment in print culture, Moseley emphasized some of the advantages of the medium in which he was working, even sometimes when he had no right to make the claims he did, as in the case of the outright deception he practiced in publishing an allegedly corrected edition of Waller

---

[108] This is the third edition of a work whose publication Moseley took over from Wakeley.

[109] See John Curtis Reed, "Humphrey Moseley, Publisher," *Oxford Bibliographical Society Proceedings and Papers* 2, pt. 1 (1927–30):57–142. Quotations from Moseley's prefaces are taken from this source and noted in the text. See also Potter, *Secret Rites and Secret Writing*, pp. 19–22 and passim, and Coiro, "Milton and Class Identity," pp. 277–89 (cited in full at Chap. 1, n. 118), for a discussion of Moseley's simultaneous marketing of prestigious single-author editions to an upper-class audience and miscellanies to a middle-class readership.

[110] It has, of course, been noted that the 1645 edition of Milton's poems was in strange company among the rest of Moseley's publications, but then Milton's courtly affiliations were emphasized by the contents and presentation of the book. On this publication, see Louis Martz, *Poet of Exile: A Study of Milton's Poetry* (New Haven: Yale University Press, 1980), pp. 3–59; Coiro, "Milton and Class Identity," pp. 286–87; and Richard M. Johnson, "The Politics of Publication: Misrepresentation in the 1645 *Poems*," *Criticism* 35 (1993): 45–71.

from "pure originalls" (Reed, p. 76).[111] In the Beaumont and Fletcher preface he advertises the absolute reliability of his texts, based supposedly on "the Originalls [he obtained] from such as received them from the Authours themselves." And the plays themselves are characterized as "the perfect full Originalls without the least mutilation" (p. 79)—that is, uncut texts rather than truncated acting versions. He reads the permanence and monumentality of print back into the composing methods of one of the authors, repeating the kind of myth associated earlier with Shakespeare, who supposedly never "blotted a line": "[Fletcher] had that rare felicity to prepare and perfect all first in his braine; to shape and attire his Notions, to adde or loppe off, before he committed one word to writing, and never touched pen till all was to stand as firm and immutable as if ingraven in Brasse or Marble" (pp. 80–81). He asserts the textual reliability for his edition of Cowley's *Mistresse* (1647): "A Correct Copy of these verses and (I am told) written by the Authour himselfe, falling into my hands, I thought fit to send them to the Presse" (p. 81). Moseley claims accurate attribution of all the texts in his Cartwright edition, refusing to add the work of other writers (as had notoriously been the case in the 1640 and 1653 editions of Beaumont's poems). Idealizing authorship and his own role in ensuring authors' fame through print, he assumes the role of protector of Cartwright's poetic canon, which was being raided by "Plagiaries" who "began to plunder Him" (p. 85) to appropriate for their own uses some of what he had written (that is, to treat the work of an author in a way characteristic of manuscript culture, as a fund of available riches). He presents himself as the rescuer of Henry Vaughan's poems from "Obscuritie" (p. 89) *in spite of* the author's wishes.

Moseley portrayed himself as the preserver of an endangered Royalist or loyalist body of texts. This is quite explicit in what he says on the eve of the Restoration in the preface to his edition of Suckling's *Last Remains* (1659):

Among the highest and most refin'd Wits of the Nation, this Gentile and Princely Poet took his generous rise from the Court; where having flourish'd with splendor and reputation, he liv'd only long enough to see the

---

[111] Moseley provided a new title page and used the old sheets of the previous edition.

Sun-set of that Majesty from whose auspicious beams he derived his lustre, and with whose declining state his own loyal Fortunes were obscured. But after the several changes of those times, being sequestered from the more serene Contentments of his native Country, He first took care to secure the dearest and choisest of his Papers in the several Cabinets of his Noble and faithful Frends; and among other Testimonies of his worth, these elegant and florid Peeces of his Fancie were preserved in the custody of his truly honorable and vertuous Sister, with whose free permission they were transcribed, and now published exactly according to the Originals.... [T]hese are the real and genuine Works of Sir John Suckling. (Reed, p. 101)[112]

Moseley, then, considered himself the main publisher of Royalist literary works in the middle two decades of the seventeenth century. That he functioned in this capacity with political and economic security says much about the power of the publishing industry and of its trade guild, the Stationer's Company, the weakness of official censorship, and the reliability of the upper- and middle-class markets for the kinds of books he printed. By the time of the Restoration, thanks partly to Moseley, the single-author edition of lyric poetry was a familiar phenomenon in the world of publication, though many verse collections appeared posthumously and few authors took the kind of care in seeing their work into print that Robert Herrick did in compiling his work for the 1648 *Hesperides*.[113]

In the Civil War and Commonwealth/Protectorate periods, however, many individual Royalist writers had their verse printed either against their wishes or allowed their work to be published only with grave misgivings. Two years after Charles I's execution, in the preface to the reader of his book of epigrams and other verse, Samuel Sheppard expressed his reluctance to publish in Cromwell's England: "I confesse my selfe guilty of no lesse then Treason against the Soveraignty of *Apollo,* and the Dignity of the Nine, to put forth any thing to publick view in this Age of Ignorance, and Ostracism of Learning, when the *Thespian* Fount is to pittyfully puddled, the Sacred Mount so sacrelegdiously Asassinated, and the *Castalian* Cave, become a cov-

---

[112] Publishers' uses of the terms "real" and "genuine," like others such as "authentic originals" and "exact copies," point to print culture's commercially driven need to claim textual superiority to manuscript-circulated works. See Marcus, *Puzzling Shakespeare*, pp. 19–25 (cited in full at Chap. 2, n. 22).

[113] See Ann Baynes Coiro, *Robert Herrick's Hesperides and the Epigram Book Tradition* (Baltimore: Johns Hopkins University Press, 1988), pp. 3–29.

ert for Chattering-Magpies" (sigs. A3v–A4r). Despite his politic poems "To the Parliament of England" and "*To his Excellency, the Lord
General* Cromwell," he seems uneasy about the timing of his work's
public appearance. John Eliot's *Poems Consisting of Epistles & Epigrams,
Satyrs, Epitaphs and Elogies, Songs and Sonnets* (1658) is presented as a
belated publication, delayed because of the political turmoil of the
times. The printer states in the epistle to the reader: "These Poems
were given me neer sixteen years since by a Friend of the Author,
with a desire they might be printed, but I conceived the Age then
too squeemish to endure the freedom which the Author useth; and
therefore I hitherto smothere'd them, but being desirous they should
not perish, and the world be deprived of so much clear Wit and
Fancy, I have adventured to expose them to thy view" (sig. A2r). The
printer emphasizes the gentility of the author and of his intended
audience, whereas the poet's own address "To his Book" (rhetorically designed for manuscript circulation, not print) expresses an
aversion to the marketplace of printed books (see especially "Pauls
Church yard," p. 8), to the middle- and lower-class readers who might
get access to the text, and to some of the members of the social elite
(that is, the "new great Lords" and licentious "countesses," p. 9).
Ideally, he says, "The only friends to whom I would commend thee,
/ Are only those to whom I humbly send thee" (p. 9). But the kind
of control a manuscript author might hope for was impossible in
print, so the poet also has poems "To the Printer, if these papers
should unhappily come to the Press" (p. 10) and "To his Stationer
if need be" (pp. 10–11). His intended audience is one of country
gentlemen and aristocrats, his ideal reader "some noble country
friend" (p. 13).

As much as publishers like Moseley did to help establish the sociocultural authority and legitimacy of poets, it was inevitable that the
publishers and authors would sometimes find themselves in conflict
within the institutional context of print culture. In his preface to the
1656 edition of his collected poems, for example, Abraham Cowley
complained about printers' "publication of some things of mine without my consent or knowledge, and those so mangled and imperfect,
that I could neither with honor acknowledge, nor with honesty quite
disavow them" (sig. a1v). He refers to the unrevised version of his
academic comedy, *The Guardian*. But then he generalizes from his
particular complaint to the problem he saw all authors facing in hav-

ing their work appropriated by publishers and printed in uncorrected, unedited form:

> From this which hapned to my self, I began to reflect upon the fortune of almost all *Writers*, and especially *Poets*, whose *Works* (commonly printed after their deaths) we finde stuffed out, either with *counterfeit pieces*, like *false Money* put in to fill up the *Bag*, though it adde nothing to the *sum*; or with such, which though of their own *Coyn*, they would have called in themselves, for the baseness of the *Allay*: whether this proceed from indiscretion of their *Friends*, who think a vast *heap* of Stones or Rubbish a better *Monument*, then a little *Tomb* of *Marble*, or by the unworthy avarice of some *Stationers*, who are content to diminish the value of the *Author*, so they may encrease the price of the *Book*; and like *Vintners* with sophisticate mixtures, spoil the whole vessel of wine, to make it yield more *profit*. This has been the case with *Shakespear, Fletcher, Johnson*, and many others; part of whose *Poems* I should take the boldness to prune and lop away, if the care of replanting them in print did belong to me; neither would I make any scruple to cut off from some the unnecessary young *Suckers*, and from other the old withered *Branches*. (Sigs. a1v–a2r)

In his own collection, Cowley claims to have exercised responsible editorial functions in presenting revised and selected texts: "Though I publish here, more then in strict wisdom I ought to have done, yet I have supprest and cast away more then I *publish*; and for the ease of my self and others, have *lost*, I believe too, more then *both*" (sig. a2r). He notes casually that many of his ephemeral texts in the manuscript system of transmission were lost. When he explains his omissions, he names specifically his juvenilia, "all those which I wrote at *School* from the age of ten years, till after fifteen" (sig. a3v), and "all such pieces as I wrote during the time of the late troubles" (sig. a4r), attempting to put behind him both his immature and his partisan work in order to claim a greater measure of literary authority. Two of the four sections of the 1656 *Poems* are comprised of lyrics, but Cowley treats each differently. "The first is a *Miscellanie* of several Subjects, and some of them made when I was very young . . . I know not by what chance I have kept *Copies* of them; for they are but a very few in comparison of those which I have lost, and I think they have no extraordinary virtue in them, to deserve more care in preservation, then was bestowed upon their *Brethren*" (sig. a4v). Treating occasional verse as ephemeral within the system of manuscript transmission,

Cowley claims little enduring literary merit for these compositions. The second section of verse, however, is another matter:

> The *Second,* is called, *The Mistress,* or *Love-Verses;* for so it is, that *Poets* are scarse though *Free-men* of their *Company,* without paying some duties, and obliging themselves to be true to *Love.* . . . But we must not always make a judgement of their *[m]anners* from their *writings* of this kind; as the *Romanists* uncharitably do of *Beza,* for a few lascivious *Sonnets* composed in his youth. It is said to be a kind of *Painting;* it is not the *Picture* of the *Poet,* but of *things* and *persons* imagined by him. He may be in his own practice and disposition a *Philosopher,* nay a *Stoick,* and yet speak sometimes with the softness of an amorous *Sappho.* (Sigs. a4v–b1r)

Cowley treats love poetry as fictional and literary, rather than as personal, social, and occasional, making it a sign of one's identity as a serious author. Though the publication of the work of Sidney, Spenser, Jonson, and Donne, in particular, lent support to this attitude, Cowley knew that he still had to overcome various prejudices against amorous verse in order to have his work in this mode accepted as worthy of preservation and respect. The association of his lyric verse in this collected edition with his pindaric odes and with his heroic poem *Davideis,* of course, was meant to dignify it.[114] But literariness and monumentality were themselves largely the product of print culture and the lyric in print was, by Cowley's time, a different kind of text from the lyric in manuscript transmission, partly due to the efforts of publishers like Moseley.

### Poetry Anthologies at Midcentury

In the 1640s and early 1650s, there were few significant published poetry anthologies.[115] Two works published first in 1640, however, enjoyed some measure of popularity—one, *The Academy of Complements,* a courtesy book of sorts that added lyric verse to its miscellaneous contents, the other, *Wits Recreations,* an anthology of short witty

---

[114] Analogously, Richard Fanshawe's *Il Pastor Fido* (1648) has some of this author's lyric poems appended to his translation of the Guarini play.

[115] For example, Samuel Pick's fifty-four-page quarto pamphlet, *Festum Voluptatis, or the Banquet of Pleasure* (1639), is a slight production.

verse.[116] Humphrey Moseley produced *The Academy of Complements*, aiming it at those on the fringe of high society who wished to learn the fashionable "eloquence" (sig. A6v) of their social betters by imitating models of their conversation, letter-writing, and verse. Like other literary miscellanies and poetry anthologies, this text reveals a basic (but commercially exploitable) conflict between its elitist contents and the democratizing effects of print.[117] Although Moseley habitually appealed to an upper-class audience interested in courtly and witty writing, especially in the Civil War and Interregnum, in this work he obviously appealed to middle-class readers. Its full title makes this quite clear: *The Academy of Complements. Wherein Ladyes, Gentlewomen, Schollers, and Strangers may accommodate their Courtly Practice with most Curious Ceremonies, Complementall, Amorous, High expression, and formes of speaking, or writing. A work perused and most exactly perfected by the Author with Additions of witty Amorous Poems, And a Table expounding the hard English words.*[118] Hoping for a broad clientele, he included in it a catalog of his publications. The ninth (1650) edition of this handbook advertised itself as "A Work perused, exactly perfected, every where corrected and inlarged, and inriched by the Author, with Additions of many witty Poems, and pleasant Songs"—a collection now containing a second "Table" or appendix, one "resolving the most

---

[116] This duodecimo volume appeared in three editions in 1640 and was also printed in 1650, 1654, 1655, 1658, 1663, 1664, 1670, 1684, 1685, 1705, 1727, 1750, 1790, and 1795. In "Milton and Class Identity," pp. 22–38, Coiro has a very useful discussion of the mid-century printed miscellanies, especially *Wits Recreations* and *The Academy of Complements*. See also Hobbs, *Verse Miscellany Manuscripts*, pp. 97–104 (cited in full at Chap. 1, n. 60).

[117] The courtesy-book function was implicit in many of the poetical miscellanies of the sixteenth and seventeenth centuries, and the kind of publication represented by *The Academy of Complements* was found as early as the Elizabethan book *The Forest of Fancy* (1579), a collection of verse and prose supposedly suitable for all tastes, but cast in the language of address to a readership of sophisticated gentlemen. This book contains not only recreational verse and prose, but also such items as model letters—for example, "A letter written by one to a ritche Widdow, wherein using earnest perswations he soliciteth his sute, and craveth to be accepted" (sigs. Liiir–viv).

[118] Consider this imitation printed in 1656: "*The Academy of Pleasure. Furnished with all kinds of Complementall Letters, Discourses, and Dialogues; with [a] variety of new Songs, Sonets, and witty Inventions. Teaching all sorts of Men, Maids, Widows &c. to Speak and Write wittily, and to bear themselves gracefully for the attaining of their desired ends: how to discourse and demean themselves at Feasts and merry Meetings at home and abroad, in the company of friends or strangers. How to Retort, Quibble, Jest or Joke, and to return an ingenious Answer upon any occasion whatsoever. Also, A Dictionary of all the hard English words expounded. With a Poeticall Dictionary. With other Conceits very pleasant and delightfull, never before extant.* London, Printed for *John Stafford* at Fleet-bridge, and *Will. Gilbertson* in Giltspur-street, 1656" (12mo). This collection mixes songs and model letters. Its dictionary (pp. 109–28) explains classical personages and deities to the unlearned.

delightful fictions of the Heathen Poets."[119] The 1684 (Restoration) edition, for example, boasts of "Many New Additions of Songs and Catches *A-la-mode,* stored With Variety of Complemental and Elegant Expressions, of Love and Courtship," the whole work "Composed for the use of Ladies and Gentlewomen. By the most refined Wits of this Age" (the fiction of a single author is finally dropped). That *The Academy of Complements* was reprinted all the way up through 1795 indicates that there was a popular market for such a text. The lyric poetry in this collection is largely complimentary and occasional, but subordinated to the general purpose of this kind of self-improvement book, the poetry anthology is a relatively poor selection of contemporary verse.

*Wits Recreations* is more significant as a printed anthology, running through many editions over the next several decades (seven by 1683).[120] Though largely comprised of epigrammatic and satiric short poems, epitaphs and riddles, the kind of witty verse often found in abundance in contemporary manuscript miscellanies, especially those associated with academic environments, this large collection contains the work of such writers as Jonson, Beaumont and Fletcher, Chapman, Randolph, Suckling, Sandys, Habington, Shirley, Massinger, Drayton, Carew, Strode, Corbett, Wotton, and Poole: antiromantic, misogynistic anti-Puritan, courtly, and encomiastic pieces make this perhaps the printed anthology closest to the collecting practices found in the manuscript tradition—though it omits the longer poems one often encounters in the manuscript collections. It shares more poems with the surviving manuscript anthologies than does any other printed miscellany of the period.[121]

Partly because of the decline of Royalist fortunes in the decade following the initial appearance of *Wits Recreations,* however, one does

---

[119] In "Milton and Class Identity," Coiro concentrates her discussion on this 1650 edition and points out that the book evolved considerably over the years. She calls Moseley "the acknowledged master of the self-help miscellany form, feeding the needs of a seemingly inexhaustable middle-class market for the tools of gentrification" (p. 27). She points out that "physically, the book was made to look as much as possible like a manuscript commonplace book, with hand ruled edges and divisions" (p. 28). Referring to the 1650 edition, she states: "The focus of the volume is sharply on social relations and class differences" (p. 31).

[120] This work was published (and continually expanded) in 1640, 1641, 1645, 1650, 1654, 1663, 1667, and 1683. See *Witts Recreations Selected from the fines Fancies of Moderne Muses 1640,* facsimile, with an introduction and indexes by Colin Gibson (Menston, U.K.: Scolar Press, 1990).

[121] See, for example, the many references to this anthology in Crum's *Index.*

not find a significant, substantial new anthology of lyric poetry for quite some time. Only in the second half of the Interregnum does the publication of poetic anthologies really revive: the most notable examples are *The Harmony of the Muses* (1654); *Musarum Deliciae: or the Muses Recreation* (1655), edited by John Mennes and James Smith (two staunch Royalists, the first of whom was in continental exile at the time of the publication); two anthologies burned by order of the authorities, *Choyce Drollery* (1656) and *Sportive Wit* (1656);[122] *Parnassus Biceps* (1656); *Wit and Drollery* (1656); and *Wit Restor'd* (1658).[123]

Material that might not have found its way into print a few years earlier was published for both upper-class and middle-class readerships. On its title page, *The Harmony of the Muses* (1654) names nine

[122] Clearly, these two books literally took the heat that others didn't (for example the bawdier *Wit and Drollery* or *Musarum Deliciae*). Courtney Craig Smith gives an account of the government's response to the two collections it banned: "On 25 April 1656, *Sportive Wit* was reported in the Council of State to contain 'much scandalous, lascivious, scurrilous and profane matter.' An order was given for all copies to be seized and delivered to the sheriffs of London and Middlesex for public burning. The men responsible for the book, Nathaniel Brooke and John Phillips, were summoned before the Council and fined. Two weeks later similar treatment was ordered for *Choice Drollery*, 'a book stuffed with profane and obscene matter, tending to the corruption of manners' and the compiler of the 1682 edition of *Wit and Drollery* writes: 'This sort of Wit hath formerly suffered Martyrdom; for *Cromwell*, who was more for Policy than Wit, not only laid the first Reviver of these Recreations in the Tower, but also committed the innocent Sheets to the mercy of the Executioners fire; as being some of them too kind, as he thought, to the Royal Partie' " ("The Seventeenth-Century Drolleries," *Harvard Library Bulletin* 6 [1952]:46–47). The full title of the second anthology signals its Cavalier social cynicism: *Sportive Wit: The Muses Merriment. A New Spring of Lusty Drollery, Joviall Fancies, and A la mode Lamponnes, on some Heroic persons of these late Times, Never before exposed to the publick view. Collected for the Publick good, by a Club of sparkling Wits, viz. C.F., B.F., L.M., W.T. Cum multis aliis. Semel in anno ridet Apollo.* The product of a Royalist cosmopolitan coterie, this small octavo text (more easily concealed than larger-format works) tried to keep the fashion of cynical, witty, misogynistic, Royalist writing alive in the hostile environment that tried to destroy it. Smith claims that the audience for the drolleries included not only young, university-educated gallants and out-of-power courtiers, but also "those who were not regularly accepted into the inner circles of the court but yet considered themselves the social superiors of the city merchants and tradesmen. It must have been among these people on the 'fringe' of society that the drollery had its beginning. They could not escape to the Continent with the court group during the Commonwealth and Protectorate, nor as good Cavaliers, could they bear the strictness of Roundhead rule without some protest. They did not belong to the nobility, yet they may have known an occasional knight or baronet. . . .The Pepyses could be associated with this group; *Wit and Drollery* (1656) was dedicated to a relative of the diarist, and Pepys was acquainted with both Captain William Hickes, the most prolific compiler of drolleries, and Henry Herringman, the publisher and probably the compiler of the first drollery of all" (pp. 48–49). *Wit and Drollery* looks like it was designed to be deliberately partisan and provocative: it contains obscene verse, merciless lampoons, and anti-Puritan pieces.

[123] See *Musarum Deliciae (1655) and Wit Restor'd (1658)*, facsimile, with an introduction by Tim Raylor (Delmar, N.Y.: Scholars' Facsimiles & Reprints, 1985), p. 8. See Raylor's discussion of *Musarum Deliciae* as the first of the "drolleries" in his introduction, pp. 5–11.

authors of the verse it contains, "Dr. Joh. Donn, Dr. Hen. King, Dr. W. Stroad, Sr. Kenelm Digby, Mr. Ben Johnson, Mr. Fra. Beaumont, J. Cleveland, T. Randolph, and T. Carew," poets well represented in the manuscript miscellanies of the 1630s and 1640s, but much of whose work had not yet been published—hence the exaggerated claim, "Never before Published." The opening epistle "To the Readers" calls attention the prestige associated with the "Names of the Authors" whose "meritorious Pens"[124] produced the work included in the collection. From the vantage point of the middle of the Commonwealth/Protectorate period, this collection appeals to a politically nostalgic yearning for verse composed much earlier by authors who lived in an age that supposedly valued poetry and learning more than the era of Cromwell did:

> Poetry in their days flourished, and they flourished with it, and gave a crown unto that which hath crowned them with Honor, and perpetuall Fame. The Genius of those times produced many incomparable Witts, who being excellent in themselves, in a noble emulation, contended who should excell each other. From hence it is we have so many admirable Pieces of Perfection derived to us, every Subject, in every particular, being so choicely handled, that what room is left unto Posterity, is rather to admire and imitate, then to equal them. There were never in one Age so many contemporary Patterns of Invention, or ever Witt that wrought higher or clearer. (Sig. A3r)

*The Harmony of the Muses* is largely a collection of love poetry, much of it libertine and bawdy: it prints the whole of Donne's "Elegy 19" ("Going to Bed") and, as a separate (similarly bawdy) poem, lines 29–46 of the elegy "Loves Warre," as well as lines 1–48 and 53–96 of "Loves Progress," the full text of which did not reach print until the nineteenth century.[125] This anthology also prints for the first time a bawdy poem found in an extraordinary number of manuscript collections (as well as in later printed volumes), a piece here named "A Maids Denyall" ("Nay pish, nay pew, nay faith, and will you, fie").[126] Revealingly, this collection also includes Carew's popular lyric "The

---

[124] *Harmony of the Muses by Robert Chamberlain,* ed. Sullivan, sig. A3r (see Chap. 2, n.13). I cite this edition within the text.

[125] See ibid., pp. xii–xvi for Sullivan's discussion of the contents of this anthology. He relates the whole collection to two manuscript anthologies, Bod. MS Ash. 38 and Oxford MS CCC 328 (pp. xi–xii).

[126] See the discussion of this piece in Chapter 2.

Rapture"—here titled "Loves Elizium" (pp. 18–23). Aware that the collection contains some obscene verse that had not yet been printed, the writer protects the collection from criticism by excusing some poems as rambunctious juvenilia: "If any shall object, that here and there the Fancy seems some time too loose for such Reverend Names, let him impute it to the lightness of the Subject, and to the heat and vigour of their early Witts, when first those Ayres were breathed forth" (sig. A3v). The same concerns manifested in the presentation of the 1633 Donne edition resurface for similar reasons.

Of the authors named on the title page of the anthology—all significant poets associated with Royalist attitudes—only Beaumont's and Cleveland's work cannot easily be found. The collection also includes pieces by Sir Robert Ayton ("An Incouragement for young Lovers," p. 7), John Myns ("*To Mr. J. W. a Parson in* Devon. *Inviting him to come up to London,*" pp. 8–10), Walton Poole ("Of Love and Death," pp. 15–16, and "In praise of black Women," pp. 16–18— the second piece the popular "If shadows be a Pictures excellence," here misattributed to "T.R."), and James Shirley ("LOVE'S Hue and Cry," pp. 34–35), Joshua Sylvester's poem "A Caveat to his Mistris" ("Beware fair Maid of Musky Courtiers oaths," pp. 66–67), as well as a series of occupation-specific comic epitaphs by one "W.M." (pp. 104–11). There is also what looks like an extended series of love poems written by an anonymous author who may be the compiler of the whole collection or one of his contemporaries.[127] In both its contents and its front matter, *The Harmony of the Muses* is an openly Royalist publication. It assumes that older authors like Donne and Jonson can be associated with more contemporary Royalist poets like Strode, Digby, and Cleveland in an anthology directed toward an embattled political minority during the time of Cromwell's rule.

Some midcentury poetry anthologies and miscellanies containing verse were advertised as being addressed to a social elite. *Sportive Wit* (1656), for example, was presented as a collection of verse produced corporately by a "Club of sparkling Wits" (sig. A4r) to be enjoyed by those who valued fashionable, sophisticated recreation; *Wits Interpreter* (1655) was aimed at a social and intellectual elite, and took satiric

---

[127] These poems are found on pp. 76–96, interrupted only by two pieces on p. 81, "To a Friend, on the word Wife" (a witty misogynistic item found in manuscript collections) and "Upon a Merchant" (a poem about the fall of Lionel Cranfield, earl of Middlesex, discussed in Chapter 2).

aim at the self-improvement books produced for the lower classes. *Wit Restor'd* (1658) has a strong anti-lower-class and anti-Puritan bias.[128] Many light, satiric, and witty anthologies were produced both before and after the Restoration, using the term "Drollery" in their titles to characterize their contents—for example, following *Choyce Drollery* (1656) and *Wit and Drollery* (1656), *Merry Drollery* (1660), *Oxford Drollery* (1670), *Westminister Drollery* (1671), *Windsor Drollery* (1671), *Grammatical Drollery* (1671), and so on. Courtney Smith has defined the "drollery" as

> an anthology of miscellaneous verse, never really dignified in nature, which was compiled by the Cavaliers for the sake of registering protest against the Puritans in a jocose, mocking, and often frankly sensual fashion. . . .The distinguishing feature of these drolleries is their quality of protest: they were compiled by and for Cavaliers as a weapon against their social and political foes. Until the Restoration brought relief, they were the "subversive propaganda" of an "occupied" people who had lost out in the field, yet were unwilling to submit to the rule (or the preaching) of the "Saints." Even with the Restoration the character of the drolleries did not change, except that the protest became more social than political.[129]

Just as many of the single-author editions of verse were obviously aimed at a Royalist social and educational elite, so too many of the poetry anthologies were meant for this same readership.

Given the steady market for self-improvement books in print culture, however, it is not surprising that some texts deliberately appealed to a middle-class readership and clientele. One such work is a courtesy book that includes verse among its contents: *The Mysteries of Love & Eloquence, or the Arts of Wooing and Complementing; As they are manag'd in the Spring Garden, Hide Park, the New Exchange, and other eminent places. A Work, in which are drawn to the Life, the Deportments of the most accomplisht Persons, the mode of their Courtly Entertainments, Treatments of their Ladies at Balls, their accustom'd Sports, Drolles and Fancies, the Witchcrafts of their perswasive Language, in their Approaches, or other more Secret Dispatches. To compleat the young Practitioners of Love and Courtship, these following conducing Helps are chiefly insisted on. Addresses, and set Forms of*

---

[128] See, for example, the poem "The Burse of Reformation" (pp. 20–24).
[129] Smith, "Seventeenth Century Drolleries," pp. 42, 45. Smith lists twenty-one of these anthologies published between 1655 and 1682.

*Expressions for imitation. Poems, pleasant Songs, Letters, Proverbs, Riddles, Jeasts, Posies, Devices, A la mode Pastimes, A Dictionary for the making of Rimes, Four hundred and fifty delightful Questions, with their several Answers. As also Epithets, and flourishing Similitudes, Alphabetically collected, and so properly applied to their several Subjects, that they may be rendered admirably useful on the sudden occasions of Discourse or Writing. Together, with a new invented Art of Logick, so plain and easie by way of Questions and Answers; that the meanest capacity may in short time attain to a perfection in the wayes of Arguing and Disputing* (1658).[130] In terms of the process of literary institutionalization at work in the English Renaissance, this work is a retrogressive one, recontextualizing poetry in the environment of the social life of the upper classes and stripping it of its growing association with the modern conception of authorship. Combining a strong snob appeal with its strategies of vulgarization, this text exploits the democratizing potential of the print medium, advertising itself as superior to the manuscript miscellanies of the elite as a source of imitable style. Attempting to reverse the traditional social inferiority of print to manuscript, the editor claims this collection is better than those found in private commonplace books (sig. A5r)—though the dedicatory epistle refers to the work as a "Table-book" (sig. A6v), a term used to describe a blank book in which texts were transcribed by hand. The preface ("To the Youthful Gentry") claims that with the right sources for imitation, any one might best his or her social betters. The editor claims: "I have known a wench of fourteen, with a few Dramatic *Drayton* and *Sidney* Quillets, put to the *non plus* a Gallant of thirty. . . . I have heard such a Lass defeat a Gentleman of some years standing at the Inns of Court" (sig. A5r). In this formulation Drayton's and Sidney's poems lose their dignity as literary monuments and become, as was literature in an earlier system, a treasury of language open to any needy user. At the same time, as the dedicatory epistle explains, the book so successfully demystifies the "mysteries" of love that it serves a curative function for those victimized by it, as exemplified in the story of the "mad lover" (sig. air) who was quickly disabused of his love illusions by perusing the text. The world of civility envisioned by this text is one from which both ro-

---

[130] This was edited by Milton's nephew Edward Phillips and was republished in 1685 and (as *The Beau's Academy*) in 1699.

mantic illusions and the "inspirations" of Puritan "Enthusiasts" (sig. a2v) are purged.

Another self-improvement book, however, John Cotgrave's *Wits Interpreter* (1655), which also includes a selection of poetry,[131] had attacked the vulgarizing potential of such works, probably specifically the earlier *Academy of Complements*, books that appealed to a "*Chambermaid* to make her beleive [*sic*], she may be easily compleated with *offensive* and *defensive* terms of Language, so to manage her Wit as if she were at a prize" (sig. A3v).[132] This text, whose frontispiece enshrines a series of writers and political figures including "Spencer," "Shakespeare," "Johnson," Randolph," "Sr. T. More," "Ld. Bacon," "Sydney," "[The Earl of] Strafford," "[Cardinal] Richilieu," and "Dubartas," appeals to "the *wiser Reader*" (sig. A3r), to an intellectually elite audience that can appreciate high-quality poetry and learning (see figure 9). Cotgrave claims to have taken great pains to secure previously unavailable texts "from the private Papers of the choicest Wits . . . from which Manuscripts of theirs . . . I crossed out whatsoever I could hear had been formerly publisht" (sig. A4r). He treats the authorial manuscripts and the printed texts derived from them with the kind of respect fostered by print culture. And to produce this text, he claims the full cooperation of many of the authors: "The *English Tongue* was never honored with a larger or a more *Accurate Collection*. . . .those Honorable Persons which furnisht me with many of these Admirable *Peeces,* were in a readiness to speak the worth of those *Copies* to the publication wherof they so freely gave their Consents" (sigs. A4r–v). In his address to the reader, the publisher Nathanial Brooke associates the question of textual accuracy ("these sheets of paper . . . are printed from [the authors'] own Manuscripts," sig. A5r) and the elevated status of literature within print culture ("these inestimable Monuments," sig. A5r) with Royalist nostalgia and politics ("the Reliques of the dead are not esteemed amongst the reformed of the Nation," sig. A5r), associating the worth

---

[131] This work was reissued in 1662 and 1671. At the end of it there is a section of poems titled "Several Love-songs, Drollerys, and other Verses."

[132] Harvey Graff argues that "female literacy gained rapidly after the Revolution, and by the end of the seventeenth century, city women's literacy rates compared well with those of men in other parts of the country" (*The Legacies of Literacy: Continuities and Contradictions in Western Culture and Society* [Bloomington: Indiana University Press, 1987], p. 155). The growth in female literacy may account for the way such a book as this was marketed.

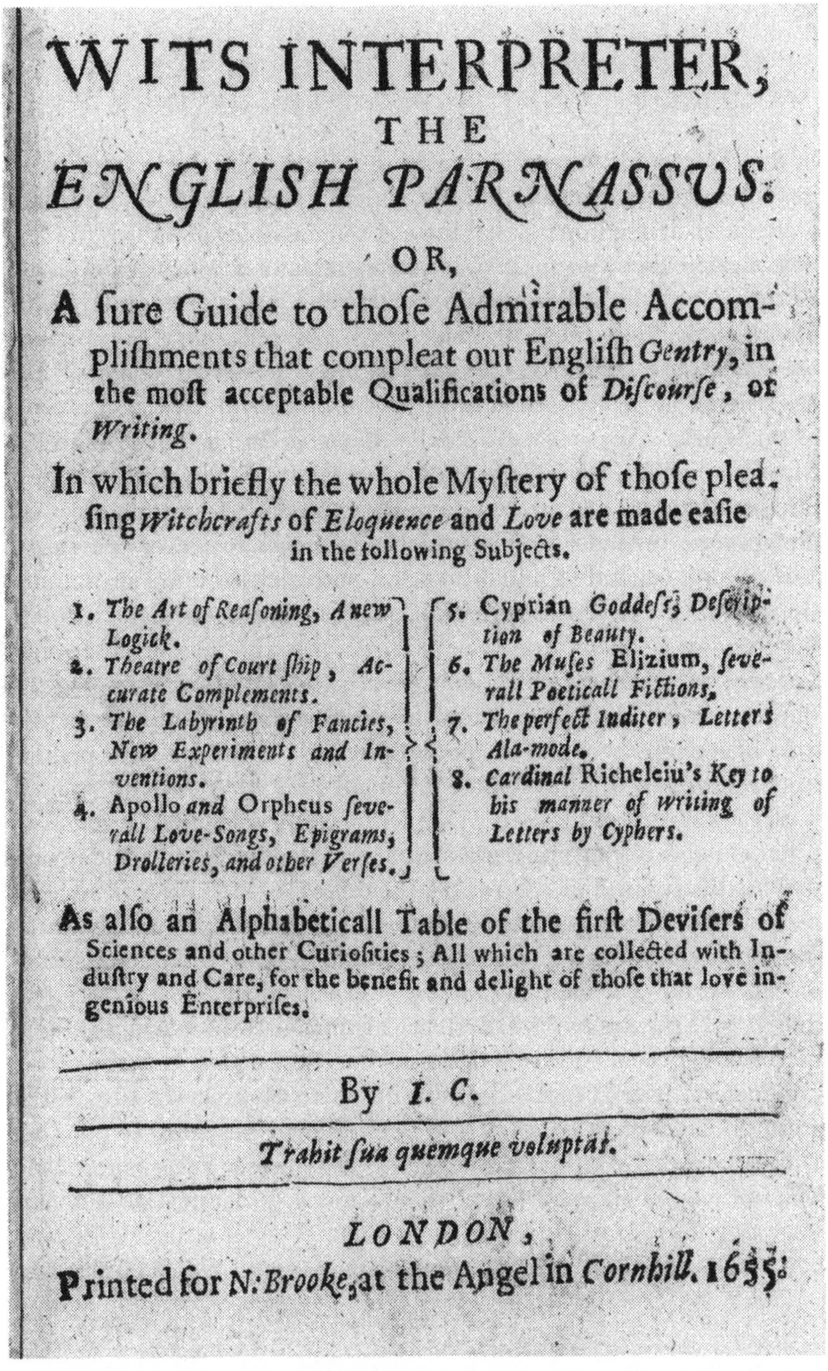

# WITS INTERPRETER,
## THE
## *ENGLISH PARNASSUS:*
### OR,

**A** sure Guide to those Admirable Accomplishments that compleat our English *Gentry*, in the most acceptable Qualifications of *Discourse*, or *Writing*.

In which briefly the whole Mystery of those pleasing *Witchcrafts* of *Eloquence* and *Love* are made easie in the following Subjects.

1. *The Art of Reasoning, A new Logick.*
2. *Theatre of Court ship*, Accurate *Complements.*
3. *The Labyrinth of Fancies, New Experiments* and *Inventions.*
4. Apollo *and* Orpheus *several Love-Songs*, Epigrams, Drolleries, *and other Verses.*

5. Cyprian *Goddess*, Description *of Beauty.*
6. *The Muses* Elizium, *several Poeticall Fictions*,
7. *The perfect Inditer*, Letters *Ala-mode.*
8. *Cardinal* Richelieu's *Key to his manner of writing of Letters by Cyphers.*

As also an Alphabeticall Table of the first Devisers of Sciences and other Curiosities; All which are collected with Industry and Care, for the benefit and delight of those that love ingenious Enterprises.

### By *I. C.*

*Trahit sua quemque voluptas.*

### *LONDON,*
**P**rinted for N. *Brooke*, at the Angel in *Cornhill*. 1655.

---

*Figure 9.* [John Cotgrave], *Wits Interpreter* (1655), frontispiece and title page. Courtesy of the Huntington Library.

of the texts with the symbolic value of a lost monarchy in calling the items "Fragmenta Regalia Aurea & Sacra" (sig. A5r). It is interesting, given the partisan appeal, that the stationer should follow this preface with a catalogue of forty-six of his publications available for purchase, a list that includes (at a time the theater remained closed under order of the authorities) three dramatic texts[133] as well as *The Queens Closet opened Incomparable secrets in physick, Chyrurgery; preserving, Candying, and Cooking, as they were presented to the Queen, transcribed from the true Copes of her Majesties own receipt-Books by W.M. one of her late Servants,* and *A Satyre against Hypocrites* (sig. A6v)—the latter an obvious attack on Puritans. Despite this presentation, the collection is actually a hodge-podge, a mixture of a treatise on logic, miscellaneous examples of wit and humor (including practical jokes and tricks) before presenting (in a newly paginated section) the main collection of poetry under the heading "Wits Interpreter: Or, Apollo and Orpheus: Several Love-Songs, Drollery, and other Verses" (sig. O1r), an anthology of (largely unascribed) serious and frivolous poetry running from the time of Ralegh through the mid-seventeenth century.[134] The impression one gets is that the editor grabbed what he could and printed it with little restraint.

Royalist nostalgia, upper-class exclusiveness, and anti-Puritan sentiments mark some of the poetical anthologies and literary miscellanies of this period (as they do other types of publication, such as single-author editions). The reissuing of the poems of William Drummond of Hawthornden in 1656, for example, in an edition introduced by Edward Phillips, was an explicitly Royalist act: this text includes "Speeches to the High and Excellent Prince Charles, King of Great Brittaine, France and Ireland at His Entring His City of Edenburgh: Delivered from the Pageants the 15th of June, 1633" (pp. 156–58), and the whole work is dedicated to Sir John Scot, "Late Director of his Majesties Chancellary, and one of the Lords of His Majesties most Honorable Pr[i]vy Councell, Sessions, and Exchequer" (sig. A2r).

There are, however, some few exceptions to the association of lyric

---

[133] "*The unfortunate Mother. A Tragedy,* By Tho. Nabs," "*The Rebellion, a Comedy,* By T.R.," and "*The Tragedy of* Messalina, By Na. Richards" (sig. A6v).

[134] Many poems popular in manuscript collections found here, for example, Walton Poole's "If shadows be a pictures excellence," Sir Robert Ayton's "Wrong not sweet Empresse of my heart," and Ben Jonson's "Come my *Celia* let us prove."

publications with Royalism. One of the stranger publications of the Interregnum is Thomas Pecke's *Parnassi Puerperium* (1659), which contains translations of the epigrams of Owen, Martial, and Thomas More along with Pecke's own "heroic epigrams." The first poem in the section of Pecke's own work is an unusual dedication to the deceased Oliver Cromwell's son, "To His Serene Highnesse, Richard, Lord Protector, etc.":

> *Augustus* was most lovely in the Eyes,
> Of *Romes* Grave Senate; who did Eternise
> His Fame; and without Arguings agree,
> To Honour him; with *Pater Patriae.*
> In a Pacifick, and auspicious Hour,
> You made an Ingresse, to the Supream Power.
> Your sweet Demeanour gives, publick Content:
> Love, Candor, finde but few, Malevolent.
> Your Father *Julius* was; *Augustus* be:
> Your Countreys Father; *Mecoena's* to Me.
>
> (P. 170)

This epigram collection—more serious than than the lighter Royalist anthologies of verse—is a rare poetic publication associated with the non-Royalist establishment (though Pecke uses the language of royalty and empire in his address to Richard Cromwell). The dozen or so poems following the dedication are addressed to prominent parliamentary and government figures, such as "Lord Chief Justive Glyn," "Oliver, St. John, Lord Chief Justice of the Common Pleas," "Lord Chief Baron Widdrington," "Sir Edmund Prideaux, Attorney-General" (pp. 170–72) and to friends and relatives. Appearing on the eve of the Restoration, Pecke's poetry collection was not exactly a well-timed publication.

What Cromwell's government banned is no surprise compared to what it permitted. With the Restoration of the monarchy, there were even fewer, or at least different, restraints on the political and sexual content of the printed miscellanies and poetical anthologies, so the number of manuscript compilations dropped off as print became more accessible as a medium and more respectable in elite culture.

Two literary collections that appeared in the year of Charles II's return clearly associate anthologizing with Royalist politics, *Le Prince d'Amour* and *The Poems of Pembroke and Ruddier*. The first combines the text of an Elizabethan Inns of Court revels with an anthology of older and more recent lyric verse, introduced by the printer, William Leake, with a dedication to the men of the Middle Temple which connects the previous unavailability of the main text with the temporary absence of the monarchy: "A Prince for some yeares past in *disguise,* and a stranger to his Native Soil, is now brought to light; and to you he comes, not for *Patronage,* but *welcome.*" Looking back on the time of the original reveling, Leake expresses Royalist nostalgia for a period in which "the *Genius* of the *Nation* [was] then heightened by all the accesses of *peace, plenty, Wit,* and *Beauty,* in their exact perfection." In defending the contents of the anthology, Leake contrasts the earlier time with "this latter ill-natured Age":

> The *attendant Poems* were the offspring of divers eminent *Wits* of the same age, and never yet appeared in publick, having confined themselves to the fortune of so *Illustrious* a *Prince;* whose *person* being waited on, and *Court adorned* with the choicest and noblest beauties of *England during his Monarchy,* it cannot be improper to have the *Muses* now appear to do honor, and pay a just duty to his *History.* In the whole *Collection* there is not any thing of the gall and venome which has mixed it self with the Ink of these last twenty years, but *wit* born long before our unhappy *intestine* divisions, and had that mark of eternity, that it is not like to grow old, but is still new, florid and innocent. (Sigs. A2v–4r)[135]

Looking back past the previous two decades of political division, civil war, and kingless government, Leake seeks to distinguish the more genial and less overtly partisan "wit" of the earlier time from the more satiric and bitter wit represented in the printed collections of the recent past. He also attributes a transhistorical character to some literary texts—a feature (or illusion) promoted by the print medium. He appeals to an audience happy about the Restoration of the Stuarts, but not just to Royalist or loyalist readers, since the Inns of Court would have housed men with varying political sympathies: he thus avoids a frontal attack on Puritans, regicides, or antimonarchical Par-

---

[135] According to Michael Rudick, the poetry collection in *Le Prince d'Amour* "derives in all probability from a MS miscellany of the usual kind compiled in the 1630s or 1640s. Of nineteen poems attributed in this, at least six are demonstrably attributed incorrectly, and most of the rest are unverifiable" ("Poems of Ralegh," p. 75 [see Chap. 1, n. 99]).

liamentarians, looking for a broad commercial appeal for his book.[136] In fact, he follows his dedicatory preface with a catalog of his publications, an interesting combination of legal, religious, historical, political, practical, military, and literary materials (including many plays). The poetry anthology (pp. 91–184) includes a selection of Elizbethan, Jacobean, and Caroline lyrics and has its own separate title page: "A Collection of several Ingenious Poems and Songs By the Wits of the Age."[137]

John Donne, Jr.'s misleadingly labeled *Poems Written by the Right Honorable William Earl of Pembroke . . . Many of which are answered by way of Repartee, by Sir Benjamin Ruddier, Knight. With several Distinct Poems Written by them Occasionally, and Apart* (1660) announces the emergence of its "elegant Poems" from "all this Noise of Drums and Trumpets, when all the muses seemed to be fled, and to have left nothing behind them, but a few lame Iambicks, canting at the corners of our desolate streets" (pp. iii–v): he presents what is, in effect, a verse miscellany containing pieces by such authors as Dudley North, Dyer, Ayton, Wotton, William Browne of Tavistock, Carew, King, Strode, Ralegh, and others under the aristocratic mantle of the earl of Pembroke and his friend. He mixes older with more recent verse gathered from printed texts, such as *Wits Interpreter, Parnassus Biceps, The Forest of Varieties* (1645), and Lawes's musical *Ayres and Dialogues* (1653), as well as from manuscript sources. It more closely resembles the manuscript collections of the previous two decades, than it does the printed anthologies of the same period: in effect, it represents the emergence into print of the kind of text that was confined to the manuscript tradition during the turbulent 1640s and 1650s.

---

[136] Although the wit of the poetry is supposed to be less intensely political than the verse of the middle of the century, the collection begins with that most political of the early Jacobean topical poems, "The Parliament Fart." It also contains Corbett's satiric poem "The distracted Puritan" (pp. 171–77).

[137] For example, "Of my Lady Anne Cecill, the Lord Burleighs Daughter" ("When I behold a woman rarely fair," pp. 102–4); Francis Beaumont's "An Elegy on the Death of the fair and Vertuous Penelope, late Lady Clifton" ("Since thou art dead, Clifton, the world may see," pp. 104–6); Corbett's poem "On the death of Queen Anne" ("No, not a quach? Sad Poets doubt you," pp. 106–8); an elegy "On Prince Henries death, 1612" ("Keep station, nature, and rest, heaven, sure," pp. 108–9); Ralegh's "Farewell false Love, thou Oracle of Lyes" (pp. 130–31), "Farewell to the Court" ("Like truthless dreams, so are my joys expir'd," p. 132), and "The Advice" ("Many desire, but few or none deserve," p. 133); Wotton's "How happy is he born or taught" (pp. 134–35); Sir John Mennis's "Upon Sir John Sucklings 100 horse" ("I tell thee Jack, thou gavest the King," pp. 148–49); and many anonymous and misattributed pieces.

Like *Le Prince d'Amour*, the *Poems of Pembroke and Ruddier* is a retrospective collection. William Herbert, earl of Pembroke, had died by 1630, and the poems he and Rudyerd wrote probably belong to the early part of the Jacobean period.[138] In addition, among the majority of the pieces in this (covert) anthology not by those two authors, there are lyrics by poets who wrote in the Elizabethan through the Caroline eras.[139] Like a number of other sixteenth- and seventeenth-century editors and publishers, John Donne Jr. found it expedient to create the impression that the authors mentioned on the title page were responsible for all the verse in the book but what he did was transfer into the medium of print items commonly found in the private collections of those who participated in the system of manuscript circulation, presenting in print to elite readers some of the texts they already knew and valued.

Something of the same social signals were implicit in the addition of occasional poems to the eighth impression of Owen Felltham's *Resolves* (1661): these pieces were composed mainly in the 1630s and 1640s as the author's "sports" and "recreations" (sig. A2v). Even though the epistle to the reader announces that the Resolves "were written to the middle sort of people" (sig. A2r) for their spiritual benefit, the poems are obviously coded as a gentleman's recreations put into print only for casual enjoyment. The poems are to be perceived as fundamentally private or coterie texts that now can safely be presented to a wider audience in print. The collection of Royalist political ballads published in 1660 as *The Rump, or a Collection of Songs and Ballads, made upon those who would be a Parliament, and were but the*

---

[138] See the discussion of Pembroke's life and poems in Waller, *The Sidney Family Romance* (see Chap. 2, n. 47).

[139] These include, for example, Ralegh's poems "The Lie" ("Go Soul, the Bodies Guest," pp. 104–7) and "A Prognostication upon Cards and Dice" ("Before the sixth day of the next New-year," p. 118); Dyer's "He that his mirth hath lost" (pp. 29–33); Drayton's "On one heart made of two" ("If that you must needs go," pp. 43–45); Ayton's "Wrong not dear Empress of my heart" (pp. 35–36); and Wotton's "Oh faithless world, and thy most faithless part" (pp. 34–35). Later, but pre–Civil War, pieces include Walton Poole's "If shadows be the Pictures Excellence" (p. 61); Carew's "Of Jealousie" ("From when was first this Fury hurl'd," pp. 69–70), "Ladies flee from Loves sweet tale" (p. 71), and "Ask me no more whither do stray" (p. 92); King's "Why slights thou here whom I approve" (pp. 81–82) and "Dry those fair, those Cristal Eyes" (p. 91); Strode's "A POSIE for a Necklace" ("Lo, on my Neck whilst this I bind," p. 100), "For an EARRING" ("'Tis vain to add a Ring or Gemm," p. 101), "On his Mistress" ("Keep on your Mask, and hide your Eye," p. 109), and "Like to a hand which hath been us'd to play" (p. 108); and two Dudley North pieces from *A Forest of Varieties* (1645), "That she is onely Fair" (pp. 26–27) and "Oh doe not tax me with a brutish Love" (p. 33).

*Rump of a House of Commons, five times dissolved,* however, had to be presented deliberately without authorial attributions since "heretofore it was unsafe, and now the Gentlemen conceive it not so proper. Tis hop'd they did His Majesty some Service, 'twas for that end they were scribbled" (sig. A1r). The descent into balladry, although politically justified, was socially demeaning. The ballad form retained the social stigma more generally extended to lyric poetry in an earlier age.

From Tottel through to the Restoration, then, lyric poetry had a fluctuating relationship with the print medium. Generally, however, some of the older prejudices against secular lyric verse were overcome and the "stigma" of print lessened or effaced through the association of printed verse with socially prominent figures, with authors who had won a measure of sociocultural authority, and, in the mid-seventeenth century, with a political and social Royalist elite. The large cultural development represented by the institutionalizing of "literature" and of modern authorship, itself largely the result of the establishment of print as the dominant medium of intellectual communication of course inevitably worked to redefine lyric texts as preservable artifacts rather than ephemeral, occasional productions.

## Some Features of the Physical Book

Since print was not simply an abstraction, but a physical medium for the conduct of social, economic, political relations, it became part of the material conditions shaping institutional and cultural change. Lyrics in print differ in some obvious ways from lyrics in the manuscript system, and books differ from manuscripts in ways that affected the basic conditions of reception of the texts they contain. Chapter 5, which deals with the relationship of poetry, patronage, and print, considers further some of the features of publication, such as title pages, dedicatory epistles and poems, addressees to readers, commendatory poems—that is, elements of the printed book usually found as "front matter." Here I would like to deal with some of the other elements of the printed books containing lyrics: typography, the architecture of lyric collections, and book size. Each influences in important ways the presentation and reception of the texts transmitted in the print medium and marks differences in the two systems of literary transmission.

Typography offers a convenient focus to discriminate some of the material differences between manuscript and print. Unlike script, type—Gothic or black letter, roman or italic—regularized visible language, although at first type was made to *imitate* different forms of handwriting, from late medieval manuscript hand to the various forms of Renaissance script.[140] Since black-letter fonts were the most common ones used by early English printers, it is not surprising that the texts of poems in poetry anthologies such as *Tottel's Miscellany* (1557), *A Handeful of Pleasant Delights* (1566), *The Paradise of Dainty Devices* (1576), *A Gorgeous Gallery of Gallant Inventions* (1578), *Brittons Bowre of Delights* (1591), and *The Arbor of Amorous Devices* (1597) were set in this type, though italic or roman fonts were used for titles and names.[141] The pamphlets of Skelton's verse and the 1568 collected edition of his work were in black letter, as were the editions of Heywood, Googe, Turbervile, Churchyard, and Gascoigne, as well as the eclogues in the first edition of Spenser's *Shepheardes Calender* (1579).

In the latter part of the sixteenth century in England, following earlier changes on the Continent, roman type came to be the preferred style for the presentation of learned writing and literature.[142] Black letter continued to be used, especially by smaller printers—for popular broadsides, for example—but poetry by the 1590s was normally set in roman typeface. One of the implications of the contrast between black-letter texts and roman texts is that the former was

[140] See Philip Gaskell, *A New Introduction to Bibliography* (Oxford: Oxford University Press, 1972), pp. 16–33. See also W. Craig Ferguson, *Pica Roman Type in Elizabethan England* (Aldershot, U.K.: Scolar Press, 1989). In the seventeenth century, however, a quaintly script-like typeface is used on some title pages of books or for frontispiece poetry—see, for example, the title page of Herbert's *Temple*, the Walton poem under the engraving of Donne in the 1635 edition, or Milton's sarcastic Greek poem under the Marshall engraving in the 1645 edition of his poems. Harold Love notes that the producer of newsletters, Ichabod Dawkes, "had a special script typeface cast" for his publications (probably to give them the intimacy and confidentiality of private epistolary communication) ("Scribal Publication," p. 141 [see Chap. 1, n. 38]). But in foregrounding script in this way, print could flaunt its technological superiority to the manuscript system, even as it appropriated some of its social cachet.

[141] Roman and italic type fonts were used in black-letter texts for names, Latin words, titles, and other purposes. For example, in Turbervile's *Epitaphes and Sonnettes*, proverbs are printed in italics or in roman type.

[142] Harvey Graff, points out that humanist texts were associated with roman type and that "only in the third decade of the sixteenth century did roman begin to replace the gothic bastarda in vernacular texts; university professors in France and Germany continued to prefer black letter, which long remained in liturgical texts. Not until the second half of the sixteenth century did popular printers acquire roman type that the public was coming to expect when their gothic fonts had to be replaced" (*Legacies of Literacy*, p. 111).

associated with the native literary tradition, whereas the latter was a classicizing mode: putting native vernacular verse in roman type, the form in which classical texts were printed, suggested that such texts were becoming canonized, monumentalized, set within a national literary tradition that was conceived as the continuation of a general literary tradition going back to such Latin poets as Ovid, Horace, and Virgil. *The Phoenix Nest* (1593), *England's Helicon* (1600), and *A Poetical Rhapsody* (1602) imitated the new practice of printing verse in roman type. The small edition of King James's poems printed at Edinburgh in 1584, *The Essays of a Prentise in the Divine Art of Poesie,* presented the texts of the poems in roman type. *Belvedere* (1600), a commonplace-book collection of poetry citations, distinguishes the strung-together quotations from one another by alternating roman and italic print. Most of the sonnet sequences printed in the 1590s were set in roman type.

Harold Love discusses the departure from print culture's initial imitation of book hands represented by the shift from black-letter to roman fonts in terms of the relative authority of manuscript and print cultures:

> The earliest printers still regarded manuscript as the more prestigious and authentic medium and bestowed great pains to make their products look as much like manuscripts as possible—modelling their types on the established book-hands and employing professional illuminators to paint in coloured initials. By the mid-sixteenth century, however, attitudes had changed and printers began emphasizing the things that gave print active advantages over manuscripts: cheapness, greater regularity of letter forms, the invariability, or near invariability, of the text from copy to copy of any given edition, and a vastly enhanced (though still incomplete) fidelity in the preservation of authorial readings. The abandonment of black-letter types for the more legible romans and italics, coinciding as it did with a marked decline in the quality of inks and paper, indicated a new confidence that print had no need to disguise its true nature or to make concessions to the prestige of manuscript. From the same period began a process by which readers began to allow the printed text a higher authority than the handwritten one. Manuscripts were discarded in large numbers—often in favour of inferior printed editions—and printing practice accepted as a matter of course that the handwritten copy for a new work should be used as waste as soon as setting was complete.[143]

---

[143] Love, "Manuscript versus Print," p. 96 (see Chap. 1, n. 93).

Such a shift anticipated a similar movement in handwriting from secretary to italic script.[144] Even after roman type became the preferred
style for printed literary texts in the last part of the sixteenth century,
however, black letter continued to be used for broadsides, ballads and
other popular ephemera far into the next century: the "native,"
Gothic type was thus associated with popular culture and the inter-
nationalist, humanist roman type with the culture of the educated
elite.[145]

In print, abbreviations were eventually expanded, punctuation was
much heavier, the superscripted characters of manuscript writing de-
scended to the level line.[146] Those forces which operated in the early
modern period to regularize orthography were largely generated by
print culture: compositors tended to convert the various texts they
set into more common forms of spelling from the idiosyncratic orthography of various scribes. The mixing of various kinds and sizes
of type fonts, along with the use of woodcuts, plates, and ornaments,
created the kinds of aesthetic expressiveness that characterized medieval, but not most contemporary, manuscripts, as the artifact that
was the book sometimes took the form of an art object.[147] The effect

[144] See Dawson and Kennedy-Skipton, *Elizabethan Handwriting*, pp. 9–13 (cited in full at
Chap. 1, n. 84).

[145] Keith Thomas discusses "black letter literacy" in "The Meaning of Literacy in Early
Modern England," in *The Written Word: Literacy in Transition*, ed. Gerd Baumann (Oxford:
Clarendon Press, 1986), pp. 97–131. Thomas points out that, contrary to the modern
intuition, "Black letter was the type for the common people. . . .Black-letter literacy . . . was
a more basic skill than roman-type literacy; and it did not follow that the reader fluent in
one was equally at home in the other" (p. 99).

[146] William Nelson claims that one of the signs of the movement from the practice of
reading aloud to silent reading to oneself is the shift from elocutionary to syntactic punctuation ("From 'Listen Lordings' to 'Dear Reader,'" p. 121 [see Chap. 1, n. 2]). However,
manuscript culture was more receptive to punctuation game poetry, verse that reads differently according to where one places the "points": see, for example, "All woemen have
vertues noble & excellent" (BL MS Add. 17492, fol. 18v) and "I hold as faith—what
Englands Church allows" (Bod. MS Rawl. Poet. 26, fol. 105r).

[147] This was certainly the case with Sir John Harington's translation of Ariosto. See Simon
Cauchi, "The 'Setting Foorth' of Harington's Ariosto," *Studies in Bibliography* 36 (1983):
137–68. Clearly, sometime in the seventeenth century the commercial value of poetic texts
increased, partly because of the higher status of authorship, but also, perhaps, because of
the "artistic" value of poetry. In "Notes on English Retail Book-prices, 1550–1640," *The
Library*, 5th ser., 5 (1950): 83–112, Francis R. Johnson points out that "the retail price
charged for the usual book from an English press remained remarkably constant from
about 1560 to 1635" (p. 89), but "about 1635, a sudden and sharp rise in book-prices
occurs [and] the price jumps at least 40 per cent" (p. 90). "Poetical works by well-known
authors seem definitely to have sold at prices above the average. For these a publisher
would set his price, not upon the prosaic basis of cost of production plus a reasonable

on the kind of occasional and social verse represented by most lyric poetry was to iconize the verbal, to reinforce the self-consciously artistic features of poetic language.

The architecture of the printed book encouraged the special arrangement of lyric poems. There was, of course, a recurring tension between the anthology model and that of the structured collection: poems could be presented as *rime sparse* or as a carefully designed sequence, but even the former appeared to have aesthetic shape in print. From Petrarch to Jonson to Herrick, authors took pains to arrange their poems in larger aesthetic wholes: print encouraged this phenomenon. Collections of miscellaneous verse continued to be printed through the Renaissance into the eighteenth century and beyond, but poems were also arranged generically, thematically, and narratively in both single-author editions and in anthologies of various sorts, including augmented editions of individual authors. Amorous sonnet sequences in particular, following Petrarch, assumed narrative form,[148] but religious poetry, following Herbert's *Temple*, was also presented in a narrative fashion as representing a kind of spiritual journey. In addition, some collections, such as the 1640 *Poems of Thomas Carew,* arranged their contents in generic or subgeneric groupings that called attention to the developed system of classification that flourished in the modern institution of literature and in the developing disciplines of literary history and literary criticism.[149]

---

profit, but upon his estimate of how much the book-buyer would pay. For poetical works by Spenser, Daniel, and Shakespeare I find three-fourths of a penny to one penny per sheet to be average" (p. 91). But since popular fiction was cheaper, "The 1598 folio edition of Sir Philip Sidney's *Arcadia* sold at the rate of one halfpenny per sheet. . . .The price, bound, was 9s." (p. 92).

[148] See William J. Kennedy, "Petrarchan Audiences and Print Technology," *Journal of Medieval and Renaissance Studies* 14 (1984): 1–20, for a discussion of some of the effects of print on poetry collections, including the encouragement of narrative structures. Cf. Annabel Patterson, "Jonson, Marvell, and Miscellaneity?" in *Poems in their Place: The Intertextuality and Order of Poetic Collections,* ed. Neil Fraistat (Chapel Hill: University of North Carolina Press, 1986), pp. 95–118, on the uses of sequencing and juxtaposition to create political narratives and messages within seemingly miscellaneous collections.

[149] In his edition of Carew, Dunlap discusses the architecture of the 1640 edition (see *Poems of Carew,* p. lxii). It is divided into a collection of songs and lyrics (pp. 1–89), epitaphs (pp. 90–99), six songs for a play (pp. 100–107), various (mostly occasional) pieces (pp. 108–35), commendatory verses (pp. 156–67), and various poems by other writers, some misattributed to Carew (pp. 168–206). This is a somewhat generic arrangement. Shawcross discusses the generic grouping of Donne's poems in the manuscripts and editions of his work in his article "The Arrangement and Order of John Donne's Poems."

Whatever shape the poems in a collection were given, it is clear that print encouraged certain forms of artful deployment that encouraged the perception of miscellaneous works as parts of artful wholes.

One of the most important features of the material book in the sixteenth and seventeenth centuries is size. It not only conditioned the use(s) to which texts were put but also came to signal much about the institutional status of a book's contents. Since most books were sold unbound, the length of a text usually determined whether it was to be regarded as an ephemeral or a more lasting artifact. As T. A. Birrell has pointed out, this was especially the case with quartos: relatively short quarto pamphlets of poetry or drama, for example, were, next to broadsides, among the most perishable of printed works, whereas, of course, quartos of much greater length would have been bound and have taken their place in one's personal library.[150] In his discussion of the "bibliotheque bleue" and other forms of popular printing in France, Roger Chartier contrasts prestigious folios with cheap quartos and octavos, associating the different publication sizes with different social and economic classes: "Contrasting intentions can be read in the material aspect of the book. For one group the book is a noble object, well-made, leatherbound, and to be carefully preserved; for the other, it is an ephemeral and roughly made thing. By its form and by its text, the book became a sign of distinction and a bearer of a cultural identity."[151] Chartier observes elsewhere that:

> From the folio to smaller formats, a hierarchy exists that links the format of the book, the genre of the text, and the moment and mode of reading. In the eighteenth century Lord Chesterfield bore witness to this fact: "Solid folios are the people of business with whom I converse in the morning. Quartos are the easier mixed company with whom I sit after dinner; and I pass my evenings in the light, and often frivolous chitchat of small octavos and duodecimos." Such a hierarchy is, moreover, directly inherited from the days when books were copied by hand. This hierarchy distinguished the book that had to be laid flat in order to be read; the humanist book, which was more manageable in its medium format and suitable for both classic and newer texts; and the portable book, the *libellus,* a pocketbook and bedside book with multiple uses and more numerous readers.[152]

---

[150] Birrell, "Influence of Seventeenth-Century Publishers," p. 166.
[151] Chartier, *Cultural Uses of Print,* p. 181.
[152] Chartier, "Texts, Printing, Readings," p. 167. Febvre and Martin also discuss the

Clearly, publication size signaled some of the ways texts were meant to be incorporated in people's public and private lives.

For lyric poetry, as for other kinds of texts, the folio was the most prestigious medium of transmission. But, of course, lyric poems usually only entered folios in combination with other kinds of texts in collected editions of particular authors. Thus, when Ponsonby brought out Sidney's collected writings in 1598 in folio form, he included the *Certain Sonnets* (printed for the first time) and a fuller and more accurate text of *Astrophil of Stella* than found in the earlier, unauthorized quartos. This precedent influenced Daniel, whose first collected works were published in folio in 1601. And Spenser's collected poetry (including the *Amoretti*) appeared for the first time in folio in 1611—*The Faerie Queene* having appeared for the first time in folio in 1609. In fact, some of Spenser's individual works, such as the *Four Hymns* and *The Shepheardes Calendar*, which had been brought out in smaller format during his lifetime, were posthumously printed in folio (in 1613 and 1617). The inclusion of Jonson's *Epigrammes* and *The Forrest* in his 1616 folio was encouraged by the examples of both the Sidney and Spenser folios. So too Drayton's lyric verse, earlier printed in quarto and octavo formats, was incorporated in the 1617 folio of his collected poetry.

For lyric poetry by itself and for many collected editions, however, the quarto and octavo formats were more usual. Gascoigne's *Hundreth Sundrie Flowres* (1573), *The Posies* (1575), and *Whole Woorkes* (1587), Daniel's 1623 *Whole Workes*, and a number of other sixteenth- and seventeenth-century poetry editions were quartos. Quarto sonnet collections were especially numerous in the 1590s, following Newman's

---

sociological associations of book size: "Quarto and octavo books . . . were only for short texts too slight to publish in folio. . . . But, from the end of the fifteenth century, anxious to ease the reading of classical authors, the Aldi launched their famous 'portable' collection. Taken up by the small humanist readership, this format was adopted increasingly at the beginning of the sixteenth century" (*Coming of the Book*, p. 88). "If the old romances of chivalry continued to appear in folio and quarto, the Latin poems of the humanists, the works of Marot, of Rabelais and of Marguerite of Navarre and the groups of poets known as the Pleiade all came out in small format. It was in this form that Erasmus' *Adages* spread through Europe, and this too was the form used for the innumerable pamphlets in which Luther and the reformers diffused their ideas. . . . For students and scholars, however, the folio was still preferred, since although it was more difficult to handle, it was more legible and it was an easier form in which to trace references. . . . the book trade in this period was, more than anything, characterized by the division between ponderous, learned tomes intended for use in libraries, and small size literary or polemical works for a larger public. Such a contrast continued to dominate the history of the book in the seventeenth century" (p. 89).

printing of Sidney's *Astrophil and Stella:* for example, Daniel's *Delia* (1592), Drayton's *Ideas Mirrour* (1594), Barnes's *Parthenophil and Parthenophe* (1593), and Giles Fletcher's *Licia* (1593) were all quarto pamphlets. Starting with *Tottel's Miscellany* (1557), the first four editions of which appeared in quarto, this format was established as the preferred one for poetry anthologies: all the editions of the popular *The Paradise of Dainty Devices* (1576–1606) were in quarto, as were *A Gorgeous Gallery of Gallant Inventions* (1578), *The Phoenix Nest* (1593), *England's Helicon* (1600, 1614), and the much slighter collections, *Brittons Bowre of Delights* (1591, 1597) and *The Arbor of Amorous Devices* (1597).

Starting with the fourth edition, however, *Tottel's Miscellany* was brought out in octavo, the format used for the large late Elizabethan collection *A Poetical Rhapsody* (1602). Googe's *Eglogs, Epytaphes, and Sonnets* (1563), Turbervile's *Epitaphs, Epigrams, Songs, and Sonettes* (1567), and Spenser's *Amoretti and Epithalamion* (1595) were octavos. Octavo books longer than pamphlet size, in fact, were more prestigious than short quartos because they were likely to be bound for preservation in personal libraries. A poet like Drayton had his work moved from quarto, to octavo, to folio, that is, from less to more prestigious publication formats.[153] The first edition of Donne's *Poems* appeared in quarto, the second and subsequent ones in octavo.

One other change in publication formats for particular works is the reduction in size from quarto or octavo to duodecimo or smaller. The smaller formats made books quite portable, if not actually "pocket books." For the 1611 edition of *A Poetical Rhapsody* the printer switched from the former octavo format to duodecimo; Daniel's *Delia and Rosamund Augmented* (1593) was reduced to duodecimo from the previous year's quarto and Constable's *Diana Augmented* (1594), to sexidecimo from quarto. Okes's separate publication of Jonson's *Epigrams* (1640) was in duodecimo. The poetic postscript to the octavo collection *Certain Elegies, Done by Sundrie Excellent Wits, with Satyres and Epigrams* [by Henry Fitzjeffrey] (1618) refers to the fashion of the portable jestbook, "a merry pocket-*Pamphlet*" (sig. G5v). Small-

---

[153] The quartos include *Endimion and Phoebe* (1595), *The Harmonie of the Church* (1591), *Idea. The shepheards garland* (1593), *Ideas Mirrour* (1594), and *Mortimeriados* (1596); the octavos *The Barrons Wars* (1603), *England's Heroical Epistles* (1597), *Poems* (1605), *Poems Lyrick and Pastorall* (1606), *Poems; Newly Corrected by the Author* (1608–13); and the folios *The Battle of Agincourt* (1627), *Poems, Collected into One Volume* (1619), *Poly-olbion* (1612–22), and *The Second Part or a Continuance of Poly-olbion* (1622).

size publications during the period of the Civil War and Interregnum also accommodated the desire for secrecy, some Royalist readers carrying about on their persons publications of a politically dangerous character.[154] Smaller books were personal possessions ready at hand to be consulted much like those small blank books students and others carried about with them in their daily business. A work such as *The Academy of Complements* (1640, 1650, 1663), which contains models of polite speech and writing for a variety of social situations, was obviously published in duodecimo format because the publisher anticipated readers' needs to carry such a text about with them. Samuel Pepys, for example, refers in his *Diary* to his own ambulatory reading: "I walked home . . . reading of a little book of new poems of Cowley's, given me by my brother."[155]

It is significant that duodecimo was the format chosen for George Herbert's *Temple,* a collection of poems obviously meant to be used almost like a prayer book:[156] this work was issued in 1633 (two editions), 1634, 1635, 1641, 1656, 1660, 1667, 1674, 1678, 1679, 1695, 1703, and 1709. Printed with an index of titles, it was a text that a devout person could use from time to time for reflection and prayer in a way similar to those editions of the psalms that appeared in duodecimo, sexigesimo, or even smaller formats. Crashaw's *Steps to the Temple* (1646) also appeared in duodecimo.

Print technology presented lyric poems in a wide variety of formats: ephemeral short quartos and octavos, longer quartos and octavos meant to be bound and kept in one's personal library, prestigious folios, portable duodecimos and even smaller sexigesimos (such as the 1638 translation of More's *Epigrams*). Size obviously affected how printed texts were perceived and used—as impermanent or as preservable, as light recreations or as literary monuments, as instruments of social utility or as books to be studied, as related to one's daily experiences or as part of an emerging canon of institutionalized literature. Print technology, of course, more generally af-

---

[154] McKenzie discusses the value of portability for such texts as the "proscribed" Douai Bible and Bunyan's *Pilgrim's Progress* (1678) (a duodecimo) ("Typography and Meaning," pp. 81–125 [see preface, n.1]).

[155] Quoted by Roger Chartier in "The Practical Impact of Writing," in *A History of Private Life III. Passions of the Renaissance,* ed. Roger Chartier, trans. Arthur Goldhammer (Cambridge: Belknap Press of Harvard University Press, 1989), pp. 141–42.

[156] This point is made by Birrell, "Influence of Seventeenth-Century Publishers," pp. 163–66.

fected the relationships of authors, publishers, patrons, and readers as print culture developed in the context of larger sociocultural change. The medium was more than the message; it was many messages.

# CHAPTER FIVE

# PATRONAGE,
## POETRY,
## *AND PRINT*

IN THE MODERN institution of literature, itself a product of democratizing tendencies that have been operating over the course of the last five hundred years, the social and economic relations of authors, publishers, and readers tend to be hidden or disguised. In the premodern and early modern periods, when literature was more obviously implicated in immediate social relations and had not yet been separated from other forms of discourse into the supposedly autonomous realm of the aesthetic, the relationships of writers, publishers, patrons, and readers were habitually the subject of explicit negotiation. After all, everyone acknowledged that literary communication was socially positioned and socially mediated: styles and genres were arranged in hierarchies homologous with those of rank, class, and prestige. The socioliterary dynamics of manuscript culture carried over into the Gutenberg era in many ways, even as print culture began to transform the intellectual, political, and social order by which it was shaped.

Responding to the heightened awareness of the culture-specific character of literary texts, recent scholarship in the Renaissance period has emphasized the importance of patronage to literary production and reception. Given the socioeconomic dependency of most writers, especially those who deliberately arranged to have their work printed, patronage was a social and financial necessity. Despite the widespread complaints about the decline of patronage,[1] dedicatory

---

[1] This subject has been extensively discussed in the scholarly treatments of the topic of

letters and poems indicate that writers and publishers sought from their patrons legitimacy, reward, and prestige. Willing or not, members of royalty and the aristocracy found themselves portrayed in print as the authorizers, protectors, even owners of a wide variety of religious, historical, scientific, polemical, and literary texts—though in many cases, their connection with the authors or publishers was slight or nonexistent and their names mainly functioned as (misleading) signs of celebrity endorsement. Through the praise and idealization that supposedly enhanced the patron's current and future esteem and reputation, writers presented themselves not simply as dependents, but also as parties to an (albeit unequal) exchange, empowered by the immediate and continuing efficacy of the print medium whose material features memorialized author and patron simultaneously.[2]

Within the literary institution developing in the context of print culture, however, another set of social relations was emerging in which the patron was ultimately eclipsed by the increasing sociocultural authority of authors as well as by the economic and interpretive importance of the reader, the "patron" of the work as buyer and consumer in the modern sense of the term "patronage."[3] In six-

patronage, and the phenomenon is part of what Lawrence Stone has argued is a slow decline of kinship and clientage as the main social organizing principles (*Family, Sex, and Marriage*, pp. 125–35 [see Chap. 3, n. 120]). I am indebted to the discussions of patronage in the following: Green, *Poets and Princepleasers* (see Chap. 1, n. 53); Peter J. Lucas, "The Growth and Development of English Literary Patronage in the Later Middle Ages and Early Renaissance," *The Library*, 6th ser., 4 (1982): 219–48; Patricia Thomson, "The Literature of Patronage, 1580–1630," *Essays in Criticism* 2 (1952): 267–84, and "The Patronage of Letters under Elizabeth and James I," *English* 7 (1949): 278–82; John Buxton, *Sir Philip Sidney and the English Renaissance*, 2d ed. (1964; reprint, London: Macmillan; New York: St. Martin's Press, 1966); the chapters on patronage in Bennett, *English Books & Readers 1475 to 1557*, *English Books & Readers 1558 to 1603*, and *English Books & Readers 1603 to 1640* (see Chap. 4, n. 6); Edwin Haviland Miller, *The Professional Writer in Elizabethan England: A Study of Nondramatic Literature* (Cambridge: Harvard University Press, 1959), pp. 94–136; Jan van Dorsten, "Literary Patronage in Elizabethan England: The Early Phase," in *Patronage in the Renaissance*, ed. Guy Fitch Lytle and Stephen Orgel (Princeton: Princeton University Press, 1981), pp. 191–206; Michael Brennan, *Literary Patronage in the English Renaissance: The Pembroke Family* (London: Routledge, 1988); and Fox, *Politics and Literature* (see Chap. 2, n. 1).

   [2] In the context of her analysis of the Elizabethan cultural system of exchanging "Objects, values, children, poetry," Patricia Fumerton concludes that dedications of poetic works "hover on the threshold of gift. . . .[P]oet and patron are simultaneously givers and takers, parents and children—both partners reap the sustaining communion of gift. In this sense, these 'gift' dedications are as much equalizers as definers of hierarchical differences: both poet and patron enter the gift circle that consumes and dilates egos, mingling selves in the hope of self-growth, peace, and culture" ("Exchanging Gifts: The Elizabethan Currency of Children and Poetry," *ELH* 53 [1986]: 270).

   [3] In introducing *The English Treasury of Wit and Language* (1655), for example, John Cotgrave states "thou Reader art the Patron of this poor Worke" (sig. A3r–v). See Karl

teenth- and early seventeenth-century editions of lyric poetry, authors and publishers balanced their dependence on the patrons to whom works were dedicated against their need to appeal to the readers or bookstall "patrons" who purchased them. One can detect, in the juxtaposition of dedicatory letters and epistles to readers, an interesting friction developing between the old- and new-style patrons, or at the least a complexity in the relationship of author, stationer, patron, and reader that was exploited by both writers and publishers to their own advantage. At issue were authorial authority, the ownership of texts, the control of interpretation, and the socioeconomic well-being of writers and publishers, that is, the roles of all those who participated in the circuit of literary production and reception.

## Skelton, Tottel, and the Poetry of Early Courtly Amateurs

The first Renaissance English poet to be published both in short pamphlets and in collected form was John Skelton. The editions of his works that survive present him as "Skelton Laureate," "Skelton Poet Laureat" or "Skelton Poeta," titles that emphasize his academic credentials and allude to his occasional courtly verse but do not seriously assert cultural authority within the print medium—something that might be claimed for the sixteenth-century editions of Chaucer's collected works, for example, Thynne's, published in 1532.[4] Skelton's poetical pamphlets contain neither dedications nor epistles to readers by either the author or the publisher: they present themselves simply

---

Holzknecht, *Literary Patronage in the Middle Ages* (1923; reprint, New York: Octagon, 1966), for the suggestion that a printer like Wynkyn de Worde broke with an older system of patronage and "courted his new patron, the general public" (p. 115, quoted in Russell Rutter, "William Caxton and Literary Patronage," *SP* 84 [1987]: 442). See also the recent work of Joseph Loewenstein on print culture and the book trade, especially the following: "Script in the Marketplace" (cited in full at Chap. 4, n. 66) and "For a History of Literary Property: John Wolfe's Reformation," *ELR* 18 (1988): 389–412.

[4] See, for example, *Skelton Laureate agaynste a comely Coystrowne* (London, n.d.), *A ryght delectable traytise upon a goodly Garlande or chapelet of laurell by mayster Skelton Poete laureat* (London, 1523) (at the end of which is a woodcut headed "Skelton Poeta"). John King points to the association of Skelton with mid-sixteenth-century Protestant radicalism and notes that the 1568 collected edition of Skelton's was the last one for 168 years: he passed out of fashion with the change of taste from moral verse to courtly lyricism (*English Reformation Literature*, p. 13 [see Chap. 1, n. 136]). For a discussion of Skelton and patronage, specifically of his relationship to the Howards, see Greg Walker, *John Skelton and the Politics of the 1520s* (Cambridge: Cambridge University Press, 1988), pp. 5–34. For a discussion of Chaucer editions, see "The Renaissance Chaucer: From Manuscript to Print" in Miskimin, *Renaissance Chaucer*, pp. 226–61 (cited in full at Chap. 4, n. 5).

as a record of what was available in the system of manuscript transmission, the sloppy appearance of the woodcuts and black-letter print suiting their ephemeral character. Pre-Elizabethan lyric poets such as Wyatt, Surrey, and the other courtly amateurs did not write for publication or allow their occasional verse to be printed. Wyatt's *Penitential Psalms* (1550) was published posthumously by the stationers Thomas Raynald and John Harrington with a dedication to William Parr, marquis of Northampton and earl of Essex.[5] But the first major publication of English Renaissance lyric poetry, *Tottel's Miscellany* (1557), self-consciously translated manuscript-circulated verse into print with a sense of some of the differences between the two media.

From the time of Caxton, of course, printers and booksellers enhanced their own position in the system of print transmission, relating to patrons as well as to authors and book purchasers in self-conscious ways as they developed strategies for marketing publications to an expanding clientele.[6] In presenting his ambitious poetry anthology to the public, particularly to that portion of it with whom he might have come in contact as the printer holding the patent for publishing common-law texts, Richard Tottel depicted himself simultaneously as a connoisseur, a patriot, and an educator, as someone doing a public service for his clientele rather than as an exploiter of texts belonging to a social and intellectual elite. His prefatory address, "The Printer to the Reader," is a clever subterfuge that both flatters his customers and aggrandizes himself:

> That to have wel written in verse, yea & in small parcelles, deserveth great
> praise, the workes of divers Latines, Italians, and other, doe prove suffi-
> ciently. That our tong is able in that kynde to do as praiseworthely as the

---

[5] The text of this dedicatory epistle is printed in *Collected Poems of Wyatt*, ed. Muir and Thomson, pp. xviii–xix (see Chap. 1, n. 134). After highlighting his status as a client to Northampton, Harrington explains that he decided, with advice from his friends, to print Wyatt's *Penitential Psalms* so that "the noble fame of so worthy a knighte, as was thee Auctor herof, Syr Thomas Wyat, shuld not perish but remayne as well for hys synguler learning, as valiant dedes in mercyal feates" (p. xix). On Northampton, see Ruth Hughey, *John Harington*, pp. 37–38 (cited in full at Chap. 1, n.7).

[6] See, for example, Rutter, "William Caxton and Literary Patronage," pp. 440–70. Rutter offers an important corrective to the notion that Caxton relied strongly on patronage, emphasizing rather this printer's techniques of advertising and selling his wares to a book-buying public. Publishers not only took it upon themselves to introduce texts through epistles to readers, but even, in some cases, they composed dedicatory and commendatory verse: for example, Richard Smith not only wrote a prose address to the readers of Henry Constable's *Diana* (1592), but also composed a combined commendatory/dedicatory sonnet for the edition addressed "Unto her Majesties sacred honorable Maydes."

rest, the honorable stile of the noble erle of Surrey, and the weightinesse of the depewitted sir Thomas Wyat the elders verse, with severall graces in sondry good Englishe writers, doe show abundantly. It resteth nowe (gentle reder) that thou thinke it not evill doon, to publish, to the honor of the Englishe tong, and for profit of the studious of Englishe eloquence, those workes which the ungentle horders up of such treasure have heretofore envied thee. And for this point (good reader) thine own profit and pleasure, in these presently, and in moe hereafter, shal answere for my defence. If parhappes some mislike the statelinesse of stile removed from the rude skill of common eares: I aske help of the learned to defend their learned frendes, the authors of this work: And I exhort the unlearned, by reding to learne to be more skilfull, and to purge that swinelike grossenesse, that maketh the swete majerome not to smell to their delight.[7]

After praising the verse accomplishments of English authors such as Surrey and Wyatt whose writing proves the worth of the undervalued vernacular,[8] Tottel defends his role in the publishing enterprise. He locates the reader midway between the nobility of Surrey and the commonness of the rude multitude, portraying his own printing of the anthology as an act of sharing what was hoarded—that is, courtly coterie literature—to the end of satisfying and edifying an educated audience interested in vicarious contact with courtly eloquence and life. There is an implied argument in this passage: just as the English tongue is equal to the Latin and Italian languages in literary expressiveness, so too are the good gentlemen readers of his book (and the stationer who serves them) equal, in some sense, to the courtly elite whose writings have been liberated into print. As G. K. Hunter has observed, such printed Tudor poetry provides "a cultured social world which the reader can join for the price of the book."[9] In serving his own economic interests, the publisher exploits the hierarchical social structure that the more democratic environment of print helped to undermine. Ignoring his own workmanlike activity of editing the poems and of designing titles to replace their lost social contexts with more generalized fictional environments, Tottel pre-

---

[7] *Tottel's Miscellany*, ed. Rollins, 1:2 (see Chap. 3, n. 31).

[8] Elizabeth Pomeroy compares Tottel's preface and its praise of the vernacular with Lorenzo de Medici's prefatory letter to the *Racolta Aragonese* (the prototypical Renaissance lyric anthology) and to DuBellay's *Déffense et Illustration de la langue Francoyse* (*Elizabethan Miscellanies*, pp. 50–51 [see Chap. 4, n. 10]).

[9] G. K. Hunter, "Drab and Golden Lyrics of the Renaissance," in *Forms of Lyric: Selected Papers from the English Institute*, ed. Reuben A. Brower (New York: Columbia University Press, 1970), p. 8.

sented himself as a class mediator taking advantage of print technology's ability to open the closed communications of an elite to a wider audience.

In his prefatory material to *The Paradise of Dainty Devices,*[10] which became the most popular of the Elizabethan poetical miscellanies (largely, as Winifred Maynard has argued,[11] because it presented lyrics that could be sung to well-known tunes), Henry Disle positioned himself as publisher between the broad readership to whom he appealed and the social and intellectual elite that included the patron to whom he dedicated the book. There is a revealing difference between the title pages of the first (1576) and second (1578) editions: the first emphasizes the quality of the contents and the status of the contributors—*The Paradise of daynty devises, aptly furnished, with sundry pithie and learned inventions: devised and written for the most part, by M. Edwards, sometimes of her Majesties Chappel: the rest by sundry learned Gentlemen, both of honor, and woorshippe, viz. S. Barnarde. Jasper Heywood, E.O., F.K., L. Vaux, M. Bewe, D.S., R. Hill, M. Yloop, with others*—but the second emphasizes the benefits to be gotten by the readership—*The Paradise of dainty devises. Conteyning sundry pithy preceptes, learned Counsels, and excellent inventions, right pleasant and profitable for all estates. Devised and written for the most part, by M. Edwardes, sometimes of her Majesties Chappel: the rest, by sundry learned Gentlemen, both of honor, and worship, whose names hereafter folowe.* Although the names of the contributors are listed on the verso of the title page, the impression created is somewhat different in this second edition: "profitable for all estates" indicates that this book is, among other things, a self-improvement manual, morally didactic and utilitarian. By contrast, the dedicatory letter to Lord Compton emphasizes the social status of the poets and the "delight" (p. 4) to be derived from reading it. Though the profit and delight of literature were supposed to apply to all, they often parted company along class lines.

The first private individual to publish a collection of his own short poems in the Elizabethan period was Barnabe Googe, whose *Eglogs, Epitaphes, and Sonettes* appeared in 1563, six years after *Tottel's Miscellany.* A kinsman of William Cecil (later Lord Burghley), whose social and political patronage he enjoyed, Googe was a devout, Cambridge-

---

[10] Text cited from *Paradise of Dainty Devices,* ed. Rollins (see Chap. 1, n. 132).
[11] Winifred Maynard, *Elizabethan Lyric Poetry and Its Music* (Oxford: Clarendon Press, 1986), p. 23.

educated Protestant whose first published work, a partial translation of Palengenius's *Zodiacke of Life* (1561), was addressed to Cecil, who helped him find service on an embassy to Spain in that year.[12] The publication of his *Eglogs, Epytaphes, and Sonettes* is excused by him with the convenient, and much used, subterfuge that protected gentleman authors from the "stigma of print," the claim that the printer was really the initiator of the project, the poet himself when he went abroad having left copies of his poems behind with a friend, "L. Blundeston," who explains in a commendatory epistle to the reader:

> I trust to fynde the thankfull now in takyng this Present from me, which not onely to shewe my good wyll . . . by preservynge the worthy fame, and Memorye of my deare frende M. Googe in his absence I have presumed more bouldely to hazard the prynting heareof, though this maye suffyce to excuse well my enterpryse, but also to styrre up thy Pleasure and further thy proffit by reading these his workes, whiche here I have Puplyshed: openly unto thee. And so (beyng unstored my selffe) I seake to satesfie thy learned or willyng desyre with other mens travaeiles. . . .Accept my goodwyll and way not the valew . . . and so shalt thou encourage others to make the partaker of the like or farre greater Jewels who yet doubtyng thy unthankefull receyte nigardly keape them to their own use & privat commoditie. Whear as beynge assured of the contrarye by thy frendly report of other mens travayles, they could parhappes be easely entreated to more frely to lend them abroad to thy greater avayle and furtherraunce.[13]

The middleman in the publishing enterprise, a gentleman to whom manuscript poetry could be lent by an author, here expresses the same attitude as Tottel's in claiming that such private treasures should be shared with the reading public: thus the printed text is a social benefaction rather than an individual writer's self-advertisement.

The presentation of the collection, however, has the marks of a deliberate authorial strategy, beginning with a commendatory poem by Googe's cousin Alexander Neville, a woodcut of his own coat of arms, and a dedicatory epistle to William Lovelace, "Reader of Grayes Inne" (p. 9), a man who shared the culturally rich environment of

[12] See William E. Sheidley, *Barnabe Googe* (Boston: Twayne, 1981), p. 21.

[13] Text cited from Fieler's facsimile edition of Barnabe Googe, *Eglogs, Epytaphes, and Sonettes* (1563), pp. 16–18 (see Chap. 1, n. 96). For a modern critical edition of this poet, see Barnabe Googe, *Eclogues, Epitaphs, and Sonnets*, ed. Judith M. Kennedy (Toronto: University of Toronto Press, 1989).

the Inns of Court, where so many young poets and translators wrote in the Elizabethan period. Neville's poem advises Googe to seek wise readers as "Patrons" (p. 4) and

> Go forward styll to advaunce thy fame
>   Lyfes Race halfe ryghtly ron
> Farre easyer tis for to obtain,
>   The Type of true Renowne.
> Like Labours have ben recompenst
>   with an immortall Crowne.
> By this doth famouse *Chaucer* lyve,
>   by this a thousande moore
> Of later peares. By this alone
>   the old renowmed Stoore
> Of Auncient Poets lyve.
>
> (P. 6)

By mentioning Chaucer and classical poets, Neville cites examples of writers already memorialized through print in the Renaissance. In leaving the social bounds of manuscript-circulated coterie literature, Googe's poems could enter an environment in which they and their author, in the face of contemporary prejudices, could supposedly win respect.

The dedicatory epistle to Lovelace, however, betrays Googe's anxieties and discomfort in publishing his verse:

Howe lothe I have ben, beyng of long tyme earnestlye requyred, to suffer these tryfles of mine to come to light: It is not unknowen to a greate nombre of my famyliar acquaintaunce. Who both daylye and hourely moved me therunto, and lytell of long tyme prevayled therin. For I both consydered and wayed with my selfe, the grosenes of my Style: whiche thus commytted to the gasynge shewe of every eye shuld forth with disclose the manifest foly of the Writer, and also I feared and mistrusted the disdaynfull myndes of a nombre both scornefull and carpynge Correctours, whose Heades are ever busyed in tauntyng Judgementes. Least they shuld otherwyse interprete my doyngs than in deade I meant them. These two so great mischiefes utterly diswaded me from the folowynge of my frendes perswasions, and wylled me rather to condem them to continuall darkenes, wherby no Inconvenience could happen: than to endaunger my selfe in gyvynge them to lyght, to the disdaynfull doome of any offended mynde. Notwithstandynge all the dylygence that I could use in the Suppression therof could not suffise for I my selfe beyng at that tyme oute of the

Realme, lytell fearynge any such thynge to happen. A verye frende of myne, bearynge as it semed better wyll to my doynges than respectyng the hazarde of my name, commytted them all togyther unpolyshed to the handes of the Prynter. In whose handes durynge his absence from the Cytie, tyll his returne of late they remayned. At whiche tyme, he declared the matter wholly unto me: shewynge me, that beynge so farre past, & Paper provyded for the Impression therof: It could not withoute great hynderaunce of the poore Printer be nowe revoked. . . . And calling to mynde to whom I myght chieflye commyt the fruytes of my smiling muse: sodaynly was cast before my eyes the perfect vewe of your frendly mynd (gentle Maister Lovelace) Unto whom for the nombred heapes of sundrye frendshyps, accountynge my selfe as bound, I have thought best to gyve them, (not doubtyng) but that they shalbe as well taken as I do presently meane them. Desyrynge you herein, as all suche as shall reade them es-peciallye to beare with the unpleasaunt forme of my to hastely fynyshed Dreame, the greater part whereof with lytle advyse I lately ended, bycause the beginnyng of it, as a senseles head separated from the body was gyven with the rest to be prynted. And thus desyrynge but for recompence the frendly receyvyng of my slender Gyfte, I ende. (Pp. 9–13)

As patron, Googe chose a friend who, as was the case with coterie literary transmission, could serve as an ideal reader,[14] a model of be-havior for the unknown readers who might buy the published book. Given the disclaimers, and given also the continuing favor of his kins-man and patron Cecil, Googe ran little danger in publishing his "try-fles."

When he published his *Epitaphes, Epigrams, Songs and Sonets* (1567),[15] George Turbervile by presenting occasional amorous and nonamorous verse to a book-buying public was obviously following the examples of Tottel and Googe.[16] Announcing a structure of love

[14] This portrayal of the patron as ideal reader makes him a figure of mediation between manuscript-circulated verse and printed literature. Other poets repeat Googe's strategy, setting the ideal patron-reader against the carping critics who might condemn the poet's works. Thomas Churchyard, for example, in *The First Part of Churchyardes Chippes* (London, 1575), combines a dedication to Sir Christopher Hatton, in which he discusses the proper way of reading his verse, with a defensive poem, "To the dispisers of other mens workes that shoes nothing of their own." In cases such as this, the actual readers were meant to imitate the reading behavior ascribed to the well-meaning patron.

[15] I cite the text from Panofsky's facsimile edition of George Turbervile's works (see Chap. 4, n. 20).

[16] One of the features Turbervile borrowed from Tottel is the method of titling or introducing poems. For example, a generalized "Lover" is invoked to produce such titles as "The Lover extolleth the singular beautie of his Ladie," "The Lover declareth howe first he was taken and enamoured by the sight of his Ladie," "The Lover against one that compared hys Mistresse with his Ladie," and so on. Panofsky remarks that the "brief po-

narrative that the final content of the collection does not realize (the first printed English lyric anthology to attempt this arrangement),[17] Turbervile self-consciously presented his work as a collection of courtly coterie poems, as patronage literature, and as a verse miscellany for a general readership. He originally dedicated the book to the countess of Warwick,[18] expressing gratitude for her acceptance of a collection shown to her previously, an act that encouraged him to expand it further in print, even as he denigrates his verse as "rashe compiled toys" (sig. *4v).[19] This apologetic attitude reappears in the epistle "To the Reader," in which he characterizes his pamphlet as "a fewe Sonets, the unripe seedes of my barraine braine, to pleasure and recreate thy wearye mind and troubled hed withall" (sig. *5r). He negotiates the respective claims of patroness and readers, telling his general audience, "For thy solace alone (the bounden dutie which I owed the noble *Cowntesse* reserved) I undertoke this slender toyle" (sigs. *5r–5v), before turning to the more important issue of reader judgment and censure:

As I deeme thou canst not, so do I hope thou wilt not mislike it at all. But if there be any thing herein that maye offend thee, refuse it, reade and peruse the reast with pacience. Let not the misliking of one member procure thee rashlye to condemne the whole. I stand to thy judgement, I expect thy aequitie. Reade the good, and reject the evill: yea rather con-

---

sies" Turbervile appends to poems and the other marks of coterie circulation "give the reader a sense of participation in the polite recreations of young literary gentlemen" (Turbervile, p. xi).

[17] See ibid., p. viii. John Erskine Hankins had earlier remarked that "Turbervile is a pioneer in English poetry. He is the first writer to publish a definite and complete sequence of poems in honor of a mistress, such as that of Petrarch in honor of Laura" (*The Life and Works of George Turbervile*, University of Kansas Publications, Humanistic Studies, no. 25 [Lawrence: University of Kansas, 1940], p. 82).

[18] Most of the works dedicated to Anne Russell Dudley, countess of Warwick, were from the late 1580s and 1590s; Turbervile's book is the earliest one dedicated to her, according to the information provided by Franklin B. Williams Jr., *Index of Dedications and Commendatory Verse in English Books before 1641* (London: The Bibliographical Society, 1962), p. 57.

[19] Hankins states that "a number of poems in the volume seem to have been addressed to [Lady Warwick] before her marriage in November, 1565; so we may assign that year as a tentative date for the earlier collection. Whether these first poems were actually printed, however, or were merely shown to Lady Warwick in manuscript, we cannot know; there are no indications of an edition of the *Epitaphes* prior to 1567, except those just mentioned" (*Life and Works*, p. 35). If Hankins's hunch is right, the original complimentary poetry to the youthful Lady Warwick might have been transcribed in a formal presentation copy, perhaps a wedding gift from the poet who was a family client. This, then, could have formed the basis for the expanded printed collection that grounded its authorization in the dedicatee's original acceptance of the verse in manuscript.

demne it to perpetuall silence. . . .But assuredlye there is nothing in thys whole slender Volume that was ment amisse of me the Writer, howsoever the Letter goe in thy judgement that arte the Reader. (Sigs. *5v–6r)

With this appeal for toleration, he then deals with the amorous subject matter of most of the collection, disingenuously claiming a high moral purpose even as he obviously appeals to the interests of a young audience:

> Whatsoeuer I have penned, I write not to this purpose, that any youthlie head shoulde follow or pursue such fraile affections, or taste of amorous bait: but by meere fiction of these Fantasies, I woulde warne (if I myghte) all tender age to flee that fonde and filthie affection of poysoned & unlawful love. Let this be a Glasse & Myrror for them to gaze upon. . . . And as I am not the first that in this sort hath written & imploye his time: so shall I not be the last, that without desarte (perhaps) shalbe misdeemed for attempting the same. (Sigs. *6r–6v)

Turbervile formulates the presentation of his poetry like a typical "Elizabethan prodigal,"[20] conscious of the educational and social denigration of amorous literature, of the readership's tendency to blur the boundary between fiction and actual experience, and, more to the point, of the market for just such ephemeral lyrics.[21] Though he characterizes himself as the "vassel" (sig. *4r) of his patroness, he appeals to the reader as a "Friend" (sig. *7r). For those who will not respond to his book with good will he writes a satiric poem, "To the rayling Route of Sycophants."[22] He performs an act of exclusion before "The Table" advertising the contents of a collection that begins, again, with an appeal for the protection of his patroness, with

---

[20] See Richard Helgerson, *The Elizabethan Prodigals* (Berkeley and Los Angeles: University of California Press, 1976), p. 6.

[21] As someone who like Gascoigne and the early Ralegh wrote in the cultural environment of the Inns of Court, Turbervile knew the kind of demand there might be for just such a collection as the one he produced, just as he knew the fashion and market for the translations he produced. Hankins cites Anthony à Wood's biographical account of Turberville, which places him successively at Winchester College, New College Oxford, and the Inns of Court (*Life and Works*, p. 5): in the two academic environments, he would have learned to compose certain forms of verse as a part of his classical training; in the latter, he would have been in a social environment that, in the latter half of the sixteenth century generated much poetry and drama.

[22] For a discussion of writers' imagining of and strategies of coping with the hostile reception of their work, see Debra Belt, "The Poetics of Hostile Response, 1575–1610," *Criticism* 33 (1991): 419–59.

an encomiastic poem to the countess of Warwick that along with the "Argument" to the work, portrays her as the fictional mistress in the poetic amorous sequence that follows. Like Samuel Daniel, whose dedication of his sonnet sequence *Delia* also treats the patroness as the addressee of complimentary love poems,[23] Turbervile defines his verse in a double fashion, first, as poetry of compliment and, second, as self-conscious acts of amorous lyricism in a tradition of such writing derived from Petrarch and the classical poets of whom Turbervile was so fond.[24] Conscious of the precariousness of his public stance as a publishing poet, Turbervile carefully positions himself in relation to patroness and both well- and ill-disposed readers, returning at the end of the collection in "The Authours Epiloge to his Booke" to the importance of the patroness's acceptance of his rough verse.

### Gascoigne and Breton

The two major publications in which George Gascoigne included his lyrics, *A Hundreth Sundrie Flowres* (1573) and *The Posies* (1575), represent sharply differing ways of presenting literary texts to potential patrons and to a general readership. In *A Hundreth Sundrie Flowres,* rather than coming to terms directly with the need to define his role as a publishing author, Gascoigne hides behind several layers of disguise. Although his name appears in the titles of poems included in the table of contents, the book does not openly proclaim itself to be the collected works of George Gascoigne. Within the fiction of its manuscript transmission from "G.T." to "H.W." to a printer "A.B."[25] (the last differing from the stationer named on the title page, Richard Smith), the book pretends to be at once an anthology of "pleasant Pamphlets"[26] and a collection of manuscript-circulated literature writ-

---

[23] Similarly, in his *Diana* (London, 1592), Henry Constable treats Lady Rich as the beloved praised in his complimentary sonnets.

[24] Turbervile translated Ovid and was influenced by Horace and the poets of *The Greek Anthology.* See Hankins, *Life and Works,* pp. 73–75.

[25] Rollins notes that "frequently 'A.B.' is used [in Renaissance English publications] as moderns employ 'John Doe' " (*England's Helicon,* 2:67 [see Chap. 1, n. 209]).

[26] *George Gascoigne's "A Hundreth Sundrie Flowres,"* p. 47 (see Chap. 1, n. 4). Further citations in the text are from this edition. In her edition of Breton, Jean Robertson points out that both Breton and Gascoigne use the term "pamphlet" to mean poem, but that Gascoigne seems to make a distinction between the two in G.T.'s prefatory letter to "F.J." (Nicholas Breton, *Poems not hitherto reprinted,* edited with biography, canon, and notes by Jean Roberton [Liverpool: Liverpool University Press, 1967], p. 200—the text I cite for Breton's works). Perhaps the term "pamphlet" (which also designates a short, ephemeral

ten by various authors made available to the public by the publisher alone. In "The Printer to the Reader," a text written (probably by Gascoigne) in the same ironic tone as H.W.'s later address to the reader, the publisher complains that, despite G.T.'s and H.W.'s opposition to publication, they are "of one assent compact to have it imprinted" (p. 47), leaving him to cope with any public censure of its contents. The most obvious traces of the printer's actual editorial activities are to be found in the awkward fit between first and second sections of the work, the former including Gascoigne's two dramatic translations, *Supposes* and *Jocasta,* and the latter being "A Discourse of the Adventures passed by Master F.J.," a collection of occasional lyrics, and the narrative poem "Dan Bartholomew of Bathe." Since Gascoigne apparently left England in haste before he was able to see the publication of his works through the press, the printer was free to follow his commercial judgment that dramatic texts should be included in the book because they were much more marketable than lyric poetry,[27] despite the awkwardness of beginning the second part of the collection with an address to the reader by "H.W." that seems to belong at the beginning of a work of "divers discourses & verses, invented uppon sundrie occasions, by sundrie gentlemen" (p. 49).

Despite all signals to the contrary, Gascoigne obviously presents his collected works as more than ephemera. Between praise of ancient poets as morally instructive in their "most feyned fables and imaginations" (p. 50) and the citation of the example of Chaucer, whose career is presented as a model for imitation, Gascoigne has "G.T." remark in his prefatory letter to the collection: "Marie in deede I may not compare Pamphlets unto Poems, neither yet may justly advant for our native countrimen, that they have in their verses hitherto (translations excepted) delivered unto us any such notable volume, as have bene by Poets of antiquitie, left unto the posteritie" (p. 50). Despite the many statements denigrating the collection as trivial, immature, and occasional, Gascoigne clearly wishes the publication to constitute a significant cultural achievement, to join the editions of

---

publication) is used metonymically to designate the poetical contents of a manuscript or printed quire or booklet.

[27] This point is made by Prouty, *Hundreth Sundrie Flowres,* p. 18. As G. W. Pigman III has suggested to me, Prouty may be wrong in this assumption and Gascoigne may have wanted to present the plays as part of his collected works. The oddity of the page numbering, as Adrian Weiss argues in a forthcoming work, probably results from the practice of shared printing.

classical authors and of the first canonized English author, Chaucer, as what the printer finally states at the end of the book is a "good rounde vollume, the which some woulde judge worthy the Imprinting" (p. 220). Although trying to use the dynamics of manuscript-circulated verse to protect himself from the "stigma" of print and the consequences of the book's salacious and scandalous content, Gascoigne nonetheless participates in and attempts to shape the institution of printed literature, the context in which texts take on a monumental character and authors assert a degree of sociocultural authority.

Once the transparent subterfuge of disclaiming responsibility for printing the work failed, the edition was banned,[28] and its author was accused of moral turpitude, Gascoigne responded in the second edition, *The Posies of George Gascoigne Esquire*, by highlighting his authorship on the title page and by prefacing the reorganized collection with three apologetic letters addressed to the ecclesiastical licenser-censors, to young gentlemen, and to the general reader. He also included twenty English and Latin commendatory poems representing the endorsement of his peers (a sign of the literary institution's capacity for self-authorization).[29] Among these, the one attributed to "The Printer" installs the poet and his works in a tradition that includes both two medieval English authors (Chaucer and Gower) and the sixteenth-century courtly amateurs whose work had appeared in Tottel (Surrey, Wyatt, and Viscount Rochford). The classification system Gascoigne adopted—"Flowers," "Hearbes," and "Weeds"—suited the medium in which the collection was being presented, allowing for fuller lists of contents (in each section) than had been provided in *A Hundreth Sundrie Flowres*. Exploiting each feature of the publication format as an author controlling the presentation of his revised and corrected collected works (that include now the completed version of the previously incomplete "Dan Bartholomew of Bathe"), Gascoigne assumed the responsibility of authorship proper to a writer deliberately participating in print culture. He refrained, however, from dedicating the book to a particular individual and thus

---

[28] See Charles T. Prouty, *George Gascoigne: Elizabethan Courtier, Soldier, and Poet* (New York: Columbia University Press, 1942), p. 79.

[29] An extraordinary example of how the preliminaries to a text can grow far out of proportion can be seen in the 1651 posthumous edition of William Cartwright's *Comedies, Tragi-comedies, with other Poems*, which has over one hundred pages of introductory matter.

from specifically associating the publication with the context of patronage.

Although Gascoigne chose no explicit dedicatee for either *A Hundreth Sundrie Flowres* or *The Posies*,[30] one finds within the collections several poems written in a patronage context—most notably two to Lord Grey of Wilton, "Gascoignes wodmanship" and the verse letter "Gascoignes voyage into *Hollande*," in which he refers to himself as "your Lordshippes bound [client] for ever"; complimentary verse to Lady Sands and Dorothy Zouche, (the deceased) Lady Grey of Wilton; and "Gascoignes device of a maske for the right honorable Viscount Montacute [Montague]." In the most famous of these, "Gascoignes wodmanship written to L. Grey of wilton," the author outlines his career, expresses his ambitions, and invites continuing patronage support from an aristocrat well disposed to assist an articulate gentleman-soldier. It is only in one of the apologetic prefaces to *The Posies* that Gascoigne makes the connection between this sort of specific act of seeking patronage and the general appeal for patronage he claims was implicit in the very act of publishing his writing. Gascoigne explains that part of his intent in making his writings available to a larger audience through print was to prove his intelligent literacy, his fitness for nonmilitary preferment or political patronage: "I was desirous that there might remaine in publike recorde, some pledge or token of those giftes wherwith it hath pleased the Almightie to endue me: To the ende that thereby the vertuous might bee incouraged to employ my penne in some exercise which might tende both to my preferment, and to the profite of my Countrye."[31] Anticipating the obvious objection that a more edifying work might have been better suited to this end, he states that he printed those writings he had available because they could demonstrate the kinds of rhe-

---

[30] In 1575, probably after the publication of *The Posies*, Gascoigne became a client of the earl of Leicester, through whom he was able to gain employment and a measure of prosperity: see Eleanor Rosenberg, *Leicester, Patron of Letters* (New York: Columbia University Press, 1955), pp. 166–72, and Prouty, *George Gascoigne*, pp. 87–88. For an excellent discussion of the relation of Gascoigne's writings to his search for patronage and preferment, see Richard C. McCoy, "Gascoigne's '*Poemata castrata*': The Wages of Courtly Success," *Criticism* 27 (1985): 29–55.

[31] Gascoigne, *Posies*, ed. Cunliffe, p. 5 (see Chap. 4, n. 72). Prouty argues that his success with the masque for Viscount Montague and the poems to Lord Grey "may have been the cause of Gascoigne's decision to publish his poems. If Grey was favorable to the work and if Montague . . . rewarded him, it would be wise to publish; by thus making his work more widely known, he might secure further patronage, even from the Queen herself" (*George Gascoigne*, p. 58).

torical skills he wished to advertise: "I thought good to notifie unto the worlde before my returne [from military service], that I coulde as well persuade with Penne, as pearce with launce or weapon: So that yet some noble minde might be incouraged both to exercise me in time of peace, and to emploie mee in time of service in warre" (p. 6).[32] In the epistle to Lord Grey of Wilton prefacing the section of *The Posies* containing the military poem "Dulce bellum inexpertis," Gascoigne narrows his appeal to someone he characterizes as "an universall patrone of all Souldiours" (p. 140) as he identifies him as one of the persons he hoped to impress ànd amuse with his earlier book. Gascoigne continued to curry Lord Gray's patronage in dedicating to him *The Steele Glas* and *The Complaynt of Phylomene.*

Without specific aristocratic patronage, of course, Gascoigne was especially vulnerable to the charges he anticipated in publishing *A Hundreth Sundrie Flowres* and was forced to answer in the prefaces to *The Posies.* Given the prejudice against amorous prose and poetry in the period, Gascoigne worried about his collected works, building into the printer's preface and the other editorial interpolations a defense of his subject matter and intentions—even as he teased the reader's imagination with allusions to the erotic content. Aware of the possible censure of "the graver sort of greybeard judgers" (p. 47), "the printer" of *A Hundreth Sundrie Flowers* assures the reader that he has "wel perused the worke" and could "find nothing therein amisse" (p. 47), in effect coopting the role of the ecclesiastical licenser. At the same time, no doubt to arouse the curiosity of book buyers, he slyly mentions the "two or three wanton places passed over in the amorous enterprise" and posits a well-meaning "discrete reader" able, as "the industrious Bee can gather hony out of the most stinking weede," to "take a happie example by the most lascivious histories" (p. 47). Emphasizing the "good moral lesson" to be derived from reading the tragedy of *Jocasta,* calling attention to the "divers godly himnes and Psalmes" also contained therein, the fic-

[32] Since the humanist educational program and its methods of rhetorical training were designed to produce intelligent and versatile men capable of useful service in aristocratic households, the government, and the Church, Gascoigne had some basis for the claim that a demonstration of his writing skills was a way of proving his fitness for preferment, but, of course, occasional and ephemeral poetry, an erotic novella, and an incomplete romantic narrative were hardly the best signs of his seriousness and maturity. As Helgerson has pointed out, Gascoigne needed to adopt the role of the reformed prodigal and finally reject such literary trifles, allowing himself only to appear in print as the author of pious and didactic works (*Elizabethan Prodigals,* pp. 44–57).

tional printer concludes that the "worke is so universall . . . as any mans mind may therwith be satisfied" (pp. 47–48), but he highlights the amorous material of the main part of the collection.

The subversion of moralism and the dispersal of literary responsibility for the publication of the whole work are inextricably linked. Recipients of the writing along the line of its transmission—G.T., H.W., the printer, and the reader—are in effect, the ones who must reconcile interest, curiosity, and pleasure on the one hand, with morality and social conventions on the other. Thus, within the frame of "A Discourse of the Adventures passed by Master F.J.," G.T. both establishes a context for literary and moral judgment and makes ad hoc observations as he sustains the narrative line of the work; H.W. assumes that a "learned Reader" (p. 49) can, as he has done, "sit and smile at the fond devices of such as have enchayned them selves in the golden fetters of fantasie" and use the work for his "owne particular commoditie" in a morally responsible way. Gascoigne makes proper reception of his writing, not its content, the issue, but the strategy obviously failed when some readers were offended by the salacious material and/or interpreted the story of F.J. as a *roman à clef.*

When Gascoigne assumed full authorial responsibility for publishing the second, revised edition of his work as *The Posies of George Gascoigne,* he addressed first the ecclesiastical licenser-censors, defending his earlier book and the revision: "It is verie neare two years past, since (I beeing in Hollande in service with the vertuous Prince of Orange) the most parte of these Posies were imprinted, and now at my returne, I find that some of them have not only bene offensive for sundrie wanton speeches and lascivious phrases, but further I heare that the same have beene doubtfully construed, and (therefore) scandalous" (p. 3). Because so much of the verse in *A Hundreth Sundrie Flowres* is rooted in the poet's social experiences, the blurring of the boundaries between the real and the fictional that was normal in manuscript-circulated occasional verse left Gascoigne in the printed edition vulnerable to the charge of "scandalizing of some worthie personages" (p. 7). Now, by assuming authorial responsibility for his printed works, he could actively define his writings as literary artifacts rather than real-life communications, thus protecting himself somewhat against the accusation of slandering or exposing actual persons.

Despite Gascoigne's stance in *The Posies* as the author responsible for the whole collection of works and despite his defense of the more frivolous amorous compositions as the follies of youth, in at least one respect he distances himself from full authorship when he tells the general readership (in the third prefatory epistle) that, of the love poems, "the most part of them were written for other men" (p. 16). Assuming the identity of the writer willing to produce verse and prose at the request of patrons or friends, a role later performed by an author like Thomas Nashe, he explains that "if ever I wrote [a] lyne for my selfe in causes of love, I have written tenne for other men in layes of lust. . . .[T]hough my folly bee greater than my fortune, yet overgreat were mine unconstancie, if (in mine owne behalfe) I shoulde compyle so many sundrie Songs or Sonets. . . . For in wanton delights I helped all men, though in sad earnest I never furthered my selfe any kinde of way" (pp. 16–17). In such circumstances, the patrons or commissioners of such verse supposedly bore much of the moral responsibility for the poet-client's productions.

In prefatory epistles to *The Posies*, Gascoigne assumes authorial responsibility for his writings, defending their fictionality (and literariness) as well as their didactic value, challenging his reader-interpreters both to indulge his youthful excesses and not to perceive what he has done as immoral or scandalous. That this work was called in by the authorities[33] demonstrates the failure of his strategy of self-protection. Without legitimating precedents, without the intervention of powerful patrons, Gascoigne could not safely translate into the public environment of print what seemed to be the thinly fictionalized private erotic escapades and recreations of a social elite, nor could he win respect for presenting as his collected works pieces whose genres and subject matter were held in such low esteem. Twenty years later things would have been different; his only choice in the mid-1570s was to prove his seriousness as a man of affairs by abandoning secular lyricism and romantic fiction to turn to the composition of public, religious, and didactic works.[34]

---

[33] Prouty notes that the Queen's Majesty's Commissioners or the Court of High Commission seized *The Posies* in 1576 (*George Gascoigne*, p. 79). McCoy observes that two other amorous works were also banned at the same time, *Restoratives to Love* and (the ballad-miscellany) *A Handful of Pleasant Delights* ("Gascoigne's '*Poemata castrata*,'" pp. 43–44).
[34] See Helgerson, *Elizabethan Prodigals*, pp. 50–57.

Nicholas Breton, whose first published work, *A Smale handfull of fragrant Flowers* (1575), is dedicated to Lady Sheffield,[35] was willing, despite the suppression of Gascoigne's *Posies* in 1576, to publish his youthful lyrics in 1577. Possibly to emphasize the harmlessness of his recreational collection, he (or perhaps the printer) titled it: *The workes of a young wyt, trust up with a Fardell of pretie fancies, profitable to young Poetes, prejudiciall to no man, and pleasant to every man to passe away idle tyme withall. Whereunto is joyned an odde kynde of wooing, with a Banquet of Comfettes, to make an ende withall. Done by N.B. Gentleman.* Though he relentlessly pursued aristocratic patronage in later publications, Breton emphasizes his gentility in this pamphlet, prefacing it only with "The Letter Dedicatorie, to the Reader," anticipating differing tastes and judgments in his audience, from whom he invites good will, promising "perhaps I wyl agaynst the next Terme, provide you some other newe ware for your olde golde" (p. 4). A young gentleman writing for his peers—probably Inns of Court "termers"[36]—relates an "as you like it" attitude to the economic transaction of book-marketing in which they were both participants. In the verse "Primordium" to the small collection, he distances himself from the "first fruites of [his] brayne" (82), his "rimes wilde Otes" (84), but his constant reference to his "Muse" marks his efforts as deliberate attempts to develop an identity as a poet which the apologetic remarks are not meant to obscure.

Breton introduces each of the poems with the kind of discursive and narrative titles found in Gascoigne, not only marking the occasional character of the pieces and revealing the patronage context in which some were composed but also providing a metapoetic commentary on his own literary development. For example, he wrote at least one poem "in behalfe of a Gentleman, who travailying into Kent, fell there in love" (p. 120) and also composed at least three pieces when "a noble man, my right good Lord . . . commaunded me to wryte him some Verses" (p. 28). The poems in the collection are related specifically to the social and literary vicissitudes of an edu-

---

[35] In this 1575 pamphlet, Breton self-consciously presents himself as a young scholar declaring literary ambitions, addressing a pious poem to a patroness as a New Year's gift, a sixteen-page octavo pamphlet.

[36] The prefatory epistle to this work refers to something he will have for his readers in the "next Terme" (p. 4), suggesting that he is addressing Inns of Court men and/or gentlemen who came to London for part of the year on legal business.

cated young gentleman who was conscious of the class hierarchy in which he functioned and of the peer group with whom he was communicating in print.[37]

## Sidney, Literary Authorization, and Patronage

One of the most significant phenomena relating the publication of poetry to patronage is, of course, the 1579 edition of Spenser's *Shepheardes Calendar,* dedicated to Sir Philip Sidney: though Spenser's own name is missing from the title page, Sidney's is highlighted, the work being *"Entitled* To the Noble and Vertuous Gentleman most worthy of all titles both of learning and chevalrie M. Philip Sidney."[38] The use of the word "Entitled" signals the passing of the work into his virtual ownership, a gesture of subordination on the writer's part in ceding property rights to a patron. It is interesting that, at this stage of his career, Sidney had no formal aristocratic title, his knighthood only being granted in 1583. The conjunction of "titles" of "learning and chevalrie" mischievously confuses the traditional feudal social hierarchy with a scale of merit associated with humanistic self-improvement, the latter one of the bases of authorial self-assertion in the face of a class system in which writers were not usually favorably placed.

*The Shepheardes Calendar* is, at once, the announcement of a significant poetic career, a coyly parodic imitation of the printing house conventions for the presentation of classical literature, and a giftgiving gesture on the part of a client who was also friend of the dedicatee. This landmark text treated the medium of print with a sociocultural seriousness lacking in most previous poetry pamphlets. Spenser's authorial self-fashioning has been discussed intelligently by

---

[37] The discursive introductions to the poems highlight not only the social circumstances of their production but also the poet's own development, the history of which can be visible in the print medium both within a single publication and in a series of printed texts such as Breton had begun.

[38] S. K. Heninger Jr. argues that "in the later stages of its composition a decision was made to recast *The Shepheardes Calender* as a reprise of Sannazaro's *Arcadia* in order to flatter Sidney, announce allegiance to him, and secure his good offices" at a time at which "Sidney was so enthusiastically imitating [Sannazaro] in his own work" ("The Typographical Layout of Spenser's *Shepheardes Calender,*" in *Word and Visual Imagination: Studies in the Interaction of English Literature and the Visual Arts,* ed. Karl Josef Höltgen, Peter M. Daly, and Wolfgang Lottes [Erlangen: Univ.-Bibliothek Erlangen-Nurnberg, 1988], p. 42).

Richard Helgerson, David Miller, and others,[39] and, in this context I only wish to provide a reminder of the chronological locus of this publication, after the early miscellanies, the editions of Googe, Turbervile, Gascoigne, and Breton, and before the prestigious publications of the 1590s, many of which were composed during the 1580s. As an author, Spenser also tried to reconcile patronage and publication, social respectability and the print medium, although his love lyrics only appeared after the more prestigious public verse of *The Faerie Queene* had established his identity as a serious national poet.[40] It was, however, the dedicatee of *The Shepheardes Calendar,* Sir Philip Sidney, whose activities both as patron and author, had more of an impact on the status of printed literature and the sociocultural authority of the publishing writer.[41]

The fashion of composing and publishing sonnet sequences or collections of songs and sonnets came to England late in the Renaissance, and it took no less an author than Sidney to inaugurate it, albeit posthumously. In the early 1580s, however, Thomas Watson published a sonnet collection with all the defensive preliminary gestures an author might use to present such work to a potentially unreceptive public. His anonymous *Hekatompathia or Passionate Centurie of Love* (1582) opens with an elaborate dedication to the earl of Oxford in which that patron is depicted both as one who caused the poems to be printed and the means for winning it approval. Watson explains that because the world knew Oxford had read and approved of his verse (in its handwritten form), "many have oftentimes and

---

[39] See Helgerson, *Self-Crowned Laureates,* pp. 55–100 (cited in full at Chap. 4, n. 1); David L. Miller, "Authorship, Anonymity, and *The Shepheardes Calender,*" *MLQ* 40 (1979): 219–31, and "Spenser's Vocation, Spenser's Career," *ELH* 50 (1983): 197–231; and Alpers, "Pastoral" (cited in full at Chap. 4, n. 7).

[40] William Ponsonby's preface to *Amoretti and Epithalamion* (1595) points out that Spenser's "name sufficiently warranting the worthinesse of the work," he makes bold to publish it in the poet's absence (text cited in *Spenser's Minor Poems,* ed. Ernest De Selincourt [Oxford: Clarendon Press, 1910], p. 370). When they appeared in print, Spenser's *Amoretti and Epithalamion* had a title page that highlighted authorship, a printer's dedicatory letter praising the poet more than the patron, and two commendatory poems arguing that Spenser should be brought home from "foreign" service because of his intellectual and literary achievements. For a discussion of Spenser's wanting to use the model of the inspired Orphic poet to break the subordination of poetry to patronage, see Jane Tylus, "Spenser and the Politics of Poetic Labor," *ELH* 55 (1988): 53–77.

[41] Van Dorsten remarks: "No matter how hard one tries to look for alternatives the new poetry had only one patron: Sidney. Against all odds and almost single-handedly, he provided the ambience and the inspiration that was to intitiate one of the greatest periods in European literary history" ("Literary Patronage," p. 200).

earnestly called upon mee, to put it to the press, that for their mony they might but see, what your Lordship with some likeing had alreadie perused" (sig. A3r).⁴² Using Oxford's blessing as a celebrity endorsement, Watson also asks him to protect the poems from malicious readers. When Watson addresses "the frendly Reader" directly, he allows him the freedom to encourage or discourage his composing and publishing further works: "This toye being liked, the next may proove better; being discouraged, wil cut of the likelihood of my travaile to come" (sig. A4v). A commendatory letter to Watson from John Lyly, the author of the popular *Euphues* (1578), himself another Oxford client, praises the love poetry to follow, alluding to his own practice of writing amorous lyrics. Finally, there follow six commendatory poems (five in English, one in Latin) praising the work and its author. Despite all this, Watson did not really entice others to write and publish love sonnets.

Once he had become for his contemporaries a Protestant martyr, culture hero, and, after the publication of his verse and prose in the 1590s, the preeminent author of the English Renaissance, Sir Philip Sidney posthumously exercised some of the sociocultural functions ascribed to living patrons, authorizing the literary texts of writers who invoked his name to legitimate the printing of their own and others' texts. If we look at the first of Newman's 1591 quartos of *Astrophil and Stella*, however, we can discover the traces of interesting socioliterary conflicts and negotiations as manuscript-circulated verse was transferred to the public medium of print. In the form preserved in the British Library copy (which alone of the three surviving copies of this quarto has preserved the front matter of the edition), Sidney's sonnets are preceded by Newman's dedication of the work to Francis Flower and Thomas Nashe's prefatory address to the readers—both of which are documents that position Sidney's text in relation to the larger Elizabethan social system. As Germaine Warkentin has cogently argued, the first of these, Newman's dedicatory letter to Flower, probably deeply offended the countess of Pembroke, who was most likely the person that brought the court pressure that led to Burghley's order to impound the edition. She would have been jealous of her own

---

⁴² Oxford is also the dedicatee of John Soowthern's sonnet collection, *Pandora* (1584), a book whose audience is identified in the "Sonnet to the Reader" as "you that are lyke us amourous" (sig. Aiiv), the group of young gentleman-amorists that would have included the earl himself.

proprietary rights to her brother's literary remains and would have wished them to appear only in the context of *her* patronage: thus the 1590 and 1593 *Arcadia* were titled *The Countess of Pembrokes Arcadia* and the 1598 folio retained this title, adding "Now for the third time published with sundry new additions" to encompass the other contents. To the countess's way of thinking, no one else had the right to patronize an edition of Sidney's writing, much less a court bureaucrat who had a reputation as a rake and shady economic opportunist.[43] Newman's dedication to Flower, then, would have galled her. And she would not have been mollified by Nashe's tribute to her as "a second *Minerva*... [whom] our Poets extoll as the Patronesse of their invention."[44] The two documents, in fact, disagree on the rights of patronage: Newman's dedication offers Sidney's text to Flower, whose "credite and countenaunce your patronage may give to such a worke" which the publisher presents as "the first fruites of my affection" (2:369), whereas the second acknowledges the countess's status as a learned, literarily skillful patroness of the arts who has some property rights to her brother's writings.

The issue of control and ownership is a touchy one in both documents. Newman, as it were, offers his publication to Flower in a gesture that cedes to him the property rights given a patron willing to countenance and protect a publication; Nashe, despite the gestures of respect to the countess, defends the theft of Sidney's sonnet sequence as a liberation of the text from its imprisonment within family and coterie: "Although it be oftentimes imprisoned in Ladyes casks, & the president bookes of such as cannot see without another mans spectacles, yet at length it breakes forth in spight of his keepers, and useth some private penne (in steed of a picklock) to procure his violent enlargment."[45] Nashe's ambivalent language condenses a rescue fantasy, an adventurous escape, and an morally sanctioned act of betrayal by a member of an in-group: he describes the kind of liberation of private texts into the accessible public medium of print that Tottel had defended in 1557 in the preface to his poetry anthology.

---

[43] See Germaine Warkentin, "Patrons and Profiteers: Thomas Newman and the 'Violent Enlargement' of *Astrophil and Stella*," *The Book Collector* 34 (1985): 461–87.

[44] *Complete Works of Sidney*, ed. Feuillerat 2: 370–71 (see Chap. 4, n. 44). Further citations in text by volume and page number.

[45] Wendy Wall cites this passage in her rich discussion of the associations of print with voyeurism and transgression, pointing out the sexual association of the Nashe's term "casks" ("Disclosures in Print," p. 36 [see Chap. 4, n. 1]).

But there is another message in Nashe's preface, implicit in his satiric tone and sophisticated pose—that the educated "Gentlemen" (2:371) who will buy and read Newman's pamphlet are the real socioliterary center of the culture, rather than the aristocrats of either the great house or the court, with their dominant structure of patronage relationships. What is being acted out is not exactly a contest between aristocratic and democratic conceptions of literature—for Nashe is still an intellectual, if not a social, elitist—but rather a conflict between the rights associated with aristocratic proprietorship and an intellectual and artistic elite's freedom of access to valued literary texts. In such a conflict, publishers could take the high moral ground of allegedly acting in the public interest, even if their basic motive were private economic gain. And they could hire someone like Nashe, a university-educated professional writer familiar with the dynamics of metropolitan culture, to defend the whole project on both social and intellectual grounds.

When Samuel Daniel took advantage of the precedent set by the publication of Sidney's sonnet sequence and published his own collection, he sought the patronage of Sidney's sister, Mary Sidney Herbert, countess of Pembroke. Addressing her as the "happie and judiciall Patroness of the Muses,"[46] he seems to have been asking the countess's permission to associate his work with that of the deceased poet-hero. Thus the function of patronage was split between siblings in an interesting way, the brother authorizing the printing of such verse and the sister serving as the dedicatee and protector. Furthermore, the countess was also portrayed as the ideal reader of the sonnets: Daniel expressed his antagonism to the general public reached through the print medium, omitting any epistle to readers and presenting the book as a gift to one person, who, in effect, became the owner of the text.[47]

[46] Daniel, *Poems and A Defence of Ryme*, ed. Sprague, p. 9 (see Chap. 4, n. 54).

[47] The format of this publication (one sonnet per page with an ornamental border at the bottom of each page) suggests that the printed text was imitating some of the features of a presentation copy of a poetry collection. Mary Lamb suggests that Daniel might have "dedicated his *Delia* (1592) to the Countess to gain a position at Wilton" ("The Countess of Pembroke's Patronage," *ELR* 12 (1982): 177–78). In the course of her discussion of the countess of Pembroke, Lamb argues that the extent of her patronage has been greatly exaggerated. Later, in the dedicatory epistle of his *Resolves* (8th printing, 1661), Owen Felltham makes his patroness Lady Mary, countess dowager of Thomond, the virtual owner of his texts since they were composed in her household: "Being (most of them) Composed under the Coverture of your Roof, and so born Subjects under your Dominion; It would have been the incurring of too apparent a *Premunire* against Equity and Justice, to intitle

Under very different circumstances, Giles Fletcher published his sonnet collection *Licia* in 1593 along with *The Rising to the Crown of Richard the third*.[48] As a former academician with a doctorate in civil law, a government servant with expertise in ambassadorial trade ne-gotiation, and the official Remembrancer of the City of London, Fletcher was a serious man of affairs who could characterize his composition of lyrics both as a gentleman's leisure activity and as a scholar's treatment of the subject of love in a philosophically serious manner.[49] Like Daniel, however, he emphasized the importance of his patroness over his reader. Whereas Daniel avoided addressing the reader directly, Fletcher expressed indifference to reader judgment in the dedicatory epistle and in his prefatory statement "To the Reader" was both insulting and condescending. After depicting Lady Mollineux as the prime mover of his love poetry (that is, an author-izer of its publication), Fletcher tells her: "For the Reader, if he looke for my letters to crave his favour, he is farre deceived: for if he mislike anie thing, I am sorie he tooke the paines to reade, but if he doe, let him dispraise, I much care not" (p. 76). Since Fletcher assumes that "our great men . . . want leasure to reade, and if they had, yet for the most part, the worse speake worse" (p. 76), he seems to be socially disparaging anyone who buys his book. Hence the comment: "Let the Printer looke he grow not a begger by such bargaynes" (p. 76). Similarly, he makes the distinction between the few gentlemen of the Inns of Court and the universities who are "onelie . . . fittest to write of Love" and those "of meane reach . . . unfitte to knowe what love meanes," that is, between those who can (Neoplatonically) conceive of love as "a Goddesse . . . not respecting the contentment of him that loves but the vertues of the beloved" and those of "a vulgare head, a base minde, an ordinarie conceit," who know only "the love wherewith *Venus* sonne hath injuriouslie made spoile of thousandes" (p. 79). He leaves the reader in an uncomfortable position both intellectually and socially, teasing him by turning inter-pretive freedom into a kind of helpless dependency.[50]

---

any other, to their owning or Protection; or to set up any forain Power, to be Supreme and Paramount, to that of your Ladiships, over them" (sig. A1r).

[48] See the *Works of Fletcher*, ed. Berry (cited in full at Chap. 4, n. 56). Henceforth cited in the text.

[49] See ibid., pp. 3–49.

[50] See the discussion of this topic in "Jonson, Authorship, and Print" in Chapter 4.

Asserting his intellectual authority and using his association with his patroness, Lady Mollineux, to reinforce his claims to gentility, Fletcher seems unusually hostile to his readership because he fears the vulgarizing potential of print, a danger against which the example of Sidney offered only partial protection, especially since as author of *Licia* Fletcher could not pretend that his love lyrics were the products of an unsteady youth. Unwilling to submit to reader censure, Fletcher finally suggests that he can dispense with patronage as well and assert the kind of authorial autonomy that the Sidney model encouraged: after expressing his gratitude to Lady Mollineux and her family, he tells the readers: "If thou mislike it [*Licia*], yet she or they, or both, or divine LICIA shall patronize it, or if none, I will and can doe it myselfe" (p. 80). In a sense, this idea of the author as his own patron is one that is implicit in the example of Sidney as it develops through the 1590s and beyond. Though thoroughly dependent in his career as a government servant on individual and corporate patronage, Fletcher could at least imagine an independence that the evolving institution of literature in print culture made it possible to conceive.

In publishing his miscellany *The Phoenix Nest* (1593),[51] the editor, "R.S. of the Inner Temple Gentleman," presented his book to the world of polite society without dedicating it to a patron and without a subservient address to readers. The commercial attraction lay in the explicit associations of the Sidney name and precedent and the snob appeal of the title page of this attractively printed quarto: *The Phoenix Nest. Built up with the most rare and refined workes of Noble men, woorthy Knights, gallant Gentlemen, Masters of Arts, and brave Schollers. Full of varietie, excellent invention, and singular delight. Never before this time published.* Largely because the printing of Sidney's sonnets lent a dignity to printed lyric collections, this book could appeal unashamedly to a well-to-do clientele.

Francis Davison's dedication of his ambitious poetry anthology, *A Poetical Rhapsody* (1602),[52] to William Herbert, earl of Pembroke, was an explicit use of this patron to establishing contact with the literarily and culturally powerful name of Sidney, the earl's uncle. Using the sonnet form for the dedicatory poem, Davison praised Pembroke for

---

[51] *Phoenix Nest,* ed. Rollins (see Chap. 4, n. 14).
[52] Text cited from *Poetical Rhapsody,* ed. Rollins (see Chap. 3, n. 11).

his "high and noble minde," "outward shape," "Vertue, Valour, Learning," and "future Hope," before getting to the genealogy of patronage and poetry of which Pembroke was a part:

> Thou worthy Sonne, unto a peerelesse MOTHER,
>   Though Nephew to great SIDNEY of renowne,
>   Thou that deserv'st thy CORONET to crowne
>   With Lawrell Crowne, a Crowne excelling t'other;
>   I consecrate these Rimes to thy great NAME,
>   Which if thou like, they seek no other fame.
>
> (1:3)

The earl, evidently, had by this time written some of his own verse, the association with which Davison sought in order to dignify his own and his brother's lyrics that were included in the anthology. Pembroke was thus one poet-patron in a family several of whose members functioned in both roles.

Many writers continued to appeal to the earl of Pembroke as well as to Sidney's sister, the countess of Pembroke, and to other members of the Sidney-Herbert families for patronage, producing dozens of dedications and complimentary poems. Once Sidney himself, as noted in the last chapter, was installed in a developing national literature that he helped to shape and elevate, he became a sign of the growing strength of the literary institution as a self-authorizing entity, less dependent than previously on traditional social and political authority for its existence.

### Jonson and the Problems of Patronage

Despite Sidney's precedent, tensions continued between patrons, poets, publishers, and readers. In the dedication of his *Epigrammes* (in the folio *Workes*) to William Herbert, earl of Pembroke, and in the poems addressed to the reader, the book, and the bookseller, Ben Jonson, characteristically hypersensitive to potential criticism, eventually insulted the other major parties in the circuit of literary production and reception. Wishing to assert a degree of personal and literary authority and independence in circumstances of obvious social and economic dependency, Jonson inevitably portrayed a power struggle taking place with these other agents.

In the epistle to Pembroke, to whom he had dedicated the 1611 quarto of *Catiline*,[53] Jonson depicts his own role in a way that ultimately reverses the power relationship between patron and client. Instead of making the usual request for aristocratic protection of his work, something that was especially necessary (given the potential for retaliation by those who might have felt satirized in the poems), Jonson reformulated the patron's function as the moral responsibility to uphold the conditions of "truth, and libertie"[54] in which he, like any serious writer, wished to be allowed to function,[55] a task he tells Pembroke he can perform, "while you are constant to your owne goodnesse." In his insightful discussion of Jonson's strategies of asserting his authority through the presentation of his texts in print, Timothy Murray notes how Jonson "undercuts his apparent declaration of subservience to his lord" and denies to Pembroke the right to judge the truth-value of his writing.[56] In a strategy he used constantly in his encomiastic poetry, Jonson instructs his social superior in his duty and challenges him or her to live up to the ideal image presented in the rhetoric of praise. Moreover, in making the conventional promise to eternize his patron, Jonson casts doubt on the worthiness of all those he praises, among whom Pembroke is the first: "I return you the honor of leading forth so many good, and great names (as my verses mention on the better part) to their remembrance with posteritie. Amongst whom, if I have praysed, unfortunately, any one, that doth not deserve; or, if all answere not, in all numbers, the pictures I have made of them: I hope it will be forgiven me, that they are no ill pieces, though they be not like the persons" (p. 3). Thus the poet patronized the patrons.[57]

---

[53] Helgerson notes that this is one of the first play quartos to be dedicated to a particular patron, a sign that Jonson had turned away from the popular audience that had poorly received his drama to an intellectually and socially elite readership that would better value what he wrote (*Self-Crowned Laureates*, pp. 167–68).

[54] *Complete Poetry of Ben Jonson*, ed. Hunter, p. 3 (see Chap. 1, n. 35).

[55] In *The Advancement of Learning*, Bacon expresses a hostility to "the modern dedication of books and writings, as to patrons . . . for that books (such as are worthy of the name of books) ought to have no patrons but truth and reason" (Book 1, A.3.ix, quoted in Brennan, *Literary Patronage*, p. 143).

[56] Murray, *Theatrical Legitimation*, pp. 79–80 (see Chap. 4, n. 66).

[57] Don Wayne argues that Jonson makes "a subtle suggestion that the poems, not the persons, are what serve to codify the standards of the good society" ("Poetry and Power in Ben Jonson's *Epigrammes*: The Naming of 'Facts' or the Figuring of Social Relations?" *Renaissance and Modern Studies* 23 [1979]: 87). W. H. Herendeen argues that Jonson's refusal to have a general dedicatee for his folio *Workes* and his decision to have individual and institutional dedicatees for the parts of the collection preceding the royal entertainments

## PATRONAGE, POETRY, AND PRINT

In the interest of protecting his own moral and literary authority, Jonson attacks the other parties involved in the system of print transmission: in addition to criticizing his patron, he attacks both the book purchasers and the commercially interested stationer,[58] everyone, that is, except the king, who is praised both as poet *and* patron. Jonson associates "Poets" and "Kings" not simply because James I was himself a published poet, having brought out both *The Essayes of a Prentise in the Divine Art of Poesie* (1584) and *His Majesties Poetical Exercises at Vacant Houres* (1591) in Edinburgh before he became monarch of England, but also because he himself was interested in elevating the sociocultural status of authorship. In dedicating to Prince Charles the posthumous 1623 edition of his brother Samuel Daniel's *Whole Workes*, John Daniel similarly associated poetry with royalty: "Sacred is the fame of Poets, Sacred the name of Princes" (sig. A2v). In his epigram to the king, Jonson names James as the person to whom his muse "should . . . flie" (9). Embedded in a publication that, perhaps self-consciously, imitated the *The Workes of James, King of Great Brittaine, France, and Ireland* (1616), the potentially dangerous and ephemeral book of epigrams, then, benefited both from the king's patronage and from publication in the prestigious folio format. As Helgerson has demonstrated, then, Jonson's laureate strategy both included and subsumed the kinds of patronage relationships that (paradoxically) *both* socially elevated poets *and* made it difficult for them to assume independent sociocultural authority.[59]

In 1602, as part of a strategy of currying the favor of the expected heir to the English throne, Sir John Harington sent a manuscript presentation copy of his epigrams with a dedication to King James

---

was a deliberate strategy on his part that allowed him an artistic and personal independence ("A New Way to Pay Old Debts: Pretexts to the 1616 Folio," in Brady and Herendeen, *Ben Jonson's 1616 Folio*, pp. 38–63 [see Chap. 4, n. 66]). "The *negotium* in Jonson's dedications and in his art generally shows his desire to deal in a literary marketplace characterized not by a medieval patronage system like that which tied Daniel for a time to the Herberts, but by a value system in which the parties involved are equals, each benefiting from the relationship" (p. 54).

[58] See "Jonson, Authorship, and Print," in Chapter 4.

[59] Helgerson, *Self-Crowned Laureates*, pp. 101–84. Martin Elsky points out that "while the printed folio of 1616 was an effective way of claiming his status as a serious professional author independent of the vagaries of courtly patronage, his conspicuous listing on the title page of the nobles to whom each of the works was dedicated still signaled his connection—no matter how uncomfortable—to the court. Whatever the psychological or social genesis of his unease, the result appears to have been Jonson's strong identification with marginality as the location of his moral and poetic activity" (*Authorizing Words: Speech, Writing, and Print in the English Renaissance* [Ithaca: Cornell University Press, 1989], pp. 106–7).

(of Scotland). Unwilling to commit them to print, he exploited them as social currency in the system of manuscript transmission, treating James as his potential patron. When the stationer John Budge brought out the posthumous editions of these poems in 1615 and 1618, he took the opportunity of dedicating them respectively to the earl of Pembroke[60] and to the duke of Buckingham. In the epistle to the latter, Budge wrote:

> This *posthume* book is furnished with worth, but it wanteth a Patron. A worthier then your selfe the Booke could not find, nor your Lordship a more patheticall Poet to Patronize. If in Poetry, Heraldry were admitted, he would be found in happinesse of wit neere allied to the great *Sidney:* yet but neere; for the *Apix* of the *Coelum Empyrium* is not more inaccessible then is the height of *Sidneys* Poesy, which by imagination we may approach, by imitation never attaine to. To great men our very syllables should be short, and therefore I make my Conclusion a Petition; That your Lordshippes acceptation may shew how much you favor the noble Name, and nature of the Poet, and Booke. Which I deigned by your Lordshippe, I shall thinke my paines in collecting, and disposing of these Epigrams well placed, and ever rest
>
> 

*Your Lordships most bounden*
servant, J.B.[61]

By invoking Sidney, Budge managed to shift his focus from the single text presented to Buckingham to the whole institution of printed literature, so that it looks as though, in asking for patronage for "the noble Name, and nature of the Poet, and Booke" he was not just asking for support for an edition of Harington's *Epigrams* but for the newly emerging identities of author and text in print culture. It is no surprise, then, that he should foreground his own important editorial functions in the literary institution of which he was part.

It was booksellers and printers, however, who had the greatest ec-

---

[60] Brennan points out that Pembroke's influence over the operation of the publishing industry was acknowledged by stationers, suggesting not only that Budge's dedication of Harington's *Epigrams* (1615) was one sign of this fact but also that "there is an interesting line of descent among some of the stationers associated with the Herberts during James's reign. Both Blount and Shawe had been apprenticed to the publisher of most of Sidney's works, William Ponsonby. Blount continued Ponsonby's practice of publishing high-class literary texts, including volumes by Josuah Sylvester, John Florio and Samuel Daniel, who all sought the favour of William Herbert" (*Literary Patronage*, p. 140).

[61] Text cited from John Harington, *Epigrams* (1618; facsimile, Menston, U.K.: Scolar Press, 1970), sigs. A3r–A3v.

onomic stake in publishing, and from their point of view, both authors and patrons were economically instrumental entities in the publication process. William Ringler, for example, discusses the unscrupulous activities of Laurence Blaikelocke, the publisher of the spurious 1640 and 1653 editions of Francis Beaumont's poetry. Blaikelocke actually published the work of other writers under Beaumont's name and finally betrayed to the Committee on Sequestration the man to whom he had dedicated the collection, Sir Robert Ducie.[62]

By the early part of the seventeenth century, the competition for patronage support for printed texts, the restricted resources of the aristocracy,[63] and the economics of the publishing industry had, in effect, changed the functions of patrons defined in and inherited from manuscript culture. Certainly publishers were more apt to use patrons' names for the purpose of promoting sales of books to a general readership than as signs of an actual patron-client relationship in the old sense.[64] Writers could normally hope for little in the way of immediate financial reward in return for dedications, though, depending on their preexisting relationships to particular patrons and patronesses, there were some real social and political benefits to

[62] See Ringler, "The 1640 and 1653 *Poems: By Francis Beaumont*," pp. 120–40 (cited in full at Chap. 4, n. 51), and James P. Hammersmith, "The Printer's Copy for Francis Beaumont's *Poems*, 1653," *PBSA* 72 (1978): 74–88.

[63] The complaints of authors about the stinginess of patrons or the unavailability of patronage are common. See, for example, Richard Barnfield's *Complaint of Poetrie for the Death of Liberalitie* (London, 1598), which bemoans his loss of patronage and the substitution of "*Good wordes*" (sig. A3r) for financial reward. Thomas Nashe continually complained about the difficulty of obtaining patronage, John Marston dedicated *Antonio and Mellida* to "Nobody" (cited in Brennan, *Literary Patronage*, p. 209), and George Wither dedicated his satiric *Abuses Stript and Whipt* (1613) to himself. In 1600, the printer Thomas Thorpe, in dedicating his first publication, Marlowe's translation of the first book of Lucan, to his stationer-friend Edward Blount, joked about the poor patronage support available for authors and publishers: "One speciall vertue in our Patrons of these daies I have promist my selfe you shall fit excellently, which is to give nothing" (quoted in Leona Rostenberg, "Plays, Verse & Masques: Thomas Thorpe, Publisher of 'Shake-Speares Sonnets,' " in *Literary, Political, Scientific, Religious & Legal Publishing, Printing & Bookselling in England, 1551–1700: Twelve Studies* [New York: Burt Franklin, 1965], p. 52). For a general discussion of the decline of patronage and the consequent complaints of authors, see the two articles by Patricia Thomson cited at note 1 to this chapter and Miller, *The Professional Writer*, pp. 129–35.

[64] Few authors or publishers, however, were as blunt about this as "N.M.," who dedicated *Certain Elegant Poems Written by Dr. Corbet, Bishop of Norwich* (1647) to Lady Teynham: "You will in the permission of your Name to be set before this Book, imitate the Custome of Kings, who set their Names on coins of Copper, as well as on those of Gold; and as the King that coines sets what value hee pleaseth on his Money, so when your name is set to this Work, I will give it what price I please, and every wise person will buy it" (sig. A4r).

hope for from the patronage system. Multiple dedications,[65] the production of presentation copies with differing preliminary matter tailored to different patrons,[66] and the displacement of part of the authorizing function onto commendatory poems[67] signal the breakdown of the old system of artistic clientage. In the new vocabulary of printed editons of poetry, the patron-function could, in effect, be transferred to those who bought books—as in Barnabe Barnes's *Parthnophil and Parthenophe* (1593), in which the printer refers to the "friendly patronages" of the "Learned Gentlemen Readers" (sig. A2r).[68]

---

[65] On multiple dedications, see Miller, *The Professional Writer*, pp. 120–21. When he published *The Scourge of Folly* (1611), John Davies of Herford, for example, included a long list of patronage poetry in two sections labeled "To worthy persons," pp. 183–229, 246–64. On the rules for arranging addresses or poems to different personages in works with multiple dedications, see Carol A. Stillman, "Politics, Precedence, and the Order of the Dedicatory Sonnets in *The Faerie Queene*," *Spenser Studies* 5 (1984): 143–48. Stillman points out that "poems addressed to noble men had to be presented according to the heraldic rules for precedence. The chief officials of the crown come first, then the peers, then the gentlemen, followed by the ladies, all ranked by the dignity of their families, offices, and titles" (p. 144).

[66] On the practice of inserting unique dedications in individual presentation copies of books, see F. P. Wilson, "Some Notes on Authors and Patrons in Tudor and Stuart Times, in *Joseph Quincy Adams Memorial Studies*, ed. James G. McManaway, Giles E. Dawson, and Edwin E. Willoughby (Washington, D.C.: Folger Shakespeare Library, 1948), pp. 553–61. Sometimes an author had his work printed only as a means to produce presentation copies for patrons and friends. Hereford, Simpson, and Simpson, for example, say of the 1631 publication of Jonson's *Bartholomew Fair*, *The Staple of News*, and *The Devil is an Ass* that the "sending out of private gift-copies to friends and patrons was the only use made of this issue" (Hereford, Simpson, and Simpson, *Ben Jonson*, 9:85 [see Chap. 1, n. 35]).

[67] See Franklin B. Williams Jr., "Commendatory Verses: The Rise of the Art of Puffing," *Studies in Bibliography* 19 (1966): 1–14. Ben Jonson, for example, wrote some thirty-five commendatory poems for other men's works, obviously thinking of peer-endorsement as one of the features of the literary institution. Williams points out that commendatory verse began as a feature of serious humanist publications and later moved to more ephemeral productions: "Lighter literature, such as English verse and fiction, began to be provided with dedications about 1570, and puffing followed in sequence. In the Jacobean years the vogue extended to frivolous publications" (p. 5). Williams also notes that "habitual writers of commendatory verses were . . . mainly literary professionals. With the curious exceptions of Sidney and Shakespeare, all the chief poets (including Spenser and Milton) wrote puffs" (p. 6). There is an unusual use of commendatory poetry in Robert Tofte's *Alba. The Months Minde of a Melancholy Lover* (1598) where several commendatory poems are accompanied by the author's answer poetry (a kind of reproduction of the practices of manuscript poetry exchange).

[68] The author's address to his book as a "bastard Orphan" expresses the hope that "some goodman that shall thinke thee witty, / Will be thy patrone," suggesting that there are no aristocratic patrons to protect it. But at the end of the text there is a group of dedicatory poems addressed to the earls of Northumberland, Essex, Southampton, the countess of Pembroke, Lady Straunge, and Lady Bridgett Manners, located just before the first and only appearance of the author's name. And each dedicatee is treated differently: Northumberland is identified as a member of the old aristocracy; Essex as a man of public

## PATRONAGE, POETRY, AND PRINT

In the case of published lyric poetry, patrons served multiple purposes: not only were they actual or wished-for dispensers of money,
social or political support and favor, offices and employment, but
also, as ideal readers and celebrity-endorsers, they were symbolic or
mediatory figures, facilitating the transition from manuscript culture
to print culture. They were part of a process in which socially restricted occasional verse was incorporated into the newly emerging
modern institution of literature, an environment in which they were
reduced to a minor feature of the publishing format as the subservient author began to enjoy prestige as a member of a new literary
and aesthetic elite. Particular poets, such as William Davenant,[69] continued to rely on old-fashioned patronage, but, as demonstrated by
the posthumous author-centered editions of Donne and Herbert,
which appeared initially without dedications to patrons,[70] poets could

---

affairs who, one hopes, might find time to read Barnes's poems; Southampton as someone
who might protect the poet from envy and scorn; the countess of Pembroke as a known
supporter of poetry; Lady Straunge and Lady Manners as great beauties, the latter urged
to become interested in the contents of the collection. Although they are ways of advertising
his social and political connections and of appealing for favor, they seem, in the format of
the book to be somewhat beside the point. See the discussion of these poems in Barnabe
Barnes, *Parthenophil and Parthenophe: A Critical Edition*, edited with an introduction by Victor
A. Doyno (Carbondale: Southern Illinois University Press; London: Feffer & Simons, 1971),
pp. xxvi–xxx.
   [69] See Helgerson, *Self-Crowned Laureates*, p. 207.
   [70] In Nicholas Ferrar's preface to Herbert's *Temple* (Cambridge, 1633), human patronage is specifically ruled out as inappropriate for such a text: "The dedication of this work
having been made by the Authour to the *Divine Majestie* onely, how should we now presume
to interest any mortall man in the patronage of it?" (sig. *2r). Similarly, James I dedicated
his collected works to "Almighty God," and Mildmay Fane, earl of Westmoreland, in publishing his religious verse, *Otia Sacra* (1648), begins the text proper with a poem that
announces the refusal to seek human patronage, a decision no doubt reinforced by his
own high aristocratic status.
   In the case of the continuing publication of Donne's works, there is something of a
reversion to the old ways. Once the younger Donne succeeded in gaining a measure of
control over his father's writings, he attempted to connect (or, in some cases, reconnect)
the works with the socioeconomic conditions of patronage. In effect he attempted a partial
rescue of his father from the open market of print to relocate him and his works in the
traditional context of literature written for patronage. The first edition of the poetry to
appear under his control was the 1650 edition: it opens with an address to the Royalist
(and nouveau-riche) William, Lord Craven, who is asked to take into his "protection" the
inspired poetry of a man who wrote before the supposed decline of civilization represented
by the kingless commonwealth period. The verse is recoded to fit it into this new context
of patronage: "Although these poems were formerly written upon severall occasions, and
to severall persons, they now unite themselves, and are become one pyramid to set your
Lordships statue upon, where you may stand like Armed *Apollo* the defendor of the Muses,
encouraging the Poets now alive to celebrate your great Acts by affording your countenance
to his poems that wanted onely so noble a subject" (sig. A4r). This rhetoric is familiar
enough in dedicatory epistles, but it is interesting to note that the sought-after patron, as

be well protected, well respected, and well installed in a literary institution made visible through the medium of print.

---

Lawrence Stone points out, is the only merchant's son in the early Stuart period to manage to buy himself a major title (for £7000): a man of enormous wealth and income, Craven was exactly the socially insecure target Donne's son needed for his flattery (see Stone, *The Crisis of the Aristocracy*, pp. 106, 146, 190, 497–98, 632 [cited in full at Chap. 2, n. 80]). In such a context he treats all of his father's verse, as he did the letters, as though they were client-patron communications.

# CONCLUSION

A YEAR or two before the 1616 publication of his *Poems,* Ben Jonson's friend, William Drummond of Hawthorndon, put out for private circulation an early printed version of the collection that he then revised for the 1616 edition (excluding some pieces that appeared in the private issue). This Scots aristocrat, who evidently had no worries about the "stigma of print," was, as his Victorian editor points out, "in the habit of issuing his poems [in print] on loose sheets, as they came out, for circulation among his friends."[1] He thus treated print as a medium that could, like manuscripts, be used to faciliate coterie communication. About the same time, John Donne contemplated publishing a very limited edition of his own verse. He wrote his closest friend, Sir Henry Goodyer: "The going about to pay debts, hastens importunity. . . . I am brought to a necessity of printing my Poems, and addressing them to my L. Chamberlain [Robert Carr, earl of Somerset]. This I mean to do forthwith, not for much publique view, but at mine owne cost, a few Copies."[2] Although he did not carry out this plan, Donne obviously thought to use publication in a very restricted way. When he published *Otia Sacra* in 1648, Mildmay Fane, earl of Westmoreland, had his poems printed in only a few copies, with the intention of restricting the distribution of the edition

---

[1] L. E. Kastner, ed., *The Poetical Works of William Drummond of Hawthornden,* 2 vols. (1856; reprint, New York: Haskell House, 1968), 1:lxii. Cf. William Drummond, *Poems* (1616; facsimile, Menston, U.K.: Scolar Press, 1969).

[2] John Donne, *Letters to Severall Persons of Honour (1651),* facsimile, with an introduction by M. Thomas Hester (Delmar, N.Y.: Scholars' Facsimiles & Reprints, 1977), pp. 196–97.

to a select group of friends and acquaintances. At the end of the work, in a poem "To my Book," Fane wrote:

> ... what alone to Friends he [the author] would impart,
> Hath not at all to doe with Fair or Mart.
> Wherefore whoever shall peruse these Rimes,
> Must know, they were beguilers of spare times.
>
> (P. 174)

There is a kind of mixed message here: the poems were recreations intended only for friends, but others, of course, were imagined as getting access to them.[3] Drummond, Donne, and Fane, no doubt, approached print with different motives: Drummond was a wealthy, socially secure aristocrat; Donne, an importunate seeker of political, social, and economic patronage who wanted to enter Church service debt-free; and Fane, a nobleman in the Interregnum who not only retained some fear of the "stigma of print" but also was politically and socially embattled. These three cases point to how the two systems of literary transmission overlapped and influenced each other, despite their many differences.

The Drummond, Donne, and Fane examples demonstrate the carryover of some of manuscript culture's practices into print culture.[4] Certainly poems, epistles, or addresses to readers or patrons or both as well as commendatory verse also demonstrate the transposition of some of manuscript culture's social dynamics into the format of printed editions. But, it should be noted, printed literature also affected the practices of manuscript transmission and compilation. Printed texts often returned to the system of manuscript transmission: keepers of commonplace books often transcribed print, as well as manuscript, texts into their collections. Both BL MS Harl. 6910 and BL MS Add. 18044, for example, contain many texts copied from

---

[3] On this book, see Annabel Patterson, *Pastoral and Ideology, Virgil to Valéry* (Berkeley and Los Angeles: University of California Press, 1987), pp. 160–61, and James Turner, *The Politics of Landscape: Rural Scenery and Society in English Poetry 1630–1660* (Cambridge: Harvard University Press, 1979), pp. 148–57.

[4] The section "Poems Found among the Papers of Sir H. Wotton," in *Reliquiae Wottonianae* (1654), pp. 506–15, contains nine poems by other (largely anonymous) writers Wotton had collected. The whole book is a good example of the transfer of manuscript materials into a printed format at a time more and more Royalist texts were emerging from the restricted environment of manuscript circulation.

printed editions.[5] William Ringler points out that that BL MS Add. 34064 also contains texts obtained from published works, including some from the 1593 edition of Sidney's *Arcadia* and the 1591 edition of Spenser's *Complaints*.[6] Joseph Hall's commonplace book, Folger MS V.a.339, has a run of poems (fol. 197r–v) taken from William Jaggard's *Passionate Pilgrim*, including the version of Shakespeare's Sonnet 138 found in that text. The Restoration miscellany, BL MS Harl. 3991 (fols. 113–15) includes thirty whole poems or extracts from the 1635 and 1639 editions of Donne's poetry, labeled "Donnes quaintest conceits" (see Beal, 1.1.69 and 258). Bod. MS Eng. Poet. e.97 has two transcriptions of old Wynkun de Worde pamphlets that reproduce the aesthetic appearance of the printed texts, as the manuscript system reabsorbs artifacts produced by a print culture that originally, by using gothic type, tried to approximate the look of manuscript texts.[7] In it there is an interesting combination of the presentational strategies of print and manuscript as a transcription of William Alabaster's sonnets is preceded by a frontispiece engraving of the poet.

People were very much aware of the coexistence and relationship of the two systems of literary transmission. For example, Bod. MS Don. c.54 contains a parody of print format in one of its items titled "A proper new ballad to the tune of why do me no harme good men or the cleane contrary way." This poem in twelve numbered stanzas about Sir Thomas Overbury's murder is set up as though it were a title page for a printed edition: "Imprinted in Poules churchyard at the signe of the yellow Band and Cuffes by Adam Arsuncke for Robert Roseairie, and are to be sould at the Andromeda Liberata in Turnbull street" (fol. 24r). A note after this in the manuscript states: "Andro: Liberata was the title of a booke made by George Chapman dedicated to the earle of Essex wife from whom she was divorst causa frigiditatis." Folger MS V.a.345, a large student anthology in which a number

---

[5] For the former, see Katherine K. Gottschalk, "Discoveries Concerning British Library MS Harley 6910," *MP* 77 (1979–80): 121–31; the latter manuscript is titled "Collections out of severall Authors by Marmaduke Rauden Eboriencis 1662 Hodsen." Rauden, whom Beal (2.1.269) identifies as "a traveller and antiquary of Guiseley, Yorkshire," self-consciously anthologizes the poems and excerpts entered into his manuscript, copying verse from printed editions of Marlowe, Vaughan, Crashaw, Drayton, Herbert, and Donne along with prose from editions of Montaigne's *Essays* and Ralegh's *History of the World*.

[6] Ringler, "Bishop Percy's Quarto Manuscript," pp. 26–39 (see Chap. 1, n. 80).

[7] On pp. 197–213 of Bod. MS Eng. Poet. e. 97 the scribe copies "A Mery prognostication" and "Here begynneth a lyttel propre Jeste Called cryste crosse me spede. a.b.c. Wynkyn de Worde."

of hands can be found, contains an opening leaf with three poems addressed to the reader ("Ad Lectorem") written by one of the individuals associated with the collection. Given that Christ Church anthologies such as this one, usually comprising several large units of verse, were copied a number of times, the addition of these three poems, imitating the format of a printed collection, is not surprising, since the readership of such a collaborative manuscript anthology was a growing one and the body of work it contained extensive.

In some surviving books both printed and manuscript verse were bound together, suggesting the compatibility of the two mediums: one such book in the British Library (BL Dept. of Printed Books C.39A.37) contains an English translation of Ovid's *De Arte Amandi* (Amsterdam, n.d.), Shakespeare's *Rape of Lucrece* (1624), *The Scourge of Venus* (1614), *Alcilia. Philo parthens loving folly* (1619), and Sir Thomas Overbury's *The first and second part of The Remedy of Loue* (1620), along with sixteen folios on which are transcribed thirty-five poems in different hands: these include lyrics by Campion, Randolph, Jonson, Harington, Ayton, and Carew, as well as other, anonymous writers. The additional poems, after the first one, are numbered one through thirty-four. Edward Doughtie notes in his recent edition that Bod. MS Rawl. Poet. 148 consists of a printed copy of Thomas Watson's *Hekatompathia* (1582) coupled with a sizable manuscript miscellany of poetry.[8]

Just as the happenstance process that characterized most manuscript compilation shaped many early printed anthologies (even the presentation of a text such as the first edition of Donne's *Poems*), the conventions of printed editions of poetry affected the presentation verse in manuscript anthologies. For instance, the arrangement by genre found in some printed editions also appears in certain seventeenth-century manuscripts. Folger MS V.a.103, an anthology begun early in the Caroline era, arranges poems under the following headings: "Epitaphs Laudatory," "Epitaphs Merry and Satyricall," "Love Sonnets," "Panegyricks," "Satyrs," and "Miscellanea." Bod. MS Rawl. Poet. 26 has some roughly generic headings for sections such as "Verses. Poems. Sonnets. etc" (fol. 1r), "Verses. Poems. Sonnetts. Morall & Divine" (fol. 13r), and "Songs. Ballads. Libells, &c." (fol.

---

[8] *Liber Lilliati*, ed. Doughtie, p. 15 (see Chap. 1, n. 8). Crum, p. 1196, lists the printed books in the Bodleian Library that also contain manuscript poetry.

CONCLUSION

21r). Univ. of Nottingham Portland MS Pw v 37 has genre headings for sections of the collection (see Beal, 2.1.158 and 257). These resemble, for example, the kinds of divisions found in Davison's *Poetical Rhapsody* (1602), which has "Pastorals and Eclogues"; "Sonnets, Odes"; "Elegies and Madrigalls"; "Sonnets, Odes, Elegies"; and "other Poesies."

The increase in authorial ascriptions in manuscript anthologizing from the mid-sixteenth to the mid-seventeenth centuries is clearly a reaction to the foregrounding of authorship in print culture. The earlier manuscript collections, especially those compiled before the 1630s, were less likely to ascribe lyrics to specific poets, and even when authorship was cited, it was usually by means of initials.[9] Despite the efforts of printers and modern scholars to identify authorship, problems of ascription still beset the canons of poets who wrote for various coterie audiences rather than for print—for example, Wyatt, Oxford, Dyer, Ralegh, and Donne. Under the impact of developments in print culture, however, ascriptions of authorship became more frequent in the seventeenth-century manuscripts, as many collectors took pains to identify the poets whose work they transcribed, especially in those manuscripts in which whole sections were given over to the work of individual writers. Many poems continued to be presented as anonymous, but such names as Donne, Jonson, Herrick, Carew, King, Randolph, Strode, and Corbett are quite noticeable in a large number of manuscripts by the middle of the century—both because authorship had by this time acquired general cultural value and because such writers were deliberately appropriated by an educated and politically conservative elite.

Other features of printed editions of verse came to mark manuscript anthologizing. Titles, for example, became a regular feature in manuscript anthologies, largely in response to the presentation of poetry in printed editions. Bod. MS Mal. 23, which looks like an anthology transcribed to be presented to a social superior, even records the titles of poems in boldface italic, demonstrating the influence of typography. Another device of the print format, the running head, can be found in some manuscripts: BL MS Harl. 4955, for example, uses "Benjamin Johnson" in the section in which that poet's work is

[9] For a general discussion of this topic see Franklin B. Williams Jr., "An Initiation Into Initials," *SB* 9 (1957): 163–78.

gathered; BL MS Harl. 6910 employs the running title "Poesyes" in a section of the collection containing ring posies.[10] David Redding argues that the running titles and poem numbering found in Robert Bishop's poetical anthology (Rosenbach MS 1083/16) suggest that the whole collection was organized from a looser gathering of manuscript copies of poems.[11] In response to the format of printed editions, some manuscripts contain tables of contents and indexes of first lines. For example, BL MS Harl. 6917 opens with "A Catalogue of all the pieces in this booke," an alphabetized index of its contents.

Mutual influence of the two systems of literary transmission was the norm, but that did not mean that certain conflicts and problems did not regularly occur, especially in the translation of texts from manuscript to print. Spelling and punctuation changes made by compositors in the printing house often changed the texts of poems being moved from manuscript to print, and sometimes serious damage was done. For example, in transferring Cleveland's poem "A Dialogue between two Zealots, upon the &c. in the Oath" from manuscript to print, the printer of the 1677 edition took the ampersand of the manuscript and earlier printed versions and expanded it to "et caetera," losing the point of the figure: the original "&c." is called "a strange mis-shapen Monster" (11), "The old halfe Serpent in his numerous foulds" (32), something it is hard to "untruss" (43).[12] *Wit Restor'd* (1658) attempts (unsuccessfully) to translate a punctuation-game poem ("The Lawyer," p. 59) of the sort one finds in manuscripts into print, but the compositor obviously didn't understand what was going on in "The Client's Transcription of the same Copy, having experienced the contrary" (I insert slashes to mark where periods should be but which this text omits and I bracket incorrect punctuation):

[10] See Gottschalk, "Discoveries," p. 125. M. B. Parkes, however, points out that late medieval manuscripts incorporate such features as marginal numbers, running titles, analytic tables of contents, alphabetical indices, and chapter titles, features that are picked up by print culture ("The Influence of the Concepts of *Ordinatio* and *Compilatio* on the Development of the Book," in *Medieval Learning and Literature: Essays presented to Richard William Hunt*, ed. J. J. G. Alexander and M. T. Gibson [Oxford: Clarendon Press, 1976], pp. 115–41). The running title is, in fact, "an ancient practice" (p. 122).

[11] See Redding, "Robert Bishop's Commonplace Book," p. 1 (cited in full at Chap. 1, n. 122).

[12] See the *Poems of Cleveland*, ed. Morris and Withington, p. 82 (cited in full at Chap. 1, n. 115).

# CONCLUSION

Lawyers themselves uphold / the Commonweale
They punish / such as do offend and steale[.]
They free with subtill art / the innocent[,]
From any danger, losse, or punishment[;]
They can, but will not keep, / the world in awe
By mis-expounded and distorted lawe
Allwayes they have, / great store of charity
And love they want, not keeping amitye.

The wit of this piece needs restoring.

The last pages of the printed edition of Thomas Pecke's *Parnassi Puerperium* (1659) deal with the issue of the printer's errors. Instead of simply inserting a page of errata, the printer himself addresses a poem to the reader apologizing for the mistakes in the text:

If you demand what kind of fate there's in't.
That Printeres cann't be faultless when they print:
One case is why this misfortune to them comes,
Is by the multitude of Individuums
Us'd in Composing. What faults are slipt here,
To curious Readers obviously appear.
For which I pardon crave; especially
For one escap't through inadvertencie.
<[line deleted]>
<[line deleted]>[13]
Some Poems said to be Mr. Tho[mas] Pecke's;
Which stile, on Him, may cast absurd rest's.
Whose modesty to clear, and Honour quit,
I say, I, not He, was framer of it.
                    J. C[ottrel]

This poem is answered by a viciously insulting piece by Pecke himself:

Upon *Cottrel*, the printer
Let a strict search quite thorow *Gotham* bee,
An Hue, and Cry, can't find A Fool like thee.
When as my Copy was grasp'd by thy Pawes,
You threw that by, to Print the Good Old Cause.

---

[13] These two lines were inked out by the owner of the copy purchased by the Huntington Library.

None might Correct but you. Base fellow know;
I such disdain, to ev'ry Rascall owe,
That I am forc'd to tell those refin't Men,
(Whose Fame may Glory in a sublime Pen,)
That to the Muses when they would express
A signal malice; They must use thy Press.
The Epigram I made, for to excuse
Erratas; durst your Impudence refuse
That's a small fault. You presum'd to subjoin
Your Dogrill Rhthmes, and Leprous Muse, to mine.
You are as Ignorant, as Clowns, who know,
No other Dialect; then Gee! Proh! Ho!
Yet in one thing, you shew'd A little skill:
*Lack-wit* most fitly dwells on *Adle-Hill.*

T.P.

Portraying the printer as a Puritan artisan more interested in publishing political propaganda than poetry, Pecke expresses a particularly nasty form of intellectual snobbery and class prejudice, but behind his complaints there lurks the old aversion to the print medium harbored by those who thought it a "stigma."

As this case and the other evidence presented in this book suggest, some of the same tensions and conflicts between private and public, manuscript and print, amateur and professional, that mark the history of the two literary systems of transmission in the sixteenth and seventeenth centuries have a long life, continuing, in fact, well into the eighteenth century,[14] for processes of literary institutionalization were inseparable from class conflicts, questions of political empowerment, the commodification of cultural artifacts, and the ideologization of art in the early modern era. I have concentrated in this book on the material embodiment of texts in manuscript and print in order to delineate some of the social history of lyric poetry within the two media through which it was transmitted, but it is clear to me that both systems require much more extensive analysis and that the most promising route to an understanding of the large scale cultural changes in which literature was implicated is through close exami-

---

[14] Focusing on such figures as Pope and Samuel Johnson, Alvin Kernan, in *Printing Technology, Letters, and Samuel Johnson* (Princeton: Princeton University Press, 1987), identifies the eighteenth century as the era in which print completed its redefinition of literature.

# CONCLUSION

nation of specific documentary remains. It is my hope that this study will encourage literary scholars who are not specialists in bibliography or textual study to explore the rich contents of the archive with open eyes and with newfound energy that can be reinforced by the excitement of discovery. There is much work to be done.

# GENERAL INDEX

# GENERAL INDEX

Compiler poetry, 171–207
  Burghe, 194–96
  Calfe, 204–6
  Catholic, 182–84
  Codrington, 199–201
  epitaphs/elegies, 173–76, 204–6
  Inns of Court collections, 179–82
  Parsons, 201–4
  prefatory poems, 171–73
  Puritan, 185–86
  Ramsey, 189–94
  Stanford, 187–89
  university collections, 176–79
*Complaint of Poetrie for the Death of Liberalitie*
  (Barnfield), 321n
Condell, Henry, 230–31
Coningsby, Humphrey, 15, 31, 38, 65–67,
  93, 139–41, 171, 176–81
Constable, Henry, 25, 47, 63, 231, 288
Conway, Viscount, 40
Corbett, Richard, 12–13, 32, 33, 35, 87,
  107n, 116, 118–19, 131, 132, 162, 169,
  247, 253, 257
Cornwallis, Anne, 38, 49, 57, 164
Corti, Maria, xi, xii
Cotgrave, John, 273, 276, 292n
Cotton, Robert, 113
*Countess of Pembrokes Arcadia, The. See*
  *Arcadia* (Sidney)
Court manuscripts, 37–40. *See also specific*
  *topics*
*Court of Venus, The* (Skelton), 212
Cowley, Abraham, 32, 254, 258, 260,
  263–65
Cranfield, Lionel, 85, 94, 105, 106–7
Crashaw, Richard, 70, 247, 260, 289
Croft, Pauline, 101n, 102
Cromwell, Oliver, 90–91
Cromwell, Richard, 277
Crown-Parliament tension, 70, 71, 88–90,
  112–15. *See also* Political poetry
Cummings, Laurence, 16, 58, 63, 64, 65,
  93

"Dampe, The" (Donne), 10
"Dan Bartholomew of Bathe"
  (Gascoigne), 28
Daniel, John, 319
Daniel, Samuel, 231, 232–33, 236, 246,
  253, 257, 287, 288, 302, 314, 315, 319
Dante, 220, 226
Darnley, Lord, 39–40, 56
Davenant, William, 323
Davies, Godfrey, 104, 125n
Davies, Sir John, 36, 37, 142, 181, 182,
  246, 322n

Davis, Sir John, 22
Davison, Francis, 73, 138, 214, 217, 235–
  36, 316–17
Dawson, Giles E., 25
*Death's Duel* (Donne), 251
*Defence of Poesie*, 229
*Delia* (Daniel), 231, 232–33, 246, 288,
  302
*Delia and Rosamund Augmented* (Daniel),
  288
Deloney, Thomas, 145
Denny, Edward, 24, 70, 70–71n, 78
*Description of Love, A*, 246
Devereux, Robert (earl of Essex). *See*
  Essex conspiracy
*Devotions* (Donne), 250
*Diana* (Constable), 231, 302n
*Diana Augmented* (Constable), 288
*Diary* (Pepys), 289
Digby, Sir Kenelm, 10, 154
Disle, Henry, 296
*Divina Commedia* (Dante), 226
"Divine Meditations by H: C:
  Philomusus" (Colman), 24
*Divine Songs and Meditacions* (Collins), 249
Dobbes, Robert, 43
Doderidge, Sir John, 16n
Donne, John, 10, 21, 24–25, 27, 37, 40,
  71, 76, 80, 113, 128, 160, 167, 168–69,
  211, 247, 269, 327
  and textual malleability, 147–59
  *See also Poems* (Donne)
Donne, John, Jr., 28, 160, 253, 255, 279–
  80, 323–24n
d'Orleans, Charles, 4n
Doughtie, Edward, 2n, 3n, 142, 328
Douglas, Margaret, 39, 40, 55–56
Dowland, John, 138, 142
Doyle, A. I., 18n
Drayton, Michael, 233, 236, 246, 257,
  287, 288
Drolleries, 271
Drummond, William, 86n, 107n, 276,
  325
Dudley, Lord Robert, 5
Dunlap, Rhodes, 69n, 170
Duppa, Brian, 32
Dyboski, Roman, 56
Dyer, Sir Edward, 9, 62, 65, 66, 126, 127,
  138, 141, 162, 163, 167

Edmonds, John, 66
Edwards, Richard, 38, 214
Egerton, John, 24, 113
*Eglogs, Epytaphes, and Sonettes* (Googe), 28,
  288, 296–99

[ 337 ]

# GENERAL INDEX

La Belle, Jenijoy, 51n
Lamb, Mary, 26, 59, 314n
Lambarde, William, 228
Lane, Elizabeth, 50
Lanyer, Emilia, 54
*Last Remains, The* (Suckling), 257
Laud, William, 110
Layout, 27–28
Leake, William, 278–79
Leare, Daniel, 13–14
Lee, Anthony, 39
Lee, Sir Henry, 6n
*Leicester's Commonwealth*, 234
Leigh, John, 260
Leishman, J. B., 143
Le Neve, Oliver, 41
Le Neve, Peter, 41
Lewis, William, 105
*Licia* (Fletcher), 233–34, 243, 288, 315–16
Lilliat, John, 6, 142, 186
Loewenstein, Joseph, xiii, 238, 240
Lok, Henry, 256
Long Parliament, 88–89, 113
Love, Harold, 11, 27, 30, 83n, 92, 283
Lovelace, Richard, 6n, 257–58
Love poetry, 75
    answer poetry, 163–66
    compiler poetry, 200–201, 202–4
    courtly, 39
    in Donne's print work, 250–52
    in Elizabethan print anthologies, 225–27
    in midcentury printed anthologies, 269–70
    and obscene poetry, 80
    and patronage, 299–302, 306–8
    and print transmission, 210, 220–22, 228, 265
    *See also* Sidney's print works; *specific manuscripts*
Lownes, Matthew, 229, 232
Lucas, Peter, 27
*Lucasta, Posthume Poems* (Lovelace), 257–58
Ludlow, Henry, 113
Lyly, John, 28, 227, 312
Lyttleton, Elizabeth, 26, 50, 52–53

MacLean, Gerald, 86n
Manne, Thomas, 23, 69, 115, 173, 205n
Manuscript collections, 10–16
    Catholic, 44–48, 51, 60
    commonplace books, 18–22, 36
    court, 37–40
    cultural beliefs in, 130

and Elizabethan print anthologies, 212, 214–15
epitaphs/elegies in, 129–30
family, 40–44
female ownership, 48–54
gatherings, 11–13
generic presentation in, 328–29
Inns of Court, 30, 31, 35–37, 67, 75–76
loose sheets and booklets, 10–11
medieval, 30–31
miscellaneous nature of, 17–18
physical features, 25–30
popular poems in, 126–33
relationships between, 13–14
running heads in, 329–30
seventeenth-century, 68–73
single-author, 22–25
sixteenth-century, 61–68
"table" books, 16, 42
transmission process information in, 14–16
university, 31–35, 63–64, 66, 75–76
Manuscript transmission, xii–xiv, 1, 207–8. *See also* Manuscript vs. print transmission; *specific topics*
Manuscript vs. print transmission
    and authorship, 211, 242, 329
    coexistence, xii, xiii, 1
    damage in transition, 330–32
    importance of, xi–xiii, 332–33
    Jacobean era, 246–47
    mutual influence, 24, 325–30
    and obscene poetry, 75–77
    patronage, 222n
    and physical format, 27–30
    and political poetry, 76, 84, 91, 94, 126
    and preservation, 227–28
    punctuation, 284n
    textual instability/malleability, 135, 137–38, 146–47, 225
    typography, 282–85
    and women, 49
Marcus, Leah, 86n
Marlowe, Christopher, 167
Marriot, John, 253–54
Marston, John, 321n
Martin, Henri-Jean, xiii
Martin, L. C., 53n
Martin, Richard, 113, 114
Mason, H. A., 7–8
Masten, Jeff, 55n, 238n
Matthews, Tobie, 113
May, Steven W., 6n, 68, 161, 187n
Maynard, Winifred, 296
McCoy, Richard, 308n
McDonald, James, 47n

# GENERAL INDEX

# GENERAL INDEX

# INDEX
## OF MANUSCRIPTS

# INDEX OF MANUSCRIPTS

# INDEX OF MANUSCRIPTS